W9-AHR-319

World
Without End

THE MIDDLE EAST

EMIL LENGYEL

World Without End

THE MIDDLE EAST

The John Day Company
NEW YORK

Published by The John Day Company, 62 West 45th Street, New York 36, N.Y., and on the same day in Canada by Longmans, Green & Company, Toronto.

Manufactured in the United States of America

Library of Congress Catalog Number: 52-12685

To my son

PETER

whose generation may yet find the solution

A word of thanks to Vera Micheles Dean, editor of the Foreign Policy Association, for gracious consent to use part of my contributions in the F.P.A. Headline Series No. 89, written by Dean Ernest O. Melby and myself; to Felice Novich, assistant editor of the F.P.A. for her help; to my colleagues and friends in the social studies department of the School of Education, New York University: Professors S. P. McCutchen, Julian C. Aldrich, Jesse J. Dossick, Alice McNiffe, John C. Payne, Durward Pruden, James H. Hanscom, Anabel Sober, Jonah Blustain, Arnold Goren for years of congenial companionship which helped to elicit such extracurricular activities as the present book. Also thanks to Charles M. Segal for having placed at my disposal the rich documentation of his Middle East collection; then to many friends in the Middle East, particularly to Ali Adibi, who seems to be the prototype of the new man the region needs; to Richard J. Walsh and Richard J. Walsh, Jr., for their spontaneous interest, which was a fruitful incentive in the writing of this book; and to Constance Campbell, for valuable editorial suggestions.

Special thanks to my wife who bore with smiling grace the burden of her "Middle East widowhood"—absences and typewriter rattle.

E. L.

Contents

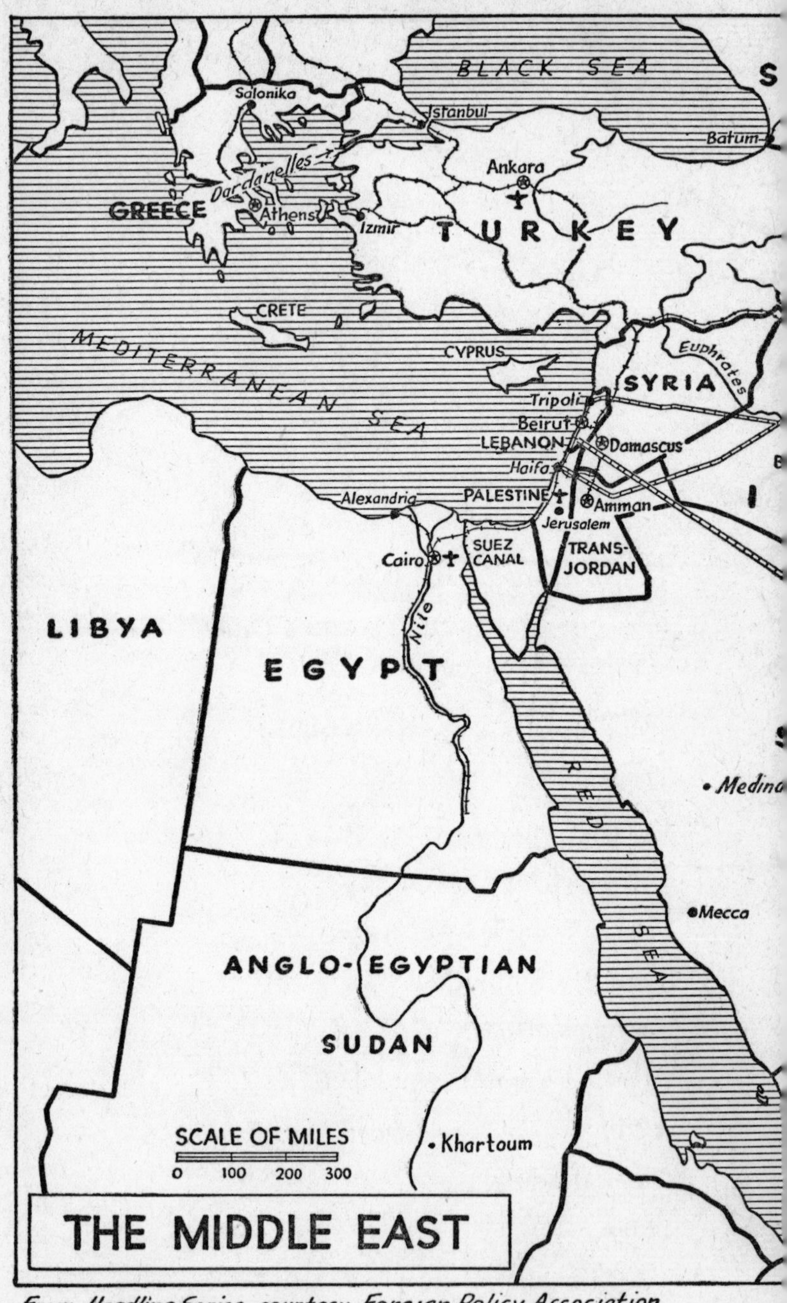

From Headline Series, courtesy Foreign Policy Association

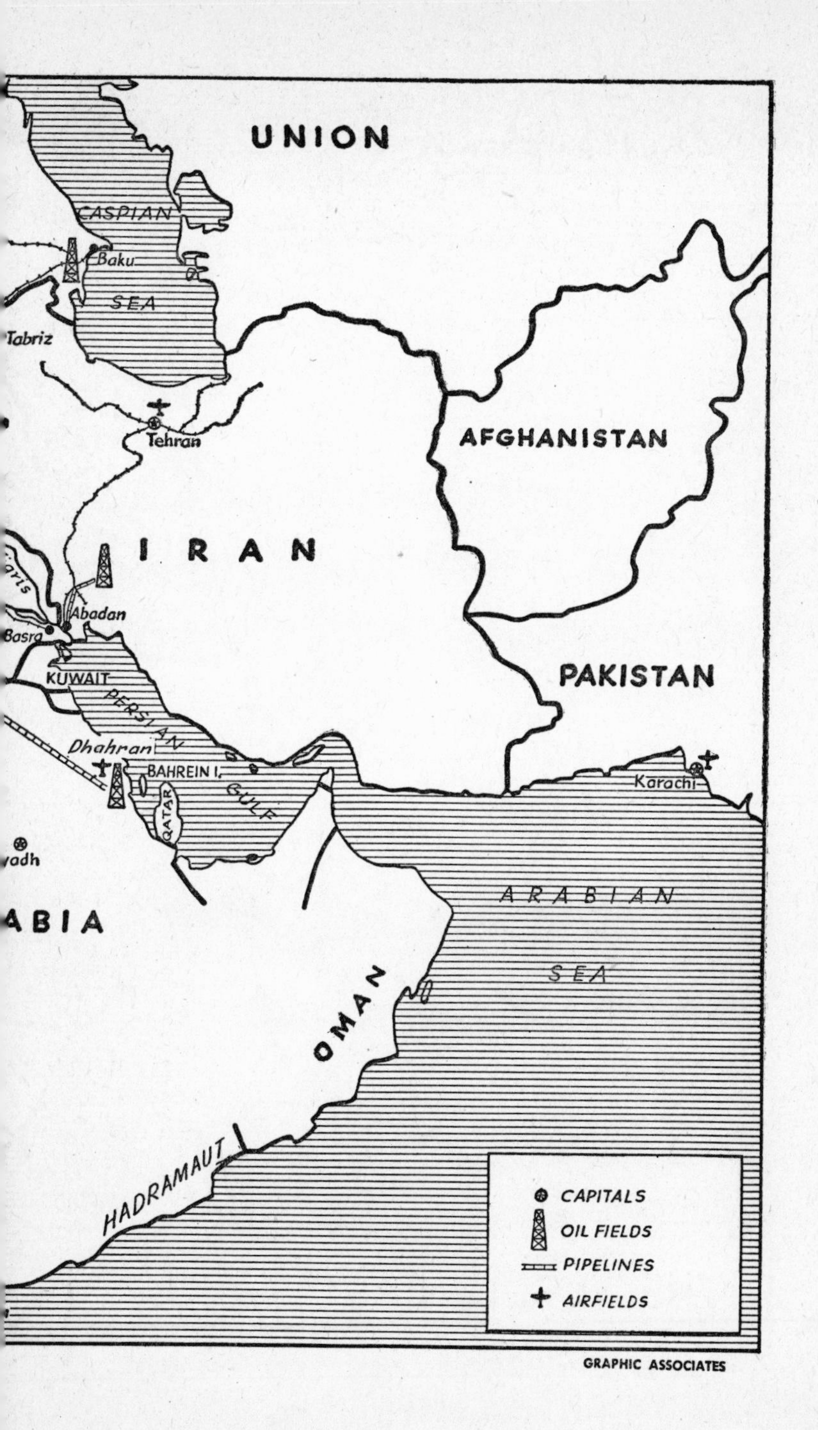

GRAPHIC ASSOCIATES

World Without End

THE MIDDLE EAST

CHAPTER 1

The Poorhouse of the World

"Eyeless in Gaza"

Two-thirds of mankind live in a global poorhouse, one of the worst parts of which is the Middle East. The region extends from Turkey's western marches to Iran's eastern boundary, and from the Black Sea to the elusive southern frontiers of the Anglo-Egyptian Sudan.[1] There are about as many definitions of this area as there are authors, but the territory here covered represents a middle ground.

The Arab countries fill out the heart of the territory. Some of them are monarchies: Egypt, Iraq, Saudi Arabia, Yemen, Jordan; others republics: Lebanon and Syria. Also there is a cluster of British protectorates around the Persian Gulf, such as the Sheykhdom of Kuwait and the Bahrein Islands. The "roof" of the region is formed by Turkey and Iran. Imbedded in the vast Arab world is tiny Israel.

What is the area of this region? It is estimated at 3,800,000 square miles, but who can honestly tell? Who has surveyed the vastness of the Arab Quadrangle and the massive mountains of the High Yemen? Not even all of Turkey has been completely surveyed. And the population? Perhaps a hundred million. But, again, who has counted the noses of the elusive tribesmen of the Nejd or penetrated into the parched wilderness of the Hadramaut?

The bulk of the region—most of the Arab countries and Iran—is part of the global poorhouse in which live two-thirds of mankind. Conditions in Turkey are somewhat better, while the

[1] For the Great Controversy about the region's name see the Note in the back of the book.

standards of Israel are on a par with those of Central Europe.

The per capita income in the poorhouse region ranges between fifty and one hundred dollars a year per head. Yet, how misleading such figures can be! There are millions in the Middle East who have hardly ever seen cash, and the "annual income" attributed to them is mostly in kind. The estimated national income is divided among the inhabitants, and the millionaire's revenue swells the pauper's share—on paper. The income of the former King of Egypt exceeded the annual earnings of thousands of his subjects' families. It was only yesterday that the League of Nations started—and only now that the United Nations is continuing—to piece together the scanty data. The result passes for statistics. Perhaps it is a series of smart guesses.

It is misleading also to rely on native knowledge about conditions at home. The peasant's horizon is circumscribed by his hamlet, and that at best. Mostly it is confined to the interests of his kin. Barring a few exceptions, the higher classes know little about the true plight of the majority of the people in their countries. The author has come across university graduates in this area so amazingly ignorant of conditions in their native lands that the proverbial foreign "expert" spending a fortnight there would have been able to collect far more information.

These educated people are not apathetic or indifferent. They are simply like people in other parts of the world, attuned to hearing and seeing the familiar sounds and sights. Living in metropolitan areas and on the Riviera, they enjoy the western comforts they take for granted. Their world has no links with that other planet which may be no more than a score of yards away. Physically they may live in the very midst of that other world, without being aware of its existence.

The privileged people with their motor cars *could* see their country. They travel long distances, passing through many hamlets which, however, they do not see, since their eyes are not focused on them. Those hamlets and their people form part of an exotic landscape, in the company of trees and wells. They are terribly ashamed of what they would see at home if they kept their eyes open. Of these swift travelers it may, indeed, be said: "Eyeless in Gaza."

The Great Polarization

Little Lebanon is perhaps the only exception to the greatest extremes of polarization in the vast world of the Arabs and of Iran. In the western world the individual's life expectancy is close to sixty-five years, while in most of the Middle East it is thirty, sometimes even less. In the poorer countries of the region one newborn baby out of three will die before reaching the age of a year. Some 90 per cent of the population of Egypt, one of the region's advanced countries, is afflicted with diseases that should not exist in our century of vitamins and miracle drugs.

"Unrelieved horror" is the life of Egypt's peasant *(fellah),* in the words of the scholarly Doreen Warriner, investigator of economic and social conditions in the Middle East. The subdued United Nations summary on social conditions in the region is no less explicit: "The great majority of the population, and especially the three quarters of the people who live in the rural areas, still largely continue to live according to patterns that were developed in the Middle East many centuries ago."

The poorest in the Middle East no longer die of starvation. They die merely of tuberculosis or intestinal troubles. They would live if they had more food, decent shelter and if somebody were to look after their health. In the twentieth century we are too civilized to speak of famine. Today there are different words for it.

At the other end of the economic scale are the *effendis* and the pashas, members of the two hundred or two thousand ruling families. They own forty thousand villages out of Iran's forty-one thousand. The property of one of them was to be confiscated recently for political reasons, and its worth was estimated at more than eight million dollars. Here is the great polarization.

The worst of it is that most of these super-rich have little of the spirit of *noblesse oblige,* the idea that private property is public trust, or even the idea that one day the situation may get out of hand. Patriots these effendis call themselves but their patriotism is no more than a holding on to their special interests and the mouthing of clichés. If reminded that the little peoples' patience in their midst is on the wane, they look deeply hurt and reply that one must understand their people. These good people want no money, are not materialistic-minded, but they do want their freedom and that means they want the Britishers out of Suez and the Anglo-Iranian Oil Company out of Iran.

Let us take a look at the people in the desert, in the village and in their urban centers. Let us see both the poor and the rich. First, however, let us observe the nomads before most of them pass out of the picture.

Under the Starlit Canopy

About 15 per cent of the Middle East population is believed to be nomadic. However, their number is shrinking, as the sown area keeps on encroaching upon the desert and governmental authority keeps on encroaching upon the type of individualism the tribesmen practice.

The majority of Middle East people, about 65 per cent, are settled in villages, in the proximity of waterholes. About 20 per cent live in urban centers.

The Hashimite Kingdom of the Jordan was believed until recently to have the largest proportion of nomads, about 40 per cent, though the proportion may have changed now because of the influx of Palestinian refugees. Strangely, the great desert country of Saudi Arabia has a comparatively smaller nomadic population, but this "guesstimate," too, has to be taken with caution, since the country is vast and the realm of the desert endless.

The West calls the Arab nomads Bedouins, but they call themselves *Badawi,* derived from the word *badw,* desert, or A'rabi. Their ancestors were reputed to have been the original Arabs before the historic explosion of the desert into the sown area, about which more will be said later.

One would think that the desert is democratic, since there man faces the most awful forces of nature where strength and character, and not prestige or birth, prevail. But is man democratic anywhere? Certainly he is not, in the desert.

Among the nomads there are several social ladders to distinction and one of these is the antiquity of blood. The genuine blue-blood aristocrats are the Arabs of the Arabs, *al-'Arabu 'l-'Aribah,* claiming that their ancestry antedates even the Patriarch Abraham, going back to the reputed progenitor of their race, after whom they are named, Yarab ibn Qahtan. How such a claim may be sustained must remain forever a mystery of genealogy.

A somewhat lower breed are the mixed Arabs, *'Arabu 'l-Musta 'ribah.* The Prophet Mohammed himself is believed to have belonged to this group.

Besides the priority of birth there is also the occupational ladder. Real noblemen among the Bedouins are the camelmen, who, because they can move freely anywhere in the desert, are not the slaves of any particular spot—the hardy camel will get through anything. The camel nomad needs no roads and he is proud to find his way in the trackless desert of sand and stone. His dwelling place under the sky is a vaster mansion than the palace of mightiest kings. For days his animal goes without water, but in the heat of the summer even the camel nomad can go only so far from the well.

Lower in the scale of social values are the tribesmen with goats and sheep, which cannot roam at will, and must stay close to the waterhole. In summer these nomads keep near the towns and have seasonal shelter against the sun. In the winter they move into the open desert, where their animals feed on the grass in the wake of autumnal rains.

Real aristocrats do not dirty their hands with work, such as patching up the tent, fashioning its poles, repairing the hearth. Much lower are the tribes performing service-station functions for the higher groups. In return for protection, the artisans serve their blue-blood masters, and some of the weaker tribes become tributaries of the strong.

Beyond the scope of a strong central authority, on the desert margins, there may still be some looting raids (razzia), which the Arabs call *rhazw.* They were considered an aristocratic and highly legitimate occupation not long ago. All of a sudden the strong men of the deep desert emerged out of nowhere and swooped down upon the passing caravan. The merchants were inclined to consider the ransom a part of legitimate business costs which they, in turn, charged to the customer. There was a tacit understanding between the attackers and the victims that the former had to supplement their earnings, but must refrain from rough methods. Wild shots in the air gave the attackers and the caravan all the thrill they needed.

This picturesque part of desert life is on the wane today, as "law and order" invest everyday life with dull routine. King Ibn Saud introduced a new code of ethics into his Saudi Arabia after having gained fame and wealth by means of the old code. He decreed the Koranic law for theft to be in full force, requiring that the thief's right hand be cut off. In the Islamic desert this is tantamount to death, because the left hand, being used for contaminated purposes, cannot touch food. So virtuous has become the policed part of the desert that a bag of gold may be left at the crossroads for days without being touched.

Whatever the social status of the nomad, he looks down upon the village wretch who is tied to his small parcel of land and does not know the exhilaration of free movement under the boundless sky. The camel nomad particularly has what the French call *snobisme du désert.*

Changing Patterns in the Desert Sand

Nomadism was thought to represent one of the lowest levels of social and economic life and therefore an atavism in the modern world. Today, however, nomadism is seen in a different light, as an elastic adjustment to certain ineluctable forces of nature. If there were no roaming tribes, certain potential food supplies in the desert and on marginal land could not be fully utilized. Thus, it is the nomads' function to turn nature's peripheral gifts into life-giving food. Because of the absence of nomadism, parts of the Middle East of the more distant past may have had to go without this food.

One phase of the great contemporary change is the attempt of the authorities to tie the nomad to the soil. Our age tends toward a centralization of authority, be it in the urbanized West or the nomadic East. The Age of Passport does not accord well with the Age of Free Movement. Most of the Middle East belonged to the Ottoman Empire in the past, but now its place is occupied by more than half a dozen countries. Within those countries there is a concerted effort to bring the entire population within the rule of the centralized law.

There are Bedouins, of course, who will sell their freedom for no price, but many others will settle readily enough if they have water and a piece of land to irrigate. The story of the great Aramco Tapline from the heart of Saudi Arabia to the Levant coast shows conclusively that wells will induce the desert people to swarm toward the life-giving source. Parts of the desert contain potentially fertile soil even though much of the stone and rubble in the open country is beyond redemption.

Experience has shown that not all settlements of the former tribesmen are successful. The point can be best illustrated by the tragic example of the Dust Bowl in the United States. The land in that region had been suitable for ranching, the American form of nomadism. Once the plow broke the soil, the thin grass covering was uprooted, with disastrous results which America will never forget. Thousands of farms became airborne, their dusty remnants deposited hundreds of miles away.

Another problem was presented in the Middle East. Surely, the Bedouin was poor, but he had his native pride. Nomadism was his way of life, to which he became adjusted and without which many of them could not live. Today many of the settlements of erstwhile tribesmen in Iran, for instance, are woeful places inhabited by human wrecks who cannot find their places in the modern scheme of life. Their sanitary habits as nomads were satisfactory but not in their settled habitations. Consequently, they are afflicted with all the plagues of the Middle East; marked for early death.

The revolution in modern transportation also affects the tribesman's ways. The camel was an all-purpose animal in the past, wonderfully fitted for desert travel. The Bedouin raised these animals and he was reasonably well off. He obtained cash, was in a position to improve his scanty fare and buy the primitive utensils needed for his tent. Today the market for the camel has been narrowed.

To be sure, it is still a useful beast; its sour milk a food staple, its droppings valued as fuel. But now the camel is more highly valued dead than alive. Its bone is used for implements, its skin for utensils, its hair for clothing and tent, and its flesh for holiday meat.

But the camel is no longer the indispensable ship of the desert. That role has now been assumed by Chevrolets and Fords, occasionally by Cadillacs. Much of the desert needs no man-made roads and one can travel on hard surface for countless miles. Because rich people demand cars, the nomad gets no cash for his camel; and yet today he needs money more than ever before to buy implements. Even in the desert one has to keep up with the Joneses.

On the other hand, sheep and goats keep on finding their markets, so that many an aristocrat of the open spaces has had to step down to a lower rung of the social level. While this may sound ludicrous to western ears, to many of the tribesmen this must be like a king surrendering his crown.

Security is the cry of our supremely insecure age and that is true even in the Arab Quadrangle. Ex-Bedouins now seek economic security in the most highly regimented occupations, as for instance the armed forces, the police, and the labor forces of the western oil companies. Some of the crack soldiers in the Arab Legion of the Hashimite Kingdom of the Jordan were former desert men.

As to the oil companies, they employ a sizable number of former nomads whom they rate highly. They can perform hard work, since the desert made them tough. Mentally they are alert and can easily adjust themselves to new conditions. However, they have no concept of time. At first, they do not understand why one must be on time, why one cannot leave the place of work without a valid cause, and why one cannot take long siestas. But they soon learn big-business discipline and then all is well with them.

New problems arise in connection with the ownership of land. The tribal chief (*sheykh*) may have been a decent fellow in nomadic life. Settled down and called upon to divide the land he may be seized with the frenzy of acquisitiveness. Often he will record tribally owned land in his own name, thus becoming the legal owner. The more ruthless members of the tribe grab superior tracts of land, while the weak must be content with inferior parcels. Still others are cast out altogether, reduced to sharecropper status, peons on the land which all of them were using in the past.

The remarkable "Lawrence of Arabia," leader of desert men in the First World War, prized the tribesmen's qualities highly. He recorded that many of them were first-rate warriors, remarkable agile, with strong, keen senses, excellent in the unpredictable warfare of the desert. They could not be easily regimented and would not tarry long in the ranks, but they fought and died well.

The Arab in his Tent

The "portable village" of the Arab nomad should command our interest. The tents are usually of black camel or goat hair. The owner's standing is indicated by the size of the tent and, frequently, the number of its poles. A traveler noticed one tent sixty feet long, ten feet wide, with poles ten feet high. The owner must have been a man of great importance, the paramount chief of a tribe.

The tent is open to the east, away from the prevailing wind. The social center of the tent is the coffee hearth. Coffee is the wine of the Muslim world and the Bedouin drinks it strong, unsweetened, sometimes spiced with herbs. To fight fire with fire, it is drunk very hot in the hot climate. When drunk in large quantities, strong coffee serves as an intoxicant.

The most influential members occupy the best spots within the tent and, naturally, the men's section, to the right, is more spacious than that of the women, to the left, even though the number of women is larger. After all, women are vastly inferior to men, as shown by the fact that they do most of the work.

The "furniture" of the tent is simplicity itself: a few sooty pots and pans, some carpets, and perhaps a few covers for the chilly season when the rains come.

The size of the tribe can be fairly well established by the number of the tents. The largest Syrian tribe at present, the Ruwalla, is believed to have more than four thousand tents. Its realm ranges from the outskirts of the Syrian city of Homs into the Jordan Kingdom. Tribes of this size are really countries within countries and one can see why governments watch them with jaundiced eyes. Tribes, especially when they are large, have an ambulatory government of their own, with the loosest of connections linking them to the central authority of the nation over whose territory they roam. Sometimes this connection is little more than nominal, a mere face-saving device. In other cases, the tribes are tributaries of the central government.

There are small tribes, too, such as, for instance, that of the Karachim in Syria's Hama district. In the deep desert there are even smaller groups, composed of a few households.

Living under primitive conditions, the people's needs are reduced to a minimum. Very simple and functional is the desert garb. The men wear long garments of a sturdy material which lasts for a very long time. During the rainy winter season they wear a waterproof cloak made of camel hair.

In the desert, where for months the face of the sun is hardly ever hidden during the day, the head and the back of the neck need constant protection. This is afforded by the traditional *kufiya* headcloth, held in place by the *'iqal,* a narrow band. These garments are highly serviceable also in dust storms. The headgear in the Arab world is more than a piece of functional clothing. It is also a mark of distinction for the crown of creation, the male. To the desert Arab, it is a diadem on that crown.

Tent Hospitality

The glamorous sheykhs of Araby live only in the capitals of moviedom. There are, of course, rich people in the desert, and this is shown by the fact that they eat well. They are attractive, and that among undernourished people means to be plump.

To be a guest in a desert chieftain's tent is not easily forgotten. The food is not only rich but also well prepared. There, as in settled Arab households, the guest is king. Middle East hospitality is fabulous, provided the host can afford to entertain. Scenes of conviviality are like pictures out of the Old Testament.

As the Patriarch Abraham served his guests personally, so does the host of today. Standing behind them, he picks out the best tidbits from the richly filled dish with his own fingers. He may be a prince, but now he is a servant, not speaking and not spoken to. Only when the meal is over does he sit down to have a chat with the guests and relish the steaming coffee spiced with cardamon.

This, of course, is not a typical picture of life in the tent. Most of the desert people eat little because they have little to eat. The diet may be some barley, wheat bread, milk perhaps, and sometimes rice, depending upon local conditions. Or dried fruit may be part of the diet, particularly dates. When an animal perishes, its remains are gobbled up with dispatch, since the heat does its work swiftly. The tribe that has done well may have a feast of meat during the annual religious festival of Bairam, following the month-long daylight fasting of Ramadan.

Many of the desert aristocrats look stunted, often malformed, because their diet is deficient in both vitamin-content and variety. More often than not, their poor development is due to the lack of enough food of any kind.

The traditional forms prevail at meals. The sexes eat separately, and precedence is established by age, the elderly being served first. Of course, few of the people live to grow really old. The younger males are served next, and after them the boys. Women can scrap over the leftovers in their quarters. The desert respects age because it betokens experience and that may mean finding the right spot for the herd, getting out of the way of hostile tribes, and commanding respect among the competing nomads.

Iran's Nomads

In Iran the nomads are often of a different type. Because of the mountains in that country, Iran practices the vertical type of nomadism known as *transhumance*. In the spring the herds are driven up the mountain slope in search of lush grass. When autumn comes the herds are driven into the valley in the wake of fall rains. These migrations sometimes involve tens of thousands and require considerable ability in organization.

Some of the larger tribes here are veritable countries within countries. This was particularly the case in the not too remote past. In their policy of penetration in those days, the British formed alliances with some of the tribes, and they also employed them as armed guards for their valuable oil plants on the well-known principle that the best robbers will become the best gendarmes.

About the Kurds, who are partly nomadic and partly settled, more will be said later. Besides them, the most important tribes of the region are the Bakhtiaris, Lurs and Qashqais.

The Bakhtiaris are very numerous and occupy the strategic regions near the oil wells and along the line of the earlier British penetration. Most of the tribesmen are very poor, while the chief headmen are fabulously rich. Some of the latter feel more at home at the gambling tables of Monte Carlo than in their rugged mountain homes. Shah Mohammed Reza Pahlavi married a Bakhtiari girl.

To the north of them live the Lurs, who gave their name to the region known as Luristan. Tartars of modern times they were once described, mountaineers of fiercely independent spirit. Reckless of lives, their own as well as others, they struck terror in the hearts of other tribesmen. Nominally Muslim, they have retained many rites that smack of paganism, venerating tombs that lack links with Islam. Their women have been observed making their obeisance to distant mountain peaks. Recently they have been forced into sullen subservience to the central authority, but only as long as its armed outposts are on hand.

The third large tribal group is that of the Qashqais, considered inferior by the others because they are of Turkish stock and not authentic Iranians, and also because they have to be satisfied with lower grade, parched land. From the high mountains they drive their herds into the enervating alluvial lowlands of the Persian Gulf.

The Middle East Village

A fabulously industrious breed of birds seems to have built the tens of thousands of villages of the Arab lands, Turkey and Iran. They look like nests constructed from whatever is the most common material of their environment. This is not the land of conspicuous red roofs and sparkling white walls. The houses blend with the landscape, and are invisible from a distance or from the air. Flying over this land, one seems to see a land of vast emptiness. Sometimes the villages are on a main road; but even then they seek to keep away from it, often hidden behind a hill. It was the law of the land that to be seen was to invite danger at the hands of marauding hosts, nomads, robbers and tax collectors.

Mud is the village building material along the Nile and in the land of the two rivers, Tigris and Euphrates. In this respect nothing has changed since Pharaonic times. The walls of the huts are "whitewashed" with mud. The mud-bricks are treated with straw, of which there is plenty, and are then exposed to the sun, of which there is even more. The edifice is crowned with a thatch of rotting reed exuding a sweetly nauseating smell, almost like an animal cadaver, perhaps because of the cadavers in the thatch.

In the Nile Delta and southern Iraq the huts are made of rotting reed and rush. They cannot be distinguished from the junglelike luxuriance of the well-watered mazes. On the other hand, most of the huts of Turkey's Anatolian high plateau are built of brown soil, which the local geologists call "Texan." On his hasty way the hurried traveler will overlook many villages, so perfectly are they camouflaged.

In the Fertile Crescent region, running parallel with the Mediterranean and curving down to the head of the Persian Gulf, the building material is likely to be stone, the polished kind one encounters on the hills of Judaea, Samaria and Galilee. It makes good sturdy dwellings which seem to absorb the heat. It is pleasant to have a siesta in the coolness of such a house.

There is an endless world of stone, too, in the wilderness of the Hadramaut, at the opposite end of the great Arab quadrangle. Some of the building rocks are purple, others are so red that they look like blue shot through with violet and yellow. In the High Yemen there are skyscrapers that consist of primitive stone huts piled one on top of the other, looking down into the precipitous canyons of the wadis. Strong fortifications, these skyscrapers must have provided excellent protection against hostile neighbors.

The huts turn unseeing eyes to the outside world; they do not want to see and do not want to be seen. There are no windows, because windows cost too much money—only crude shutters and those are luxuries. They keep out the sun's rays, since the sun is curious also and wants to see dark corners which are better left in darkness.

A room is a man's castle—that is, his hut, his home. He feels secure in it, and probably sometimes he even feels happy. He looks around and surveys the world he owns. There are the rusty kitchen utensils, inherited from his forebears. How many generations? Who knows and who cares? Then the rags on which the family sleeps: these are another luxury protecting the household from having to rest on the naked floor with the bugs. But those little creatures are sly and eventually they share the rags with the humans, the one well-fed and the other hungry.

When there is a marriage in the family another hut is glued to the old one; then another one, and so on, until finally there is a small compound that swarms with people at bedtime. Where do they all sleep and what about the happy human cravings? Everybody sees everything, everybody knows everything, and consequently they are nervous. They are not aware of their state, however, and therefore the problem is not acute. Luckily for them, they have never studied psychology, let alone psychoanalysis.

Upon occasion, of course, they do run wild; when their skins are soaked too full of sun and their stomachs are too empty; when too many babies are screaming; when somebody steps on a head in the dark.

Then there are sick people, groaning, always groaning; they are not only sick but want to *show* that they are. They have no doctors and they crave sympathy, which they give to themselves but not to others. Groaning people are unpopular. Sometimes there is an old woman in the family—maybe forty—and she turns up with some fantastic concoction which she gives to the patient. If he does not die of it, the concoction is bound to gather fame. If he dies of it there will be a brief scuffle for the dead man's estate—his place on the rags.

Where misery is boundless, as in the rich Nile valley, there are frequent suicides and occasional murders. Not too many, though, because people have no arms, not even knives. Choking a man to death is an easy way of disposing of him, but that requires a strength which many lack.

And so the family grows, dwelling-units mushroom, glued into each other around the courtyard—and the compound is ready. It is surrounded by a wall, neither strong nor high, and affording no protection, as walls should. It is made of mud or stone, again depending on the dominant raw material. It keeps curiosity out, so that the women can go about their business unmolested. The protection of the wall is mainly psychological. It separates you from the world; and that is good, because the world is bad.

Within the walls there is the yard and in it there are heaps of dirt of all kinds. There may be dried dung if the family is well-to-do and has animals. There are small piles of some food or other as well as nondescript articles which must have been collected in the course of many years. Then there is the hearth, placed in a concealed nook of the yard so that the women shall not be exposed to greedy eyes. And why should eyes be greedy when seeing such women? Perhaps because, there being nothing better, even these poor creatures appear attractive.

The huts have no trace of the *haram,* about which the western world has heard. That is a luxury for the rich, who have a place for it. At home the women are not veiled; their men folk know them, and strangers are kept outside the walls.

Within the family the rule is patriarchal. An elderly male—grandfather, father—is the household head. He is the ruler of the sons, their wives and children, the unmarried females. When the girls marry, the jurisdiction over them is transferred to the head of the household of the bridegroom's kin.

The Architects were Goats

The planners of the villages were unpredictable goats in the remote days when they still found forage in these parts. It is their whims and the creases of soil erosion that the alleys follow. In the foothill regions the villages are built on the slope, on bare rock, stopping on the margin of the alluvial land where fertility begins. The peasant wanted to be near his soil, yet it was too precious to have houses built on it.

Another problem is faced in the villages of Egypt. They were built on the banks of the Nile and in the Delta, sites many of them may have occupied not for centuries but millennia. Therefore, they occupy some of the world's best soil, fit for the most intensive type of farming.

On the other hand, the population fertility of the country is high and the need for living space is pressing. Villages would have to grow and new villages would have to be founded. However, if people were allowed to expand further onto the rich farm land, they would crowd out the food and Egypt would become a charnel house. Hence, it has become the law of the land that villages must not grow in size and no new villages may be founded on fertile ground. The overflow of people must be absorbed by the existing settlements within their confines, or the population surplus moves into urban centers. In order to solve this problem a drastic suggestion has been made to the effect that Egypt's villages should be transferred to the desert edges where they would not fill up valuable space.

Farm people in the Middle East mostly live in villages and towns, not on the farm. These centers are near wells and their size determines the extent of the place. To live on the farm would mean using up valuable land for purposes other than production, and this would be wasteful in a region where land is such a boon.

Also the settlement centers provide protection for land and people. Armed hosts were ravaging the land in the past and the villages served as defenders. The desert is never too far from the sown area and the desperate people of the great wasteland could not afford to think twice about food-gathering methods. Again, the village was to serve as a bulwark.

The villages are so spaced that the land between them should be under their effective protection. The outer limit between settlements is also determined by the pace of the donkey. That phlegmatic animal cannot be hurried, wise as it is in the ways of Middle Eastern life. Two miles an hour is about all even the sturdiest stick can get out of it. The peasant can afford to walk two hours to the field, and two hours homeward. The outer limit of village land is therefore about four miles.

Café Society in the Middle East Hub

Man's worst enemy may be man, but he is also his best friend. People want to talk or just gaze and listen in unison. For this there are several institutions, of which the most universal is the café. It has no neon signs to attract the customers, who are thoroughly familiar with its location. Nor is it anything like the Café de la Paix of Paris. The café clientele consists of habitués who can afford to loll around a large part of the day and pay the price of a cup of the syrupy brew.

Cafés are often near the entrance of the village or at the intersection of roads, so as to enable the customers to keep an eye on the world—their world, the village. The architecture is simplicity itself. There is usually a terrace covered with canvas or reed, exposed to the prevailing breeze, and from there the customer can really see everything of importance in his miniature universe. Behind the terrace there is the café proper, its walls bare except for the chromo pictures of an American soft-drink bottle.

The furniture of the café is almost modernistically functional. It consists of a few backless low stools and an assortment of small round tables, on which the *nargileh* or water-pipe is placed. The café habitué seems to have a glorious time puffing at the water-cooled pipe and, in intervals, sipping his strong coffee. The radio provides him with the best entertainment he fancies: the wailing strains which the westerner finds so hard to accept as music; the familiar recitals from the Muslim Holy Script, Koran; the latest news. Sometimes the café clientele plays cards or a kind of checkers, but more often it engages in familiar gossip, talks politics or just gazes into nowhere—seemingly the most satisfactory form of entertainment, judging by the expression of rapture on the beholder's mien. Such communions with nothing may come closest to the earthly realization of *nirvana*, being submerged in the endless nothing, feeling no pain, the mind devoid of thought.

Unless the village is very poor, it also has a guest house which is a social center where men chat, listen to the radio or hear the headman (*mukhtar*) transmitting the latest word from the higher-ups. Solemn family occasions, such as marriages, also depend on these guest houses. The "home" is inadequate, small, dark, crowded, lacking even the low benches which are indispensable for conviviality. In republican Turkey one of the great innovations of the founder of the republic, Mustafa Kemal, was the establishment of Peoples' Houses as social centers. He believed that his regime could be brought closer to the people through such places.

The threshing floor is another meeting place for the country man and is also popular with the boys. Here there is always life, choice gossip, delightful beefing about conditions in the village and the entire broad world. Here there is also hard work, but life is always hard where the motive force is a man's hands.

In parts of the Middle East the house of worship serves as a social center too. In small places particularly it is often a matter of etiquette to repair to the mosque for the five prescribed daily prayers. Besides being uplifting, it provides a welcome interruption of work. The leader of the prayer may also be the leader in the village.

Old customs never die. In Turkey, for instance, the mosques were under a heavy shadow during the revolutionary reform phase of the republic under Mustafa Kemal. He exposed them as symbols of the bad old times, of the age of the great shame, when Turkey was the dying man. It was Kemal's idea that the Peoples' Houses should take over the social functions of the mosque. But the new "Prophet" of nationalism seems to have waged his war against the old Prophet of Islamic creed in vain. In most Turkish villages of today the mosque seems to have regained its previous importance.

The Christian church plays an important role in the small republic of Lebanon, where all Christian creeds taken together have a small edge over their Muslim fellow citizens. In these villages social life is "bi-polar," centered around the mosque and the church. This was not always so. There was the time not long ago when the mosque fought the church and made its life miserable. Those days are gone, not because the Middle East has become more tolerant but because it has become more intolerant. In those days the mosque felt itself crowded out by the church in the mountains of Lebanon and responded with violence. Then the guiding institution was the house of worship, often perverted to serve as the instrument of intolerance.

Today the Middle East has a new God, much stronger than the God worshiped in mosque and church. That new God is the Nation. The mosque and the church get on well together because they are no longer important. What counts today is nationality, "Arabism." Both Christians and Muslims of the Lebanon are Arabs and their supreme loyalty goes to the Godlike State. The lukewarm leftovers of loyalty are solemnly dedicated to creed.

For many Lebanese there is also another social center and that, strangely, is the local post office. The reasons for this curious selection are not hard to find. Among all the Arabs the Lebanese are the most footloose and they have large overseas colonies, particularly across the ocean, mainly in the United States. In the lives of the Lebanese people remittances of overseas funds and mail from the kin in America play important roles. Numerous are the links knotted together in front of the General Delivery window.

Women are Also Human Beings

Women have not been mentioned so far in connection with social life. Frankly, they do not count much. In the larger towns one sees a woman occasionally in a café but that is probably not considered proper. In the villages they are not seen in public places, with men around. Still, their need for gossip is not less than that of the male animal, and so they have their social centers which, however, are almost invariably linked with work.

The traditional meeting place for women is the village well, which, in many places today, may be the mechanical water-pumping station. It is there that the rural grapevine works with that lightninglike rapidity which is so surprising to the outlander. Also women are in the open-air community "laundry." pounding away at clothing in the same way Hagar must have done it ages ago. The chatter of their gossip forms a subdued counterpoint to the swishing of the clothes.

Even in the most tradition-bound families of the Arab world women of character and common sense can reach honored positions, becoming the centers of their homes. In Turkey there are women judges, deputies, bankers, plant managers. In Israel the road to the highest positions is open to them. Women have the right to vote in some Arab countries and they are rapidly freed of trammels. Egypt's "Daughters of the Nile" follow in the footsteps of prewar England's "suffragettes."

The Land of D.I.P.

When considering census figures about Middle East national income one is reminded of the saying, "There are three types of lies: plain lies, damned lies and statistics." No two sets of figures will ever jibe. However, one thing is certain: Iran and the Arab countries, with the notable exception of Lebanon, are incredibly poor. Turkey is very poor. Nor is Israel rich.

What the figures make clear about the Arab countries and Iran is that its people do not live—they merely vegetate. A recent Rockefeller Foundation study of selected villages in Egypt brought out the fact that more than 60 per cent of the families investigated had monthly incomes between $2.90 and $14.50, and 5 per cent had even less. Some 30 per cent had incomes between $14.50 and $29, and only the small remainder earned more than that amount. Another study showed that unskilled farm labor in Egypt received about 22 cents a day for work which was irregular throughout the year.

The Department of Commerce in Egypt's Ibrahim Pasha University recently produced even more devastating figures. It showed that the entire country's income on the eve of the First World War was 150,000,000 pounds sterling and remained stationary in old currency values (without the watering effect of inflation) for the next forty years. And this in spite of the very great increase of population. During the same period the per capita annual income in Egypt actually declined from about twelve to seven and a half pounds. At the same time the total national income of the rest of the world increased considerably.

Money income, of course, is sometimes completely unknown in rural areas. There are regions in the rich Nile valley where all income, including the farmer's produce and the laborer's wages, totaled not more than fifteen to twenty dollars during the entire year. What can a man buy for such paltry sums, and how can he support himself and his family?

A true picture of the conditions is not conveyed by money comparisons. What can one say about the all-pervading filth of poverty, the terrible diseases and the ignorance of the majority of the people? Even clean water is a luxury. As Doreen Warriner points out in her study, *Land and Poverty in the Middle East,* the pattern of village life in this area is near-starvation, pestilence, soil erosion and an unbelievable degree of economic exploitation. "There is no standard of living in the European sense—mere existence is accepted as a standard."

Lebanon falls into a different category, partly because she receives considerable sums from overseas. Turkey is a "plutocrat" with an annual estimated per capita income of $125. She was greatly aided in reaching this level by her ability to keep neutral during the Second World War. She sold her valuable mineral and farm products to both sides at high prices.

The per capita annual income of Israel in 1949 was $389, representing the only western standard in the region. This figure, too, is subject to corrections because of the distorting effects of inflation and immigration. While the country is in flux it is well-nigh impossible to give a realistic picture of its living standards.

Whose Fault Is It?

Since Asia is a global poorhouse, we should not be surprised to see poverty holding the Middle East in its grip. Yet, this region is so close to Europe, is linked with it through so many bonds, that it appears to be almost its extension. In Europe one is not used to such low standards. Also, the Middle East is adjacent to the Soviet Union and that country thrives best on situations of this sort.

Let us see, therefore, what accounts for this poverty.

Nature, of course, is one factor and a highly important one. The area forms a part of the world's arid and semi-arid belt, extremely poor in important natural resources. Oil is something new in this territory and its influence on living standards will not be felt until later. But nature is not the sole explanation, because, unbelievable as its sounds, not all farming resources of the region are fully exploited, great though the need is for them.

Then there is the climate, which exerts its influence. Is it enervating? It is in certain parts, especially around the Persian Gulf, in large parts of Iran, on the Red Sea. However, what could be more delightful than the climate of Egypt? In most of Turkey the climate may be said to be stimulating and on the coast of Levant, the eastern Mediterranean region with its dense human settlements, the climate is no more enervating than that of southern California.

There is much sunshine in the region and neither clothing nor shelter is a great problem. As a general rule, human beings respond only to energetic goads. Here two of the three goads are absent—food remains. This may be one reason why the Middle Eastern man is not more dynamic.

What about the psychology of the inhabitants? You can place a certain type of people in the very midst of a treasure house and soon they will be surrounded by abject poverty. Traditions may be debilitating, customs antisocial.

What about kismet, the hand of fate? It is, indeed, a Turkish word, derived from the Arab's *qismah,* portion, lot. The spirit of Islam is that of submission to God but that is not different from the philosophy of other monotheistic creeds. This is a point, however, that deserves attention. Turkey's great reformer, Mustafa Kemal, did blame Islam for the backwardness of his country. The Middle East mentality, exceptions apart, is saturated with the idea that earthly life is short and that man should concentrate on the eternal. One might as well take it easy in this ephemeral life. What does it all matter? *Malesh.* It matters naught.

The influence of Islam may have been to encourage a static attitude, as opposed to the overheated energy of the West. "It is better to walk than to run; it is better to stand than to walk; it is better to sit than to stand, and it is better to lie down than to sit." Do not exert yourself, take it easy, and what is tomorrow in the company of eternity?

The western world has been able to reconcile its religious beliefs with a dynamic emphasis on one's mission in earthly life. In our present-day life, religion, at best, is a restraining influence, not the motive force. Perhaps we can better understand the Middle East if we think of the Middle Ages for a moment. Nationalism is likely to make short shrift with Islam, as it made short shrift with Christianity. And nationalism is an appallingly dynamic idea, entailing the maximum of competition within and between the nations.

The Ottoman Heritage

The Middle East is also the victim of the Ottoman heritage. Most of this region was under the Sultans' rule for five centuries, a reign dynamic only in military matters. The motto of that regime was to take and not to give; a locust plague, which left the Arab world denuded. Where the Ottoman official set his foot, no grass was to grow.

Such a heritage etched itself deeply into the minds and ways of the people. What was the sense of exerting oneself, or just working? The more you had the more was taken away from you. If one's neck was stuck out, it was chopped off. It was best to say nothing and do nothing, because otherwise one was bound to arouse attention and that meant jealousy.

Then the Ottoman Empire collapsed in our own century, republican Turkey was born and the Arab states were set up. This was the signal for the oncoming of the Golden Age, but instead of that the Middle East saw the dismal dawn of the Iron Age. The Ottoman Turkish officials were replaced by native Arabs, the very kin of the bulk of the people. Let there be justice in the land, so that the poor should not die of their poverty. Let the locust-ravaged land be made to bloom under the beneficent rule of fellow Arabs.

The shadow of the past turned out to be extremely long. The heart of the fellow Arab was hard as rock. He commiserated with the poor and kept on robbing him. He was worse than the Turks, because he was familiar with native wiles of evasion. Also, he obtained reinforcements from an unexpected quarter.

The new Arab countries were taken in tow by two of the

world's most advanced nations, Great Britain and France. They acquired mandatory rights in the heart of the Arab world. As progressive nations they deemed it their duty to rule with the consent of the governed. But who were those people? Certainly not the inarticulate millions, the submissive masses, trained to obedience throughout the ages, forever complaining but never acting, since they were unorganized and too tired, sick and poor. It was the "two hundred families" in each of these countries, with their *savoir-faire,* well-oiled machines, selfishly articulate public opinion which was the only opinion the region produced. The enlightened mandatory powers could not ignore them without ignoring the most elementary rules of "democracy."

France and Britain had the mission of training these countries in the art of self-government. It was also their mission to maintain law and order. The western governments could not start revolutions to put the masses into the driver's seat. Besides, what would those people do in their lofty perch? By failing to co-operate with the native governments, the western countries would have been remiss in their mandatory duties.

Had there been no France and Britain there might have been a better possibility for the forces deep below to rise. However, the very fact that Great Britain and France were present cemented the hold of the ruling oligarchies. This confronted the world with a strange spectacle.

Countries where Great Britain and France were not called upon to perform their high mission made attempts to break the hold of the dead hand of the past. Turkey, no longer an Ottoman empire but a republic, staged a massive revolution. A similar attempt was made also in Iran. Even Ibn Saud, sovereign of one of the most backward Arab countries but not subject to "enlightened" foreign tutelage, was in a position to introduce reforms which the far more advanced Levantine countries, under their French and British mentors, lacked the power to launch.

Who else was to blame? The lack of capital, obviously, and an entire assortment of negative qualities: lack of technical skills, low health standards, and antiquated, destructive land policies. For a long time there has been an anarchic "system" of land registration in the Middle East. Feudalism was rampant in the region under a variety of names, and it paralyzed the workingman's will power. He knows he is engaged in a hopeless struggle against odds he cannot overcome. And it is no use to work either. For more can be accomplished by devious ways. What counts is not what you know, but whom you know.

The sharecropping system also frustrated initiative. Leases were for short periods and the landlord always found ways and means to cheat the tenant out of his share. "The injurious effect of the existing welter of uncertainty upon both the agricultural prosperity of the country and public order can hardly be exaggerated," said Sir Ernest Dowson in a study undertaken in the thirties.

All or Nothing

The Middle Eastern landlords are, indeed, further removed from the peasants than were Europe's medieval feudal lords, most of whom had their manors on their estates and thus could not help being in contact with their serfs. Also they had to become acquainted with the countryside because of their hunting grounds. There are neither manors nor hunting grounds in the Middle East. The landlord lives in the city, in Paris or more often in a luxurious villa on the Riviera.

Since the owner is absent, he has a manager on the premises. He represents power; the sharecropper has no protection, except in heaven. The manager may be a pious man performing his ritual ablutions according to the very letter of the law; but since he has no tenure in his employment, he will refuse a peasant water until he receives a bribe.

The Prophet must have been familiar with these problems, for the Koran says that the rich man is not to exploit the poor and is not to charge usurious interest. The effendi is the staunch pillar of society and so it is not for him to break the law. The interest he charges is not usurious. However, he forces his cultivator to acknowledge receipt of twice the amount of loan he actually obtains. Then the effendi performs his religious duties with a light heart, knowing well that his will be the bliss of Paradise, of which he receives a glimpse on earth itself.

Many are the ways through which the Koran's social-minded

injunctions may be circumvented. There was the recorded case of the effendi in Gaza whose lands rounded out five thousand acres. He wanted to help his tenants and so he bought a tractor. Then he raised his tenants' rent from one-third to one-half of the produce and this left them just a little worse off than they had been.

How much does the tenant get for all his work? Conditions are different in various parts of the region, but often he receives no more than one-fifth of the farm produce he grows. One-fifth of it goes to the landlord for the land, another one-fifth goes to him for the water, a third for the seed and a fourth for the livestock—altogether, four-fifths to the landlord.

The owners of the so-called dwarf farms in the Middle East are not much better off than the landless tenant and labor peasantry. The owners of small farms, very often not more than half an acre, cannot even afford to eat the food they raise. They live on cheaper products and whatever they can pick up in the fields.

Only 13 per cent of the cultivated land was owned in 1947 by two million peasants of Egypt, the most populous of all Arab countries. At the same time, 36.8 per cent of the land belonged to 11,000 landlords. There were plans afoot in the country to add some four million acres to the eight million cultivated ones and to distribute the accrual among the small and landless peasants.

One of the richest effendis of Egypt was the former King Farouk I. After he had been forced to abdicate in midsummer 1952, an inventory of his landholdings was to be made. Only estimates were published, and these varied widely. The most extravagant estimate was that he owned about one-third of the cultivated land of the country. According to the most conservative estimate he owned 20,000 acres outright, had partial interest in other estates, had mortgaged a considerable part of his land in order to salt away a portion of his fortune in the United States, Brazil, and Europe. His fortune was reported to amount to between a quarter and a half billion dollars.

At the other extreme of the Middle Eastern world, in Iran,

it was reported[2] that fully 40,000 of her 41,000 villages belonged to the rich landlords. A previous estimate placed ownership of half of the cultivated land in the hands of some hundred thousand landlords out of an estimated total population of eighteen million. The Shah of Iran alone was reported to have 2,167 villages as his own private property. More public-spirited than the rest of the effendis, he wanted to sell the land on terms favorable to the peasants.

To take another example, in Syria, which is one of the more advanced Arab countries, fully 60 per cent of the cultivated land is effendi-owned, while in the northern parts of the nation the percentage is eighty. In the Hama district of that country 110 villages out of 114 passed into the landlords' hands in recent times and four of their effendis owned 80 of these villages.

The Middle Eastern farmer suffers also from extreme fragmentation of land, particularly where it is arable. This is due largely to ancient customs of inheritance. As a rule, landed property descends to the offspring, each male sharing equally and two females equaling one male. In the Lebanese village of Bar Elias, for instance, the fragmentation has gone so far that 5,285 acres were divided into no fewer than 32,643 plots. A person may own a fruit tree on the neighbor's land and occasionally no more than a branch of a tree. One of the worst curses of the East is to wish a person bad neighbors.

A Midsummer Night's Dream

The midsummer of 1952 saw the incubation of great changes in Egypt and Iran, pivotal Middle Eastern countries. After the expulsion of King Farouk I the land reform was announced.[3] The Palestinian war, four years before, may have provided the impetus of the change. "The men of the Egyptian army were too lean," an observer said, "the officers too fat." Now some of the men at least were to put on weight. Nobody was allowed to retain more than 200 acres of farm land. Peasants were to receive allotments of from 2 to 5 acres. The reform was to be

[2] *The New York Times,* August 6, 1952.
[3] *The New York Times,* August 13, 1952.

carried out in five years. The expropriated landlords were to be compensated according to prewar value, some 40 per cent less than the market value after the war. The newly created peasants were to reimburse the government, which was to effect the purchase, in thirty annual installments. The average value of farm land was said to be $914 per acre, four times the prewar value. Under the plan, 2,200 owners holding 1,167,000 acres were to lose 727,000 acres. Fewer than one-tenth of the landless, of whom there were some million and a half, were to benefit, and besides there were the dwarf owners, who could not make a living on their property.

The Ministry of Social Affairs was to supervise the distribution of irrigation water and fertilizers, and the new peasant proprietors were to organize themselves in farm co-operatives. Where would they receive the tools and capital, especially for cotton raising? And would they know how to run a farm?

At about the same time, Iran also announced far-reaching reforms. Landlords were to turn over 20 per cent of their harvest, to be divided among peasants working on the land and rural co-operative societies. The Premier's decree also abolished remaining feudal dues and forced labor charges burdening the peasantry in parts of the country. The Minister of Agriculture was instructed to spend $30,000,000 on irrigation and half of that sum on farm tools. A National Council was set up to put these measures into effect and also to set up consumer and credit co-operatives providing low interest loans; and to establish marketing organizations.

Were these plans to mature, or were they to join the grand parade of lofty projects devised by new regimes? Where was Iran, for instance, to get the funds when she was in arrears on the government officials' pays? Was this merely a midsummer night's dream or the beginning of long-overdue reforms?

The Tragic Paradox

There is a great shortage of land in the Middle East and yet only a portion of the Middle East poorhouse is actually under the plow. The thousands of western tourists visiting the Holy Land must have noticed the ruins of agricultural terracing, showing that much more of the soil was cultivated in the past than at present. This is even more dramatically evident in Mesopotamia, the site of the "Garden of Eden," which at one time supported many times her present population. Many tracts could be redeemed from swamps and others from the desert. It has been shown in Palestine that even the most hopelessly boulder-strewn mountain slope can be turned into orchards, with patience and hard work.

The reliable United Nations Food and Agricultural Organization is the source of the estimate that not more than one-half of the potentially available land in the Middle East is actually used. Worse than that, less than one-fifth of the cultivable land is cropped annually, according to a study of the equally dependable Royal Institute of International Affairs. An official French study undertaken in Syria revealed the shocking fact that not more than one-sixth of the total potential irrigation area of that country was so used—half a million out of a possible three million acres. It is estimated that Iraq tills only one-fourth of her tillable soil. It has been found that even in Egypt, which was presumed to have pushed the limit of land cultivation to the boundaries of the desert, it is possible to bring additional land under the plow. After the expulsion of King Farouk another one of the ambitious plans was to wrest millions of acres from aridity.

It is a tragic fact that effendi resistance plays a large part in the existence of this paradox. In the Middle East there are large tracts of land available for cultivation, some of them belonging to the State, while others belong to religious foundations (*waqf*) for the ultimate benefit of charity. More often than not the managers of the State land and the religious foundation land are the effendis themselves. They fear that opening these tracts to land reform would change the existing picture and diminish their importance.

Meet Ahmed Pasha

Ahmed Pasha is the head of one of the twenty, forty or two hundred families which form the nations. The name of that nation may be Iraq, Syria, Egypt or Iran. Yet, Ahmed Pasha is the government, and he is the parliament (*barlaman*), and he is the people. The democratic structure is impressive, and parliaments meet to discuss problems, sometimes with much heat. Governments come and governments go but Ahmed Pasha remains forever. The choice may be between Ahmed Aboud and Ahmed Hilaly or a few scores of other Ahmeds or Mustafas or Suleimans. "Democracy" consists of a certain amount of rotation between this Ahmed and that Ahmed. When the one is in power he loots the treasury and calls the other one a robber, and the other way around. There are a few honest Ahmeds, but they do not last long. They are run out of the magic circle, denounced as unpatriotic, because among thieves it is dishonest to be honest.

Ahmed Pasha is the eternal effendi. The following was reported from London via *The New York Times* on July 7, 1952.

> A dispatch in *The London Daily Express* reported today without official confirmation that Ahmed Aboud Pasha, millionaire Egyptian industrialist and financier, was responsible for the downfall of the government of Ahmed Neguib el Hilaly Pasha, who resigned nine days ago. The newspaper alleged that Ahmed Pasha's campaign cost him £1,000,000 ($2,800,000).
>
> In a dispatch carrying the dateline Geneva, Switzerland, *The Express* said that when Aboud Pasha, one of the principal figures in the Egyptian sugar industry, heard that Hilaly Pasha intended to nationalize the industry, "he decided the government must go."
>
> *The Express* reported that two of Aboud Pasha's associates in the affair approached Jefferson Caffery, the United States Ambassador, and told him that the Middle East defense plan sponsored by the United States and Britain would go forward if he would put pressure on King Farouk to dismiss Hilaly Pasha.
>
> Instead of going to the King, Mr. Caffery reported the conversation to Abdel Khalek Hassuna Pasha, the Foreign Minister, the newspaper reported.
>
> Hilaly heard about it, was disgusted at the intrigues and immediately resigned . . .

The effendis and pashas own the countries, and the question arises: How much do they contribute to the upkeep of their nations? Again the outside world must stand aghast at what it finds. In all the Middle East Arab countries and in Iran, the bulk of the government revenues is derived from indirect taxes—imposts on consumption which weigh more heavily on the poor since they have to spend all their money on them. In a part of the world where land is the greatest revenue producer, the equitable tax would be on land, especially absentee estates, and those are precisely very lightly taxed, if at all. It was but recently that a land tax was introduced in these countries and even this turns out to weigh more heavily on the poor, partly because it is regressive (the tax rate declines with increasing income) and partly because the effendi cannot be compelled to pay the tax.

Here are a few significant facts for purposes of illustration.

In the republic of Syria indirect taxes in 1950 accounted for £ Syr. 45,600,000, as against direct taxes of £ Syr. 5,800,000. (The official rate of exchange was $2.80 per Syrian pound.) In Egypt the "Land Tax, etc." in the fiscal year of 1950-51 amounted to £ E 24,000,000 (a great increase over the previous year), out of a total revenue of £ E 206,000,000. After a raise in the rate, tax on incomes up to £ E 5,000 was 15 per cent, and it is only very rich people who make so much money in a wretchedly poor country. In the great housecleaning in the midsummer of 1952, it was announced that annual incomes of £ E 50,000 would pay eighty per cent. The proviso was, of course, in case the taxpayers could be found on the premises.

In Iran's 1949-50 budget, indirect taxes amounted to 578 million rials, against 1,160 million in direct taxes.

Tehran announced in midsummer of 1952 that the government was planning to impose a 2 per cent tax on all land. The same rate was to be paid whether the land was the half acre of the small peasant or the hundreds of villages of the grandee. However, there too the grandee considered it execrable manners to pay taxes and most of them knew how to evade payment. When Iran had an American Treasurer General, Morgan Shuster, before the First World War, he had to use force to collect taxes from the large owners and was successful only in part.

The Plagues of Egypt

The plagues of Egypt and of the Middle East are far more numerous than the Biblical Ten. Again statistics must be eyed with caution because, as an Egyptian health authority warned, "for every recorded case of specific disease there are hundreds of cases of absence of full health due in part at least to malnutrition."

The most unsanitary place of any civilized part of the world, according to a Rockefeller Foundation study was the Egyptian village. Conditions there were seen as worse even than in India, China, and the sorest spots of the West Indies. Using a scale on which a community with proper sanitary standards scored 106.5 points, India, China and the most wretched islands of the West Indies registered 53.2–Egypt, 23.8.

The villages observed were all close to Cairo and, therefore, presumably under the cultural influence of a world metropolis. Yet nearly all the inhabitants of these places were afflicted with amoebic dysentery, while 89 per cent had trachoma. There are few more tragic sights in the Middle East than sightless children whose pus-filled eyelids are covered with flies. (Allah has sent the flies and no man should destroy them.) Six per cent of the investigated people were half blind and one out of a hundred was totally blind. About 65 per cent of the inhabitants had intestinal worms; 5 per cent had pellagra; more than 6 per cent syphilis; 2 per cent contracted typhoid fever every year; and 6 per cent were typhoid carriers.

About 92 per cent had the dreaded disease *bilharzia,* which is decimating countries like Egypt and Iraq where there are irrigation canals. Through the skin of the fellah's bare legs the minuscule parasites of this intestinal affliction work their way from the soggy soil into the human body. Once within the intestinal tracts they proliferate at a prodigious rate. All over Egypt and in parts of Iraq one sees these living ghosts, mere shadows, a burden to themselves and their kin. The parasite virtually carves out their intestines, leaving them hollow shells, climaxing their agony in a nightmare of suffering from which the great release is blessed death. To purify drinking water would save countless lives, but the project to do so in Egypt, for instance, would cost three quarters of a billion dollars and the government revenue for fiscal 1950-51 was only half a billion dollars.

Malaria has been the great killer in this region too, as in the rest of the great poorhouse of the world. Until recent times nearly all the inhabitants of Iran's Caspian shore were afflicted with it. Close to a hundred per cent of the malaria incidence was in the vicinity of Palestine's Lake Hullah, under the interbellum British regime. Today the miracles of insecticides have cleaned up much of the region.

Old ways are still considered the best in many parts of the Middle East. The thoughts of the sick turn to the "religious-medical practitioner," the barber phlebotomist, the wisewoman and the cupper. Female patients shun the male doctors as if they were Satan in disguise, and there are very few female physicians.

Most of the hospitals are horrid places, barely one degree better than jails, and the patient who is shipped there is ready to recommend his soul to Allah's mercy. The author wanted to visit a Cairo clinic some time ago but he beat a hasty retreat when he caught a glimpse of the interior. It was not part of his plans to contract an eye ailment in a hospital.

Distressingly low is the number of qualified physicians in most of the Arab countries and Iran. Even in Turkey there were only 4,590 physicians in 1947. The entire Kingdom of Iraq, with its population of some five million, had 569 registered physicians in 1945, and more than one-half of these were practicing in Baghdad, the capital, which comprises one-tenth of the population of the country. In Iran there is one doctor for every 63,000 inhabitants. A visiting United States health team saw one single physician looking after 33,500 cases in an Egyptian health center. At the other extreme, there is one physician for 380 inhabitants in Israel.

Many people die prematurely in this region of Arabs; but the birth rate is very high, ranging between 25 and 60 per thousand, compared with 15 and 16 in Great Britain and the United States. The increase of population is so great in parts that every half a century the population is doubled and this creates another problem. In Egypt, for instance, the population pressure is already tremendous. Also, in Egypt the death rate is highest in the world.

The Great Illiteracy Belt

The region of the globe in which the Word was born is today a part of the world's great illiteracy belt. In Saudi Arabia and Yemen the illiteracy rate is highest, perhaps all the way up to 95 per cent. In Egypt it is estimated at 75 per cent, while in Lebanon it may be only 25 per cent. In Jordan some 28 per cent of the children of school age go to school, and in Iraq about 39 per cent. Four-fifths of the children of Iran do not go to school and there, too, 90 per cent of the entire population is believed to be illiterate, and this in spite of the fact that a compulsory literacy law was placed on the statute books years before.[4]

In parts of the Middle East the only school is still the ungraded *kuttab,* where the child memorizes the Koran and learns the barest elements of the three R's. He stays there for a year or two, then he or his family gets tired of scholarship and he goes home. The fellah can seldom afford to spare even the children from work.

Hundreds of thousands are registered in the compulsory lower schools of Egypt, but only a few thousands remain in

[4] As part of the great "housecleaning" program of the summer of 1952, the Iranian government was to launch a radio education program intended to teach every peasant who is capable of it to read and write. The program called for the setting up of high-powered receiving sets provided by the United States Information Service in Tehran. The first equipment to be installed in fifteen test villages was to have loud speakers so strong that they could be heard for four miles. Simple texts for learning to read and write basic Persian were to be placed in the peasants' hands together with notebooks and pencils. The equipment was to include a dynamo to provide electric light for the groups following the lessons in the village streets. The program was to be broadcast every night from six to seven. As there is nothing to do in an Iranian village at that hour it was believed that there would be few peasants not willing to listen. The rest of the program was to be divided into three parts: ten minutes devoted to sanitation and health, twelve minutes to basic agricultural problems and the remaining time to activities designed to improve the economic lot of the peasants. (From a Tehran dispatch by Albion Ross in the August 25, 1952, issue of *The New York Times.*)

the fifth grade. In Iraq, Jordan and Syria no more than 5 per cent remain in the upper grades.

This lack of interest in education is due to several causes. One of these is the heritage of the Ottoman Empire, which did not believe in secular education, only in a little learning of the Koran. The teachers were frequently as ignorant as their pupils. Boys have some commercial value doing chores in the house and on the fields. Girls are not supposed to know the Koran, and some members of the older generation consider it godless to let them go to school. Very few of them do. There is now a tendency, however—in certain Arab countries at least—to open up educational opportunities to the girls.

An important factor militating against education is the spirit of *malesh,* that nothing matters, that it is best to take things easy and not to burden one's brains with useless knowledge.

Then there is the ingrained suspicion of the government. The school is mostly a government department and therefore it is the enemy. There must be some sinister motives behind the governors' attempts to teach the young and therefore they must be resisted.

The school feels its close connection with the government and acts accordingly. The teacher is a functionary and belongs to the class of the governors, expected to keep aloof from parent and child, who occupy a subordinate position in the scheme of things. Some of the teachers are familiar with the modern educational methods in the West but the climate of opinion in most of the region does not encourage experiments with progressive education. The school has hardly anything to do with life. It would be beneath the teacher's dignity to concern himself with the problems of the parents and children.

Then there is the fear that the more people know the more questions they are bound to ask—and no questions should be asked. The Koran is considered safe, in spite of some of its "revolutionary" passages, since people read it by the rote, without trying to understand its meaning or to put its social precepts into practice.

Recently in the Middle East, an American educator was among a group of people discussing the problems of the region and offering solutions. Education was the answer, the American thought, but the response to his suggestion was less than enthusiastic. A member of the party was thoroughly aroused and he was definitely against schooling for more people. "Schools are the breeding places of communism," he orated. The American was surprised by this violent opposition and he was even more flabbergasted when he learned that the uncompromising enemy of public education was a teacher himself.

Another persistent enemy of education is poverty. The observation of an American educator in southern Iraq is typical of much larger areas. He noted there that even parents who would have liked to send their children to school could not do so. In the first place, the children lacked proper garments. Then, how was a poor peasant to pay for pencil and paper?

The advantages of education in improving the standards of life of the people are not well known in the region. A survey conducted in Alexandria revealed that a literate person in Egypt earned twice as much as the illiterate in the same type of job. It also showed that the ratio of disease among the children of educated mothers was only 3 per cent, against 83 per cent in the case of illiterates.

There is an increasing number of Middle Easterners who are aware of the importance of education in raising the standards of their countries. They know that higher education means higher living standards, less dependence upon foreigners, and a greater degree of self-determination. They also know that one can read the importance of a country in its educational record. No matter how eloquent a statesman—and Arab statesmen can be very eloquent—their efforts will be discounted if exerted on behalf of millions of illiterates.

One of the most potent forces behind mass education in the region was the famous blind author and educator, Dr. Taha Husayn, former Minister of Education of Egypt, himself of fellah origin. The motto he observed in and out of office had a modern ring: *To pursue knowledge is like water and air, an inalienable right to which every citizen is entitled.*

Asked how his ambitious program of free education was to be financed, he replied: "It is not my business to provide all that [finances]; all I have to do is ask, and it is up to the Minister of Finance to find the means."

Higher Education in the Middle East

A truly pioneering work was initiated in the Middle East by the foreign schools of higher learning. In this respect, America has played a notable part. Robert College in Istanbul was founded during the War Between the States, in 1863. When the writer recently visited the Grand National Assembly of Turkey in Ankara in the company of a distinguished former faculty member of Robert College, he was shown the members of the legislature who were graduates of that American school. It was revealing to see how much the college contributed toward the building up of a politically articulate citizenry.

It was five famous young men educated at the Syrian Protestant College at Beirut whose secret society signaled the Arab awakening. Today that school is named the American University of Beirut, internationally famous, whose 2,500 students belong to thirty-seven nations but are still mainly Middle Eastern. The graduates of the American University have played distinguished, and often historic, roles in their countries, in the world of universal scholarship and global statesmanship.

The French and British also have many important schools in this region, particularly in Lebanon, Syria and Egypt. One of the most famous schools is the Université de St. Joseph in the Lebanon.

It is unfortunate, though, that so many of the young people in the Middle East should want to go to schools of higher learning for extraneous reasons. In the Muslim world, caste divisions are not hard and fast, and they vanish at the sight of the proper diploma. University credentials open the door to the fellah offspring into the exalted company of the effendis. That alone would not be reprehensible. However, very often graduates believe that by spending a few years at a school of higher learning they have bought themselves immunity from work for the rest of their lives. Studying appears to be a negligible factor in the universities of Egypt. The students seem to be on strike more often than in their classrooms. After graduation many of them appear to be only too ready to accept the higher government positions and other "glamorous" occupations.

Some of the educated young people begin to notice the world around them and they may talk quite freely in private conversation about the things they know. However, the journalist or editor who displays so much insight and knowledge loses both when he goes into print: *What is all this talk about the great polarization of wealth?* he writes. *And what is all this nonsense about the need of a measure of economic democracy? We are all patriots and we know nothing about polarizations. The poorest as well as the richest in our midst will gladly lay down their lives for our freedom, the only thing that counts. We are sick and tired of imperialism. Out with the British! Down with the American!*

This land of the Koran is also the great bookless and newspaperless world. Egypt has a few good newspapers and the bare beginnings of book publishing. But even so, not more than 20 newspapers circulate per thousand persons in Egypt, Turkey and Syria. The most highly literate Arab country, Lebanon, claims 81 copies of newspapers circulating for a thousand inhabitants, while the corresponding figure in adjacent Israel is 235 copies. In the Kingdom of Yemen there seems to be no regularly published newspaper, while in Saudi Arabia there was none until recently.

It may be said that most of the Middle East has skipped the age of the newspaper and is now in the very midst of the radio age. The radio is, of course, the great revolutionary influence in the region and more may be heard about its all-pervasive influence in the future. A United Nations survey says that Saudi Arabia has 2 radios for a thousand persons, while in Iran the number is 3, in Iraq it is 6, in the Lebanon 36 and in Israel 123.

Great are the problems of radio broadcasting because of the many dialects which diverge from literary Arabic. Therefore, the villager frequently fails to understand his own native tongue as it comes over the airwaves. The Egyptian State Broadcasting Company has attempted to solve this problem by offering popular programs in the colloquial language.

A Glimpse of the Turkish Village

Before turning to the Middle Eastern towns, let us catch a glimpse of the Turkish village. The rural problems of Israel will be mentioned in another connection.

"In most of rural Turkey there is scarcely an indication of change since ancient times," an American team of the Twentieth Century Foundation reported shortly after the Second World War. The hand tools are of primitive design, the plows are wooden and their furrow is shallow. In the spring when much of the work has to be done, the plows are drawn by small oxen, weak and emaciated animals. However, in the four years up to 1952 the number of tractors increased from 2,000 to 25,000, due to American aid.

The interior of the Turkish hut is not much richer than that of the average Arab and Iranian. Perhaps it is a trifle more cheerful, with some rugs and low benches around the wall, and a few copper utensils besides the sooty pots and pans. The Turks eat a little better, too—hominy of wheat, yoghourt and, on occasion, a little pounded meat spiced with garlic (*pastima*). The well-to-do peasant has a richer house which may have mosaic decoration, separate quarters for women, attractive carpets, more sunshine and air. But that is the exception.

Most Turkish villages—and there are more than eighty thousand of them—are dismal places blending into the dun landscape, displaying the familiar swallow-nest effect, revealing the fear of trespassing on fertile soil and the even greater fear of being seen. Anatolia has been in the past one of the world's most important highways for hungry, restless people always on the go, lured ever onward by the mirage of hope—man's eternal hope of finding something better, a place to rest. In the west of the country and in parts previously inhabited by such nationalities as Greeks and Armenians, the standards of houses are higher, closer to European dwellings.

Primitive is the word written all over the Turkish countryside. The peasant has no refrigeration and must dispose of his produce, especially meat, very quickly. He totes the carcass to the mart where he is at the mercy of the middleman. His position is all the worse because all farmers have to take their produce to the market at the same time, thereby causing a disastrous glut.

Co-operative farming would help the farmer greatly, but he lacks the capital and organizing gifts. Not more than one-tenth of the total sales are effected through co-operative marketing. The government set up a Central Office of the Product of the Soil some time ago, but it is not geared to concern itself with the small producer, in greatest need of help.

There is one advantage the Turkish village has over its Arab and Iranian counterparts: the polarization of wealth is far less pronounced. Under the old pre-World War I regime of the Ottoman Sultans, a disproportionately large part of the landed wealth was in non-Muslim and foreign hands. When republican Turkey was established, much of the land was nationalized, a process which helped the Turkish cultivator while ousting the hated alien. As the result of land reforms, about two-thirds of the formerly landless population have been provided with their own small plots. Republican Turkey is alive to the dangers of the vast concentration of landed wealth. Theoretically, no owner may retain more than a thousand arable acres. Four-fifths of the farms are smaller than 240 acres. Even so, 5 per cent of the total acreage is over 1,200 acres (1949 figures), and a little over 400 farms consist of more than a million and a half acres.

On the Turkish countryside the contrasts are great. Nothing could be more incongruous than the traffic on the republic's highways. Moving at a snail's pace there is the ox cart with its disk wheels, the form of which has not been changed since man invented the wheel. Next to it there may be the armed juggernaut Turkey received from the United States for armed defense.

The contrast between Ankara's modern government quarters and the "Stone Age" looks of the Turkish village makes one pause and wonder. The founder of the republic, Mustafa Kemal, was the most thorough reformer, who could change everything except the people themselves. We shall return to this point when taking a closer look at Turkey. The miraculous Orient can not produce practical, everyday miracles. To quote the French proverb: *plus ça change plus c'est la même chose.*

A Glimpse of Paradise

When Mohammed, who was to become the Prophet, came within sight of Damascus on his travels he was overheard to say, "This looks like heaven, of which there can be only one. And mine is not of this world."

Even where Islam rules, the Middle Eastern countryside is pre-Islamic and its villages must have looked no different under the Hittites, the Assyrians and the Babylonians. When Mohammed's creed vanquished these regions, it gained control of the pivotal positions, leaving the countryside to fend for itself and, eventually, to conform to urban leadership. This was good strategy, and besides, the human cattle could far better be shaped in the urban centers.

In the proper setting, with the right slant of the sun, the Middle Eastern town can present a beautiful picture. We have seen the village as secretive and dull, burrowing itself into the unfeatured landscape. The town, on the other hand, is nakedly exhibitionist. While the village wants to be overlooked, the town wants to show off its strength, so as to impress and scare away the potential enemy.

Many of our western cities smell like exudations of some evil spirits of the earth. Especially from a distance, they are shrouded in an atmosphere which is not nature's. That atmosphere is composed of the gases of the intestines of the earth pumped into the air by mammoth plant chimneys.

The Middle Eastern city, on the other hand, stands out clearly in the crisp air, one step above the surrounding countryside in the foothill regions, so as not to trample on life-giving soil. It forms a geometrical figure of clear-cut outline, easily encompassed with the eye.

The first houses of the town stand guard self-consciously as if proud of their audacity to venture into the front line, facing the wide open world in whose unfathomed depths grave dangers may be lurking. Isolated houses beyond the front line are almost nonexistent; the town was built for the protective warmth of serried ranks. Suburbs are known only in the large and recently built cities.

Looking down upon a cluster of satellite dwellings near the center, the protective mosques stand guard—jealous hens watching their chickens. Other landmarks are the effendis' mansions flaunting their marble glory, and the government offices, not decorative but spacious, since authority wants to impress with size.

The blemishes of the individual dwellings are smoothed out by the shimmering sunshine. The blue paint on the houses brings luck, of course, and it also forms an engaging color scheme in conjunction with the impeccable white. From a distance life is concentrated in sights, not in sounds, and the cosmic silence absorbs the cacophony of the markets.

The town stands at the meeting of natural features, which may be the intersection of important roads, the debouching of a river wadi from the hills into the plains, or the juxtaposition of the arid country and the sown. Sometimes it may be the confluence of slender streams, a natural harbor, a religious shrine. Whatever the town's justification, it becomes inevitably a mart.

Scents and Sounds of the Bazaar

Cosmic silence pervades the town when observed from afar but cosmic cacophony enwraps it when one is in its midst. Its heart is the bazaar, a word denoting "market" which the world borrowed from the Persians. Nature dominates the outlines of the town, but man dominates its intimate details. He drowns the town in full-throated sound, talking, shouting incessantly, as if afraid that in stopping talk he would cease to breathe. Talking is life, the creation of personal history, one's projection into the universe; it is momentary immortality.

The bazaar is good because it is cool even on the hottest days. The sun does not reach its narrow alleys, its maze of galleries, its stone steps leading up to unexpected heights and down to surprising depths. Tattered fabric flapping in the breeze covers the alley and the sound is as cooling as the wind. Protruding balconies also conceal the secrets of the bazaar from the curious sky. The wealthy merchant may keep vigil on his balcony to see that his menials are working, while he sips his coffee and loves life.

The scents and sounds of the bazaar are more informative than formal signs would be. The aroma of the alley tells the world what spices are on sale. The sound of the coppersmith's hammer is different from the tinsmith's. The world of the embroiderer is different from that of the sandal-maker. The open-air food store is open to all the world, even to the flies, whose number is myriad. The cafés and taverns tell their noisy tale. The tautly filled lambskin gourd of the waterboy is inviting—but the Middle Eastern bazaar is being rapidly "coca-colonized."

Competition is keen in the bazaar, the scene of concentrated life. The stakes are higher than in the fellah's narrow world and life is more pleasant in the shaded breeze. The shopkeeper throws himself into the argument with all his heart, and without a heart he is even more convincing, because then he is acting, and man is always more sincere when acting.

Selling in the bazaar is more than a science, more than an art; it is a way of life, it is life itself. The westerner, bungler that he is in understanding the depths of the human soul, does not understand the bazaar's sales technique. Man is so made that he wants what he cannot have and does not want what he can have. It is for the artist-scientist merchant to build up an atmosphere to panic the prospective customer into the purchase. The merchant artist of the bazaar knows how to play on the complicated instrument of human hopes and fears. He also knows that his bargaining partner is bent on getting pleasure out of the act of purchase; and so does the merchant himself.

Ritual is probably a more correct designation for the act of bazaar-sale than haggling. It enriches one's experience, provides diversion and renders life spicy.

The opening move is made by the merchant, who asks a price that includes not only his own overhead but also those of his ancestors all the way back to the Prophet's flight from Mecca. He wants to show that what ignorance may consider a mere bauble is the most precious jewel of the universe. He would be a fool unworthy of the Seventh Heaven if he were to rob himself of this unique gem.

The inquirer, on the other hand, wants to prove that nobody could be more disinterested in the merchandise, which he considers utterly worthless. Then he makes a reluctant offer, eliciting full-throated laughter from the merchant. The two appear to be so far apart that nothing more need to be said.

That is absolutely wrong, of course, because now the table has been cleared and real work begins. If the haggling is sufficiently vocal, idlers will be attracted. Then it becomes the goal of the participants so to fascinate their audience that it is unable to budge. Humorous quips are injected into the argument, with ogling side glances. Gradually, almost imperceptibly, the merchant climbs down from his dizzy peak, while the buyer climbs up, until they reach the point where their minds meet and the sale is effected. It is surprising how often the price thus reached comes close to the prevailing market price. And meanwhile, they were having a grand time.

In Iran, particularly, the bazaar wields considerable political influence, comparable to guilds and western trade associations. In some bazaars the trade association is blended into a political pressure group, very much like our lobbies. In the Middle East the town wields an incomparably greater influence than the isolated village because it contains great wealth, political pressure power and often the only effective public opinion.

The Pull of the Town

The town population of the Middle East is increasing very rapidly. Within ten years up to 1947 it had increased 53 per cent in Egypt, against a mere 20 per cent over-all population increase. Turkey's urban population increased by 37 per cent in the ten years up to the end of the Second World War, against a national population growth of only 7 per cent. The Iranian capital, Tehran, doubled its population from half a million to a million within a single decade. Similar and even larger increases have been registered in Amman, capital of the Hashimite Kingdom of the Jordan, and in other towns.

Urbanization is not only an economic and social phenomenon but may also become a political one. The town is potentially more explosive than the village. Common political action coalesces more easily in crowded city quarters. It has been in urban centers that revolutionary action has been unleashed in recent times. Careful attention should be given therefore to this type of accumulation of political combustible material in the Middle East.

In the town the poverty-stricken Arab or Iranian sees the "man from the moon" in his luxurious car, driven by his chauffeur. In his home village he had no opportunity to see such a person, a man whose very existence was so nebulous as to be almost unreal. In the town the ex-villager cannot help seeing ostentatious wealth. He emerges from his warren in the native quarters and sees the European streets, with their incredible display of luxury. He sees the beautiful mansions shut off from the contamination of the world by high walls, in the midst of trees, overlooking a fountain where water, the essence of life, is wasted.

At first the new town-dweller looks at the scene dully, and his attitude is that this is not his world, none of his business. This may be heaven and he may get there after death. But, after a time, he begins to ask: Why? And then the trouble begins.

He talks this thing over with some of his companions in the café, at the crossroads, in the bazaar's streets. Something is wrong, but what is it? He is told that all this is the fault of the British because they are along the Suez Canal, in the Sudan; or that this is the fault of the Anglo-Iranian Oil Company in Abadan. He is also told that all would be well if the British were out of Suez, the Sudan, out of Abadan. He is further told that the heart of the trouble is that the Jews have stolen Palestine.

The town-dweller turns this information over in his mind. All this makes sense to him. It is his patrimony that the British, the Anglo-Iranian and the Jews have stolen. Slowly the idea percolates into his receptive mind. He is an individualist, dependent upon himself. Or at best, upon his kin. Outside of his family he is not used to collective action. He does not trust other people. What does he want? What do they want?

He is slow to move. The sun is good and to rest is sweet. A man who is underfed does not like to move too much. Movement requires energy and that he has not got. So he sits down in the gutter and turns things over in his head, slowly, very slowly. After a while he begins to notice that he is poor, wretchedly poor, and that there are people who are so rich they do not know what to do with their gold. There are the streets, the mansions, the luxuries, the food in the display windows, the food in the . . . the food, the food. He notices that he is hungry, and there is the food, so close to him, and there are the people in Suez, Sudan, Palestine. But he does not know what to do.

Then he learns it. He is told that he is an Egyptian, the proud son of an ancient race—and Iranian, and in what cave were the British hiding when Persia was already a world power?—an Iraqi, the greatest and noblest of the great. He learns about his nationality, and that is something new to him. He had thought of himself only as a Muslim, and that he is, but he is also an Egyptian, an Iranian, an Iraqi, a Syrian, and all others. Nation—that is the great thing. If the others in Suez, Sudan and Palestine would not steal his patrimony he would have enough to eat. He must assert himself. He hates the West and does not know that the hated West has made him nation-conscious. What is wrong with the world and why he has not got enough to eat become suddenly clear to him: because he is being robbed of his birthright.

He must take it back. Out of nowhere there arise the people who go in the same direction in which he is moving. And more people are swarming out of the warrens of the native quarter, with sticks, and some of them with firearms, and all of them are shouting. At first he was diffident but now he takes courage, because he is in company, surrounded by a mass of heavily breathing people, and they all are becoming courageous. He picks up the words others are shouting: "Down with the British, the vampires, leeches." If he could see himself, he would see a strange sight: eyes aflame, cheeks flushed, lips forming inarticulate sounds. All his frustration rushes toward his lips, surging with an elemental heave from his innermost being. It is a primeval frustration and his lips shape the primeval howl of the deeply wounded man.

In front of him there is the rich foreigner's hotel, the Britishers' warehouse and now he sees nothing but a piece of treasure. It may be a pair of shoes, a shawl, a piece of meat. It is his, will be his, and he had been despoiled of his heritage. Now he is going to get back what is his by right. The next moment the hotel is in flames, the store is looted. Everybody is running away. In the distance there are a few shots. As he runs he gulps down the food he had barely time to grab. What kind of food it is, he does not know. Food. And for a moment he feels the peace of the contented stomach descending upon him. Food, rich food from the rich man's table, and now he is eating it, because he is an Egyptian and he has just participated in the great riot of Cairo. And it all had been because of Suez, and because of the Sudan.

A few days later he will die, in agony, because his shrunken stomach could not take the rich food. But at least once in his life he ate good food, and plenty of it, costly food, from the rich man's table.

The Industrial Revolution

Factory smoke does not darken the sky of the Middle-Eastern town. All over its millions of square miles there are not so many industries as one can find in a few city blocks of Pittsburgh and Leeds. The Middle East's "industrial countries" are Turkey, Iran, Egypt, and now, Israel. Most of the industries are small, mainly processors of native products, such as textile and flour mills, cement plants, small chemical factories and the beginnings of metallurgy. What the Middle East calls industry is handicraft —carpet weaving, jewelry, bazaar work. Israel may become the first country of the region to develop an industry in the western sense of the word.

The Middle-Eastern "industrial countries" are today where Yorkshire must have been over two centuries ago. Small plants are being erected and occasionally an attempt is made to help the peasants work at home during the slack season. Several reasons account for the scantiness of industries. Most of the people are poor and cannot afford to buy industrial products beyond the irreducible minimum—pots and pans. The population is mostly sparse, except in the river valleys and on the Levant coast. Transportation is inadequate. Also, this is part of the great colonial area where western nations have sought to cultivate their markets.

Nor is there much "risk capital" in the Middle East. In Egypt there is some native investment, and also that of resident aliens —Armenians, Greeks, Italians, some British money, and now American capital is being wooed.

Probably because of the lack of private capital, the governments themselves went into business in Turkey and Iran. The former country devised the system of *étatism,* under which the entrepreneur is the State and the accent is on national welfare. Industrialization in the State of Israel forms a chapter in itself, so more about it later.

And there are all the sicknesses of incipient industrialization, with few remedies and often without even the knowledge of remedies or the desire to apply them. If it is Allah's will that children should die in the factories, what can mortal man do? And so children are perishing in the plants. The Egyptian parliament passes a bill introducing labor-protecting devices, and everybody feels good about it. Let those —— foreigners come and we shall show them something! Have you got such wonderful laws in your books? No, but where are those wonderful things? We don't see them in the plants and it means nothing if they are only in the books. . . . The impertinence of the infidels, may Allah roast them alive.

How can one find out what is going on in those factories? You ask the government offices what is the average wage of the industrial worker and they say, "How do we know?" Then a United Nations investigating committee comes along and it is told a figure, almost any figure that sounds good. The patient investigator writes to the governments asking for information, and there is no answer. Then he writes to the embassies and legations of the Arab countries, and again no answer. Or there is this answer: "We shall write to our home offices for information"—and it never comes.

Then there is a riot among the textile workers of Alexandria [5] for living wages. What are the wages of those workers? "Twelve to eighteen piasters a day." (Thirty-six to fifty-four cents.) One

[5] Reported in *The New York Times,* Aug. 13, 1952.

of the "ringleaders" was sentenced to be hanged. The textile workers wanted a considerable increase in their wages: up to seventy-five cents a day. Is that enough? Yes, if your stomach is shrunken, but if you try to loot again, do not steal food or you will die.

The employer says that wages are low because labor productivity is low. That is true but how can the productivity of underfed workers be high? Also, the worker came but recently from the land, where he took his time under the sun. Plant discipline is not in his blood, and labor turnover is high. The wage-earner decides to go home and try his hand at something else. Absenteeism is high, too, and western plants could not operate under such a system. People are not only hungry but also sick if they are not well fed. When will the employers learn that there is a link between the wages they pay and the markets they gain? Of course, the *other* employer should pay the higher wages. Minimum wage laws? Your effendi will answer: "But, *monsieur*, you do not understand our people, they are not money-minded, they want no minimum wages, all they want is freedom. The British should evacuate Suez and the Sudan."

"Egypt has led all other Arab countries in enacting major social security legislation." [6] Then the same authority quotes *The New York Times* reporting on the Egyptian government old age pension scheme. In rural regions the basic pension will be $31.60 *a year*, while the maximum pension for an Egyptian worker with a substantial number of family dependents will be $83 a year.

Unemployment figures would be significant but they are spotty. When hands are hired, one sees crowds of applicants around factory gates. Even 36 cents a day is better than starvation, and industry cannot absorb all the unskilled labor.

And the labor unions? They exist in some countries on paper. Again Israel is the notable exception and more will be said about its remarkable Histadrut. In the Arab world's most important industrial country, Egypt, the unions were recognized in 1942, and the British may have had something to do with

[6] *Challenge and Response in the Middle East*, by Hedley V. Cooke (Harper) 1952, p. 76.

that. The latest available figure shows only 120,000 registered members in a country of twenty million. However, organization on a national scale was forbidden, and so was organization among certain categories of urban labor. But the trade union laws look good on paper, and in case you are one of those supercilious foreigners you are reminded that Egypt has the oldest civilization in the world.

Reform is in the Air

The Idea about the collective responsibility of society originated in the Middle East, but it has taken practical form in the West. It is the function of society to provide the minimum protection of the individual, to safeguard him against economic hazards beyond his control. Now the application of the Idea is reaching the Middle East, haltingly, very haltingly. "Reform is in the air." Unfortunately, the sentence may be read literally. Certain measures of reform have been taken, others are about to be taken, while much of the real reform is up in the air. There is also the difficulty of telling plans and realizations apart. One thing seems to be sure: there is a stirring in this area such as it has not seen since the Prophet's days. "At the present time," a recent United Nations survey said, "the Middle East is in the grip of a social upheaval, the causes and ingredients of which are varied and complex." They are varied and complex, indeed. From the West comes the word that it is society's duty to help the common man so that the hungry shall eat, the sick shall receive care, and the illiterate be taught. Ruling minorities in large parts of the Middle East would like to close their ears to the word. However, not all the gods of the vast desert could hold out against the might of Allah in the plenitude of time.

Then there is the effect of the newly found oil wealth which will form the subject of another chapter. With the passage of time its influence is bound to wax.

Plans and Realizations

All the self-governing Arab countries have drawn up plans (with the possible exception of Yemen, about which scarcely anything is known) to raise living standards. With few exceptions they are on a limited scale and their implementation is even more narrow. The object of some of the more ambitious plans is to settle the nomads, a process that has been going on for years. Such land reform schemes frequently serve the interests of the sheykhs more than those of the common man.

More important appear to be the various river schemes which most of the Middle East countries have. They have received a great impetus since the fruitful visit of the United Nations Commission for the Economic Survey of the Middle East, also called the "Clapp Mission," after Gordon Rufus Clapp, chairman of the board of the Tennessee River Valley Authority. If anywhere in the world, the river authority system is justified in the Middle East. It was a revelation to the public-spirited people in the region to find that there was so much wasted water power in the area.[7]

The Kingdom of Iraq is particularly well suited for large-scale land reclamation. It is believed that the region of the Two Rivers, Tigris and Euphrates, supported many times its present population in distant times. Even today the visitor can see the ancient canals and terracing. One of the most ambitious plans is that of the Wadi Tharthar, which is a usually dry river between the two rivers. By developing it, Iraq could gain 3,500,000 acres of land, which added to the million-acre Habbaniya scheme might become the largest water-control project in the Middle East. The first loan which the International Bank for Reconstruction and Development ever granted to a Middle East country was the $12,800,000 to the Iraqi government for the flood control stage of the plan.

The Kingdom has already undertaken water control plans. One of them is the Dujayla Project, so named after an expanse of land to the south of Baghdad, to help place some 180,000 acres under cultivation, dividing them into 60 acres each, for distribution among tribal and farming families. It is thought that during the first four years of the plan's operation not more than some 800 families have benefited from it. A Royal Institute

[7] From another source, the United States Department of State, Saudi Arabia learned that her arable acreage could be increased at least tenfold by drawing upon underground water alone.

of International Affairs study quoted an expert, Dr. Seton Lloyd, to the effect that even though the Dujayla scheme has been in effect for four years "the mechanism of assignment has so far proved imperfect, and the co-operative organizations which would be indispensable to successors only now under discussion."

The oil bonanza has induced the Kingdom to assign petroleum royalties to a Development Board to work on a five-year plan of economic and social development, mostly water control. It set up a Development Board in the spring of 1950. One of the weaknesses of this plan was pointed out by Hedley V. Cooke, former member of the Middle East Planning Staff of the Economic Co-operation Administration, that no important measures have been taken for the co-ordination of the plans of the interested countries or even for the efficient exchange of information about the movements of the rivers. The interested countries are Turkey, Syria, and Iran, besides Iraq.

Mr. Cooke sized up the Iraqi situation rather pessimistically: "If present indications are any criterion, it can be predicted that most of the land benefiting from the irrigation will, through one means or another, fall into the hands of great landlords." [8]

The Hashimite Kingdom of the Jordan alone among the Middle Eastern countries "has consistently shown enthusiasm" toward the Survey Mission's recommendation. The country appeared to be eager to carry out these plans not only in order to raise living standards but also to absorb the Palestinian refugees within its frontiers. Also Jordan seems to be free from the more blatant forms of nationalism.

The proposed river system of the country is pivoted on two "part-time" tributaries of the Jordan. One is the Wadi Zerqa, to the north of Amman, Jordan's capital, and the other one is the smaller Wadi Qilt, reaching the Jordan from the West, to the north of the Old Town of Jerusalem.

The Lebanon has real rivers, fed by the rain captured by her high mountains, some of which are snow-covered much of the year. Small as the republic is, it has an all-Lebanese river, the Litani, cradled between the Lebanon and Anti-Lebanon ranges, in the fertile Beqaa valley. The stream then turns boldly west-

[8] Cooke, *op. cit.* p. 199.

ward, reaching the Mediterranean north of Tyre. The other substantial stream is the Hasbani River, which enters Israel before reaching her Lake Hulah. The execution of these schemes is largely dependent upon the peaceful co-operation between Israel and her neighbors, the establishment of the Jordan River Valley Authority.

Syria is entertaining a project considered by experts the most suitable for the raising of her living standards. It is the Ghab Valley scheme to drain a swamp covering some 85,000 acres close to a densely populated region. It also offers possibilities for the generation of water power.

Also, there is the Jezireh Scheme in the northeastern part of Syria, adjacent to the Turkish and Iranian frontiers. With the help of the Allies, the region was subjected to large-scale World War II development. Even so only some 800,000 acres out of a possible cultivable area of 2,500,000 acres are now under cultivation. The Jezireh is said also to offer possibilities for a considerable increase in the raising of Syria's living standards.

Then, there is Iran's ambitious Seven-Year Development Plan, undertaken in 1948, which was to involve an outlay of 650 million dollars. It was to "increase production, expand exports, provide prime necessities for the people within the country, develop agriculture and industry, discover and exploit mines and underground resources, particularly petroleum, organize and perfect means of communication, improve public health and carry out any kind of operation for the development of the country," in the words of George V. T. Burgess, secretary and treasurer of Overseas Consultants, an American organization of engineering, construction and consulting firms engaged by the government of Iran to assist in the execution of the plan. Its ultimate purpose was to raise the people's standard of living. It was to be financed to a large extent from oil royalties. Then Iran nationalized the Anglo-Iranian Oil Company, thereby paralyzing oil production and rendering the execution of the plan impossible. Here was one flagrant case of divergence between a magnificent plan and utter failure of execution.

Because of the Truman Doctrine, Turkey was the recipient of American largesse more than the other Middle Eastern countries. She received large amounts from America both under that famous doctrine and the Marshall Plan. She received, among many other things, thousands of tractors, enabling her to increase her cultivation by 20 per cent and to export large quantities of grain to Europe. Even so, most of the country's ten million tons of grain produced in 1950 was cut with sickles, not even scythes, threshed by animal-drawn sleds and winnowed by being tossed in the air. Turkey's coal production was expected to increase by about one-third and chrome production by 40 per cent, under American guidance. Thousands of Turkish mechanics and technicians were trained in centers set up by American specialists to teach them in the use of modern tools.

The Middle East was looking forward to the implementation of America's Point Four Program, so named because it was the fourth point of President Truman's Inaugural Address on January 20, 1949: "We must embark on a bold new program for making the benefits of our scientific advances and industrial progress available for the improvement and growth of underdeveloped areas. . . ."

The Point Four Program was meant to help countries help themselves. More than a half of the amount appropriated under it was to help the Arab states in reclaiming land, developing water resources, improving basic experimentation and extension services. A considerable amount was to improve public health and sanitation services as well as education—and particularly vocational education. One of the projects under the Plan was, for instance, to clean out ancient cisterns in Jordan, constructed in Roman times to catch rain water and, over the centuries, allowed to fill up with silt. Another project was to manufacture soap from olive oil, still being done by methods used in Biblical times.

This enumeration of some of the more important plans clearly shows that the reforms are on a modest scale. Sidney Sherwood, a consultant of the UN Economic Survey Mission to the Middle East, pointed out that while the countries were crying out for development, the governments were in no position to support ambitious projects. He also called attention to the anomalous situation that in many countries of the region the national budgets were balanced. "But balanced budgets and absence of debt are hollow virtues," he commented, if the governments cannot help themselves.

Yet much could be done. At an international symposium held in Jerusalem in 1952 it was shown that 800 millions of acres of accessible deserts throughout the world could be economically irrigated and produce more crops than naturally watered areas now under cultivation. Many of these deserts are in the Middle East. The poorhouse of the world need not be a poorhouse.

"The Sacred Dissatisfaction"

No major social revolutions have taken place in the Middle East for centuries. The so-called revolutions in Persia and Turkey were imposed from above. They were not spontaneous explosions of the popular will striving to achieve a better balance in the social and economic structure. Curiously, few parts of the world show more of the symptoms of organic troubles that usually lead to revolutions. Where else can one encounter such great extremes of wealth and poverty and such limited efforts to establish a better balance? It is not from a long distance that the Middle East looks at the new era in the western world—the era of social justice, the Age of the Welfare State. The region we are looking at is in the very backyard of that progressive western world.

The stresses and strains in the Middle East indicate the presence of social forces that are inevitably pressing for revolutionary earthquakes. The warning signals are numerous. The chronic presence of the Middle East on the front pages of the newspapers has a deep significance. Something is stirring there, but the issues have not crystallized clearly, leadership is not yet on hand. Millions of people are groping for self-expression, but they have not yet found themselves. What do they want? Nationalism, independence, freedom? These are the words they mouth, but they mean bread. They hate the foreign oppressor, but who oppresses them really? Their own effendis. Yet, these very effendis are the mouthpieces of xenophobia. This is a typical case of "diversion," the sociologist says. The accusing finger is pointed at the "colonial oppressor," who is no longer either colonial or an oppressor. But people, especially illiterate people, always live in the past, never in the present. There is that tragic lag. And so the effendis keep the devil's cauldron of hatred complexes busy by pointing to the misdeeds of the oppressor in the past—if he was really an oppressor.

The device is as ancient as social organization. And it works, for long periods, for centuries, decades, and then all of a sudden it ceases to work. Then there is an explosion and the revolution turns against the merchants of hatred, generating its own hatreds against the pacemakers of the past. Is this period approaching in the Middle East?

It is a strange phenomenon that when people are too miserable they are not ripe for revolutionary outbreaks. Wretched people, mired in the most profound depths of misery, may look like human beings, but they only "vegetate," whereas human beings act. A man whose body is hollowed out by bilharzia cannot act. A person must have some food in his stomach before he rises in wrath against his fate. The ignorant person can be easily deceived.

The paradox is that conditions are improving in the Middle East, and it is for that reason it approaches the revolutionary threshold. The fabulous wealth of oil does not seek out the poor man's pockets, but a small part of it seeps into the land of D.I.P. Even the mild innovations which the dominant minorities of these countries have undertaken help to strengthen the revolutionary upsurge. Yes, the social security laws, the clinics and irrigation canals. Because all these help man to become man, to tear up his roots and walk like a man.

American money also helps to bring about that revolution, and yet the official policy of the United States frowns on revolutions. Then there is little Israel, clothing the old message in a new form, showing that it is possible to have the Word take shape in the Land of the Word. Also, crouching behind the mountains of the north is the Soviet Union, a constant challenge and reminder, playing the role of the proverbial catfish.

Where are the leaders of the inevitable purification? Who need it most? Obviously, the fellaheen. But the leader will not arise in their midst. They are browbeaten, lacking in courage, training and the knowledge that are required for the organization of the Great Chaos. It was not a fellah of the Faubourg St. Honoré, but an effendi of the Faubourg St. Germain, Count Mirabeau, and other members of the privileged classes, that launched the great liberation. Why the effendis of France? Perhaps because they were outraged by what they saw, or perhaps because they were patriots of the deed and not of the lips and because they knew that never could a nation of beggars become *la Grande Nation.* And also, perhaps, because they hoped for historic roles and more lucrative employments in the new order. Who knows?

And so throughout the modern history of revolutions. It was not an undernourished worker in Petrograd's Putilov Works that headed Russia's bourgeois revolution of the First World War, but a pasha, Prince Georgi Evgenievich Lvov. And Lenin himself was not one of *les damnés de la terre,* about whom the revolutionary anthem sang, but a member of the higher social classes. And when Turkey's time came to rise, the leadership was not in the hands of the tattered Anatolian peasants but in the manicured hands of a prominent army general, Mustafa Kemal, who was something of a dandy. And elsewhere in Europe, in Asia, everywhere, it was people from the effendi class who sounded the keynote and led the revolt.

In the Middle East, too, the leader is bound to be a member of the ruling class, an Ahmed Pasha. Not all effendi are opposed to change, not all of them are antisocial-minded. Among them and among the "intellectuals," college professors, journalists, or just decent middle-class folks, there are plenty whose eyes are open and who behold the horror that the Middle East may face unless the ruling classes yield to the inevitable change. But they have not yet dared to show themselves, their thoughts are incubating in the obscurity of private conversations. They have received no encouragement from the British and are receiving the cold shoulder from America. And the catfish is in ambush, to stir up the troubled waters.

CHAPTER 2

In the Beginning There was the Land

A Glimpse from the Umayyad Mosque

A reminder of the Middle East's ancient history is the Umayyad Mosque in Damascus, the capital of Syria. It is believed that in Assyrian times it was the site of the shrine of the god Rimon, he to whom Babylon's people gave the name of Adad. He was Thunderer to both of these peoples, the good god of fertility and of rain. The god of storms he was also, and his wrath laid low the grain of the land. The Deity of Damascus is the name under which he is mentioned in the Old Testament.

Then the Egyptians ruled over this city, which they called Darmesek or Dimashka, and they, too, had a shrine to one of their deities on the site where the Umayyad Mosque stands today. The story of that Egyptian deity trails back into prehistoric times.

The shepherd king, David, who was "ruddy and withal of beautiful countenance," humiliated Rimon with Jehovah's might. He is believed to have erected a shrine to the only God he knew on the site of today's mosque.

The Romans swept in after several centuries and they built a temple to Jupiter Tonans, the Thunderer, on the hallowed site. And after Rome had embraced Christendom, Emperor Theodosius the Great had the Basilica of Saint John the Baptist built where the mosque stands today.

It was in the seventh century that the Muslim Arabs came but they let the Basilica stand for seventy years, that famed "Traveler of Islam," Ibn-Battuta told the world. One half of it was used as a church during that period, and the other half as a mosque. The Caliph El-Watid built the mosque, which was pillaged by Tartars, victimized by fire, finally yielding to the present house of worship toward the end of the nineteenth century. It is also known as the Great Mosque.

Older than the Umayyad Mosque is the city of Damascus, perhaps the oldest urban settlement in the world. What story could be told by its many layers of rubble, each of them the burial ground of a defunct culture? This was the great workshop of history, of which Damascus is the center.

Today again the Middle East is in the very center of history.

Crossroads the area was in the past and crossroads it is again. At the intersection of East and West, it is the hub of the great aviation route between Orient and Occident. It is the site of two of the world's most important waterways, the Straits and the Suez Canal. The Middle East is known to be the world's richest petroleum well; and the role of oil as the lubricant not only of global economics but also of strategy needs no stress.

In a world deeply fissured by diplomatic and ideological conflicts, the importance of the Middle East today is even greater than in the past. It is the region which is of the utmost importance both to the western world and to the Soviet Union. Possession of this region may mean all the difference between victory and defeat. The area is the site of one of history's great conflicts, between dominant minorities in many of its states and unhappy majorities. Also, the Middle East is the site of the western-minded State of Israel, thus creating a problem by inviting comparisons.

With a tremendous history and a future which appears to be fraught with potentialities, the world faces the Middle East with awe. There mankind's history began. Will it be the scene of a new rejuvenation, another beginning? Or will the Middle East hasten the end of one phase of mankind's life? Were the burning bush and the thundering mountains graphic illustrations of the endless span of history? Truly, it is a world without end.

The Arab Quadrangle and the Fertile Crescent

What is the physical setting of this drama? The most prominent feature of the region is the presence of deserts. Endless deserts, some of them the most extensive in the world. Deserts of stone and rubble, mostly, also deserts of sand. Then there are oases, scattered far apart in the vastness. Also great rivers, on the banks of which the history of western man began: the Nile, the Tigris and Euphrates, the Jordan. There man the animal became Man the Man. They were the scenes of his dawn of conscience. From there we have received our own Occidental heritage, nearly everything that counts.

Then there is another dramatic feature of the region, which Professor James Henry Breasted called the Fertile Crescent because of its shape and also because of its contrast with the dominating landscape. Mountains which give rise to streams, slopes with trees and peaks with snow. It was in a part of that hill country that man first beheld his God.

Then there are other mountains, too; huge massives of plateaus, scoured by rain and wind, with wrinkled hides that look like the skin of pachyderms. There is also the greatest natural phenomenon of the region, and it deserves a special word: it is the great *Graben*, the rift.

Its dramatic quality is best illustrated by the incident which Great Britain's famed Field Marshal Allenby, commander in chief in Palestine, told Professor Breasted toward the end of the First World War. Allenby's forces were pushing northward the Ottoman empire's armies. One morning the Field Marshal sent a dispatch to his War Office in London, which read: *At dawn, our bombing planes, flying six hundred feet* below *the sea, bombed the Turkish positions in the Jordan valley.*

Six hundred feet below the level of the sea, and yet the planes were flying more than six hundred feet above their targets in the Jordan valley. This is the most spectacular natural feature of the Middle East, this gash in the skin of the earth, the deepest depression, nearly 1,300 feet below sea level. This is the Great Rift.

And then the Dead Sea, the waters of which hold about 25 per cent of solids in solution, five times as thick as ocean water. No body of water can be more frightening in its wrath, and no body of water contains such inexhaustible treasures in minerals which man can use. Nearby was laid the scene of that terrible judgment of sin, told in the story of Sodom and Gomorrah.

Then the Rivers

The "miracle" of the Nile is another historic feature of the Middle East. Without that stream man could not look back upon Egypt's history, and some twenty million inhabitants of that country could not live. Yet the Nile receives no single tributary for sixteen hundred miles.

Emptiness reigns for millions of square miles all around like story book scenes depicting the first day of creation. Then suddenly, the miracle. The slender green thread with its swarming human life, the most densely populated strip of land, covering but a few miles on either bank. Then the Delta, criss-crossed with irrigation canals, and green, very green, life within the grip of death. Humus soil reaches down to seventy feet, unique in the Old World.

Then the Twin Rivers, and between them Mesopotamia, the other cradle of western civilization, today's Kingdom of Iraq. A quick comparison with the Nile. The banks of the Egyptian stream are crowded, and the Land of the Two Rivers empty, with space for many more millions, but under a different regime. The terraces are there, and the ruins of the canals, to show that there was life where there is no life today. And they also tell another story, which nobody in the Middle East likes to hear. Why can't we speak about the miracle of the Tigris and Euphrates as we speak about the miracle of the Nile? Because of their different natures? Yes, but the substance is the same . . . water. Nobody likes to listen to the explanation, or possible explanation. The Nile acquired its most miraculous qualities with the coming of the British. Until then Egypt, too, was empty. The Land of the Two Rivers belonged to the Ottoman Empire, decadent, dying, grasping on to whatever it could hold, always grabbing, never giving. "Colonization" is not always deadly.

The Arab Quadrangle, to the southeast of Mesopotamia, has never been surveyed; much of it has never been explored. It is a subcontinent in flames in the dry season. The Arab world looks at it from Mecca and calls the territory to the left of it *El-Shemal,* which means the Left, and the region to the right *El-*

Yamin, which means the Right, and which is also the name of the least known of the Arab countries.

The bulk of the square-shaped Arab peninsula is occupied by Saudi Arabia, a new name given to it by its founder, King Abdul-Aziz ibn Abdur-Rahman al-Faisal Al Sa'ud, better known to the western world as King Ibn Saud, a picturesque and dynamic monarch. This was that original Arabia from which the Arabs burst into the world, east and west, staging one of history's most dramatic dramas, the barbarian desert overrunning the cultured sown and creating a higher form of civilization.

The Arab Quadrangle's shores are washed by the hottest seas in the world; the Persian Gulf waters with a summer temperature of 95 degrees, and the Red Sea, which runs an annual average of 84 degrees.

And so we reach the Fertile Crescent, which gave the world the land of Philistines, Palestine; Phoenicia and Assyria; Babylon and Elam; and, above all, Judaea. Here stand the cities that marked man's march from material conquest to brotherly love: Tyre and Damascus, and Jerusalem, on top of a hill as if to symbolize the heroic climb from lust to love, an aspiration more than a reality, but an important climb just the same.

The Fertile Crescent and its hinterland also produced Byblos, which was to see its name enshrined, and Susa, as well as Babylon and Nineveh.

The western pivot of the Fertile Crescent is what the Arabs call Jebel Musa, the Mountain of Moses, and what we call Mount Sinai. The crescent is not very fertile here, excepting after the rainfalls. Nor is there much vernal green in the Negev, the inverted pyramid, resting on the Red Sea's Gulf of Aqaba. Here the observer is overwhelmed by nature, as though it had been caught in the travail of creation and was presenting scenes from the beginning of the world.

The Fertile Crescent stretches beside the eastern Mediterranean. There are patches of green on the slopes, in the river beds, wadis, on gently undulating foothills, where the hills force the eastbound clouds to disgorge the treasure of water they had accumulated on their travels over the midland sea. Here are the heights of Judaea, so well known to the western world, continuing in the gentler hills of Samaria; then there is a break in the landscape, the Plains of Israel. They are plains on a miniature scale but refreshing to the eye, which is led to the rounded dome of Mount Tabor and then to Lower Galilee, cradling the town of Nazareth.

Galilee—the Ring—so called because there the Gentiles ringed around Israel. The scenery is capped in the north by mighty Hermon, the birthplace of rivers which, in turn, give birth to life.

Grandiose and rugged, often shrouded in mist, the mountains of Lebanon and Anti-Lebanon attract attention. They are the sanctuaries of many religious sects, because dissidence means persecution and that in turn makes man cherish his creed all the more.

Our eyes follow the Fertile Crescent. We had left behind the Hashimite Kingdom of the Jordan, and the republic of Lebanon. Now we are on the Syrian coast and pause for a moment before bidding good-by to the Arab world. In the western haze we catch a glimpse of Cape Andreas, a long finger on the island of Cyprus pointing in the direction of the Hither East.

Then the Fertile Crescent swings eastward away from the Mediterranean, forming a bridge between it and the Persian Gulf. To the north it looks at the massive weight of the Anatolian plateau. At the Cilician Gate the Turkish and Arab worlds meet, speaking different languages, having different backgrounds for much of their history. The mountains rise higher as we proceed southeastward, and reaching the fourteen-thousand-foot peak of Cilo Dag, we may be able, on exceptionally clear days, to have an object lesson in at least one of the great problems of this region: from that mountain peak we may be able to cast a glance at the tall mountains in the haze-covered distance, where another world begins—the Soviet Union.

The mountains now pick up the trail of the boundary of Iran, and there we are in still another world, speaking a language different from Arabic and Turkish, an ancient history which has seen more ups and downs than any of its neighbors. We are now in the Zagros range, which seems to soak its feet in oil. On one side there is Kirkuk, in the Kingdom of Iraq, and on the other side there is the mosque of Solomon, Masjid-i-Sulaiman, a center of Iranian oil production.

The larger part of the Middle East belongs to the Arab world. The entire Arab world, of course, is much larger. From Egypt's western desert frontier station of Es Solum to the Atlantic Ocean the distance is more than two thousand miles as the crow flies and most of it is Arabic, comprising the newly constituted Kingdom of Libya and portions of France's overseas empire, Tunisia, Algeria and Morocco. In the latter the predominantly Arabic urban dwellers are mixed with the Berber rural population. These African regions are so far to the west that it would be far-fetched to include them in the Middle East.

The Poor Rich Land

Bread, too, not only the Word, came from the Middle East. Wheat is thought to have been first raised there, as far as the West is concerned. Also barley. But what about today? What about the Garden of Eden of Mesopotamia, the milk and honey of the Holy Land, Egypt's granaries? The Middle East is poor in the products of the soil, poorer than it need be. Man's ruthless hand placed a heavy toll on its resources. Much of today's poverty is caused by him. Wheat is still the ruler in most of the Middle Eastern grain producing regions. It requires little money outlay, of which there is little, much labor, of which there is much; it sates hunger quickly. Naturally the Middle East is ages behind the open-air wheat factories of the Middle West.

Yet, the sun has not stopped in the Middle Eastern sky. Egypt's long-fiber cotton enjoys great fame in the world. Fears have been expressed that the country might become a Cotton Kingdom, at the mercy of the hazards of monoculture. Tobacco in Turkey is, of course, famous, and opium is also important, in that country and in Iran. Wine is not for Muslims, but they like grapes, and so there are vineyards in favored locations of the Middle East. Biblical Canaan, the land of Milk and Honey, was really the land of grapes; her broken-down terraces of today were prosperous vineyards on the slopes of hills.

Then there are the citrus groves, dark foliaged, perfumed in the proper season, delights to the eyes. There is sugar cane and bananas, rice, olives, almonds and figs.

The enumeration may sound impressive, but a warning is in

order. Only 2 per cent of the land in Iran is fit for use and not more than a fifth of that is under cultivation. In Lebanon and Syria, too, only about 8 per cent of the land is actually in use. Also today the King is Cattle, and not Wheat. Cattle strains in the region are not noted for quality, quite the reverse. Animal husbandry is not for poor people. As in biblical times, there are the sheep and the goats gathered around the well, and in the twilight hour wending their way home. The Muslim world is enjoined from eating pork, and so pigs are raised only in minority areas, if at all.

In spite of the productive areas, desert is still the dominant quality of the region. Perhaps it is this contrast that has inspired so many poets to sing the beauties of the fertile spots. Beautiful to behold are the Plains of Sharon and the Plains of Israel. In the Lebanon, the Beqaa valley has caused the lips of generations to sing. Then there are the Hauran and the Jezireh in Syria, the Shatt-el-Arab in Iraq, the wheatfields of the Hashimite Kingdom.

Not only is the Middle East poor in the gifts of the soil but it is also subject to the devastations of plagues, among the worst of which are the locusts. They are almost human in their habits. Individually they are harmless, but let them band together and see what happens then. They darken the sky, and as they descend upon verdant areas they make them charnel houses for animal and man alike. On this one issue the East and West appear to be ready to co-operate. An antilocust crusade several years after the Second World War enlisted the joint work of the United States, the United Kingdom and the Soviet Union in a highly effective "Operation Killer."

It is an ill wind that produces no delicacies. In certain regions of the Middle East locusts are eaten when roasted. It is recorded that in Damascus a bag of appetizing locusts costs four Syrian pounds at a time when elsewhere they had devastated the land.

The Fishes of the Sea

The Middle East is rich in seas: the eastern Mediterranean, the Persian Gulf, the Caspian, the Arabian and the Red seas. Where the land is poor, man turns to the waters for his livelihood. Yet, little food is hauled out of the waters here, and for this partly man and partly nature are to blame. Closest to the great population centers of the Middle East is the eastern Mediterranean, which, unfortunately, is poor in fish. It is fresh water which provides the calcium salts many types of fish need and the eastern Mediterranean is deficient in that substance, except for the estuary of the Nile, which is its only important fishing ground.

One day, perhaps, a candidate for the degree of Ph.D. will write a dissertation on "World Empires and the Poor Fish." He may make out a good case that Byzantium, the ancestor of Constantinople, the present-day Istanbul, was built on its site at the Straits because of the fish. In the Black Sea, winter storms and ice conditions force the fish to migrate toward more placid waters in the Aegean and in doing so they are forced into the bottleneck where Istanbul guards the Straits.

The Persian Gulf should be rich in fish, since it has plenty of new water, the contributions of the Tigris and Euphrates. Many of its species are edible. The commercial use of its turtles, sharks and narwal whale is great, and the Gulf is rich in them. There is some fishing in the region, but not enough. The blame lies, perhaps, with folk habits. At the present time the personnel of American oil companies is trying to convert the local people to the realization of the importance in their lives of fish.

The pearl fisheries of the Persian Gulf are the most important, of course. Today, however, they are struck by the blight. Cultured pearls these days are so highly cultured that they cannot be distinguished from the real thing. Therefore the pearl industry largely belongs to the past.

What about the Red Sea and the Caspian? The answer to this question makes clear that more than the fisherman and his equipment are needed for good fishing. Supposing you catch fish in the Red Sea—how do you transport it and where are your markets? The shores of the sea lack transportation facilities as well as population centers. The Caspian is famous for its caviar, but that industry belongs to the Russians, in accordance with an international pact signed shortly after the First World War.

In the Darkness of the Earth

Today an important measure of the importance of a region is its wealth in minerals and metals. Where does the Middle East fit into this picture? The answer to this question would have been "Nowhere," until a short time ago. Now, however, the region is known to have the world's most fabulous oil wealth. In regard to the other treasures of the insides of the earth our knowledge is limited, and future surprises cannot be ruled out.

It is strange indeed that so little should be known about the physical qualities of a region which has been longer in western history than any other part of the world. One reason is the secretiveness of the Ottoman empire, a drowsy realm which had little interest in minerals and metals until it changed its mind about them in its declining days. And that realm was the ruler of most of the Middle East.

Britain and France, exercising mandatory rights over most of this region after the Ottoman collapse, wanted to sell their products to these countries and were not eager to help exploration. Also they concentrated on the solution of political questions.

As things stand at present, the Middle East is near the tail end of the list of the industrial raw-material-producing countries—always excepting oil—which is headed by the Soviet Union, the United States and the Union of South Africa.

The only country producing sizeable amounts of minerals and metals is Turkey, the third largest producer of chromite and the ninth largest producer of antimony, an important ferro-alloy.

While the quality of Turkish coal in the Eregli-Zonguldak area is good, its quantity is small. The Turkish soil contains quantities of iron ore, copper, zinc and lead. The region must have been richer in nature's gifts in the distant past. It was the Hittites, whom Turks consider as their ancestors, who are credited with having been the first to make iron. Gold was also a famous product of the region. The legendary home of the Golden Fleece is northeast Anatolia, where even today pieces of oily fleece are used to wash golden particles out of the river silt. The memory of famous marble quarries is perpetuated in

Turkey's Sea of Marmora, and the region is said to have once held the world's monopoly of meerschaum. The island of Naxos was rich in emery.

The region has very few known deposits of first-class iron ore, except in Egypt, not far from Aswan. Egypt's forbidding hinterland produces such desert products as sandstone, pumice, common salt, also granite, basalt and gypsum. The Dead Sea is alive with chemical products, about which more will be told in the chapter on Israel. In the interwar period the Palestine Potash Company extracted mineral salts through solar evaporation. Potash salts were used as fertilizers, while bromine was employed, among others, for explosives and lethal gases, and this at the very foot of the mountains where brotherly love was first proclaimed to man.

When all this is said, we have enumerated most of the items of the mineral wealth of the region. A meager list, indeed.

CHAPTER 3

History Unlimited

Then Came the Conquerors

At the crossroads again, as in the past, today's Middle East must be seen in its historic perspective. It is only in their proper setting that current events gain significance.

Strange land indeed, this Middle East, which rose so high and fell so low.

It gave the world the Word. The Semite had to be a monotheist, said Ernest Renan. The Semite was the man of the desert where nature was uniform, with none of the mysteries of the woodland, the groves, the variety of vegetation. Within each tribe there was only one god, and that fact too favored monotheism. Men were used to fastening their minds on one sovereign deity, and conspiring with that habit was the desert, uniform and bare.

But we cannot tarry at that early epoch, since we want to know what is the historical heritage of the Arabs, the Turks and Iranians today—the three largest groups in the area. No need to retell the story of Israel, known to all of us from the Testaments.

Because the Middle East was the crossroad, after the Word came the sword. It was wielded by that hurricane in human form, Alexander III, the son of Philip of Macedon. Barely in his early manhood, he had the insight of great creators and great destroyers. He saw the world in perspective, many centuries ahead of his time. There was to be one world or none, and of that one world he was to be the head.

Then came Rome, as it was bound to come, since the Middle East was the pivot of three continents. Her great contributions were the law and communications, closely related and summed up in one word: order. Without law there could be no roads and without roads there could be no law. The Romans followed the laws of their dynamism and pressed onward to the very edges of the world—the world as known then. On the margins of the sown area the desert began and that was as far as they could go, the end of their world. They did not know about the world beyond the great silence, which was to overwhelm them. Magnificent remnants of imperial ambitions in such ruins as those of Heliopolis are the mementoes of Rome's conquering ambitions. The Syrian metropolis, Antioch, in those days was said to have a population exceeding the number of the residents of the country's three largest cities today.

The sword of the mightiest empire was blunted: all swords of all empires are. Against the debilitating forces Rome sought to save herself by turning to the Word, when it was too late. She was the physical force seeking strength in brotherly love. Christianity became the imperial creed under the Edict of Milan, and Constantine the Great was its author. It was to be the new foundation of the old empire. The Word was to triumph over the sword.

But the *urbs* could not escape its fate, it was entrapped in its own greatness. Protection needed further security, and the defensive power of Rome became diluted. Aggressive Rome had to defend herself in all four corners of her world, while beyond the *limes* (the imperial boundaries) hunger gathered momentum. The hunger-driven force of the barbarians cracked the imperial walls.

Since its scope was endless, could not the empire rejuvenate itself? Where the Bosphorus meets the Marmora Sea, on the banks of the Golden Horn, there stood venerable Byzantium. It too was situated in a strong strategic position, at the intersection of global trade routes but away from the main barbarian pressure. This city of Constantine the Emperor, to be named Constantinople, became the guardian of the Eastern Roman Empire for well nigh a thousand years.

This was the Second Rome, the youthful one, which adjacent Asia was to know as "Rum." Later, the name was applied to Rumania, Rumelia and all of western Christendom. The eastern Orthodox church was to flourish on the Golden Horn, holding sway in the Middle East, to the desert edges and in Egypt. In the northeast, in the presence of the mountains and the million dangers lurking in their shadows, the Eastern Empire was forced to make a halt before reaching the Zagros mountain range. Beyond it reigned the Persians' Sassanid dynasty, steeled and broken in a welter of gruesome regicides. This indestructible Iranian royal family held its own for four centuries.

Byzance and the Sassanids mutually weakened one another in endless wars. The Byzantines shared the lot of those who by insisting on the letter of the law lost sight of its spirit. Countless disputants were to determine the real nature of Jesus Christ, and the number of variations of their views was endless. Soon the contestants forgot the essence of the religion, remembering it only in order to score points.

The eastern realm wanted to continue the work of the West. As there was one God in heaven so there was to be only one

Emperor on earth. This involved Constantinople in many wars, and attempts to crush many rebellions.

What made Constantinople so "Byzantine," meaning submissive to force, sycophantic, evasive? "The curse of the East," some people call it. Fatalism cheapened the worth of honor, the worth of life. The strong smashed their way to power irrespective of the price in human lives. Only the ruthless represented the end, while the meek were the means. The eastern world was ripe for a change.

Then Came the Arabs

The Prophet Mohammed was dead in 632 A.D. and the Arabs erupted from the desert into the sown. This was one of history's most remarkable eruptions. The faithful were to reap their reward in heaven a thousandfold, and they could only gain by death. The sole loss they would sustain was hunger's thralldom. Tackling the eastern Roman empire seemed to be a bold undertaking, but its might turned out to be largely a myth. At this point our history begins and it is still a living memory.

It was birth from darkness into light for the Arabs, as Thomas Carlyle said. They had been a poor shepherd people roaming in the desert since the beginning of time and to them came the Hero Prophet with the Word. Within one century afterward Arabia was at Granada, on one side, and at Delhi, on the other.

At first the Arabs practiced the well-tried ways of the guerrillas, out of their element in the shadow of great cities and in the land of waving grain. Then they drew courage from unexpected victories and success fed on more success. Their valor was compounded by the weakness of Byzantium, whose realm they entered. In reality that zone was a power vacuum which the Arabs were to fill.

Not more than seven thousand of the Arab fighters entered on the historic mission which was to end with the conquest of half the world. Quickly they learned how to fight in concerted action under common command. Their numbers grew as the defeated asked for the privilege to join the victors. Also the Arabs recruited new forces along their line of march.

From Medina, desert capital of the Arab world then, the

warriors were warned not to cross the Nile, beyond which they might be beguiled by the wiles of the western world. However, they disregarded this warning.

Commander of the Arab forces was 'Amr ibn-al- 'As, and he it was who first beheld the radiant countenance of the city of Alexandria, one of the most important metropolises in the world. In distant Constantinople, Emperor Heraclius pondered how to save this matchless jewel of his far-flung realm. While he kept on pondering, the Arabs increased their pressure. No matter how long the monarch meditated, he could do nothing in the absence of a sea force. Even so the city held out for many months, but finally it was taken.

A report of 'Amr to Medina in 640 A.D. reveals the impression the great city made on the desert warriors. "In this city," he wrote, "there are 4,000 palaces, 4,000 baths, 12,000 dealers in fresh oil, 400 theatres and places of entertainment, 12,000 gardeners, and 40,000 Jews to pay tribute."

It was said of this Arab warrior that he had the matchless library of Alexandria supply the furnaces of public baths with fuel. "If their contents are in the Koran, they are not needed, and if they are not, they should be burned." Some doubt has been cast on the authenticity of this oft-told tale. When 'Amr's warriors came, the library was long past its one-time glory.

One of the first prizes of the conquering Arabs was Egypt, and it is Arabic culture that it nurtures to this very day. Remarkable indeed was the metamorphosis. In the past the land of the Nile had its Pharaonic ways, on which the sediments of many successive cultures were deposited: Hellenistic, Roman, Byzantine, blended with Persian and a conglomerate of Levantine. All of these were submerged in the great upheaval, with Arabic surviving.

It did not take more than a dozen years after the death of the Prophet before the Arabs had gained mastery of what today we call Syria and Iraq, besides Egypt. They also broke down the resistance of parts of Persia which had contained even the legions of Rome.

Westward the onrushing hordes of the Arabs rolled in their incredible march. On the North African coast they absorbed the kinsfolk of the Egyptians, known as the Berbers, mainly of the Hamitic strain blended with Roman survivals and barbarian ethnic scraps. The feuding chieftains of this land of sown patches in the midst of desert waste had long felt the paralyzing hand of the nominal master, Constantinople, and were delighted with the change.

Strengthened by the Berbers, the Arabs raced onward and between the years 670 and 697 covered the massive top of Africa, once the granary of Rome. Then they crossed the narrow water separating Africa "the dark continent" from Europe which was then even darker. One of their leaders was a warrior by the name of Tarik and the rock which he beheld on the European side was named after him "Tarik's Mountain," or, in Arabic, "Jebel Tarik," from which our distortion of that name in the form of Gibraltar.

In Europe the Arabs defeated the atomized lands of the Visigoths of Spain, conquered the Pyrenees and made their way into southern Gaul.

Was it possible that these wild sons of the desert should top their unbelievable victories by gaining also western Europe? Thence they might be able to cross the Rhine and force the heart of Europe to accept their reign. Everything seemed to be possible after the achievements of the Muslim hosts, which had covered thousands of miles in their global march. In fact, nothing stopped them until they were almost within sight of Lutetia —Paris. The highwater mark of their conquest was the Loire river where finally they met reverse at the Battle of Tours in 732.

The Arabs also struck out against the East with amazing success. They defeated Persia's Sassanids, the last king of that line being assassinated by one of his own satraps. Nor was this the end of the Muslims' victorious march. Leaving behind the Afghan land, they ascended India's mountain ramparts, then descended into the valleys of the south-Asian subcontinent. By doing so they created one of the burning issues of our own days by the introduction of Muslim culture into India. The new State of Pakistan is one of the great historic results of the Muslim conquest.

The center of the eastern empire, Constantinople, repelled the Arab onslaught. The Arabs were inferior in naval warfare. It was the weakness of the eastern metropolis which saved it, rather than its strength. It had stout defenses, which betokened a great fear. Withal, they deterred reckless aggression.

Most of the Mediterranean now became part of the Arab world. The Levantine conglomerate that had fallen previously under the influence of Byzance adopted the Arabs' tongue and creed. Most of the Arabs of today are the descendants of this ethnic mixture, former Christian people and not of the "Arabs of the Arabs," erstwhile desert nature worshipers.

Reaching for the Stars

After the march of the armies, it was the onward march of man's inventive genius that erupted in the Arab world. In the next few pages we shall see that it was this spirit of the East that nurtured the spirit of the West back again into life. Then, too, there was an Arab Awakening, infinitely richer than the contemporary one. It led the way to the reawakening of the western mind.

When the inquisitive mind of the Arabs came into touch with Europe's cultural traditions, a cross-fertilization resulted which was to astound the world. Arab culture produced its richest flowers on what is Spain today. Of tenth century's Cordova it was said that it eclipsed all of Europe's cultural centers. A century later it was overshadowed by Seville, which attracted the best minds in the western world. Then, again, Toledo excelled these cities. Through them Europe's great universities in Bologna, Padua, Paris, were stimulated into life.

Arab learning was extremely hospitable and that may have accounted partly for its success. The parallel with American hospitality to learning is too obvious to be overlooked. There, too, fame attracted fame, as the keenest minds were seeking recognition in the halls of Arab learning.

Literally, the Arabs were reaching for the stars. The greatest names in their midst busied themselves with celestial mysteries, immortalizing their names as the frontiersmen of astronomy. How could it be otherwise? The Arab's sky pervaded his life.

In the desert he was in constant communion with it, setting his course by the stars. When, later, he embarked on his world-conquering course, the stars served as the guides of his seafaring craft.

One of the great achievements of Arab scholarship was the rediscovery for the western world of Aristotle's realism. This was the beginning of a new way of life which is ours today, the life of reason, practical, pragmatic, guided by research.

Arab medicine also formed the bridge between that of the Greeks and our own. Galen says "Nay" and Hippocrates "Yea" and so the Arab scholars studied both, transmitting the fruits of their labor to succeeding generations.

"Miracle of the World"

To name even the most important of Arab scholars would disrupt the framework of this chapter. Only a few of the most famous will be mentioned here.

"Miracle of the world," *stupor mundi*, was the designation given to Avicenna, whose full Arabic name was Abu-'Ali Hussein ben Abdullah ben Hasan ben 'Ali ibn-Sina, he who graced the world at the turn of the first millennium. He was Turkestan-born, so that today his birthplace is in the Soviet Union. Yet, so vast was the scope of Arab learning in those days that he became a beacon of Arab scholarship. Where was one to begin the enumeration of his gifts and where to end? Such giants are no longer born. His work spanned fields as far apart as medicine and metaphysics, logic and philosophy, mathematics and theology. Poet he was, too, and also a statesman. The works he produced endured for centuries. His famous *Canon of Medicine* was used as a handbook until the seventeenth century, not only in the Eastern countries but in the medical schools of Paris and Leyden and Montpellier as well. *The Book of Recovery* of Avicenna fills 18 volumes, an encyclopedia, large portions of which were republished in Iran until recently.

It is said of this scholar that he dealt with the physical law of freely falling bodies, that he suspected the existence of microbes and that he spoke of the connection between the diseases of the brain and other organs.

Then there were the other eminent scholars of the Arab awakening, such as Averroës, whose name is linked to a great paradox. A Muslim, he is considered a pacemaker of scholasticism, which was to attempt to provide Christian faith with a rational basis. He and the equally famous Avempace cultivated fields that encompassed astronomy as well as jurisprudence, grammar and zoology, medicine and philosophy. They kept on piercing the hard surface of traditions in an age famed for its attachment to the "cake of custom."

The hospitality of Arab genius was revealed in the large number of Jewish scholars writing in the Arabic tongue. One of the most notable of these was the court physician of twelfth century rulers over Syria and Egypt, the famous Saladin. The physician was Rabbi Moses ben Maimon, known also as Maimonides and Rambam. His famous *Guide to the Perplexed* was composed in Arabic, but he also wrote in Hebrew. He tried to reconcile Rabbinic Judaism with the Arabic form of Aristotle's philosophy. In an age where the tendency was strong to judge a man merely by the company he held and the creed he professed, Maimonides wanted to know what the individual was attempting to do with his God-given gifts. To this early humanist the individual was the sovereign and the measure was man. He extolled the saving grace of socially useful deeds in an age which praised the virtues of asceticism.

Avicebron was another great Arab scholar of the Jewish faith, with the ancestral name of Ibn Gabirol. He wrote Hebrew poems in Arabic meters and he, too, was one of the precursors of scholasticism, which Christian philosophers were to practice.

"You, Too, Speak Arabic!"

Our debt to the Arabs is clearly reflected in our English tongue, in many words of which the extent of our obligation is marked. Our "Arabic" numbers are, of course, of Indian origin, but getting them to us the Arabs were the go-betweens. Their word "*sifr*" for our zero resulted in our "cipher."

The Arabs' pioneer role in calculations is marked in the name of algebra, derived from the original "*al jabr,*" meaning the "reunion of broken parts," and thus to put together. The people who gave us that word led the way in trigonometry, the measurements of specific gravity, infinite quantities, plane and spherical surfaces, conic sections. The great Arabic scholar, al-Farabi, who himself was of Turkish origin, appears to have come close to the discovery of the logarithm while working on the problem of musical intervals.

The Arabic words in our language sometimes have an authentic Anglo-Saxon ring. What could be a more typically American drink of our South than the julep? Yet, it is an authentically Oriental word meaning "rose water."

The United States spends more money on alcohol and "soda" than any other country or, for that matter, continent. In the case of alcohol, there is, of course, the telltale Arabic article, "*al.*" Strangely, the word itself in the Arab original means "eye-shadow" or "powder for painting eyelids." The modern meaning of alcohol was derived from the fact that both it and eye painting consist of highly rectified spirits.

The United States is the classical land of soda and one shudders at the thought of what would happen to our pharmacies if it were removed from the national diet. Yet nothing could be more Arabic than this word, "*suda.*" Unexpectedly, it means "splitting headache," which would be more appropriate to the name of alcohol. But the paternal grandfather of *suda* was sodium carbonate and that is where the scene was set for the splitting headache.

Then, again, could there be a more typical American farm product than alfalfa, the very name of which exudes the scents of Middle Western farms. Yet no word could be more typically Arabic, meaning simply "grass." To continue with farm products, America is both the largest producer and exporter of cotton. Again we are face to face with a pure Arabic word, spelled in the original as "*qutun.*"

If we were to ask strangers to name one of the best-known American institutions, many of them would mention the tariff. That too, is an Arab word, meaning "schedule." It was brazen Arab mariners who set up business for themselves at the meeting place of the Ocean Sea and the Mediterranean, at the entrance of the Strait of Gibraltar, levying toll from the passing boats.

The name of this island became known as Tarifa, because of the schedules the ships had to show.

Another well-known western institution is the magazine, of which the United States seems to be the largest producer and consumer. And what a good Arabic word it is, too, "*makhazin*," storehouse—a storehouse of stories in this case.

Admiral sounds very English, too, and that is as it should be. Did not the English rule the waves for centuries? And now it seems to be America's turn. It is only right that the nations having the largest navies should provide the title of the highest officers. Yet the word is Arabic, derived from "Al Amir," the leader. The Arabs were famous navigators at one time.

There are the names of chemical substances (chemistry itself is derived from alchemy, an Arabic word), such as alkali, ammoniac, niter, borax and sulphuric acid. Then, the famous fabrics named after places in the Arab world, such as damask (Damascus), muslin (Mosul) and tabby, meaning cloth with stripes of different colors.

Unknown Arab History

What happened to the Arab empire after that mad dash to east and west, covering a span of nearly six thousand miles, which planted the Prophet's banner on the peaks of the Pyrenees and the Bay of Bengal? The inevitable happened, of course, since no central government could maintain itself in regions so far apart and so divergent in interests. That heavenly city, Damascus, was the center of the Arab empire of the Umayyad dynasty for about ninety years, up to the middle of the eighth century. Then the center was removed to Baghdad, where the Abbasid dynasty ruled. Nominally this ended in the thirteenth century, but that date was nominal, indeed.

What could be the connecting link between the heart of the Orient in Baghdad and the heart of the Occident in Seville? Already under the previous dynasty the Arab world empire began to fall apart. A Moorish emirate was established in Cordoba, later transformed into a caliphate. The atomization continued apace.

The drought-ridden East disgorged another hungry horde in

the form of the Seljuk Turks in the eleventh century, Turanian in tongue, akin to Mongol and Finn and named after Seljuk, of the Turkish tribe of Ghuz. The East was the land of the famine-stricken dust bowls, while the West was fat and flabby. On the remains of the Eastern Roman empire the human vultures were converging. The Seljuks were booted out by their own Osmanli kinsmen, hungrier and more ruthless, who had little to lose. Vast North Africa and Spain had become wholly independent, but the religion and language lived on.

Then came Hulagu, the son of Tului and the grandson of Genghis Khan, the Mongol miracle, brother of Kublai Khan and Mangu Khan. He was the Hulagu who laid siege to Baghdad, seized and sacked the city in the thirteenth century, overthrew the Abbasid caliphate and ended the Arabs' eastern global rule. He it was who invaded Syria, then captured Aleppo and magnificent Damascus. He, the noble of nobles, was then defeated by a slave, the Sultan of Egypt of ignominious birth. Thus Hulagu was compelled to see the light and he embraced Islam, rather than die. The world was not to be his but his descendants were to rule over Iran for a century. The Tartars destroyed the Arab universal empire and in the process they also destroyed themselves. Another chapter of Middle Eastern history was to start.

At this point the western man is disposed to assert that the Arabs sank into oblivion for centuries. The case, however, was different. True, the Arabs had shot their bolts in the political and cultural fields, but their productive period was not over. On the contrary, their genius turned to new fields to till. They turned their attention to trade and travel, producing remarkable merchant adventurers who anticipated the various western trade companies. The ancestors of today's landlubber Arabs were enterprising seafarers who ventured into the monsoon-swept Ocean, penetrated into the coastland of the desert and jungle in Africa, swept into the Far East.

Someday the amazing story of the spices will be told in great detail, and particularly what the world owes to cinnamon and clove. What does civilization owe to the heavy silks from the

East which the royal ladies and gentlemen of the West craved? Then there is the story of ivory tusks and slaves.

Yes, the Arab traders took risks as they set sail for India's Malabar coast, rounded Cape Comorin, sailed up the Coromandel shore, called at the Ganges estuary, and left their mark on the Bengal country. There even today some 85 per cent of the inhabitants are Muslims.

Long before the enterprising Spanish, Portuguese, English and French missionaries, sailors, merchant adventurers, these Arabs swept into the vastness of Asia's distant lands, where they met Hinduism, Buddhism, also fetishism and animism. While trading with the natives they gave them Allah. Thousands of miles from the Prophet's birthplace the rulers of Malaya's jungle lands are still called Sultans, because the majority of the indigenous population is Muslim.

As the Arabs ventured into the world of uncharted oceans they found the ten thousand islands of the Indonesian archipelago. What happened as a result of this encounter is clearly written on Asia's face. A world apart from Mecca, in the maze of the islands, on Java, Borneo and Sumatra, on countless other islands, Islam prevails. It is only because of the mixture of alien blood that the entire population is not Muslim today, but even so some 90 per cent of it follows the Prophet's law.

The Arab merchants moved onward, to the very ends of the world, dealing in spices, precious stones, also furs and slaves. These sons of tropical lands pressed into the frigid regions of the north, into the Baltic country, leaving numerous Arab coins along the route of the original Russian settlements. Indeed, it was Arab writers who first described the original land of the "Russ" as an island covered with woods and marshes; an erroneous description, but pioneering, just the same.

Because the Arabs were everywhere it was their "Code of Saracens" which parts of the western world attempted to follow up to the eleventh century, representing the first medieval attempt to safeguard the rights of noncombatant populations in a world at war.

Carried by the Arabs, Islam became the first cosmic creed, embracing the entire world from the Pyrenees to the Philippines.

Nor was Islam only a "horizontal" religion, along the beltline of the globe; it also became a vertical one. To these doughty Arab traders the "Dark Continent" was not dark. They left their mark on Africa's eastern coast, and penetrated deep inland in pursuit of the treasures they sought. Many remnants of their earlier rule are being uncovered in spots where no eastern influence had been thought to exist. Arab merchant kings are now believed to have set up their realms in distant Africa. Nor did the open seas hold any horrors for these enterprising monarchs of exotic trade. Hundreds of miles from nowhere, in the far-ranging Seychelles Islands of the Indian Ocean, Islam holds an important place, and so it does on the islands of Mauritius and Reunion, in wind-swept oceans, many miles from Madagascar.

Arabs were the most famous travelers of the fourteenth century but the fame of none of them equaled that of Mohammed ibn-'Abdullah ibn-Battutah, whom the world knows simply as Ibn-Battuta. This Tangier-born traveler spent a quarter of a century in the crossings of Asia, Africa and Europe, covering some 75,000 miles, not counting deviations. He went to India via Constantinople, then across the Black Sea to Central Asia. He went to China as the representative of the Sultan of Delhi. He visited every Muslim country of his time and other lands as well. When the gatekeepers of Constantinople caught a glimpse of his exotic garb they muttered "Sarakini," since a Saracen there was an unusual sight. He crossed the Gobi desert of many horrors.

He also tackled the Sahara desert, reaching the edge of another world at Timbuctoo. As a good Muslim he turned his incurable "wanderlust" to good account by making four pilgrimages to Mecca. He combined spiritual bliss with earthly pleasures on his first trip by marrying two wives as he moved along. The records of his travels may be read with relish even today.

A Christian Interlude

To deliver the Holy Land from the infidel was the call of Pope Urban II, in Central France's Clermont in the autumn of 1095. Christendom was relapsing into barbarism as brother's hand was turned against brother. When every free man wore arms and wanted to display his valor, surplus energy could be well used for the liberation of the Holy Land. Christendom in Constantinople was fighting with its back against the wall, on the point of being engulfed by the Islamic tide. It cried out to the West in despair. If it could be saved, could the East and West not be reunited?

Also, the mighty north Italian cities of Genoa and Venice were losing ground as the "Saracens" showed signs of wresting the lucrative East and West trade from their hands. The merchants held that permitting the profits to pass into unhallowed Muslim hands would be a tremendous loss to the Christian world.

Then, too, there was an abundance of ambitious younger sons and a shortage of good land in Europe on which to establish fiefs. By extending the way of the West to the East, could not the younger sons' problem be solved?

Not the least important was the religious ecstasy that seemed to sweep the masses in an age when social tensions were mounting. People began to realize that religion was not merely for the lips but also for the heart. The weird practices of the age indicated profound upheavals. Flagellants were roaming the countryside, and the residents of monasteries could no longer find their vocation between the overcrowded walls. The crusade might become a unifying force, making all of Europe the dwelling place of Christ's sanctified hosts, heeding the word of the Pontiff, the vicar of Christ on earth.

The words of the Pope produced unexpected results. Weather-beaten warriors burst out sobbing, the listeners were raised to the highest pitch of exaltation and seized by frenzy, the crowd demanded immediate deeds. And so the period of crusades began.

The crusaders were noble knights and humble monks, priests and husbandmen, beggars and lepers, murderers and hermits, harlots and saintly women. They walked barefoot and in rags, rode on superb chargers, wore tatters and royal mantle. How many of them were there? Perhaps a hundred thousand, perhaps three times that number. They ascended mountains and lost their way in the woods, crossed plains, forded streams, were scourged by rain and snow. They were welcomed in churches, set upon by bandits, killed by marauders.

Finally, the war-bent pilgrims reached the Holy Land, those of them that survived, and carried onward by frenzied zeal overwhelmed Jerusalem. When night fell on the Holy City on July 15, 1099, the crescent of Islam had been replaced by the cross of Christ. The slaughter was terrible, according to descriptions in contemporary accounts. The blood of the conquered ran down the streets until men splashed in gore as they rode. The crusaders went to the Church of the Sepulchre as night fell and put their bloodstained hands together in prayer. On that day in July the first crusade came to an end.

The Christian fighters formed the conquered parts of the Middle East in their own image. They set up feudal states for the bold young blades of the West, in Antioch and Edessa, in Tripoli and they established the crowning glory of all, the Kingdom of Jerusalem.

These domains, however, had no depth and behind the crest of hills a few miles away the Muslim world began. A short distance farther, Damascus was in Islamic hands. The best grain land belonged to the "infidels," and so defense favored the holders of the hinterland. The soil over which the crusaders held control was mainly on the shores, choked with sand and swamp, providing them with scant food. And most of the knights of the cross were thousands of miles away from home. The Christian island in the midst of the Islamic sea could not maintain itself. The crusaders fell out among themselves as Christians took the stronghold of Constantinople. So this period of history ended some two centuries after it began. The last bulwark of the crusaders, the town of Acre in Palestine, yielded to the Islamic hosts in 1291.

History casts a long shadow in the world, particularly in the Middle East. The mark the crusaders left in the Levant is visible there even today, and not merely in the form of ruins. Among the crusading hosts the French played a leading role and their language was to become the universal tongue (*lingua franca*) of the Middle East. Even today when the unlettered Middle Easterner means the Westerner he will say *Franji*, the Frank, the French. The French were the first to obtain concessions from the Ottoman empire in times to come. It took the form of "capitulations," exempting them from the jurisdiction of the native courts and placing them under their own administration. In more recent times the French became protectors of Catholics in the Middle East. When Christians were persecuted in the second half of the last century, France was called upon to offer them succor. After the First World War the best regions of the area were assigned to the republic of France as mandates.

Many crusaders unable to reach home found sanctuary in the mountains of Lebanon, adjoining the Holy Land, and there their descendants live to this very day. It was during the crusades that the Maronite Christians of the Lebanon decided to enter into communion with the Church of Rome. Until then they were a dissident group, holding to the monothelete doctrine, under which Jesus was represented as having only one will, although having two natures, human and divine.

Highly important is the fact that French feudalism in crusading times established a pattern which the tide of times has not been able to change. Feudalism is still rampant in the region, as it was then. Long after the crusaders had been forced to yield, land in Syria continued to be held in fief for military service. The spirit of feudalism also survived in the form of the taxation system, under which tax collection was farmed out to pashas, to squeeze the most out of the human cattle so as to have an excess over the sums to be delivered into the Ottoman imperial treasury. Today, too, the long shadow of feudalism is still a blight on the land.

Then the Locusts

When the Arab rulers were weakening in Baghdad, they sought to hold on to their power by maintaining human stud farms of strong and sturdy slaves. The only people that could be trusted, they held, were slaves in need of the master's feeding hand. They forgot that if allowed to wax in strength the slaves could become masters. That is precisely what happened.

At first the slaves formed a praetorian guard, and as the rulers' power waned, theirs began to grow. They formed a dynasty which adopted none of the magnificent surnames of "Glorious" and "Perfect." On the contrary, it called itself "Chattel," since that is the translation of the word "*Mamluk,*" under which it became known.

The history of the Mamluks was summarized in the designations of their dynasties, of which there were two. The first was called Bahri, from the Arabic word "*bahr,*" sea, since the masters had established a human stud farm on an island off the Nile. From those humble beginnings the slaves rose to positions of the highest authority in the Islamic world.

The name of the second Mamluk dynasty also indicated a place of detention. The members of this branch were called Burji, from the native "*burj,*" tower, from which the western Burg, where they were kept under close control. With their headquarters in Egypt, these Mamluks ruled over much of the Middle East after the crusades. The whip in their masters' hands had been their trainer and with it they were to train their own subjects.

Endless conflicts broke the strength of successive rulers and by neutralizing them a power vacuum was created in the Middle East. And then came the Ottoman Turks.

The Turks Stayed Long

The Seljuk Turks had been ground up by Allah's slowly working mills, and the road was open for the next wave of invaders to step over their dead bodies. These were the Osmanli or Ottoman Turks, so named after Osman, whom the world also knew as Othman, and who died in 1326.

When the Osmanli first appeared on the well-known warriors' highway of the Middle East, they were hungry, desperate and unspent. In less than twenty years they conquered Asia Minor, the Turkey of today, extending their sway all the way to the Straits. However, Constantinople held out, protected by its stout walls and location. In the interior of Asia Minor the conglomerate of Eastern Romans, a Hellenized mixture of ethnic groups, were exposed to the victors' abrasive force and most of them became Turks. On much of the coast, near the seas that offered the chance of refuge in case of too oppressive rule and linking them to the bulk of the Greek communities, the original settlements retained their Greek speech and Christian creed. It was only after the First World War that they were largely wiped out, in an age of intolerant nationalism and of genocide.

Why did the descendants of Hittites, Phrygians, Latins, Greeks, Persians and Arabs become absorbed in the new organization? This was not accomplished mainly by fear induced by the threat of death, Professor Arnold J. Toynbee reminds us. Nor did the Turks kill off the original inhabitants they found and settle the land with their own people. The eyewitness evidence is clear. Today a large number of the Turks looks anything but Turkish and the prevailing type is Alpine, a branch of what the German Nazis used to call Aryans. Had the natives been wiped out, the Oriental type among the Turks would be more pronounced. Their greatest man in the twentieth century, Mustafa Kemal, looked like a Minnesota Swede.

The Turks were a handful against millions of settlers. The new rulers needed workers, soldiers, administrators and, above all, they needed taxpayers, and so it was their policy to have the natives collaborate with them. Later their elite troops were converted Christians, and some of their highest officials were of non-Turkish descent. Had the Turks depopulated the country they would have cut the pillars under their new land.

The facility with which the crescent ousted the cross appears to be a mystery only at first sight. In the Byzantine empire the common man may have had human features, but he was treated as a beast. He was trained to accept orders without question and when the Turks came he accepted them, too.

The Turks, on the other hand, were cattle growers and in that work they learned how to deal with human beings. This is what they did and their policy was successful: you give the cattle a chance to eat and then you form a herd, within which there is no individual opinion, only the crack of the whip and the frightful bark of the dog. You improve the strain of the cattle, and this they did by kidnaping Christian children and raising slaves they trained to high positions, sometimes the highest in the State.

"Osman was a fighter and something of a political organizer," wrote Professor Donald Everett Webster in *The Turkey of Ataturk.* "His heirs were fighters and rulers. For the other qualities needed in the populace of a successful empire the Ottomans relied upon the contributions of the peoples they found and conquered and governed, among whom they lived and whom they came to appreciate. Horsemen do not become workers–producers–and the Osmanlis were horsemen."

At the feet of these horsemen the world was crumbling, as they answered a call which was history's. It was in 1356 that they crossed the Dardanelles, and for the first time in their turbulent career the Turks entered the Balkans, never to leave it again.

Here a parallel with the previous Muslim conquest forces itself on the observer's attention. Several centuries before, the Arabs had also crossed a waterway, Gibraltar, and forced their way into Europe. That was the westernmost of the three great European peninsulas. The Ottoman Turks crossed the Dardanelles and they were now in the easternmost great southern peninsula of Europe.

At the time of the Arab invasion, Europe's extreme peninsular west was the weakest, a power vacuum. Meanwhile, however, the Christian nations had filled out the West. The weakest spot was now within the shadow of those sturdy Byzantine walls. That was the Balkans which, for centuries was the trouble spot of the world. No longer under the effective control of a strong power, those rugged mountain chains and ranges of southeastern Europe became the home of fragmented ethnic groups that fought and mutually weakened one another.

The Arabs, centuries before, had to push their way toward Paris. When defeated there, their world rule crumbled. Likewise, the Turks also had to fulfill their dynamic destiny in trying to drive their advantage to the very limit and so they pushed right to Vienna's walls. Before that happened, however, history was to witness a startling event.

The Story of Constantinople

Like a lighthouse in the Muslim sea, Christian Constantinople stood out. Between it and surrender were only its powerful walls: five miles in length was the Wall of Theodosius, stronger than any that man had ever seen. Against those walls Turkish waves were beating, and one after another the imperial city lost its links with the outside world. Up the Bosphorus the Turks had built a wall of their own, from which they could look down into the heart of the doomed capital, which was also its own country. Turkish caravels controlled traffic with the West. Emperor Constantine, of the Paleologue family, read the writing on the wall. The Roman church seemed to be willing to let his capital fall a prey to the Turks because it was considered schismatic. Let then the eastern and western churches unite, and Constantinople was surely worth a Roman mass. The Emperor did not count with the fanaticism of his priests, and the union was prevented. What was to save the sacred city on the Golden Horn?

His exalted predecessors had dispatched ardent appeals to the rulers of the West, bespeaking their aid. Could Their Christian Majesties tolerate St. Sophia's falling into pagan hands? Could they surrender Christ's last outpost in the East? Theologians may wrangle over fine details, but East and West were the fighting knights of Christ.

These frantic calls for help found polite ears in the West, but they found no readiness to help. The Popes saw the peril more clearly than the secular Princes but their attention, too, was riveted on a myriad other problems. The Crusades had been tried and they had failed.

The Ottoman's Sultan was Mohammed II, a young man of twenty-one when he ascended the throne. "The Conqueror," "The Great," "The Victorious," he was called. As hard as the iron of his cannons was he, and nothing could sway him from his way. From his commander's tent on an elevation he saw St. Sophia every day, taunting him, challenging him to action. He would have no rest until the proud city of Christ was humbled by Allah. In Hagia Sophia he must hold his Friday *selamlik*, public worship. He could have starved out the city, but that might take years and he was impatient. Besides, a Mohammed II does not win wars in that manner. He must accomplish the impossible, even though the Wall of Theodosius had defied his stoutest cannons. He scoured his lands in Europe and Asia to find a master worker to build a cannon to be equal to that wall. Finally he found one, a Hungarian and a Christian by the name of Urbas, who knew how to build such a mammoth.

The siege began on April 6, 1453, and for a last moment the city justified its early past. Not more than eight thousand defenders were able to stand up against an attacking army of a hundred thousand. The heavy battery swung into action and its massive stone balls battered the walls. The Emperor led the spirited defense. His were all soldiers of Christ, their weapons hallowed by their dedication, and so would be their deaths.

The Emperor was hoping that the Princes would send him a force of relief. Daily the noncombatant populace mounted the inner walls, gazing intently toward the Sea of Marmora where they expected to see the Christian galleons' swelling sails. Week after week the walls held out. The crack troops that tried to scale them were cut down, and so were the regulars and the special troops of Spahis and Janizaries as well. The walls were dented, the breaches were gaping, but the defenders filled them again.

For the final assault Mohammed gave the signal on May 29th. His patience was wearing thin. Again the defenders shook off the attackers. A miracle might happen. The old and lame prostrated themselves in Hagia Sophia, praying for divine deliverance. Meanwhile, the cannon balls crashed, the iron ladders clattered, the hot oil swished and its victims shrieked. In the general pandemonium it was unnoticed that an inner gate, known as Kerkaporta, had been left open by the defenders, presumably in the excitement of the final agony. However, the attackers did not overlook that opening and through it they began to pour into the city, Mohammed II riding at the head of his victorious troops. The dead body of the last Emperor of Byzantium was found.

Thus the Eastern Empire ended and thus a dream went up in smoke. In an impregnable position on the Straits the Turks entrenched themselves. They made Constantinople their capital and nothing was to halt their irresistible advance. Europe woke up with a start, as the enemy was on the very threshold of the

West. The Turk had become a world issue. "The master of Constantinople," Napoleon was to say, "was to rule the world."

From then on until the end of the First World War the history of the Middle East was largely the history of the Ottoman empire. Included in it were the Arabic lands, and again the top of North Africa. Bleeding from many wounds, weakened by generations of strife, the territory we call Iran today was again largely immune to the alien onslaught. Persia, indeed, seemed to have countless lives.

So the Ottoman Turks followed the law of their own nature, pressing the advantage they possessed to the very limit. In front of their new possession there was chaotic southeastern Europe. Who but themselves were called upon to rule over this cockpit? And from there Europe's great Transcontinental Highway along the majestic Danube River led them directly into a dramatic gap in the mountains. To the north began the wreath of the Carpathian Range, while to the south were the foothills of the Alpine system. The gap contained the imperial city of Vienna.

The master of Constantinople was not yet the master of all Europe but the master of Vienna would find Europe at his feet. Masters of Vienna were the Habsburgs and in front of the walls of the imperial city the East and West clashed in one of the most dramatic battles of recorded history. The battle took place in 1683, and its results were uncannily similar to those which Charles Martel scored not far from Paris nearly a thousand years before.

Retreating from the high mark of their invasion the Ottomans settled down in the Balkans. However, there the parallel ends. No Avicenna or Averroes of the Turks enriched the cultural heritage of the world. Nor did the Turks make their fame in world-wide travel and international trade. No Turkish style of architecture revolutionized the world, as the Moorish had done. The Turks' trail was not marked by the enrichment of philosophy and science, and our languages have not been made more expressive by Ottoman contributions. The Turks were a military race and a very efficient one at that. The only vestiges they have left are the ruins of fortifications, deep down into Europe, on the banks of the Danube. But they had folk poetry.

Lest one misunderstand history, it should be made clear that there was a vast difference between the worlds the Arabs knew and the one the Turks encountered. The former found a period of transition and waiting, the "Dark Ages," and anybody with a light had a tremendous opportunity. The Arabs had such a light.

The Turks, on the other hand, burst into Europe in an age of great intellectual stimulation which reached its apogee in the Renaissance. Even today that period stands as a high-water mark of intellectual fermentation, the Age of the Giants. The Turks were said to have got it started with the seizure of Constantinople, resulting in the dissemination of Greek scholarship and Byzantine art, the invention of printing and the discovery of America. The Renaissance had already begun with Petrarch and the Italian humanists in the fourteenth century.

There was another basic difference, too, in the mark the Arabs and Turks left on the world. The former had made their contribution to the world and then they dropped out of history for centuries, submerged in the vast Ottoman Empire. They re-emerged as nations only after the First World War.

The Turks, on the other hand, never collapsed as a nation. They entered a stage of rapid decline after their defeat on the Danube valley. Then it seemed as if they were to be wiped out altogether, and what a czar called the "sick man of Europe" would become the dead man of the world. Possibly this did not come to pass not because of the strength of the Turks but because of the weakness of the Great Powers which feared the consequences of a fratricidal fight for the family heirlooms of the deceased. But the fact is that the Turks have a continuous history.

They have always had a tremendous racial pride. Once a global threat, history does not deny Turkey's strength. This pride was as characteristic of the Turks in the past, when they controlled a huge empire, as it is now, when their country is confined to only a small portion of what was once theirs. Today that part is only Anatolia and a toehold in southeastern Europe.

After their great successes the Turks were far less solvents of alien blood than the Arabs had been, and this is also explained by their racial pride, which stayed the mixing of their own with the "defiled" blood of others. (It was during the Korean War, in which Turkish soldiers participated, that medical students of Istanbul, capital of republican Turkey, donated plasma to be airmailed to United Nations hospitals when the public objected to Turkish soldiers in Korea receiving transfusions of alien blood.) To be a Turk meant to be a Muslim (and that is not true of all Arabs) and if one was a Christian, an Armenian, a Greek, or a Jew, he was not only the follower of a different creed but of a different breed. These other minorities received the right to organize themselves in self-governing units, *"millet."*

Thus the Ottomans had constructed a nationality state in which the ruling Turks were surrounded by many satellites. The majority was formed by the "minorities"—Arabs, Armenians, Greeks, Kurds and many others. It was a dynastic state, not a national one. The Turks of the higher classes called themselves Osmanlis, not Turks. The so-called "Young Turks" at the beginning of our century called themselves so only in the West and in foreign tongues. At home, however, they translated this designation into Turkish by calling themselves "Young Osmanlis."

It is impossible not to see the parallel between this state and the Habsburg Empire. It may also be significant that the two of them were adjacent for a long time. Both of them were located peripherally, covering the bulk of eastern Europe's ethnically atomized region. Neither the Osmanli nor the Habsburg dynasty could therefore afford to identify itself with any of the component nationality blends.

While both empires lasted they could not help employing identical principles of rule. The ruling minorities in both countries had to use the device of strengthening themselves by weakening the majorities through the application of the principle of "divide and rule." The members of the many groups composing these states were not aware of the invisible hands regulating their mutual hatreds.

It was no coincidence that both dynasties expired at the end of the First World War. This was the end of the dynastic way of life and the resounding triumph of the nation and the National State.

"Dolce Far Niente"

The Ottoman Empire was floundering in the mire of its incompetence early in the twentieth century, in need of rejuvenation if it was to survive. This was not the age when nations could afford to take things easy, do nothing. The new life-giving elixir was nationalism, which appeared to have miraculous life-giving qualities. That was also the view of the young officers of the Ottoman army, exposed to western influence in the Balkans. Their headquarters was in Salonika on the Aegean Sea, at that time in the Ottoman Empire but now an important port of Greece. The rejuvenation was to be effected by the Young Turk Revolution of 1908, spearheaded by the Committee of Union and Progress.

The magic word among progressive Turks then was "Constitution," which came to mean to them progress, prosperity and happiness. That was what the Young Turks wanted. The old regime was so decrepit that it yielded to a mere show of strength. The young revolutionaries appeared to be westernizers, therefore liberals, and the minorities of the Ottoman Empire hailed their efforts with delight. They expected great things from an enlightened rule.

The Awakening of an Empire

At this point today's Middle East history begins, and it is the history of nationalism in the region. The "Old Turks" normally left their majority "minorities" to their own devices, to rule themselves under their own autonomous systems of government, *millet*, virtually nations within the supernational dynasty. Occasionally the Old Turks lashed out at the minorities, massacring recalcitrant groups, mainly Armenians.

The Young Turks promised freedom to the Ottoman minorities, but it was a liberty beneath the Turkish nation's heel. The old Ottoman Empire could do it, but a modern nation state could not tolerate minorities with special rights, such as worshiping their Gods in their own languages and in their own ways. It could not permit a place for God in man's heart unless it was the national god. It expected every member of the national community to give his all to the national cause. The modern nation's claims on the citizen are far stronger than the claims of even the most intolerant creeds.

This was particularly true of the Young Turks, exalted by the discovery of the delights of nationalism. With the zeal of the convert they put into effect the lessons they learned in the West. Instead of greater freedom, the nationalities lost whatever liberties they had under the flabby old regime. Most numerous of these nationalities were the Arab subjects of the Ottoman Empire, their land extending endlessly from Aleppo to Aden and then deep into the center of Africa.

The Arab Awakening began shortly before the outbreak of the First World War. In Paris, intellectual homeland of many Levantines, the first meetings of the nation-minded Arab intellectuals began. The first sign of Arab awakening was the formation in Paris of the Young Arab Association, "Al jam'iya al'Arabiya al-Fatat," the aim of which was to gain freedom from Turkish rule.

A group of Arab officers in the Ottoman Empire also banded together in an organization of their own, magnificently called "Solemn League and Covenant." Since a large part of Arab officers came from Mesopotamia, this group consisted of what today we would call Iraqi. The organizations were so secretive that they knew little of one another.

At the very time this movement began the creative use of classical Arabic had all but ceased. Old authors were ignored while modern Arab poetry was merely a copy of archaic models. Members of the higher Arab social classes affected to speak Turkish and this went also for the "plotters." It was only later that a new school of young Arab writers emerged, engaged in the task of rendering the tongue more pliant for the expression of modern thought.

Other Arab organizations came into being, but their number continued to be limited. Right in the lion's den, Constantinople, there was an Arab literary club. In Cairo another body, styling itself "Party of Ottoman Decentralization," appeared.

This was not a mass movement, of course. The masses of the Arab people were not familiar with the newfangled idea of nationalism. They spoke a language which was different from that of the Turkish officeholders, but that meant little. The Turkish officeholders were Muslims and so were they, and that meant much. People either belonged to the Islamic world, in which case they could hope to enter heaven, or they did not belong to it, in which case they were infidels. This was the basis of their classification.

The Arab fellah did not like the Turkish officeholder just because he, too, was a Muslim. The Turks were scoundrels because they always oppressed the people, but Arabs probably would have been no different. What mattered was not what strange language you spoke. Were you part of the government? In that case you were obnoxious and a crook.

There was no general agreement among the Arab rebels either about what they wanted. In those days the Ottoman Empire seemed to be destined to endure throughout the ages, in spite of all its weaknesses. If nothing else, it was the jealousy of the Great Powers that was to keep it alive. Some of the Arab plotters were thinking only of some form of self-government within the empire. Others, in turn, were dreaming of nationhood.

Not all of these were idealists dedicated to a consecrated cause. For that they were too deeply steeped in the traditions of the Ottoman Empire. Many of them were thinking of better jobs and higher government positions in a native administration. Many of them would have abhorred the thought of sharing their nationalism with the dirty fellah.

At the Bedside of the Sick Man

The Ottoman Empire seemed to be disintegrating at the time of the outbreak of the First World War. Its revenues covered no more than one-seventh of its expenditures, and its debt charges alone amounted to nearly one-third of the imperial income. Turkey was a bankrupt country.

Shortly before the outbreak of the Great War the Ottoman Empire had lost its last foothold in the Balkans, retaining only the European approaches to the Straits. Egypt, nominally Ottoman, had been occupied by the British and soon was to be proclaimed their protectorate. Italy had invaded Tripolitania, which in years to come it was to combine with Cyrenaica into Libya.

In the past, Britain underwrote the independence of the Ottoman Empire, in order to keep the Russians from warm water outlets. However, great changes had taken place in recent times. The Armenian massacres in Turkey had aroused British public opinion, and leading statesmen in London had denounced the "unspeakable Turk." Britain had stripped Turkey of her control of Egypt; also, she was now in possession of Cyprus, which formerly belonged to the realm of the Sublime Porte.

Nevertheless, as the First World War approached, Britain appeared to be eager to keep Constantinople out of the German camp and offered to guarantee her territorial integrity. The Germans, however, were more aggressive and they could point to the fact that the British were now the Russians' allies and what could be a more hideous sin in Turkish eyes? Finally the Reich pushed the Sublime Porte into war against the Triple Entente of Britain, France and Russia.

From the German point of view this appeared to be a master stroke. With Turkey in their camp, the Central European Powers controlled the great Eurasian landmass from the North Sea all the way to the Persian Gulf. This enabled them to operate with the aid of highly prized lines of internal communications (after Bulgaria had joined their ranks) so that they could throw their forces from one imperiled point to the other with little delay. This also meant that the Allies were split right in the middle. The industrially advanced western Allies were not in a position to send arms and ammunition to Russia via the Straits. They had to employ the long route halfway around the globe.

Revolt in the Desert

The weakest link of the bastion over which the Germans stood watch was the Ottoman Empire. It was weak inherently, and also because seven-tenths of its people were non-Turks, potential aliens and perhaps enemies.

In the early weeks of the First World War the giants of the West had come to grips in France. It was the plan of the Reich to rush into that country and deliver the mortal blow in the first round. The blow was powerful but not mortal. Then the combatants settled down to the life of troglodytes, the awful war of attrition. Periodically, one or the other of the opposing cave dwellers attempted to break loose and thus end the paralyzing deadlock.

At the other end of the embattled world, Allied thoughts and ambitions surged. Could not the British help to break the deadlock by tackling the Turks, whose realm was on the verge of the grave? Once the Ottoman Empire was knocked out, the Allies could break the deadlock by smashing open the back door. In British government offices in Cairo these thoughts were entertained by strategists.

In Mecca, the Holy City of Islam, there was an elderly Arab leader who was nominally subject to the Sultan's order but virtually independent of him. As a member of the family of Hashim, he was of the Prophet's own seed, this Grand Sherif of Mecca, Husayn ibn-'Ali. Being a real Arab of old stock, he derided the Sultan's claim to pose as a successor of the Prophet Caliph. The Sultan, after all, was only a Turk and not an Arab. Also, the Arabs should have their own country, and he should be its head.

Two of the Sherif's sons, Feisal and Abdullah—both of whom were to play historic roles—established contact with the office of Great Britain's far-famed soldier, Field Marshal Lord Kitchener, first Earl of Khartoum, former Sirdar of the Egyptian army and Governor General of the Sudan. The Arab emissaries had a bold idea. There should be an Arab revolt against the Turks, engineered with Britain's help. For this London should recognize an Arab Kingdom in all Arabia (except Aden, a British colony), in Palestine, Syria and Mesopotamia.

Before the British could assent to this plan many contingencies had to be considered. How good were the Arabs as soldiers? Military operations in the Middle East would suffer in the wake of an Arab rout. Then, too, was it in Britain's interest to see the Ottoman Empire eliminated? It had served a highly useful purpose in the past as a punching bag for the Russians, containing them in their icy vastness—with British help, of course. And what would be the consequence of an Ottoman collapse? Would the Arabs have the faculty to fill out the void and if so would they be amenable to British advice? London also had to give thought to the claims of Paris, which considered itself paramount in the Levant.

The upshot was that Britain decided to take the risk. As a result of this decision, the British High Commissioner in Cairo, Sir Henry MacMahon, and Husayn in Mecca engaged in a historic correspondence. Since the region was overrun by spies, the greatest secrecy had to be observed. The letters were not signed and the messengers carried them sewn into the leather of their boots.

The British were very cautious at first, not sure whether Husayn was not forwarding their letters to the Sultan. Then they were reassured. On July 14, 1915, they made their offer to Husayn: "Great Britain recognizes the independence of the Arab countries and agrees to the proclamation of the Arab caliphate for all Islam." Their dispatch of gold and grains to the keeper of the Holy Places was an earnest of their intention.

The British offer was too general and the negotiations had to continue. What did the British finally promise to the Arabs? Lawrence of Arabia—Thomas Edward Lawrence—stated in a letter to the *Times* of London that the government in London promised to recognize the independence of the Arabs south of latitude 37 degrees, except in the provinces of Baghdad and Basra, and except where Britain was not "free to act without detriment to the interests of France."

Winston Churchill, Secretary of State for the Colonies, on the other hand stated in the House of Commons on July 11, 1922, that "an undertaking was given to the Sherif of Mecca that His Majesty's government would recognize the independence of the Arabs within certain territorial limits, which specifically excluded the districts of Mersina and Alexandretta and the portions of Syria lying to the west of the districts of Damascus, Homs, Hama and Aleppo."

West of that line was the region in which the British believed the French were entitled to consideration. London is said to have kept Paris and Petrograd informed of these parleys.

There was another set of negotiations resulting in a secret

pact concluded on May 16, 1916, known as the Sykes-Picot Agreement, after the negotiators: Georges Picot, a French diplomat and Sir Mark Sykes, whom his biography describes not only as a foreign office adviser but also "breeder of sheep and horses, master of foxhounds."

This agreement provided for the division of the spoils in the Ottoman Empire, the demise of which it anticipated. Britain was to have a free hand to set up an administration in Mesopotamia's Baghdad and Basra districts, in which the Indian Office took a deep interest. France was to have similar prerogatives on the coast of Levant and deep in the heartland of Turkey in the north. An international regime was to be set up in Palestine, but Haifa and Acre were to go to Britain. The coastal region of the Hejaz was not to be touched and over it the Sherif ruled. A serious conflict of interests was in the making. The Arabs considered Palestine their own land, inhabited by their kin. On the other hand, many Jews considered it their ancestral home.

The Much Promised Land

Political Zionism was now some two decades old, advocating the creation of a homeland for the Jews. This was the issue on which the British government took the next important Middle Eastern step.

British interest in the Jews' connection with Palestine was not new. As far back as 1838 Lord Palmerston instructed the first British vice-consul to Jerusalem "to afford protection to the Jews generally."

This was a humanitarian move but also something else. Each of the major nations with special interests in the Middle East used a religious group in the Holy Land to further its diplomatic interests. It would not have sounded well for a Great Power to demand special rights in the Holy Land. It sounded much better to do it while advocating the rights of a religious minority in the Sultan's realm. The French regarded themselves the protectors of the Catholics, and this in spite of the fact that Paris and Rome were certainly not on the best of terms. The Russians represented themselves as the guardians of the Eastern Orthodox, using them as diplomatic pawns. The Germans began to take a lively interest in the Protestants of the Holy Land. There was only one more religious group in Palestine without an advocate—the Jews; and Great Britain saw her chance.

During the Great War Britain's interest in the question of Palestine and the Jews was revived. Already in the spring of 1916 the British Ambassador to Petrograd wrote about it to Russian Foreign Minister Sergei Dmitrievich Sazonov: "The attention of His Majesty's government had recently been drawn to the question of Jewish colonization in Palestine. Numerous and most influential sections of Jewry in all countries would highly appreciate the proposal of an agreement concerning Palestine which would fully satisfy Jewish aspirations."

What was Britain's object in creating another issue in the Middle East? Was not the scramble for the Arab lands fierce enough? Obviously, the British government professed to be motivated by humanitarian motives in espousing the cause of the Jews. In the new Jerusalem of the future old injustices were to be removed. The Great War was represented as a crusade for the oppressed and the weak. Who were more oppressed and who were weaker than the Jews? The world remembered the endless persecutions the Jews suffered in eastern Europe: the pogroms in Bessarabia and Russian Poland, in Rumania, also the ritual murder charges of the recent past in Hungary and in Bohemia.

It was suggested that in thus advocating the Jewish cause the British government was thinking less of Palestine than of the United States. London thought that Jewish influence in America was strong and this was one way of gaining its good will. Also it was suggested that in espousing the Jewish cause the British government wanted to make an impression on the influential Jewry of Germany and Austria-Hungary.

Those who liked to suspect British motives further whispered that far from complicating the Arab problem, London was simplifying it by injecting the Jewish issue. The Arabs were to get a part of the former Turkish land after the war. However, it was not in Britain's interest to invest the Arabs with too much strength, and the Jews in Palestine were to serve as the counterweight. The old, old story of divide and rule.

Then Czarist Russia dropped out of the war and the United States joined the belligerents. It took time before the American war effort gathered momentum. The long-deferred settlement of the "Jewish problem" was to be one of the first steps leading to the eagerly awaited new world order.

The Zionists wanted Palestine as the National Home of Jewry, while the English concept was different. Like so many others, these details were overlooked for the duration but they came back to plague the world. Finally, on November 2, 1917, Foreign Secretary Arthur James Balfour wrote a famous letter to Lord Rothschild, a leader in English Jewry, which contained Britain's official position in regard to Palestine. This letter is known as the Balfour Declaration. The Foreign Secretary wrote:

> Dear Lord Rothschild,
> I have much pleasure in conveying to you on behalf of His Majesty's government the following declaration of sympathy with Jewish Zionist aspirations, which has been submitted to and approved by the Cabinet: "His Majesty's government view with favor the establishment in Palestine of a national home for the Jewish people, and will use their best endeavors to facilitate the achievement of this object, it being clearly understood that nothing shall be done which may prejudice the civil and religious rights of the existing non-Jewish communities in Palestine, or the rights and political status enjoyed by Jews in any other country." I should be grateful if you would bring this Declaration to the knowledge of the Zionist Federation.

The Jews in the Allied countries acclaimed this declaration as a historic document laying the bases of the Jewish State. The British government did not contradict this interpretation at the time but did so after the war, when "Jewish influence" was no longer needed. Then it made the important point that not a word in the Declaration mentioned Palestine as *the* Jewish State, but merely mentioned *a* Jewish homeland in Palestine with no territorial designation. The inference was that if the British government wished to interpret this as a ten-square-mile "homeland" the Balfour Declaration's specifications would have been met.

The feast of promises culminated in the British cabinet promising to a representative committee of Arabs that they should keep as their own the territory they conquered from the Turks. This led the caustic Lawrence of Arabia to comment in his record of those events, *The Seven Pillars of Wisdom:*

> To help the downcast Turks and to show us that it could give as many promises as there were parties, the British finally countered document A to the Sharif, B to their Allies, C to the Arab Committee, by document D to Lord Rothschild, a new power, whose race was promised something equivocal in Palestine.

Then he continued:

> Old Nuri Shaalm (a Bedouin chieftain), wrinkling his wise nose, returned to me with his file of documents, asking in puzzlement which of them all he might believe. As before, I glibly repeated, "The last in the date," and the Amir's sense of honor made him see the humor. Ever after he did his best for our cause, only warning me, when he failed in a promise, that it had been superseded by a later intention!

Lawrence of Arabia

Meanwhile the revolt in the desert had its start, beginning around Mecca and moving up the coast. In a war that saw tens of millions of people under arms, the Arab contingent amounted to little, some 30,000 to 40,000 men armed with all kinds of weapons ranging from modern machine guns to antiquated rifles and knives. Most of the warriors were tribesmen, joining for the fun of it, for the loot, or to follow a popular leader. The idea of an "Arab nation" meant little to most active participants. The British ran into difficulties when handling the Arabs. They could not mix or combine the tribes, nor could they use one in the territory of the other. The men fought as long as they liked, and left when the spirit moved them, and returned, or not, after having enjoyed the company of wives. There were no organized ranks and there would have been no way of holding them anyway; not in the desert, where the army always had to be on the move—a nomadic army in a nomad country.

"The actual contingents were continually shifting," Lawrence wrote, "in obedience to the rule of the flesh. A family would own a rifle, and the sons serve in turn for a few days each. Married men alternated between camp and wife, and sometimes a whole clan would become bored and take a rest."

The Arabs' secret weapon was the desert which they knew and which was unfamiliar to their Turkish foes. For the Turks to pursue the tribesmen into the desert would have been as suicidal as sailing into an uncharted sea full of dangerous reefs. Camel-raiding parties, as self-contained as ships, could cruise confidently along the enemy's frontier of civilization, sure of unhindered retreat into their desert element which the Turks could not explore.

The most effective weapons of the Turks were terror and big cannons. They cut their prisoners' throats as if butchering sheep. The Arabs were their subjects and fighting against the Ottoman realm was high treason as well as sacrilege.

The Turks had cannons which were not too effective but made an awful noise. The Arabs were not afraid of bullets nor of dying but thought death by shellfire awful. It seemed to Lawrence that only heavy guns could restore their self-confidence. Useful or useless, the big guns were, at any rate, very noisy.

The British leaders of the Arab revolt came. It was not easy for them to maintain contact with the Sherif, because the holy cities, Mecca and Medina, were out of bounds for them.

Britain sent some of her very good men into the desert. There was Sir Charles Wilson, remembered because of his notable deeds in the Sudan of another day. It was he who had seen the British triumph over the natives in the Sudan. Britain lost no wars in his generation and he was filled with confidence.

The Commander in Chief arrived, Sir Reginal Wingate, another great veteran of the Sudan war and a scholar as well, Kitchener's successor as Egyptian army Sirdar and Governor General of the Sudan. Later, the great Lord Allenby himself was to be in supreme command, after the Arab irregulars had broken out of the desert into the sown areas of the Levant.

However, it was the exploits of a youth in his twenties, T.E. Lawrence, which the world remembers most. At twenty-three he had already acquired a reputation as an archeologist, a member of a British museum expedition into the Euphrates country. Thence he went to Syria in search of the crusaders' churches. In Syrian hill-towns he learned Arabic, which he spoke with a British-university accent. The Palestine Exploration fund called upon him to survey the Sinai peninsula, a matter of strategy rather than scholarship.

Not a heroic figure, Lawrence was small and thin, with finely chiseled features and high color. Those who knew him intimately asserted that he often blushed like a young girl. He had the magnetic quality of a leader of men and while appearing to be modest he had tremendous self-confidence. Lawrence was sincerely fond of the Arabs and they liked him. Because of his small stature he had been turned down for active military service. Attached to the geographical section of the War Office in London, Kitchener had him transferred to intelligence in Cairo, where he set up the Arab Bureau. He had no military commission when presenting himself to Husayn in October, 1915. The Sherif's son, Feisal, appealed to him greatly, more than the other sons: Abdullah, who was too clever; Ali, too clean; and Zeid, too cool. Lawrence wrote:

> Then I rode up-country to Feisal, and found in him the leader with the necessary fire, and yet with reason to give effect to our science. His tribesmen seemed sufficient instruments, and his hills to provide natural advantage. So I returned pleased and confident to Egypt, and told my chiefs how Mecca was defended not only by the obstacle of the Rabegh, but by the flank-threat of Feisal in Jebel Subh.

Lawrence called himself "Sherif Hassan," observed the Islamic rituals and went into the desert to preach war to Muslims, against other Muslims. He reminded the Arabs of their past, when they were the terror and hope of the western world. He described the rich towns of the Turks, filled with loot. He read the desert Arabs' minds and knew that the excitement of war relieved the monotony of their poverty-stricken lives. He turned their energies from feuds into warfare, opened the gates not only of heavenly but also of earthly paradise. He impressed them with his knowledge of sand and stars. He rode as well as the best of them on horse and camel.

When water grew scarce and the tribesmen murmured, he merely smiled and led them to a well. But he gained his greatest fame for his exploits along the Hejaz Railway, the line from Damascus to Medina by way of Deraa and 'Amman and Ma'an, which was to have been the Muslims' short cut to heaven and was now to be the Turks' short cut to victory.

The Turks had beaten Feisal's troops at Medina because they had the line. It was patrolled by Turks operating with German armor. In this instance man beat the machines, because carrying heavy armor meant for European roads was a disastrous undertaking in the desert.

Lawrence organized wrecking parties which operated with great precision. Word of mouth spread his fame in the desert and what he may have lacked in inches he possessed in the tribesmen's fancy. He became the legendary "El-Orens, the Engine-Wrecker."

It was difficult for the Turks to maintain a front against an army of ghosts and that is what soldiers operating in the desert were. The Turks could not come to grips with these phantom men and so they had to retreat. Meanwhile Allenby was pushing them back on the western side of the Fertile Crescent.

Sherif Husayn proclaimed himself "King of the Arab Countries." He had rallied the Arabs on the Allied side and felt entitled to receive the highest reward. A naïve person, he thought nothing more than a proclamation was needed to unite Arabia. It is said of him that he trusted Britain's word so implicitly that he did not insist on a detailed pledge. From this one can deduce that he was not a diplomat. He did not heed Lawrence's warning to one of his sons, Feisal: "I begged him," that remarkable Englishman said, "to trust not in our promises, but in his own strong performance."

Numerous chieftains were not ready to exchange one authority for another. Ominous rumblings were heard in the deep desert where the ruler of the Nejd was sharpening his sword. Ibn Saud trusted no one's promise, but he did trust his own strong deeds. During the war he kept aloof, accepting subsidy from British agents, as he had little to fear from the Turks. Should his power wax he would cast aside the Sherif of Mecca, and it was not Britain's colonial custom to back the weak. Still, London was embarrassed and we may be certain that the British leaders of the Arab revolt let their voices ring. London consented to have Husayn assume the title of the King of the Hejaz, the American equivalent of which would be the Grand and Exalted Potenate of Death Valley.

In the Wake of Victory

Still, this was not the final settlement and so Feisal went to Paris, where the mighty of the earth converged. He was accompanied by Lawrence. To both of them this was as much part of the war as engine-wrecking. The frail Englishman had become a living legend and we may be sure he wanted to use his hypnotic eyes on the framers of peace. These attached an efficient and pleasant guide to Feisal to reveal to him the charms of Paris, so as to take his mind off perplexing problems.

"As the representative of my father, who led the Arab revolt against the Turks on behalf of the British and French," the Olympian peacemakers heard themselves addressed by Feisal, "I am here to ask that the Arab-speaking people from the line of Alexandretta-Diyarbekir, southward to the Indian Ocean, be recognized as an independent sovereign people under the guarantee of the League of Nations."

In a memorandum Feisal wrote: "I am confident that the Powers will observe basic undertakings which motivated Arab participation in the war."

His father showered letters on the Big Four which oozed with lofty sentiments and were jammed with pearls of wisdom. The more impatient he grew, the more flowery his style, and the more often he wrote, the less attention he received.

It took some time before the Arab problem was placed on the agenda. President Wilson suggested that a commission of inquiry should be dispatched to ascertain the peoples' wishes. The French disliked the idea, the peace negotiations were consuming too much time, and besides, everybody knew that France had been the protectrice of the Levant since the crusaders' days. The Italians were dejected at the thought that although victors, their own Allies treated them as if they had been defeated; and besides, for the moment they were concerned only with the problem of the Dalmatian coast. As to the British, they knew all they wanted to know about the Middle East and considered another investigation another day wasted.

Feisal was now completely lost amidst the glories of Paris, and he was demoralized, too. When his big moment finally came, he was treated as a petitioner before his judges. He became panic-stricken at the last moment and let himself be inveigled into signing a document which was the death sentence of United Arabia.

The difficulty was not merely Husayn's naïveté, or Feisal's desert-born chivalry. Lawrence, who thought of himself as a westerner ennobled by contact with the noblest desert people, remained a westerner in that he condemned failure and extolled success. Now he wrote in summary:

"Feisal was a brave, weak, ignorant spirit, trying to do work for which only a genius, a prophet or a great criminal was fitted."

The great weakness of the Arab case was neither Husayn nor Feisal; not even Lawrence or the Olympian peacemakers. We have to turn to Lawrence himself to find the basic cause of the great failure, to him who loved the Arabs and came to think that they had been betrayed.

This is what he said about the Syrians and by that he meant the entire Levant, the dwelling place of the most politically articulate Arabia:

> Their distinctions were political and religious; morally they differed only in the steady gradation from neurotic sensibility on the sea coast to reserve inland. They were quick-minded; admirers but not seekers of truth, self-satisfied; not (like the Egyptians) helpless before abstract ideas, but unpractical; and so lazy in mind as to be habitually superficial. Their ideal was ease in which to busy themselves with others' affairs.

Lawless from childhood, they obeyed their fathers only through physical fear; and later their government for much the same reason. It was something new they wanted, because the passion for politics went with their superficiality and lawlessness. Always discontented with the government they had, few of them thought out a working alternative. And fewer still agreed upon one.

The End of the Rainbow

There came into life a Syria, a Transjordan, and an Iraq, under British mandate. Husayn had not bargained for this.

The Foreign Office had knifed the Arabs in the back, Lawrence thought, and he was not the only one to think so. Yet he seemed to ignore his own findings, that in most of the Arab world there was no political entity larger than the clan, the village, and those, too, were unintegrated, voluntary, informal. Even the best-taught Arabs showed a curious blindness to the importance of the country. Some cried out for an Arab Kingdom, which would have been a theocracy. The Arab Christians of the region demanded protection, privileges without obligation.

> The master-key of opinion lay in the common language [Lawrence continued] where also lay the key of imagination. Muslims whose mother tongue was Arabic looked upon themselves as the chosen people. Their heritage of the Koran and classical literature held the Arab-speaking people together. Patriotism, ordinarily of soil or race, was wrapped to a language.
>
> A second buttress of a polity of Arab motive was the dim glory of the early Chaliphate, whose memory endured among the people through centuries of Turkish misgovernment. The accident that these traditions savored more of the Arabian Nights than of sheer history maintained the Arab rank and file in their conviction that their past was more splendid than the present of the Ottoman Turk.

This was the Arab weakness in those days and also in years to come. There had been too many years of Turkish rule and too deeply ingrained habits of feudalism—the idea that property, not man, was the ultimate measure.

Now the Arabs' hectic postwar history began. Amir Feisal, of whom Lawrence thought so highly, moved into Damascus exercising the authority delegated to him by Allenby. That authority was called Occupied Enemy Territory Administration East. The Syrian coast and Beirut were retained under direct British rule.

The western world took scant notice of the "cold war" raging in the Middle East shortly after the First World War. The conflict was between England and France. The former had to yield to the latter under the pressure of events, but now that the war was over, London wanted to oust Paris. The two antagonists carried on their feuds through stand-ins. Britain's was Feisal, trying to establish himself in Damascus. London observed him with that subdued curiosity which is British diplomacy's inimitable trait. Feisal had himself proclaimed King of Syria in the spring of 1920—a king for a day. He was to be the King of a Greater Syria, which was also to include Palestine and what today we call the Jordan. His father was still the King of Hejaz. With these two thrones in the Hashimite family, was Britain's wartime pledge of Arab independence redeemed? The French had not forgotten about their "sacred obligation" in the Levant, however. So while the British stood aside, the French army units moved into Damascus and pulled Feisal off his throne. Thereupon, he appealed to the British for protection. The British representative congratulated General Henri Joseph Eugene Gouraud on his victory over Feisal.

Northeast of Syria lay Mesopotamia, renamed Iraq, and several of her officers had taken part in the desert revolt. Some of them had been Turkish army officers, as, for instance, Nuri es-Said, who was to become Prime Minister many times and about whom more will be said.

These Iraqi patriots wanted to have important government jobs and not crumbs from British hands. The virulent nationalistic society of Iraqi Covenanters in Baghdad was to further their aims. When the patriots found large British contingents in the country and their fancied nationhood transformed into a protectorate, there occurred a violent explosion, in which thousands fell.

This was one of the many explosions to rend the Middle Eastern sky. The British trusted Feisal and now he was a king without a job. He was an Arab of the Arabs, and that was good. He would serve Britain well, and that was good, too. But he belonged to the majority sect of Islam, *Sunna,* while most of the Iraqi belonged to the minority sect of *Shi'a,* and that was bad. Yet, it was not an insurmountable obstacle and so he became the king of the newly created Kingdom of Iraq, which owed its existence to a diplomatic horse-trading. Would Iraq exist today if there had not been a cold war in the East?

The King's Parade

The other son of Husayn, Abdullah, was to have become the Iraqi king and now he found himself without a throne. Luckily, the Arab world was large and there lay an amorphous region beyond the Jordan shading into Ibn Saud's desert realm. Over that Transjordan area the British exercised authority. So the diplomatic carpenters started fashioning another country on the margins of the desert and the sown. This is how the Amirate of Transjordan came into life as part of the Palestine mandate, yet a separate entity over which the Damocles sword of the Balfour Declaration did not hover.

The population of this country was small, estimated at less than a quarter of a million at that time. Yet, Abdullah was to play a role much greater than the size of his country.

> The Arabs thought Abdullah a far-seeing statesman and an astute politician [Lawrence wrote]. Astute he certainly was but not greatly enough to convince us always of his sincerity. His ambition was patent. Rumor made him the brain of his father and of the Arab revolt, but he seemed too easy for that. His object was, of course, the winning of Arab independence and the building up of Arab nations, but he meant to keep the direction of the new States in the family. So he watched us and played through us to the British gallery.

Lawrence watched him, and carefully at that. The more he saw of him the surer he became that the Amir was too balanced and too humorous to be a prophet, especially the armed prophet to lead revolutions. During the physical struggle, when magneticism, devotion and self-sacrifice were needed, Abdullah was too complex for a simple purpose. In peace, after success, his value would come perhaps.

Abdullah was full of cabals, overcharged with what the haughty Occident calls the Orient. But he was also human, in a good Oriental sense of the word. One could talk to him, and even convince him on occasion. Not a fanatic was he, nor a monomaniac. He was somewhat too conscious of his flexibility. He admired the British and wanted to outsmart them sometimes, just a trifle, to show that he was not inferior to them. Britain's talent for appearing to be always just and for wrapping her own aims in the larger goals of civilization impressed Abdullah, and he was also impressed with the British ability to press an advantage to the very limit one day, then change the course in response to the whim of a new wind. Abdullah wanted to be the master of compromise.

He was also proud of being many-sided and that he was indeed, although not always to his own good. He was convinced and some of his readers believed that his poetry was good. He took delight in the voluptuous cadences of words, the rippling rhythm, the attractive sense for the sake of the beautiful sentence.

Abdullah was also considered an excellent chess player, one of the best in the Arab world. He believed that rulers of men should attempt to achieve mastery on the chessboard, to teach them how to wriggle out of tight corners when all avenues seem to be barred.

He never stood on ceremony but jested with all comers. Yet, when he fell into serious talk, the veil of humor seemed to fade away. He could be undiplomatically outspoken in his choice of words. He called his Saudi Arabian fellow monarch a bloody-handed butcher, then smilingly shook hands with him.

His great ambition was to realize at least a part of the Greater Arabia which had been the aim of the revolt. That part was to be the Greater Syria, and was to include not only Syria but also Iraq and Transjordan and perhaps Lebanon. Obviously he and his Hashimite family were to rule over this country and thus the Prophet's seed was to come into its own.

At one time his productive brain played with the idea of a Fertile Crescent unity, originally launched in Iraq, including the same countries and Lebanon more definitely, and perhaps also Turkey in some loose relation, even though the latter was not an Arab land. Once his ancestors may have played historic roles in Cordova and Toledo and so he roamed as far afield as Spain. He must have presented some schemes to that country's Generalissimo Franco. He pursued a farrago of plans, and only one of these might have been better.

A Doughty Desert King

Abdullah was the ruler of Transjordan, his brother Feisal was the King of Iraq and their father Husayn was the King of Hejaz. There were three thrones in one family and the gods are notoriously jealous. However, men are even more so. Out of the desert swept danger for King Husayn. To be a king in the desert one must be strong and ruthless, not kind and weak. People have no use for the meekness which great religions laud.

That danger swirled out of the desert, just like a dust storm. In the great Arab Quadrangle historic events were brewing. Previously, explorers reported ruins and mirages, and glittering lakes of salt which craven camels crave. They used to return into the sown with stories of phantom towns where wind and winter rains whip the soil into weird shapes. They spoke of savage frontiersmen who shot at sight and then invited the survivors into their tents. Now, however, they came out of the desert to speak about a great king.

Newspapers of the West began to take an interest in King Ibn Saud because of his rich married life. His biographer and friend, H. St. John B. Philby, reported that the monarch was married more than 150 times, and that seemed to beat even the highest Hollywood figure. At the age of seventy-five, Ibn Saud became a father for the sixty-fourth time. From history's point of view it was more important that this tall man with the flashing eyes became the gravedigger of the Hashimite dream of United Arabia, and the founder of a strong desert Arab Kingdom.

His ancestors lost their patrimony in the lawless law of the desert. It was in the first year of this century that the young man in his early twenties launched his campaign to retrieve his heritage. He collected some two hundred determined men under his command, and his object was to recapture Riyadh, the capital of his ancestors, from the foe.

He selected fifteen men for the final assault, according to the narrative of his biographer, and they entered Riyadh by night. They forced an entry into the house opposite the fort sheltering the enemy governor and from there they moved into the fort. When dawn broke, Ibn Saud was the master of the capital and soon became the monarch of the heart of the Arab desert country, Nejd.

The law of the desert was lawlessness in those days, and raid (*razzia*) a highly respectable way of life. Ibn Saud suppressed these practices with ruthless hands. Supreme ruler of the region and not a mere tribal chief, he recognized only one law and that was his, presumably based upon the Koran. History repeated itself, but in reverse. Centuries before, the creed of the Prophet swept out of the desert, and now the creed of the West swept into the desert, the new religion of nationalism. "He boldly seized upon the latent fanaticism of his countrymen," wrote St. John Philby, "as an instrument for the creation of a non-tribal or pan-tribal element out of tribal material to leaven the mass into the semblance of a homogeneous nation."

How would nationalism look in the desert setting? Ibn Saud shed blood mercilessly before he was accepted as the father of his people. The desert was to cease to be lawless or it would cease to be the desert. The prototype of a hundred colonies to spring up within the next fifteen years was the flourishing town of Artawiya, with some hundred thousand inhabitants at present. Pastoralism may be lawless, but agriculture is obedient, and so parts of the desert started to bloom like a rose, with well-watered orange groves and orchards, fields of barley and wheat. Still there were more men than food and the country was scourged by famine.

If you destroy life you must also create life and that Ibn Saud knew well enough. He also knew what was the punishment for strong gods who failed to charm water out of the clouds. So he had to become the rain-making god.

In order to have more water he had need of better watered space, and also he had to give peace to his people so that there would be no need for men on horseback, no need for war leaders to contest his claim to the throne. Ibn Saud saw his role in the historical perspective of Manifest Destiny. There was one Allah in the desert and there was to be only one King there, and his realm was to seek its natural boundaries. This also meant new wells and new places of settlement.

The unfortunate King Husayn was sitting on his rickety throne in Mecca, meditating on the fact that he had Britain's promise to have Arabia. He had himself proclaimed the King of the Arabs, but whatever your title, it is the law of the desert that the weak must go—and King Husayn was weak. King of the Arabs meant that Ibn Saud was to recognize this weakling as his superior. This was an affront that rankled. Still, here was the germ of an idea—Arab unity. Yes, let there be unity in the desert, and Husayn the weak-kneed must go.

However, Britain was in honor bound to side with Husayn, the nominal leader in the late desert war. But Ibn Saud launched his campaign to oust this British protégé. London warned the desert king that Husayn enjoyed Britain's confidence and suggested mediation, which took place in proper form and produced no results, also in proper form.

Now that Britain had done what she could, she washed her hands of the war, standing aside as Ibn Saud invaded the Hejaz in 1924. Ibn Saud found that the best way to command respect was by slaughtering a suitable number of people and this he did by massacring the inhabitants of Ta'if, one of the larger desert towns. King Husayn again appealed to the desert to rise and protect him, but this time his pleadings went unheeded. In a few months the war was over and Ibn Saud was King of the Hejaz and Sultan of the Nejd, later changing the name of his country to Saudi Arabia.

Fallen low now was ex-King Husayn, he of the House of the Prophet, former Grand Sherif of Mecca, King of the Hejaz, King of the Arabs, leader of the revolt and ally of Britain.

He escaped from Mecca and the British could do no more than to provide him with an asylum on the island of Cyprus, where he spent many brooding hours reliving the years of his near-grandeur. His heart was in the desert, which was his home, and so he expressed the desire to live with his son Abdullah on the edge of the desert. There he faded into a mere shadow of his formerly confident self and became a recluse, torturing himself with bitter memories. It was into a better life that Allah called him in the year of 1930 of the Christian era.

Another Maimed Soul

The revolt in the desert was over, and its real leader, T.E. Lawrence, assumed another form in a new reincarnation. He had suffered the fate of heroes of spectacular achievements. He became a legend and his exploits grew in stature as the years passed by.

Lawrence the engine-wrecker reverted to a scholar's life. Learned societies deemed it an honor to have him in their midst, archeologists solicited his assistance, and All Souls College called him to Oxford. Placid outwardly, he was racked by an inward storm. His mysterious desert life had wiped out his zest for the adventures of scholarship. Now he was harassed by a sense of guilt. He who had stirred up the Arabs and led them into battle for their freedom now bitterly realized that Arabia was enslaved. The hopes he inflamed had been in vain. How could he face his desert friends?

The people he met in drawing rooms and at cocktail parties repelled him. All around him rose the walls which racial strains could not level, and he was being stifled. The beneficiary of the learning of the West, he weighed the Orient and the Occident and found the latter wanting.

"Why do you love the East so much?" blank-eyed society ladies asked. They saw only its thirst and hunger, its filth and vermin. He could not tell them that in the desert he had friends, while in the drawing rooms he had none.

But he could think only of his great love and obsession. He had tasted the excitement of gambling with one's life, with other lives, too, and facing the question every morning: "Will I see the night?"

Now he faced a more tormenting problem and it would not let him rest. In the desert he had failed because he had remained a scholar. The stones with which he had become familiar in his excavations always told the truth, but diplomats seldom meant what they said. Men lied and called it diplomacy, and the greater the lie the better the diplomat. It was his mistake that he had not known this.

He tried to redeem his past by urging the governments to honor his country's pledge. He wrote letters to the *Times*. Naturally, the British government could not change its course, and the new order was enshrined in pacts sanctified by self-interest and usage.

Lawrence could not return to the desert but the desert could still depend upon him. He was summoned into the Colonial Office by the omnipresent Winston Churchill to serve as an expert on Arab affairs. It was he who had urged the British government to make Feisal King of Iraq, a small payment on a large loan.

He was dissatisfied with the activities of the Colonial Office and he resigned. The victim of changing moods, he shut himself up in his library and was not seen for days. He reappeared haggard, a fixed smile on his lips and a film over his eyes. Then he was swept into spells of overpowering energy. He wanted action at any price and enlisted in the Air Force as a mechanic.

His assumed name was "Ross," showing the arrogance of the immortal. His restless mind turned to the classics of Greece and he published a prose translation of the *Odyssey*. It was in 1935 that he was killed in a motorcycle accident. He was driving very fast. People who read significance into every human action would say that he wanted to commit suicide.

The Arab world now crystallized itself in half a dozen countries. Let us pass them in review.

On the Mountains, in the Plains

Antioch and Aleppo, Sidon and Tyre, Beirut and Damascus have long been well-known places in the world. This was famed Syria, along the route of the conquerors between the Tigris and the Nile. Yearly the pilgrims' caravan inched its way from Damascus to Mecca. The road in the opposite direction, toward the northwest, led across the Cilician Gate into Asia Minor. Other important roads also radiated out of Syria and because of her pivotal location a strong military power there was bound to become a mighty power in the Middle East. After the First World War it was France which held this land, the New France of the East.

An undeclared war was raging between the two former Allies in the East, as we have seen. The most interesting chapters of that history were written in invisible ink.

It was *une histoire triste,* a sad history indeed, this postwar history of France in the Levant. In the territories under her supervision peace was temporary, conflicts were chronic. France regarded herself as the missionary of the greatest civilization, of which she was ready to present a part to the Levant. Schools teaching French and the ubiquitous Alliance Française, an active cultural organization, began to mushroom. The French were ready to receive the Levantines as wards if they learned to speak their tongue, willing to relish Corneille and Racine. The Levantines might have been happy to enjoy these classics had it not been for the fact that French banks and trading companies moved into Syria in their wake. It was the caustic comment of a French-tutored Levantine: "Classics plus seventy-five per cent."

Divide and Rule

Syria presented greater difficulties to the French than the British mandates presented to London. In the first place, the leading Arab classes were more nation-conscious here, precisely because they were more western-minded. France insisted that they should be thankful to her for extending to them the benefits of her superior culture. Syria, which at the outset included the Lebanon region, had a larger ratio of educated Arab people and it was hard to convince them of the superiority of any other country.

The French also found some opportunities to impose their rule upon the region. This area was ready-made for the application of the principle of divide and rule, because of the large number of minorities and sects. French interests were best served by carving the region into several states and balancing one against the other. So they carved the Republic of Lebanon out of Syria, a small enclave no more than 25 to 50 miles wide and some 135 miles long. This was a political device and it is worthy of notice that even after the French went, the Republic of Lebanon remained. Vested interests have endless lives, no matter who creates them.

France expected the Lebanese Christians to do their duty by rallying to Paris. She seems to have overlooked the fact that today we live in a world of nations, not of religions. The Lebanese Christian came to consider himself an Arab and it is a paradoxical fact that he learned this when in Paris. Besides, France's credentials for the protection of Christians were none too good. The dominant Christian sect of the Lebanon, the Maronites, were strongly church-minded, while the French republic was antichurch.

Trouble, Trouble . . .

Great empire builders of the stamp of Morocco's Marshal Lyautey were not produced in the Levant. The proconsuls Paris sent into the region were mostly party wheelhorses who considered the exotic Orient just the right setting for the display of their dazzling Machiavellian gifts.

The first major trouble of the region exploded in the hills of that strange religious sect, about which more will be said, the Druzes. The French made the mistake of rushing artillery into that rugged country to crush the uprising of 1925, which probably would have died down after the mountaineers had had their fling. The invading forces lost and from the hills the revolt spread to Damascus. The authorities seem to have lost their heads and started to bomb the city from the air. Since Damascus is an ant heap of humanity, we may imagine what carnage was caused. This was a novel way of disseminating French culture in the bazaar. From there the conflagration spread to the Lebanon and for years there was no peace in France's mandates on the Mediterranean coast.

The British "Plot"

London knew how to yield to pressure with grace, and so the British piloted their protégé, the Kingdom of Iraq, into the League of Nations in 1932, thereby setting the authentic seal of independence on that country. To the French in the Levant this appeared to be a sinister plot to render their position untenable.

Among the Arabs, the Iraqi are considered less advanced than the Syrians and Lebanese. If Iraq is independent, why should Syria and Lebanon remain subject to foreign rule? The French officials saw the emancipation of Iraq as an invitation to the Arabs under their rule to cause even more trouble.

The mid-thirties seemed to be the most auspicious time for Middle Eastern people to demand more rights. This was the Age of the Great Revolt, the age of the Communists and Fascists, two movements of discontent. The Communists called on the Middle East to take stock of its plight, and Mussolini thought he gave the East a great gift when offering himself as Islam's protector. France saw the arrival of a New Deal government under the premiership of the Socialist, Léon Blum.

When out of power, the Socialists of France were inclined to espouse the colonial peoples' cause, and when they got into power Syria and Lebanon asked for independence. Eventually, Paris reached an understanding with Damascus and Beirut under which the two Arab countries were to become independent in three years. However, France was to have the right to maintain armed force bases in the Levant and to enter into alliance with these countries. But, as it often happens in France, the progressive government fell and the conservatives came in. The pact was never carried out.

Meanwhile the Levantine sky, too, became overcast; a general war was threatening. The friendship of the Turks, to the north of the French Levant, became of increasing importance to Paris. On the other hand, the Turks were pressing for the rectification of their frontier with Syria, so as to incorporate the territory known as the Sanjaq of Alexandretta, in which many Turks lived. Also the region had a good harbor.

Eager to keep the Turks on their side of the fence, the French concluded a pact of mutual assistance with them in 1939, a part of which provided that they were to turn over the Sanjaq of Alexandretta to the Turks, and this was done.

This does not sound like a very exciting event and yet it had important repercussions. The French mandated territories had never liked their mentors and now they liked them even less. They blamed them for giving away a part of their own country. The Turks did not join the Allies during the war, so that the profit the French drew from the bargain was nil.

The Levant in the Second World War

While in a global war the entire earth is important, the Levant's role was of paramount importance. The plan of the enemy, the Axis, seemed to be to execute a vast pincer movement down the Caucasus and across the Nile. The junction between the Fascist forces may have been somewhere in the Levant.

When France fell during the Second World War, Syria and Lebanon fell, too. The so-called Vichy government, which collaborated with the victorious German Reich, assumed the reins in Damascus and Beirut. The Germans appeared to have a golden chance to launch their own Revolt in the Desert, this time against the British. Prospective Nazi Lawrences of Arabia descended on Middle East capitals, headed by Herr von Hentig, head of the Near East Department of the German Foreign Office.

The raucous voice of the Axis blared words into the Arab world from Berlin and Bari, telling the people to rise against the eternal oppressor, the British. Loudest "Voice of Free Arabia" was that of Amin al-Hussaini, former Grand Mufti of Jerusalem. He was an expert on "Jewish world conspiracy," and knew how to solve the "Jewish problem." It was he, according to some observers, who concocted the hideous plot to slaughter all the Jews the Nazis could find. He was a Semite of course, because he was an Arab, and the Nazis professed to detest the Semites. Yet that made no difference, since Germany's omnipotent leader could change even Semites into authentic Aryans.

Word was conveyed to the Middle East world that the Fuehrer himself was the Prophet's descendant. Mohammed was a desert Arab and Arabs are Semite people. This, too, made no difference. The Nazis knew that black turns white through the hypnotic quality of constant repetition. Thus the worst anti-Semite of the age became a Semite in Arabia.

Stories of the Arabian Nights variety were' told about the Fuehrer, whose superhuman power seemed to surpass the might of the Middle East's legendary Alexander the Great. Would the name of Alexandria be changed into Adolfia after the war? In the shadows of the bazaars Hitler mustaches were sprouting. Not only the people of the mansions but also of the huts were to see how the immense power of the Fuehrer ground the once mighty Frenchmen (Franji) into dust.

The Vichy representative in the Levant was General Henri Dentz, who shared the prevailing view that the wave of the future belonged to the Fascists. When the Nazis seemed to be riding the very crest of that wave, in the spring of 1942, a pro-Axis premier took over in the neighboring Iraq. This may have been the beginning of a tidal wave of pro-Axis sentiment. Premier Rashid Ali al-Gailani was an ambitious politician who tried to ride the crest in the company of a group of pro-Fascist Iraqi colonels, picturesquely called the Golden Square because there were four of them.

In order to help Rashid Ali, General Dentz opened his airfields to German planes. Had the coup succeeded, not only Syria and Lebanon would have been lost to the Allies but what was known as the Third Reich could have become the First Reich of the world.

Another War Between the Allies

On June 8, 1941, the Levant war between the British and the French began. On that day Imperial and associated forces crossed the frontiers of Syria and Lebanon under the command of General Sir Henry Maitland Wilson, and one of the component forces was the pro-Ally Free French unit under General Georges Catroux, a faithful follower of General Charles de Gaulle, the leader of the Free French.

It was expected that the Vichy forces would offer only token resistance, but that was not the case. General Dentz resisted, and he would have welcomed German assistance but it was not forthcoming. The Third Reich was preparing the knockout blow against the Soviets—quick victory, after which the Middle East fruit was to be plucked.

The Vichy resistance was strong but the Allied forces overcame it. Significantly, it was on the national holiday of France, the 14th of July, that General Dentz sued for peace. Speaking on behalf of the Free French, General Catroux addressed Syria and Lebanon: "Henceforward you will be sovereign and independent. . . ." Speaking on behalf of His Majesty's government, Sir Miles Lampson, the British Ambassador in Cairo, endorsed this proclamation—a significant and ominous fact.

Time passed and independence did not materialize. Pressure in the region increased for the implementation of the Allied pledge. Finally General Catroux, acting as Plenipotentiary of Free France in the Levant, took what seemed to be the decisive step by proclaiming the independence of the two States. However . . . this was independence on paper only, as French officials continued to occupy key positions. The expectant native statesmen regarded this as a betrayal of the Allied pledge. And now the second phase of the cold war between the Allies (French and British) began.

The Free Die Hard

The British insisted that the French must turn over the government to the local people—Britain's word was involved. Again this was done—on paper. Now the United States backed up the British. The war was still being waged and the Middle East was considered an important junction point and staging area. The French said they were ready to grant independence to the two countries but on one condition—that they were to maintain their armed force establishments in the Middle East. They did not say that this was no more than the British had in the Middle East. Neither did the British say that there was a vast difference between the French and themselves, especially after the war.

Things dragged on and then in midsummer 1945, when the Allied world was talking about freedom and democracy and while the French resisted the evacuation of the Levant, Syria and Lebanon rose again. This time the British acted promptly, with the approval of America. They issued an ultimatum to the French to pull their troops out of the Middle East. At long last this was actually done.

This was the end of the long tug-of-war between the French and English. In the first place, the British did not want the French in the region but could not prevent their moving in. Throughout the interwar period, London was irked by what it considered the bungling Middle Eastern policy of Paris, which tended to compromise the West. During the Second World War France's weakness was revealed, and there was no more reason for Britain to put up with her.

French rule had raised the cultural standards of the region considerably but had done little to raise its economic levels. The proconsuls did next to nothing to do away with the fatal effendi rule. Land reform had been undertaken only on a small scale, in limited areas, and no large-scale attempt had been made to industrialize the region. The Levant was to continue as a purveyor of raw materials and the consumer of France's industrial products.

Independence Means Oppression

Now that the French were out after the Second World War, did the Syrian and Lebanese governments take steps to relieve the sufferings of the common man?

The postwar history of Syria has consisted largely of attempts to solve two problems: to thwart the Jewish people's efforts to establish their homeland in Palestine, and to prevent Syria's neighbors from changing the Arab status quo.

Syria was opposed to Jewish Palestine on the same ground as the other Arab countries: that Palestine was an Arab land to which the Jews could raise no claims. The unavowed reason was, of course, something else again. Syria has a system with a strong feudal undertone, and the effendis feared that a democratic Jewish State in close proximity would introduce "wrong ideas" into their people's minds, teaching them that it was possible for the common man to lead a human life.

Syria also took an active part, mostly, in opposing the Greater Syria scheme of Transjordan's Abdullah. She feared that this would mean the rule of the Hashimite dynasty, as, no doubt, it would have meant it.

The Age of Violence

In mid-May of 1948, Syria joined other Arab countries in the march upon Israel with the idea of overwhelming her. Instead of that, she was overwhelmed herself. This defeat produced a reaction which incubated for months, and it was only in March 1949, that it erupted into a coup d'état, the leader of which was Colonel Husni Zayim.

This enterprising Syrian had been an officer in the late Ottoman army and was conversant with recent Turkish history. The record of the founder of the Turkish republic, Mustafa Kemal, had made a great impression on him. The march of progress in Syria had been impeded by the French tutelage, but now the road was open to introduce great reforms.

It was on the pattern of Kemalist reforms that Husni Zayim attempted to introduce his own New Order. He shared the belief of his illustrious model that it is the nation that must command the citizen's undivided loyalty and therefore the dead hand of Islam must be weakened. Not as drastically as Kemal, he effected the separation of Islam and State. He also held that the nation that kept its women in seclusion was only half a nation, and so he introduced feminine suffrage, a bold undertaking in the Arab world. He held that the solution of the problems of modern life could not be based solely upon the Koran, written for another age, and so introduced a modern civil code. First among people in high authority, Colonel Husni Zayim took notice of the majority of the people, noticing that they were desperately poor and that it was absurd to expect them to score victories on the battlefield while afflicted with disease, ignorance and poverty. He wanted to increase the productive capacity of Syria, to increase public works and to create full employment. In the foreign field he favored the close cooperation of Syria, Iraq and Jordan.

Then something happened. Evidently, the Three Power Scheme was in conformity with British plans. They had found the Arab world too amorphous and wanted to create a new and more solid core. This plan did not please King Ibn Saud, because it would have weakened him, in comparison with the stronger Arab coreland. What did not please the ruler of Saudi Arabia did not please the United States either, because of American oil interests in that country. The Egyptian government did not like the plan either. Husni Zayim paid a visit to Cairo and returned home, a changed man. What pressures had been exerted on him? Was he offered money? Was there a Great Power in the background?

Now he changed his ways. He who had given the impression of a puritan, became an epicurean. He moved into luxurious quarters, bestowed the rank of Marshal upon himself, and had himself called the Head of State. He started to lead the life of a despot surrounded by personal bodyguards. He seemed to forget about his recent Kemalist reforms, and the former leader of the Syrian New Deal became the leader of an anti-New Deal. Eventually, fate overtook him. He became the victim of a murder plot, the details of which are extremely nebulous.

Husni Zayim dead, Syria swung back momentarily to the British Foreign Office concept of Greater Syria. For a moment a radical group calling itself the People's Party was in the saddle, but its heads lacked the late colonel's compelling personality and their attempt at innovations followed the way of all previous attempts. A third coup took place within a year, headed by another army officer, Lt. Col. Adib el-Shishakli, who, in turn, was opposed to the Greater Syria scheme. By that time people got tired of the kaleidoscopic changes and instead of naming names began to speak about this statesman as a Standard Oil man and that politician as a Shell man. Syria is an important transit land for oil pipelines.

The Center of the Middle East

Under the long Ottoman rule over the Arab world, Baghdad remained an historic name but not an active participant in history. Turkish officials appointed to posts in the Mesopotamian metropolis reached their destination by circumnavigating the huge Arab Quadrangle (after the Suez Canal had been cut) and then sailing up the Shatt-al-Arab river, a trip that consumed several weeks. No wonder governors were left largely to their own devices. If they did not embezzle too much of the state funds it was because the climate was enervating and sometimes also, because they were honest. As a rule, the administrators swaggered, the effendis ruled, and people died like flies in the fall.

The British felt they had to take an interest in the region for good reasons. Iraq is looking toward India and the London governments were bound to take an interest in everything that looked in that direction. There was a time, in the opinion of diplomatic wiseacres, when all parts of the world seemed to be looking toward India.

Iraq acquired a particularly important role in the British scheme of things when it turned out to have a basement well-stocked with oil. During the First World War Anglo-Indian troops moved into Mesopotamia and fought the notable campaigns about which the world knows. London could not let this territory fall into other hands.

Iraq for the Iraqui

No parent ever really believes that the child is sufficiently mature to leave the family nest and no Great Power ever believes that its ward is ready for independence. Britain shared the view with other mandatories that it was her "sacred duty" to protect her reluctant charges against the hazards of life. In Iraq as well as elsewhere in the Middle East, Britain wanted to perform her duty in her own special way. She grew mighty in the world partly because of her great institutions, the greatest of which was Parliament, where men learned to thresh out their problems instead of threshing out one another. She felt it her bounden duty to carry out her mission by leaving parliaments in her wake. Those parliaments were set up, but the great transformation seldom came.

The only political experience the mandated people had was autocracy. Under the system they long endured, the enemy was the government and the less one had to do with it the better it was for all concerned. In turn, the governments fell into the habit of extracting all they could from the people. The Turkish pasha was the enemy in the past and now it was the local pasha, and both of them were equally ruthless.

Perhaps the parliamentary system in Iraq would have worked if there had been more political parties representing different sets of interests. However, there was only one politically articulate class, that of the pashas, and there was no effective middle class of sufficient weight. Should the British have attempted to create a middle class in order to produce the conditions favorable for the operation of parliamentary democracy? They felt they were restrained from taking that course by the very frame of reference of their stewardship. Since the pashas were strongly entrenched, nothing short of a revolution could have dislodged them, and the British did not feel it was their function to foster revolts. Thus the parliamentary containers created by the British were filled with autocratic substance.

It will be recalled that Iraq's king was Feisal and he knew well enough that he could not operate without British aid. London knew this, too, and so it trusted him. He was ready to sign pacts with Britain granting her the right to "advise" the government of Iraq. Translated into everyday language this meant that the British continued to rule.

Dissatisfaction was rampant in Iraq, too, but there again it was hard to keep together cause and effect. Because bread was scarce and people felt miserable, many of them thought that if they had their own people in power, not being advised but actually governing, all would be well. Dissatisfaction burst into disastrous revolts.

Still, the British were less unyielding than their neighbors, the French. Gradually the scope of Iraqi self-government was expanded, until in 1930, Baghdad and London signed a pact which two years later resulted in the independence of that Middle East Kingdom.

The British did not, however, relinquish all their rights in Iraq. Great Powers seldom do. They had their way through the intermediary of a set of trusted friends of whom the most prominent was Nuri as-Sa'id Pasha.

The Indestructible Nuri Pasha

Nuri Pasha became known as Iraq's hardy political perennial, whose name had been associated with his country's politics beginning with the First World War. Up to the present he has served twelve times as his country's Prime Minister. Born in the oil-rich Kirkuk district, he and his family led the life of well-to-do Arabs in the Ottoman Empire. He attended the Turkish military college in Constantinople and became an officer of the Ottoman army six years before the First World War, during which he served in the desert with Lawrence, eventually becoming a top commandant in Damascus, companion and adviser of King Feisal and chief of staff in new Iraq. Lawrence described him as a man whose courage, authority and coolness marked him as an ideal military leader. He had the ability of getting at the core of a problem, expressing it in homespun language and conveying the impression of sincerity.

He was called a "British stooge," but that was true only to the extent that he believed Iraq needed Great Britain as a friend and adviser. First-class statesmen are in short supply in the Middle East and therefore Nuri's numerous appearances at the head of the government. Once a statesman, always a statesman.

The Death of a Statesman

Britain's loyal friend King Feisal was also a competent statesman. He, too, realized that it was safer for a Middle Eastern country to be counted among Britain's friends, rather than among her foes. Unfortunately for his country, which needed a man of his caliber, he died an early death in 1933. He was followed by King Ghazi, twenty-one but immature for his age, one of those people who believed that they kept abreast of a fast-moving age by driving at breakneck speed. He broke his neck in an automobile accident after six years of highly undistinguished rule. After his death the throne was occupied by the child King Feisal II, whose maternal uncle, Prince Abdul Illah, kept the country safely within the circle of British satellites.

With the coming of the Second World War, attempts were made to line up Iraq with the Axis and it was then that Rashid Ali staged the coup to which reference has already been made. Even after his defeat, unrest kept on convulsing the country and broke into the open with sporadic rebellions involving one of the major tribes, the Barzanis, who made common cause with the irrepressible Kurds.

During the war, Iraq was one of the Middle East Allied pivots, headquarters of the British Tenth Army and, later, of "Pai-force" (Persia and Iraq Force) and of the Polish army, in the course of its Odyssey. After the war the inevitable Nuri Pasha kept on popping up, engaged in the promotion work of the Fertile Crescent scheme dear to the heart of London's Downing Street. Many influential circles frowned on the plan, partly because they suspected Britain's busy hand and partly because they were apprehensive that Jordan's ambitious Abdullah would play the leading role in their enlarged fatherland. They also feared that further attempts at the realization of the project would disrupt the tenuous bonds of Arab unity.

Rioting broke out in Baghdad toward the end of 1952, and an army officer, General Nuriddin Mahmoud, assumed the premiership. The causes of the riots were deep-seated and the instigators may have been inspired by communism. Articulate public opinion in Iraq expressed the hope that the new regime would take prompt steps to relieve the unbearable burden of mass-poverty.

Egypt at the Crossroads

Egypt is to the Middle East what the Middle East is to the rest of the Old World—the crossroads. She faces Europe and yet her very life is the gift of Africa. The Suez Canal, entirely within Egypt, is a life-artery of trade and strategy of the East and West. In the Arab world, too, Egypt occupies a central position as the country with the largest population. She is in the vanguard of education, industrialization and westernization, and this in spite of the fact that the bulk of her people are abysmally poor.

What should be Egypt's role in the world of today? Should she play the role that was Prussia's a century ago, striving for the unification of states with similar background? In order to do that she must first become truly independent, free of foreign troops on her soil. Or should she cut her bonds with the Arab world, as of little use to herself—poor relations not worth cultivating?

At any rate, Egypt's international relations are bound to be transformed as national sentiment waxes. Too long has she been forced to follow, secured and "protected." Yet the country still lacks leadership rooted in a sufficiently homogeneous public opinion expressing a coherent policy.

We have seen Egypt at the end of the First World War, finally detached from her previous nominal dependence upon the Turks. Now she was a British protectorate. The First World War meant good business to the people who counted and their number was never too large.

In the wake of the war—which was to be the "last"—a Messianic age was to save the world. "National independence," "self-determination of nations," were the new divinities. In Europe and the Middle East one country after another became independent, large countries and small, some of them microscopic. And here was Egypt, a protectorate. Egypt, the birthplace of western man, the site—in the words of Professor Breasted—of western mankind's "dawn of conscience." If the Estonians, Latvians and Albanians had their nations, were not the Egyptians entitled to their own country?

Here was an opportunity to represent a popular cause and it met the man it needed in the person of Saad Zaghlul Pasha, not just one of the pashas but a different kind, of fellah origin. His early education was sketchy in one of the country's wretched villages, learning the Koran by rote, seeing most of his fellow students drop out of school. What was the use of reading when one had no letters to read, or writing when there were no letters to write? There was no use trying, since the road was always barred. But this young man was driven onward by an inner fire. He did not want to be one of the nameless ones, a human cipher. If one could learn, one could become a lawyer and from that point the road might be cleared . . . even in Egypt. Al Azhar was his next goal, Egypt's famous theological university.

Eventually, he became a lawyer and found his way into politics. Yes, the road could be cleared even in Egypt for a young man who knew his own mind, knew the language of his age, his environment. Nationalism, nationhood, these were the magic words. One must represent a popular cause, in order to be able to represent his own interests, to multiply his own strength. He worked his way into the higher social strata; it could and still can be done in the Middle East with education, some money, the right associates. He came to occupy high positions in the State, ministerial posts, first Minister of Public Instruction, then Minister of Justice.

Then came the great watershed, the war, which was to bring salvation to the unfree, and there was a popular cause, independence. It was not a cause that many of the fellaheen readily understood, but they could grasp it, too, in due time. It was comprehended by the few who counted and they counted because they could comprehend it. Zaghlul Pasha became head of the Nationalist Party, whose program was: Break the ties to Britain and let Egypt have her independence.

The British did not like this and so they imprisoned him in Gibraltar, in the Seychelles islands, and that was good for Zaghlul Pasha. He had leisure to think, to draw up plans, to work at the expense of the British empire, which he fought. "Self-determination of nations" resounded throughout the world. Britain was a champion of that new creed. Let Egypt become independent, Zaghlul insisted. Let us take our cause to the architects of the new world of more purified substance who are working on the future in Paris. The British did not let him go to France. Let us take our cause to the British government, surely they would have to listen. But he could not leave Egypt. Then we must speak to the British High Commissioner in Cairo. At long last that turned out to be feasible. Zaghlul Pasha led a delegation to Britain's representative. He and his fellow delegates had a lot of time to think of what they were going to say while waiting for the interview in the antechamber of the mighty. Finally they were admitted, but the interview proved to be fruitless. That was not the only important thing. The important thing was that they had a delegation (*Wafd*) and it was this fact the Egyptian nationalists dramatized. They called their party the Wafd and that was the only major political party of Egypt, with a well-knit organization and a national apparatus.

The Record of the Wafd

Year after year they reiterated the call: Independence. To many Egyptians the word came to possess a magic ring. The British, tired of so much noisy agitation, were applying drastic measures to crush it, but the Wafd kept on, making more noise, confronting London with its professions of faith and its record in Egypt.

Finally, in 1922, the British decided to take action. They proclaimed Egyptian "independence" and permitted the country's nominal head, Sultan Fouad I, to change his title to the more exalted rank of King. But . . . the most important attributes of national sovereignty, such as defense, remained in British hands. Also the British undertook to protect foreign interest in the country and they retained their hold on the "Anglo-Egyptian Sudan."

Zaghlul died in 1927 and was succeeded at the helm of the Wafd by Mustafa el-Nahas Pasha, big-time political operator, former judge and lawyer, ex-exile, who now became Secretary General of the Party. His position was important but he lacked Zaghlul's magnetism. Yet, he was to achieve more in his chosen field than his illustrious predecessor, not because of his ability but because of the revolution that was sweeping the world.

This revolution hit Egypt in reverse. It had been unleashed by Germany, Italy, Japan, known as the Axis powers, filling the air with their plaints that they were the disinherited nations of the world, have-nots, lacking elbow space, "*Lebensraum.*" In the heart of Africa, adjoining the Anglo-Egyptian Sudan, was the independent empire of Ethiopia under her own native ruler. This was the last independent native country in Africa, with no special Great Power attachment. Fascist Italy pounced upon her in 1935, in application of the principle of immorality it advocated: to the stronger belong the weak. A year after this event the British reached an accord with Egypt under which she was to become independent.

The architect of that independence was Italy's dictator, Benito Mussolini—again in reverse. Egypt was now situated between Africa's two Italian realms: Libya in the West and Ethiopia in the East. Could not Mussolini link up these two territories by banking upon the disaffection of the Egyptians? It was far better to keep the Land of the Nile quiet.

The independence Egypt gained was hedged around. Britain retained the right to maintain armed force establishments in Egypt, mainly in the zone of the Suez Canal. The accord was to run for twenty years.

Upon the death of King Fouad, his son of sixteen ascended the throne under the name of King Farouk I. Years passed and the boy grew to young manhood. Before the world stood Farouk I ibn Fouad, King of Misr, Lord of Nubia and the Sudan, Sovereign of Kordofan and Darfur, Chevalier of the Order of Annonciade, of the Order of the Seraphines, etc. etc. He was the son of Queen Nazli, who in her middle age still wore traces of her former beauty. Later he was to disown her, and she was to take refuge in California.

Fouad had been a dour person, an ex-exile, ex-Italian army officer, enthroned by his British protectors during the First World War. He had ascended his throne without a penny and when he died two decades later, he had a fortune of some fifty million dollars. Nazli was Fouad's second wife, a debonair beauty known in all the aristocratic night clubs of the western world.

Farouk was to be brought up in England in the manner of a young English aristocrat. He was to excel in all gentlemanly sports and to have his education climaxed by a training period at the Royal Academy of Woolwich.

But Downing Street proposes, and Allah disposes. Though he achieved some fame among aristocratic dowagers as the most perfectly behaved boy in the world and as free-spending "Prince Freddy" among tradesmen, Farouk was not destined to get the final patina of a British gentleman. His father died. The year was 1936 and Farouk was sent home to be enthroned under a Regency. Two years later he was crowned.

In Abdin Palace

The young King made his home in Cairo's Abdin Palace, straight out of the Thousand and One Nights. It had a museum collection of chinaware, fantastic tapestries and elaborately expensive furniture. Farouk became the owner of other dream palaces. The Kubbeh in Cairo was occupied by his mother and some of her daughters. In the summer capital, Alexandria, he had two other magnificent palaces, Ras el-Tin and Montazah.

From the beginning Farouk was the creature of Egypt's two hundred families. His spiritual tutor, the Rector of Al-Azhar, Mustafa Al-Maraghi, was a strongly pro-Axis scholar and he undertook to de-Anglicize him. On the other hand, the British influence was exerted on him by the great Egyptian geographer and explorer, Hassanein Pasha.

The court camarilla in those days included several highly placed Italians living in Egypt, headed by the palace architect, Signor Verucci. This man, the virtual major-domo of the Abdin Palace, was also strongly anti-English. Another strongly Italian influence was that of the Mosseri banking house, which had a mortgage on much of the country. The court camarilla also included trading, shipping, agricultural and industrial interests, represented by such persons as Hafez Ramadan Pasha, former Minister of Justice, and Fikri Abaga Bey, both leaders in the die-hard nationalist Vatan party and powerful courtiers.

The youthful King was encouraged to take life easy. He became an habitué of the supersumptuous Gezireh Sporting Club of the capital, of the ultra-exclusive Anglo-Egyptian Union, of the Royal Automobile Club and of the Club Mohammed Ali.

He excelled at polo, tennis, even at boxing, and was on the point of becoming a daredevil driver when warned to take it easy lest he imperil the royal succession. He acquired a cavalcade of luxurious motor cars, ten Rolls Royces in the first string, about fifteen Cadillacs in the second. As a youth he lent a royal hand to archeological excavations, and later started collecting antiquarian copies of the Koran, coins, watches, stamps and pornographic pictures.

Once a royal playboy, he became a royal fat man. Fat is more admired than muscle by Egypt's common man, since it means that a person has plenty to eat. Even though Egypt is thoroughly Muslim and Allah is the Great King, Egyptians still retained a tendency to Pharaoh-worship and Farouk was popular at first.

In those days he worked hard at being King. In order to visit his people he attended a different mosque every Friday. He also liked to travel like Harun Al-Rashid, "incognito," in one of his luxurious cars or in his equally resplendent royal yacht *Mahroussa.* "Make way for His Majesty the King in disguise," was the signal of his coming. The cry was intoned by his Royal Body Guard of handsome young men wearing clinking mail chains on their shoulders.

Wherever Farouk went, his subjects quivered with eagerness to bask in the light of his smiling countenance, and the line of royal march resounded with the fervent prayer: "Peace on Him and all His Descendants."

As evidence of his interest in his subjects, the King made a bid for hundreds of thousands of sandals in the United States, to be distributed among his people as a royal gift. The plan failed to materialize, but the good intention of their ruler was duly made known to the grateful millions.

The Great Estrangement

The great estrangement between Farouk and his English mentors occurred during World War II. The Axis was within striking distance of Suez and the King decided to join the winning cause. He had to be careful because Cairo was the British Middle East Command headquarters. Nevertheless, early in 1942 he appointed a strongly anti-British and aggressively pro-Italian premier, Ali Maher Pasha. The Premier was made acquainted with the British plans for the defense of Egypt. Shortly thereafter British intelligence found the plans on the dead body of an Italian general staff officer.

One morning thereafter the British Ambassador in Cairo, Sir Miles Lampson, later Lord Killearn, and Lt. General Robert G. W. H. Stone called at the Abdin Palace. The Ambassador bluntly told the King that he must either remove the Premier or —as Egypt's ex-King—take the next plane to South Africa. He drew the curtain aside to reveal the British tanks at the palace gate and New Zealand troops surrounding the royal residence. The King signed the appointment of the new premier, Mustafa Nahas Pasha. "You leave me no choice," he was reported to have told the Ambassador, "but I shall never forget." It was also said that for hours after this humiliating incident the King went around the palace, crushing priceless china.

The war over, Farouk's capital became the Mecca of the Arab world's Britain-haters, best known of whom was the former Grand Mufti of Jerusalem.

The Age of Violence

Something was very definitely wrong with things Egyptian, as revealed by that country's fiasco in Palestine.

It happened in the month of May of 1948. The British pulled out of Palestine and the State of Israel came into being. To the Arab world this was an abomination and a challenge. Palestine was Arab and Arab it was to remain. To enforce the Arab countries' view their armies converged upon the little state, not yet fully constituted. In the shadow of the mammoth-like Kingdom of Egypt, Israel seemed to be pitifully small, indeed.

Egypt's army was filled with self-confidence. It crossed the Palestinian frontier and marched up the coast, encountering little resistance. The Egyptian press kept the public informed about the heroic exploits of the country's armed forces, which seemed to eclipse those of Napoleon's Grande Armée. Not a word became known to the public of what happened after a victorious march.

It did not know that the army's weapons were faulty because of corruption in high places. Nor did it know that there was no co-operation among the units of the invading Arab forces, that the Jordan troops let the Egyptians flounder in their inefficiency. They did not know that most of the soldiers of the "glorious army" were too debilitated to give a good account of themselves on the field of battle. Nor did people in Cairo, in Alexandria, in the Delta, on the banks of the Nile, know that little Israel pushed huge Egypt out of most of Palestine. At the critical moment Great Britain intervened and reminded Israel that London was bound to Egypt by means of a pact of mutual help. Otherwise, Israel might have been tempted to make a dent in the Egyptian homeland.

As long as people did not know, all was well. So the retreating Egyptian army was given a victory celebration in Cairo. But, the

Middle East is no different from the rest of the world. Even if people read no newspapers and even though they obtain distorted news on the radio, truth somehow manages to come through, and so Egypt learned about the arms scandal, which was traced to highest-ranking army officers and even into the court.

When something of this nature happens there must be a change and the elections early in 1950 brought it about. After having prowled and howled in the wilderness for years, the Wafd came back with a resounding victory, again headed by Mustafa Nahas Pasha. The King opposed it but was impotent to act, afraid that a frustrated Wafd might be a more dangerous enemy.

The new government announced an Egyptian new deal, in line with the new spirit of the world, justice for the common man—even the fellah was a human being. The Wafd introduced reforms and they were good. We saw some of them in connection with the economic and political conditions of the country. But they were not enough. Besides, the Wafd became afflicted with the occupational hazards of power. Once it seemed to be safely ensconced it did not want to antagonize the pasha power, became pasha ridden and gradually lost interest in reforms and gained a corresponding increase of concern with Egypt's foreign affairs. Why were British troops in Suez? Why was the Anglo-Egyptian Sudan in London's hands?

Said a British writer, Philip Toynbee, in a *New York Times Magazine* article: "Since the Wafd came overwhelmingly into power it has done less than nothing to put into effect the reforms which figured so nobly in its program. An observer at a session of the Egyptian parliament would find it hard indeed to distinguish between the figures who lounge on the massed government benches, and the little groups of 'reactionaries' who oppose them."

The End of the Road

It happened on a warm night while most of Cairo slept, at the end of July, 1952, that a soldier thrice-wounded in the war with Israel, Major General Mohammed Naguib Bey, proclaimed himself army commander in chief, surrounded the royal palace with armored cars and made the government resign. In a nationwide broadcast the General said that corruption and bribery were the main reasons of Egypt's failure. "They are the main reasons for the troubles in Egypt's political and economic life."

Three days later the General forced King Farouk I to abdicate and to leave the land. The Egyptian press was allowed to pour its venom on the former king, who was described as a lecherous scoundrel battening on the country's life-forces, the cause of its misfortunes. If the street crowds of Cairo could have laid their hands on the former ruler he would have been torn to shreds. And this in the land where Pharaoh-worship survived all changes of regime. Great, indeed, is the power of the tribal god that delivereth the rain. But woe to the god of the tribe that faileth to cause the sluices of the heaven to open.

Then came the dawn of the new day . . . and people disappointed in frustrated expectations so many times in the past expressed the fear that it might have been the dawn of no more than one day only. The titles of Pasha and Bey were abolished. Even the highest-born was to be Mister, *sayed*. Word came from above that the fez was soon to go and there was some talk about adopting a national uniform.

The Pipe and the Man

It was a *junta* of army officers that helped General Mohammed Naguib carry out his *coup*. There had been in existence a clandestine organization of Free Officers. Among these Germans played an important role. These were veterans of Rommel's famed *Afrikakorps*, freed from war prisoner camps after the war or who had made their way to Egypt from the Reich, with the aid of friends. They had been engaged as military instructors under the King Farouk regime to lick the army into shape. There must have been about 500 of them, some of them with known names. There was, for instance, General Fahrbacher, as good a member of the former Nazi S.S. élite as Africa has ever seen. Well known were also Marine Captain Baron Theo von Bechtolsheim and Korvettenfuehrer Sprecher. Great were the reputations of General Muenzel and of S.S. Officer Tiefenbacher, the latter of whom was to train the Egyptian police. It seems that these ex-German officers were to function as the Egyptian army's brain-trust.

The hand of well-known organizers was obvious in the execution of the coup, and Egyptians are not famed for a high degree of discipline. The plotters seized the capital's nodal points and their operations gave evidence of the quiet efficiency of specialists. German terminology was too obvious in the official communiqués of the plotters: "The move was effected with lightninglike rapidity," "Instantaneous action." General Naguib himself kept on using the most typical German phrases, as, for instance, when he spoke about Egypt's "place in the sun."

The coup was the outcome of long suppressed resentment. During the Second World War the rich became much richer and the poor even poorer. Everybody spoke about the *ghaniyy harb,* war rich. Then came the Palestine fiasco, rumors of corruption, the incredible conduct of the King. There was corruption and inefficiency everywhere.

General Naguib was of Sudanese birth, the son of a police officer. Several times he was wounded in the Palestine war where he saw the real state of Egypt's affairs. A modern person, he smokes a pipe (and Islamic puritans shun tobacco) and even drinks a glass of wine (and wine-drinking is sin). He acquired only one wife, as do most Egyptians, and became the father of six children, the name of one of whom was Farouk.

He began the great housecleaning with the aid of his *junta.* Prominent politicians were jailed, former leaders of the Wafd and other parties, such as the Liberal-Constitutionalists and Saadists; also persons formerly too close to the throne. A new day was to dawn for Egypt.

General Naguib discovered the fellah; for the first time a mighty man set eyes on the peasant. Never had anything of this kind happened, under the rulers of ancient or modern Egypt. He went among the peasants, paid visits to the country's towns. People wanted to rush him, to touch his uniform, to kiss his hands, their savior, a new Pharaoh who was to help them. They would have trampled him underfoot if he had not been protected. With bloody skulls some of his admirers were beaten back and yet they tried to come back, to grovel at his feet.

The new regime dug up the dirt about the old order, announced the great reforms; no titles, but land for the people, and a human lot for the fellah. No longer was the name of peasant to be a word of degradation.

What strange practices were brought to light? There were five government officials to supervise one street-cleaner in the capital. And then there was the story of the mules of Cairo which made people laugh and cry. They were needed for garbage disposal and mules are so constituted that once a week they must receive a laxative if they are to earn their keep. (Or so at least the press reported.) The amount appropriated for this purpose was so large that the poor beasts would have perished if there had been no graft in government circles. And now there was to be no corruption, or so at least people thought. Something new under the blazing sun.

Artifice is Mightier Than Nature

Among all the artificial nations of the Middle East none was more synthetic than Transjordania, which was later to assume the name of the Hashimite Kingdom of the Jordan. If there had not been an insistent Abdullah who had to be provided with a vacant throne there would be no Kingdom of the Jordan now. And yet today that country's people get ecstatic about its beloved flag of black, white and green, with the vertical stripe and star.

The Land of Moab and Edom is the name under which the student of Biblical history knows this region. This was the Romans' wall against the desert dangers, the terminus of the civilized world. The ruins of Petra, Jerash and Kerak still brood over the frontier's silence. History dies hard in this area and therefore it may not be surprising that the modern name of Transjordan was anticipated many centuries ago in the medieval French name of Oultre-Jourdain. Part of this region was also known as the Lordship of Montreal. Under the long Ottoman rule this was an unimportant part of the Syrian vilayet, and to the Arabs this region never meant too much. They raced across it at the time they burst out of their desert confinement, their eyes beguiled by the abundant resources of the Mediterranean coast.

After the First World War, Amir Abdullah had his eyes on the Baghdad throne, instead of which he received the easy chair in Amman, primitive capital of primitive Transjordan, carved out of Palestine. No sooner was it established than it faced hard problems. Adjoining it was the realm of the same King Ibn Saud who had chased Abdullah's father out of Mecca. Even at the present time the boundary between the two countries is not definitely drawn. Matters were further complicated when both rivals wanted to have a window on the Gulf of Aqaba, which is a distant corner of the Red Sea. Ibn Saud had an extensive seacoast and to him it was a matter of honor that the despised foe should receive no valuable award. To Abdullah it was to be his only toehold on a sea. Finally, he received Aqaba, and the world knew that Britain had a hand in this award. Abdullah was her satellite.

In the Middle East a Great Power can pick up bargains. Abdullah's little thirty thousand square mile country was poor and it had to have a British subsidy, which amounted to £5,000 a month. In the United States there are plenty of individuals with larger incomes.

Three years after the First World War, Transjordan saw the creation of her armed force, the Arab Legion. According to some people, it would have been more correct to call it the British Legion. Its first commander was Captain F. G. Peake, leader of the Camel Corps during the desert war.

He was one of those British expatriates who loved simple people unsullied by competitive greed. He held that people in desert lands and on the margins of the sown were far more human because they were in the presence of nature's constructive and destructive might. Among the virtues he found in the desert was frankness and loyalty. Obviously he idealized the great open spaces of the East, but he did elicit those virtues.

Later the Legion's command was assumed by a man who became far better known to the outside world, Brigadier John Bagot Glubb, known as Glubb Pasha. A Jordanian who was born a Britisher; he was extremely successful with his Arab fighting men. There was nothing spectacular about him. He was matter of fact but he, too, had that undefinable something which may be called leadership quality. People liked him because he liked them, spoke their language, even Bedouin dialects. And that was different from the attitude of officers in other Arab armies, speaking a language which, even though Arabic, the common soldiers did not understand.

The Arab Legion came to play an important role. It was never too large, reputed to be about 14,000 men strong. It attracted people not only from the Jordan region but also from other parts of the Arab world, and some of them came from very long distances, from across the Red Sea, from the Sudan. It turned out to be an all-purpose army, performing the duties not only of the soldiery but also of the police. The Legion was more than useful for Abdullah because it stood between him and his neighbor, Ibn Saud, who might have been tempted at one time to do to him what he had done to his father, the Sherif of Mecca. Having the Legion command in British hands he was under London's protection. In the Arab-Israel War it was this force which gave a good account of itself.

In 1930 Transjordan gained her "independence" of the usual kind, combined with an alliance. The British had the right to retain their armed forces in the country. In 1946 Amir Abdullah assumed the title of King and shortly thereafter Transjordan's name was changed to Hashimite Kingdom of the Jordan.

This was a significant change. By carrying the name of Jordan and not *Trans*jordan, the King gave notice that he was going to raise a claim to the other side of the river in case the British evacuated Palestine. This was opposed to the policy of some of the loudest Palestinian Arab politicians who claimed the country for themselves. The name of Hashim in the designation of the country was a reminder that Abdullah outranked all the other rulers in the Arab world because he belonged to the Prophet's own family.

Abdullah did occupy much of the Arab part of Palestine after Israel had been established, adding some two thousand square miles to his kingdom. This was against the policies of the most aggressive Arab leaders, headed by the former Grand Mufti of

Jerusalem. They formed their own government in Palestine's Gaza strip, which was in Egyptian hands.

Jordan's king was attempting to create a larger Arab coreland in the heart of the Middle East, his Greater Syria scheme. This incensed his Saudi Arabian and Egyptian neighbors, not to mention certain Syrian and Lebanese factions.

His Arab enemies denounced him as a "British tool" and "Jewish agent." He did go along with the British, realizing that his weak country might be crushed by stronger neighbors without London's help. Also, he was the only one among the Arab rulers to maintain proper relations with Israel.

It was while visiting the Mosque of Omar in the walled-in town of Old Jerusalem in midsummer 1951 that Abdullah fell a victim of foul play. He was assassinated. The trial of the murderers disclosed the fact that the plot had been hatched in Egypt.

Heir to the throne was his son, Amir Talal, about whom it had been said that at one time he had attempted to shoot Glubb Pasha. Whether this was true or not we do not know, but we do know that he was in a Swiss sanatorium for mental and nervous cases when his father died. At first an interim regime was established but eventually he ascended the throne. It was believed that he had pledged his word to the British to pursue his late father's policy. A few months later it was announced officially that his condition was such that he could no longer occupy the throne. The conservative French daily newspaper, *Le Monde,* of Paris, reported on this occasion: "Talal became insane again when the British found he did not want to play their game; was friendly with Egypt and unfriendly with Iraq." He was deprived of his crown by the Parliament's decision and was succeeded by Crown Prince Husein, his young son.

The Plateau and the Center

When you are on the plateau, close to the seas, you want to insure yourself against surprises from them, and so you descend to the coast—in case you are in Arabia and you are a king. We have already encountered Ibn Saud, whose original home was the Nejd, meaning "Mountain Plateau." Therefore he wanted to insure the coast and the British permitted him to do so, to descend to the Persian Gulf, which was completely misnamed and whose correct name should have been the British Gulf. They kept him away from that Gulf in various places where they had their protectorates.

Ibn Saud could be trusted because he nearly always knew where his interests lay and those interests lay mostly with the British. He also could be trusted because he had the rugged honesty of the desert warrior and he accepted a monthly stipend of $25,000 without much ado.

It must be said of Ibn Saud that he had what Friedrich Nietzsche called the "third ear," an organ that was attuned to sounds that were inaudible to people with only two conventional ears. This way he learned that while the British lose plenty of battles they like to win the last battle, the one that really counts. So, Ibn Saud sided with the British during the First World War, without antagonizing their Ottoman enemy too much, just in case. . . . However, the King's favorite enemy, the ruler of the region known as Jebel Shammar, sided with the loser and now found himself without a friend. What was he to do, all alone in the world? Ibn Saud gave him the answer. He had him escorted into his own capital as a prisoner and then took his country.

A ruler as unscrupulous and successful deserved credit and that was accorded to him when Britain recognized him as the head of an independent Sultanate in 1921. With that go-ahead signal flashed to him, he extended the boundaries of his country to the nebulous frontiers of Britain's coastal sheykhdom protégés.

Ibn Saud then conquered the Hejaz, and that means "Center Land." From that position he extended his realm farther south on the Red Sea coast, into Asir and the Tihama lowlands. This section was very far from the heart of his realm and its leaders staged a revolt against him, seeking the aid of the adjacent High Yemen, whose ruler, Imam Yahya, was ready to help for Allah's greater glory and in expectation of rich loot.

Desert barriers could not contain Ibn Saud and off he marched against the revolters in the distant lands, reconquering Asir and occupying Yemen. This was his chance to round out his realm to the remotest points of the Red Sea. Also this was his chance to reveal true statesmanship. Instead of conquering Yemen, he sealed a pact with her ruler and suffered no loss for his pains. Had he annexed Yemen he would have also annexed a lot of trouble, to keep the mountain region in check and not to get involved with the British.

Ibn Saud's third ear also relayed the information to him that the British would not lose the Second World War either, and this at a time when many people in the Middle East were selling Britain short. He dispatched one of his numerous sons to Britain's headquarters to exhort the Muslim soldiers in the ranks to fight until victory. Also he gave the Allies permission to build a large airport at Dhahran, in the Saudi Arabian oil country.

The international stature of Ibn Saud was recognized when the President of the United States met him on board an American warship in Egypt's Great Bitter Lake. The spectacle must have pleased the Prophet. The King had his own sheep brought on board, to have his meal prepared in the traditional way. "Unclean" Christians were not to touch the food he was to eat.

It must have been a sight for the gods to see the head of one of the most advanced countries in the world engaged in earnest conversation with the head of one of the most backward of countries. One of the most refined products of the West, the President, seems to have cast his spell on the Eastern king.

On Saudi Arabia's royal flag is inscribed the Koranic text: *There is no god but God and Mohammed is the Messenger of God.* The color of Saudi Arabia's banner is the Prophet's own green, with the sword of Islam. In the name of the Prophet and with the sword, Ibn Saud made himself the master of the great Arab Quadrangle and a mighty potentate in the Islamic world.

The Land of the Moon

A sword is also the emblem of the Kingdom of Yemen in the southwestern corner of the Arab Quadrangle. That country looks down upon the busy Red Sea and yet its interior is little better known than Tibet. While Egypt has been described as feudal, Saudi Arabia medieval, Yemen has been characterized as Biblical.

Few outsiders have ever seen Yemen's capital, Sa'na, a walled town with eight gates, which must have looked the same in the Prophet's time. The famous granaries of Upper Yemen must look very much like those that served Joseph so well during his stewardship. East by north of Sa'na is the famous Saba, a distance of but six days' travel by the speediest ox carts. Most of the people of the kingdom are addicted to a drug called *qat*, which saps energy and destroys even the last traces of efficiency.

Yemen may be compared to a hedgehog the British lion has been loath to touch. All around her Britain holds strong points, including the Aden crown colony.

The kingdom of the mountains has dared to defy the British because of its location. It was not until 1934 that the ruler, Imam Yahya, consented to conclude a "truce" with Britain's delegates (since peace cannot exist between Muslim and non-Muslim countries), and a strange document, indeed, it turned out to be. The declaration of good intentions was there but it contained no agreement on the thorniest subject, the question of controversial land. "What Allah has put together, let no man tear asunder," the Imam said, and, obviously, Allah put together every piece of land he claimed.

Even after the pact had been signed no British representative was allowed to reside in the State. English entomologists in search of strange specimens needed all the help diplomacy could offer—compounded by patience—before they were admitted into the country for scholarly research.

The title of the next chapter of Yemenite history might have been "High Politics in the High Mountains." Nothing succeeds like success, the well-worn axiom says, but nowhere is it truer than in this region.

Success seemed to crown the efforts of Fascist Italy in the later thirties. Across the Red Sea, in Africa, she was carving out a colonial empire for herself. The Imam of Yemen was not remiss in hitching his star to that of Mussolini. While keeping out the British, he admitted Italian engineers into his country, and also he admitted Fascist arms.

Nothing fails like failure in this fata morgana land. When the Fascists toppled from their high estate, the Imam promptly thrust a deft stiletto into their backs. Those whom he had welcomed a short time before were now ordered jailed. Still he retained a measure of dignity in that he did not jump on the Allied bandwagon, either. His country became a United Nations member, in spite of the fact that it failed to declare war on the Axis in due time.

Yemen is not one of the countries whose name the reader finds on front pages every day. It was in the headlines, though, on February 17, 1948, when His Majesty the King of Yemen, Imam Yahya b. Mohammed b. Hamid ed Din found his gruesome end at the hands of assassins. Two of his nine sons were also killed. Among primitive people it is not uncommon to kill the old and weak, so that they shall not live on the community's meager resources. That is not, of course, the custom even among the most primitive people of the Quadrangle. However, kings must not give the impression of being weak, and that was the impression Yahya gave. He had to die at dagger's end in what was, in effect, a palace revolution.

The revolters' success was short-lived, however. They were defeated by the heir apparent, Saif al Islam Ahmad, who conquered the capital, executed the plotters, and proclaimed himself Imam. Precipitately, Yemen dropped out of the news. However, it seems that the forbidden land is no longer forbidden, having opened its gates to explorers for uranium. Civilization is on the march.

The Arab League

The Arab dream had been one nation indivisible, from Casablanca to Aden. Whose dream? That of dreamers, poets and other useless people who think the thoughts of millions. Not the dream of practical politicians, who dream their own individual dreams because they want government jobs. The more numerous the governments the larger the number of jobs.

That Greater Arabia might have been even larger than the United States. Then, there was *Arabia irredenta,* from Casablanca to Es Solum, including Morocco, Algeria, Tunisia, and

Libya. From Egypt to Yemen, however, the dream could take shape.

Great Britain thought that was what the Arabs wanted. It just goes to show that even the most accomplished diplomats make mistakes, because, evidently, this was not what the Arabs wanted. Or at least those Arabs that counted, the people who qualified for high government positions.

London could not afford to have a sullen Middle East in one of the world's most strategic positions. Iraq was in the throes of a rebellion, Egypt was restless, and soon Axis armies were to besiege the gates of the Nile. British Foreign Secretary Anthony Eden spoke up on May 29, 1941, and his words alerted the Arab world:

> The Arab world has made great strides since the settlement reached at the end of the last war, and many Arab thinkers desire for the Arab peoples a greater degree of unity than they now enjoy. In reaching out toward this unity, they hope for support. No such appeal from our friends should go unheeded. It seems to be both natural and right that cultural and economic ties, too, should be strengthened. His Majesty's government for their part will give their full support to any scheme that commands general approval.

What form was this Arab unity to take? Naturally, the shape that would best promote Britain's interests. It was London's faithful friend, Nuri Pasha, Iraq's hardy perennial, who submitted a plan to the Arab countries. And, lo and behold, it found favor promptly in British eyes. This was the old British plan of the Fertile Crescent, to include Lebanon, Palestine, Transjordan, linked with Iraq through federative union.

The French considered this project as being directed against them and they had not been consulted. Such a Greater Arabia might also exert a strong gravitational pull on the French North African dependencies. Was it Britain's plan to break up the French overseas union? Whatever the answer, the Arabs did not like the plan either.

On February 24, 1942, Britain spoke again and this time, too, it was through Anthony Eden. He rebuked the Arabs for having offered no plan commanding general approval. He made it clear that the "initiative in any scheme would have to come from the Arabs themselves." Again he offered British support in the preparation of unity. After this repeated prodding the Arab League came into being. However, it was not to be a union of states, but a loose league of sovereign nations.

In the autumn of 1944 the delegates of the independent Arab countries met and formulated the Alexandria Protocol, as it came to be known, delineating the charter of the Arab League. On the basis of this the Covenant was drawn, establishing the League, and it was signed by the delegates of Egypt, Iraq, Lebanon, Saudi Arabia, Syria, Transjordan and Yemen. Egypt was to play a particularly important role in the League, the headquarters of which was established in Cairo, and it was an Egyptian with ambassadorial rank, Abd al-Rahman Azzam Pasha, who became its first Secretary General. When he resigned in the autumn of 1952, another Egyptian statesman, Abdel-Khalik Hassuna, took his place.

The object of the League was described as the strengthening of the ties between the participant states, the co-ordination of their political programs, the preservation of their independence and sovereignty, and the consideration of the affairs and interests of the Arab countries.

The participating countries were to co-operate in a large number of economic and financial matters, too, including trade reciprocity, currency, tariffs, also communications. Further, they were to co-operate in cultural and social questions, public health, matters of nationality, visas and passports, the extradition of criminals and the execution of judgments. The Arab League council was to meet twice yearly, and Egypt provided not only the Secretary General and headquarters but more than 40 per cent of the budget of the League.

The Record of the League

What has the League accomplished since its inception? Some harsh words were said about its record in a report which Dr. Nazim el-Kudsi of Syria submitted to the Arab League itself in the winter of 1951:

> The Arab League has failed Arab hopes. It has been lavish in demonstrations and words, but barren of results and deeds. Everybody knows that its prevailing spirit is out of harmony with the times, the rapid succession of events and their gravity because it has not taken the constructive road in any field, be it defense, economics, culture or social affairs. The individual Arab has not felt its existence because it has not secured anything for him and has not achieved any goal.

In *The World of Today*, published by The Royal Institute of International Affairs, in May 1951, an author wrote:

> The truth is that unity is not the natural condition of the Arabs, and has never existed. . . . The picture afforded by the Arab League so far is one of dismal and often deliberate failure. . . . The League became, and to a very large extent still remains, the chosen field of inter-Arab struggle rather than the expression of a united Arab world.[1]

Jordan's King Abdullah described the League as "six severed heads stuffed into a sack."

In its most crucially formative years the Arab League seemed to concentrate on the Palestine question, to the exclusion of all other problems. It engineered the boycott of Jewish goods from Palestine which, incidentally, damaged the Arab states more than the prospective victims. It maintained a constant barrage of threats against Israel, talking about the "second round" and the "Israeli danger." In the political field, too, it helped to push the French out of the Levant, even though the initiative was taken elsewhere.

Among other negative acts of the League was its condemnation of the Hashimite Kingdom for her annexation of Arab Palestine. Several of its members went so far as to suggest that Jordan should be thrust out of the fold. Lack of unanimity forestalled the consummation of this plan.

A positive step, at least on paper, was taken in the spring of 1950, when the Arab League drafted a collective security pact. Aggression on any of its signatories was to be considered aggression against them all.

[1] Quoted by Harry N. Howard, United Nations Adviser, Bureau of Near Eastern, South Asian and African Affairs, Department of State; at the January 1952 conference of the Academy of Political Science.

The Treaty of Joint Defense and Co-operation set forth that members of the League were moved by the desire of their peoples "for the realization of a closer union for the common defense of their States and to safeguard peace and security in conformity with the principles and objectives of the Arab League Charter and the United Nations Charter. . . ."

A Permanent Military Committee was established to report to the Common Defense Council, composed of the Ministers of Foreign Affairs and of National Defense. An Economic Council was also set up.

How the collective security features of the Arab League will operate, only the future can tell. Was its impressive apparatus established mostly to crush the little State of Israel in times to come?

Would the Arab League be the nucleus of a Muslim League to encompass half of the globe? But then what was it that Indonesia and Lebanon had in common? Or Saudi Arabia and Pakistan? Yet, Pakistan did take the initiative of convening an International Islamic Economic Organization. It met, discussed problems and left things pretty much where they had been. Would there be much point in setting up an International Christian Economic Organization? Ours does not seem to be the age when nations can be organized along religious lines.

It used to be said about the defunct League of Nations that while ineffective in dealing with prostitution in diplomacy it was effective in combating white slavery. What about the nonpolitical work of the Arab League?

The Arab League has sponsored conferences of social scientists, archeologists, engineers and physicians. It set up an Arab news agency, promoted the exchanges of scholars on a moderate scale, drew up model treaties and drafted aviation pacts. At one of its meetings a large amount of useful material was made available about the poverty of the region.

The League took steps to conserve valuable Arabic manuscripts in various parts of the world. It announced a prize on the subject: "What are the obstacles delaying the progress of the Arab world in matters political, social, economic, cultural and moral?" As part of the League's recent program it sought to encourage writers to treat subjects of common importance to the member states; to have foreign works translated into Arabic, producing films representing various aspects of modern Arab civilization for diffusion among the Arab states and abroad. At a meeting of the Cultural Office of the League the recommendation was made that it should lend its support to attempts to produce a generally acceptable colloquial Arabic language.

The plans are modest but they are good. The question is how many of them will take shape? It has been suggested that in order to render the Arab League's work more effective it ought to be informed that there are other countries, too, besides the State of Israel.

CHAPTER 4

The Tortuous Story of the Straits

On Land and Sea

The Straits have been longer in Middle East history than any other problem. The modern phase of this history began when Russia became a Great Power and Turkey's forces waned.

History has not known in modern times a truly Great Power without access to warm waters. Russia became vast but not great because of her isolation from important sea routes. The Black Sea was locked by the Straits; the Baltic by Scandinavia's Narrows. Murmansk beyond the Arctic Circle was barred by the tempestuous northern ocean and its remoteness from the center of Russian life. The Arctic waters were ice-bound and the Far Eastern waters of Russia were out of the focus of international life.

In the second part of the last century there was a remarkable American naval officer who wrote one of those books that few people read but many remembered. He was Alfred Thayer Mahan, who wrote a book whose title revealed little about its exciting content: *The Influence of Sea Power Upon History, 1660-1783.* The volume was published in 1890, at the very time when Britain appeared to be at the pinnacle of her power. Admiral Mahan sought to show that a world power must be in command of the seas and, conversely, that command of the seas involved world power.

A generation went by and a new school of thought arose, which linked geography with politics and therefore became known as the school of geopolitics. Best known among these was the German General Karl Haushofer. In the middle thirties of our century he made another kind of guess about which he wrote books with such intriguing titles as *Macht und Erde* (Might and Earth), *Weltmaere und Weltmaechte* (World Seas and World Powers). Also he edited the *Zeitschrift fuer Geopolitik,* which many people considered one of the most exciting publications of the continent. The General and his disciples held the very reverse of the Mahan thesis. They maintained that not the control of the seas but dominion over the great landmasses of the Heartland of the World Island, from the Elbe river to the Amur in Far Eastern Siberia, could assure the rule over the world.

The history of the past seemed to support the Mahan thesis. It was the powers controlling the seas that won the two World Wars. Will that again be the case in the future? One day Russia may reach the Atlantic Ocean, and in that event her problem of cracking open her "icecage" will have been solved. This is not likely to happen, however, without very serious consequences. Meanwhile her closest approach to warm waters is by smashing the bottleneck of the Straits. There too the United States stands guard. But will she keep on mounting the guard for long? And the Soviet Union is right next door.

The Straits link the Black Sea with the Aegean, and the Soviet Union is the most important Black Sea power. Together with her satellites she controls all but the southern shores of that sea.

Her Black Sea ports, of which Odessa and Sebastopol are the most famous, are close to the country's great population centers, and to one of its great industrial and farming areas. However, in order to reach the Aegean the Soviets would have to pass through the tortuous Straits and there the trouble begins.

Those Straits are really too small to have caused so much trouble. They begin with the Bosphorus, the frailest of the three links of the chain. It is only eighteen miles long and so slender that it can be easily swum at its narrowest point, where it is only six hundred yards. Even at its widest it does not cover more than two and a half miles.

The next link is the Sea of Marmora, which is really a salt water lake a little over four thousand square miles, with a length of one hundred seventy-two miles. The most "romantic" part of the chain is the third and last link, the Dardanelles, forty miles long and ranging in width from one to four miles.

History on the Rampage

The name *Bosphorus* comes from the Greek *ox-ford.* Greek mythology is somewhat mixed up here. It tells the story of Io who, in the form of a heifer, swam the Bosphorus. According to the myth, Io had been changed into the heifer by Hera, wife of Zeus, who was jealous of the Thunderer's affection for the daughter of the river god Inachus. Although Io was a heifer at the time, her feat is traditionally connected with the name of the strait.

The Dardanelles were known to the ancients as Hellespont. The cloud goddess' daughter Helle and her brother Phryxus were involved in one of those marital scrapes of their parents for which the gods of Greece were famed. Their father, Athamas, fell in love with Ino, who was not a nice woman at all. She hated her lover's children and, like the real villainess she was, she ordered the grain roasted before it was sown, attributing the damage to famine. The Greek gods had solutions for such problems and Athamas consulted an oracle who, it seems, was in Ino's pay. The oracle ordered Athamas to offer his son as a sacrifice, which he was about to do when the cloud goddess sent a golden ram to take her children away. They reached the

Straits safely but there Helle turned giddy, fell into the sea and was drowned; thence the name of Hellespont. Why the cloud goddess could not do anything about that, we are not told.

The question of the Straits was already old when Helen of Troy was still radiantly young. Not because of her bewitching eyes were those thousand ships launched in the Trojan War but because the Greeks were loath to pay the toll Troy's people exacted.

Control of the Straits then passed to the Greeks, who made profitable use of them after they had smashed Persian might at Salamis. Then the Greeks swept into the Black Sea, plying their trade in meerschaum and salt, spices and gold. Over the East the Greeks asserted their supremacy in the region of the Straits, and when they were ousted from it they lost their supremacy in the Middle East.

When Emperor Constantine turned Byzantium into Constantinople, the question of the Straits again became a burning issue. From the time of New Rome until the present this problem has been the root of many wars. "Whoever is master of Constantinople, is master of the world." These were Napoleon's words and who could speak on that question with more authority?

The rulers of Constantinople sought to reconstruct a world empire from the Straits. They succeeded momentarily when fat Justinian was the autocrat, and Theodora, the flashy daughter of a keeper of bears, was empress. Their great general, Belisarius, conquered more land than Napoleon the Great. However, the gods were jealous at New Rome's might and barbarian hordes were their instruments of destruction.

Death swept out of the desert sand when Allah's banner inspired the Arabs to fanatical deeds. They won everywhere but were repelled near the Straits, so that the fearless warriors of Islam were beaten to retreat. Danger threatened the Straits again from the Christians of the West, bent upon a holy mission and unholy trade. They had set out to exterminate the Muslim "pagans," who desecrated the blessed shrines of Christ. In the great crusades the faithful marched to redeem the Grail from the infidel and their souls from temptation as well. They set stunned eyes on purple-robed merchants of Venice, proud

Pisans and pompous Genoese on their way to Palestine. The rank and file of the Christian Crusaders did not suspect that some of the Christian traders had struck a deal with the pagans. How could they suspect the cupidity of Christian Venice and that it would cause the downfall of Christendom in the Holy Land and, centuries later, on the Straits. Instead of fighting the Muslim, the Venetian merchants bribed themselves into influential positions in the councils of Constantinople. Then they "bored from within," causing dissension, diverting attention to fancied dangers, preparing the ground for the fatal attack which was to yield the Straits to Venice, "Queen of the Adriatic Sea." From there they wanted to control the trade with India and fabulous Cathay, with no fear of rivalry from the Greeks.

Finally, in the middle of the fourteenth century, the waters of the Dardanelles reflected the Islamic Prophet's green banner. On three sides the victorious Turks were closing in, but for another century the strong walls of the imperial capital held out. The Christian rulers of the city were also strengthened by the Mongol invasion which weakened the aggressor Turks. Then, in the middle of the fifteenth century, Constantinople became Turkish, the capital of the Ottoman Empire.

At first the Turks established a complete monopoly of trade and only Turkish boats were permitted to sail into the Straits. Had that Empire remained strong, and Muscovy in the mists of the North weak, there would have been no Eastern Question and no Problem of the Straits. However, that was not to be.

At the turn of the seventeenth century the chronic stage of the Straits question began. For some time then the Russian empire had been in the ascendant to the north of the Black Sea. Having acquired the "top of the world," Russia had a huge land but no access to warm waters, and yet such an access would have meant not merely an increase of foreign trade, but an influx of the fertile spirit of the West, a commanding voice in the council of Great Powers, and a higher scale of life.

Warm waters lured Russians in many quarters but nowhere were they closer than at the Straits. The shores of India and Iran were also washed by warm waters, but the topography of these countries represented formidable barriers. The "roof of the world" would have to be scaled before the Russians could reach the Indian plains. Even if they overcame all these obstacles, they would have reached "back-waters" for a European Power. Had they managed to ford the sandy waste of Iran and scale her barren rocks, they would have acquired only a sea hemmed by inhospitable, torrid shores and far from the high roads of trade.

The Straits were precisely what Russia needed and wanted. They commanded the exit gate of the Black Sea, near the shores of which the empire had built up its "Pittsburgh of the Steppes," in the Don and Donetz basins, in close proximity to Russia's population centers.

Besides, Holy Russia regarded herself as the lawful heir of the Greek empire. Moscow was the Third Rome, after the loss of Second Rome on the banks of the Straits. The Second Rome, in turn, represented true, "orthodox" Christian catholicism in the Russians' eyes.

Now the Second Rome was in the sacrilegious hands of the Turks and a new crusade was in order to free it from the "pagans" and reconsecrate eastern Christianity's magnificent shrine, Hagia Sophia, on the shores of the Golden Horn. Russia had thus a religious mission and, incidentally, she would also gain control of the Straits and break the bottleneck that kept her away from the highly coveted warm waters. Religion and national interests offered a perfect blend, and every Christian country should have understood and promoted Holy Russia's consecrated course. However, the British did not understand it. They cared nothing about the Second Rome, but they did care a lot about their own imperial interests and lifelines.

The Black Sea was then an Ottoman lake and as a first step Peter the Great of Holy Russia demanded freedom of navigation for Russian ships on it. The Turks were indignant: "The virgin waters of the sea must not be polluted by Russian boats." Not only the Russians but they, too, had their ideas about religious missions and consecrated waters. If the services of the sacred waves were to be enlisted, Russian cargoes must be stored in Turkish vessels. The wrathful Muscovite was not to be trifled with and he led his boats against the Turks at the beginning of the eighteenth century. This was one of the score of wars the two countries were to wage in the course of two centuries.

The energetic Catherine, Czarina of all the Russias, had the cunning to devise a plan to break the Turks' stranglehold on the Straits. Round the Rock of Gibraltar her Baltic fleet sailed into the Mediterranean, to the very walls of the capital of the Ottoman realm.

Then, something happened which was to happen again and again. At the crucial moment Russian determination faltered and the ships of the Czarina withdrew. Just the same, Ottoman supremacy in the Black Sea was broken and in the treaty of Kuchuk Kainarji of 1774, Russian merchant ships acquired the right of free passage across the Straits. The date of the pact is significant. It was two years after the first partition of Poland, which catapulted Russia into Central Europe. "Peace is indivisible," another age was to say. "Success is indivisible, too," history teaches. Russia's increased weight on the Vistula, in Poland, also increased her weight on the Straits.

A Strange War

As the life forces of the Ottomans were ebbing, Russia's gargantuan appetite grew. "We have a sick man on our hands"—and who should be the heir? Closest to the deathbed was Russia, the expectant heir. Also, "Holy Russia" considered herself engaged in a crusade against the eternal infidel. It was Russia's sacred obligation to redeem the desecrated Christian shrines on the Golden Horn.

As the major powers sought entering wedges into the Ottoman Empire, wrapped in idealistic ideology, the Russians set out to protect the Orthodox Christians of the Holy Land, which was part of the Ottoman realm. Religion was an important tool in the arsenal of aggressive national policy. The British were not taken in by Russian asseveration. They knew only too well that when a Russian foreign minister pontificated about the Holy Land, he meant the Straits. This time the "bluff" of St. Petersburg must be called. The occupant of the throne of France was Napoleon III, whom his adversaries called Napoleon the Little.

He wanted to gild his tarnished name and redeem French glory in Russia. Napoleon the Great was beaten in that horizonless country, but Napoleon the Little was to score. He was also in favor of calling the Russian bluff.

The time was 1853 to 1856, and the name of the conflict was the Crimean War. It was a strange war indeed, one of the most haphazard of major conflicts, a tragedy of errors. In some ways it still had the trappings of a medieval joust, in which gallantry played a role. But it was also the first of the modern wars in which not individual valor but the machine was to play the dominant part. It introduced the trench warfare which was to change the nature of modern wars. The Crimean War provided the inspiration for "the Lady with the Lamp," Florence Nightingale, reformer of hospitals and sanitation. That war stirred the patriotic fancy of Tennyson, whose "Charge of the Light Brigade," describing a dramatic episode of Crimea, was recited by millions. It aroused the deepest pity in the heart of a young Russian volunteer, and the world was made richer by Leo Tolstoy's descriptions of war scenes.

The challengers in the war were a motley crowd: Britain, France, Sardinia and the Ottoman realm. Most important of these were the British. As always in those days, they were concerned with the road to India and all roads seemed to lead to that fabled land. Sprawling into infinity on top of the Old World was Russia. Should that mammoth break into the open, Britain's imperial lifeline would snap. Russia must be contained within her icy quarters.

Least important of all the belligerents was Turkey, on whose behalf the Western Allies were waging the war. Nominally independent, even a Great Power, she was no more than the catspaw of the West, the whipping boy of the British, their leading satellite.

The Russian czar, Nicholas I, was confident. A literal-minded person, he compared the size of his country with that of his opponents and drew all the incorrect conclusions. Besides he knew, even if the pride-ridden western countries did not, that Russia was the champion of a sacred cause. He thought the British were bluffing, the French emperor was beneath his contempt and the King of Sardinia made him laugh. Besides, in case of a war his faithful ally the Emperor of Austria would leap to his feet to help him. Had he not saved the Habsburg dynasty from a very serious danger just a few years before?

In the autumn of 1853 Russian forces moved into Turkey "not to make war but simply to secure material guarantees." The Habsburg emperor did not leap to his feet to help Nicholas. The Allies now had their *casus belli* and the Crimean war began.

Military strategists have not been able to decide yet which of the two sides conducted a more wretched campaign. As events were to show, the Allies picked out a good point on which to force the issue, the Crimean peninsula where they could bring their naval supremacy to bear upon the Russians. It was isolated from the heart of Russia, barred from it by lack of communications. On the other hand, the Allies would have done far better if they had been equipped with good maps. In that case, probably, the war would not have dragged on and on.

The most important point of the Crimean peninsula was Sebastopol, and the Allies made their landing some fifty miles north of it, encountering little resistance at that point. The French advanced on the shore and the British tried to keep step with them inland. The numerical strength of the Allies was weak, but Russian resistance was not too strong either. Not that the Russian soldiers were not good fighters. Following their priests, who carried miracle-working icons into the battle, they marched unhesitatingly into the path of death. In bayonet charges the *mujiks*, peasants, were particularly strong. "The bullet is a fool, the bayonet is a fine fellow." But the Russian supply lines were not working, so that the defenders had to go on short rations, and eventually household animals, and later, cats and rats were devoured. The Russian officers owned their men body and soul.

The war dragged on. In retrospect the weakness of Russian strategy is patent. What has been Russia's main strength? Space. It was General Space that defeated Napoleon and not Field Marshal Kutuzov. Also, it was General Space that defeated Hitler. Instead of accepting battle on a limited territory where their weakness was revealed, why did the Russian high command not let the Allies lose themselves in endless space? It did not do it.

It is said that people cannot die of a "broken heart," and yet that is what must have happened to Czar Nicholas I. He died while the war was still going on. The incredible happened. The pygmies gained the upper hand over the giant, the unclean scored over the dedicated cause. The contemporaries assert that the Czar did not want to live. A sickness which he could have fought off under normal conditions took him away.

On March 30, 1856, the Treaty of Paris sealed Russia's fate. Not only were the Straits forbidden to her but she had to destroy her own Black Sea forts and not erect new ones. That body of water was neutralized. Also Russia had to abandon her claim to protect the Orthodox Christians of the Ottoman Empire. The Danube was turned into an internationalized river. Turkey, on the other hand, was admitted into the European concert, as a reward for good behavior. The British remained masters of the seven seas. The death sentence was pronounced in Article XI of the Treaty of Paris which provided: *The Black Sea is neutralized; its waters and ports, open to the merchant marines of all nations, are perpetually closed to the flags of war of the powers possessing its coasts and other powers.*

The Straits question seemed to be settled for a long time, but the settlement lasted a mere fifteen years. While the other powers were busy in western Europe, Russian Foreign Minister Prince Alexander Mikhailovich Gorchakov denounced the principal provisions of the Paris Treaty. The Black Sea was neutral no more, but the Straits remained closed to war vessels.

The Ebbs and Tides of Diplomacy

Against the Straits the ebbs and tides of diplomacy kept on beating. Again Russia tried to break out of her ice-bound coop and this time she won the war. However, she lost the peace. The year was 1877 and the Russian belief that Christians needed to be saved in the Ottoman Empire was stronger than before. This time the Czarist forces tried to bypass the Straits, sweeping directly into the Balkans overland. While Turkish resistance was considerable, the Russian steamroller was well oiled, and the Czar's armies moved within sight of Constantinople's countless minarets. The armistice of San Stefano with a badly beaten Sultan turned the Balkans into Russia's advance post. Bulgaria was to dominate the peninsula and Moscow was to dominate Bulgaria.

However, there was always an England, which quickly organized a countercrusade against the Czarist crusade. The western powers agreed with London that to bury the Ottoman Empire then would have precipitated a fight among themselves for the dead man's estate, and that they wanted to avoid. Nor could they afford to let Russia liquidate the Sultan's realm. Should the Ottoman Empire collapse and the Russians gain a foothold on the Golden Horn, the laboriously constructed balance of power would be upset. The Congress of Berlin "deflated" Bulgaria, showed Russia her place and wrote "finis" to another chapter of the history of the Straits.

Then in 1907 the radical change of fronts took place. For generations Great Britain contained Russia, keeping the "bear" chained to its cage. And now Russia was treated in London not as a "bear that walketh like a man," but like a man, even as a gentleman. The accord provided that the Czarist empire was to have its own sphere of influence in northwest Iran. At the same time British influence was to prevail in the southeast of that country. Between the two regions was a neutral zone, a buffer region.

What accounted for this incredible turnabout? Russia had been badly beaten in her war with Japan a few years before. A humiliated Russia was no danger to the British and also it would be more easily amenable to accept a satellite position in the global system of London.

At the same time Germany's strength grew, as she no longer had to fear the massive might of what the world had thought of as the Russian giant. The German Reich now felt it was her mission to be the dominant power on the European continent. That was precisely what the British did not want, fearful that the European balance would be upset. The dramatic change had its logical explanation.

Still, it aroused doubts about the intuitive power of diplomacy. Could not the British, with their well-organized diplomatic system and intelligence service, have foreseen that the Russian "giant" was stuffed with feathers? Why the deep-seated apprehensions about the "glacial strength" of the monumental Muscovite?

On the eve of the World War, the question of the Straits forged to the fore again. Bosom friends now with the Russians, the English reversed themselves and recommended strongly that the Straits should be neutralized. In the past they had always wanted to keep it wide open. Then they had the commanding position along the Dardanelles but now the Germans had the strongest positions in the region of the Straits. Reich General Liman von Sanders was the commander in chief of a Turkish Army corps in Constantinople. While the British had been watching the Russians, the Germans stole the show. Neutralizing the Straits would have also neutralized the Germans.

The World War broke out before this idea could be further pursued. Nominally Turkey remained neutral at first. A few days after the outbreak of the war the German warships, *Breslau* and *Goeben,* cast anchor in the Golden Horn. The Turks should have interned them, in accordance with the prevailing law of nations, but the Sultan's government did nothing of the sort. Instead of that, it "bought" the ships, which were given new names but retained their old crews. The Straits were now played into German hands.

The World War was no more than a month old when an incident of great import occurred just outside the Dardanelles. A British destroyer stopped a Turkish warship and forced her to turn back. The following day the Ottoman Empire closed the Straits to all ships. A month after this incident, the Turkish fleet, including the two Reich ships, went on maneuvers in the Black Sea. Without advance warning they began dropping shells on Russian ships and ports. The imperial government of Russia declared war on Turkey. For the entire duration of the war Russia was most effectively isolated, cut off from her western Allies. This was a disastrous situation. Russia in those days was still short of heavy industries, but long on man power. The western Allies, in turn, had those industries and they needed more men. Had they been able to supply Russia's inexhaustible reservoir of men, the strength of that country would have been bolstered.

In the second year of the war the western Allies sought to break this vicious blockade and they staged the tragic campaign of the Dardanelles. The Turks put up a spirited fight, led by the brilliant German High Command. The shore-based batteries of the defenders proved too strong against the challengers' ships that had to be provisioned from across the seas. The British suffered one of the most spectacular reverses of the war, in their own element, the sea, at the hands of a reputedly inferior enemy, the Turks.

Britain's great wartime leader, David Lloyd George, had to admit: "Russia and Rumania were not defeated by the German and Austrian armies, but by the Dardanelles. . . . These narrow Straits imperiled the chances of Allied victory. They certainly postponed the victory for probably two years."

A far more exciting drama was being played behind the diplomatic smokescreen, spectacular though the sea fight may have been. One of the most well-known rules of diplomacy is that the best time to take advantage of a friend is when he is hard pressed. That was the situation now. The British were fighting with their backs against the wall. This was the time when the Russian diplomats in their best cutaway suits turned up and pressing a revolver against John Bull's temple declared in a quiet voice:

"Give us the Straits or else. . . ."

They said that their country's morale must be bolstered. What were the Russians fighting for anyway? They had not been apprehensive about the Germans, whose policy was directed mainly against the British. Public opinion in Russia would be stiffened in favor of continuing the war to the very end if the country's legitimate demand for the Straits would be met. The Ottoman Empire was now siding with the foe and what would be more natural than that the Second Rome should be reunited with the Third Rome?

In the early spring of 1915, finally, Russia's secular dreams were to come true. An agreement over the Straits was reached between the British Secretary of State for Foreign Affairs, Sir Edward Grey, and Sergei Dmitrievich Sazonov, Russian Minister of Foreign Affairs. For the first time in the history of the relations of the two countries, Britain assented to the solution of the problem of the Straits in accord with Russian desires.

In this secret treaty the Russians were promised the Turkish capital on the Golden Horn and the adjoining territory facing the Bosphorus and the Dardanelles on the European and Asian sides. This was complete triumph for the Czarist regime, but the inscrutable fates again forestalled the consummation of the deal. After this tremendous diplomatic victory, Russia, fighting on the side of the victorious Allies, lost the war. The agreement about the Straits was published by the Soviet government almost as soon as it had seized the reins.

Beautiful Swiss Places

The war was drawing to its end and, innocently, America's President Wilson proclaimed in the twelfth of his Fourteen Points: "The Dardanelles should be permanently open as a free passage to the ships and commerce of all nations under international guarantees."

The "sick man," Turkey, was treated as if he were dead. The best parts of the heartland of the former Ottoman Empire were assigned to the victorious powers to rule, as spheres of influence or mandates. Only the mountainous core of Anatolia was to be retained by Turkey. The Straits were to be internationalized, but this provision never entered into force. The Turks rose against the peace settlement, defeated the Greeks, who were nearest at hand, and forced the Allies to rewrite the peace pact.

In the beautiful Swiss city of Lausanne a new treaty was signed in 1923. The region of the Straits was demilitarized; no fortifications or bases were permitted. A Commission of the Straits was established with jurisdiction over the area. If Turkey were threatened by war, France, Great Britain, Italy and Japan agreed to protect her. Merchant ships could use the Straits at all times, except for enemy vessels when Turkey was belligerent. Warships also had the right of passage in war and peace, except for enemy warships when Turkey was involved in war.

The international administration of the Straits continued until collective security and the League of Nations began to weaken under the revival of German and Italian strength. In the light of this situation, Turkey asked for a revision of the Treaty of Lausanne and this demand was heeded. The delegates met in the summer of 1936 in another Swiss city, Montreux. There were the usual banquets in their honor and informal excursions to the rocks of Naye, seven thousand feet above sea level. Lake Geneva was placid and the air invigoratingly cool. Beautiful scenery is recognized as a useful instrument for creating good will among the nations. Who could remain indifferent to such a gorgeous setting? Within the radius of a few hundred miles some of the happiest documents of diplomacy have been signed.

In keeping with the spirit of the place, the Turks were serene, but they were also firm. The Soviet delegates were grim, but they backed up their Turkish colleagues. In those days the U.S.S.R. and Turkey were known as the Siamese twins of the diplomatic world. It was Moscow's view that whatever benefited the Turkish friends was also good for the Kremlin. The English diplomats were flawless in dress and accent, but they were far more impressed by the Italians than by the scenery. They were inclined to like what the Italians disliked, and besides, they wanted to strengthen their fences in the East. In a world just on the edge of something pretty bad, Turkey's friendship could be courted by yielding on the matter of the Straits. After some horse-trading, the Montreux Convention was signed on July 20, 1936.

It was a victory for Turkey. The Straits Commission received its walking papers, and international control was terminated. The Turkish republic acquired the right to fortify the Straits. Some of the most important provisions of the Convention were the following:

In time of peace Black Sea Powers obtained the right to send warships through the Straits without limitation of number, type or tonnage except that they must pass in single line. This provision favored the Soviets, the most important of the Black Sea Powers.

The aggregate tonnage of vessels of war which outside powers were permitted to send into the Black Sea was limited to 30,000 tons, and any single power was authorized to dispatch only two-thirds of this total. Again this provision favored the Soviet Union by keeping the narrows closed to an unlimited tonnage of nonriparian nations. The stay of these outsiders was limited to twenty-one days in the Black Sea.

In time of war, Turkey being neutral, vessels of war were not to be allowed to pass through the Straits except in cases of aid rendered to a State victim of aggression in virtue of a treaty of mutual assistance binding Turkey. The validity of the convention was twenty years.

The More it Changes . . . .

Early in the Second World War, the period of the Stalin-Hitler co-operation, the Kremlin asked for a free hand in dealing with Iran. Also it was urging the Reich to let the Soviets also "share the responsibility" of gatekeeper at the Straits. When the war was over in Europe but not yet in Asia, President Harry S. Truman set forth the following thought in reporting on the Potsdam Conference among the major Allies in the summer of 1945:

> One of the persistent causes of war in Europe in the last two centuries has been the selfish control of the waterways in Europe. I mean the Danube, the Black Sea Straits, the Rhine, the Kiel Canal, and all the inland waterways of Europe which border on two or more States.
>
> The United States proposed at Berlin [Potsdam] that there be free and unrestricted navigation of these inland waterways. We think this is important to the future of peace and security of the world. We proposed that regulations for such navigation be provided by international authority. . . .

The war in Asia over, a new era began in the relations of the former Allies. The Montreux Convention was subject to revision in 1946, and the Potsdam Conference agreed that steps should be taken in that direction. The United States was the first government to act by presenting a note to Turkey on this problem. It suggested an international conference to seek a solution for the Straits problem on the basis of our four main principles which it set forth.

Merchant vessels were to be free to use the Straits at all times. As to the Black Sea Powers—and of these again the Soviet Union was the most important—not only their merchant vessels but also their warships could use the Straits at any time. On the other hand, non-Black Sea Power vessels of war could use the Straits only on United Nations authority, specific consent of the riparian powers and an agreed limited tonnage in times of peace. The Montreux Convention was to be modernized, the United Nations replacing the League of Nations and Japan eliminated as a signatory.

Reacting quickly, the British government accepted the American proposals as a basis for discussion. A few days later the Turkish government did likewise. Then the Soviets spoke up on August 7, 1946. They mentioned more details and what they said pleased neither the West nor the Turks.

The first three proposals of the Soviet note were substantially identical with the western proposals in regard to merchantmen and warships. The dynamite was packed in the last two proposals:

> The establishment of a regime of the Straits, as the sole passage leading from and to the Black Sea, should come under the competence of Turkey and other Black Sea powers.
>
> Turkey and the Soviet Union, as the powers most interested and capable of guaranteeing freedom of commercial navigation and security in the Straits, shall organize joint means of defense of the Straits for the prevention of the utilization of the Straits by other powers for aims hostile to the Black Sea countries.

What, indeed, could be more equitable than that the powers most vitally interested in the defense of the Straits should organize its defense? Great Powers like this kind of co-operation, forming a team between the lion and the lamb. Soon, of course, the lamb was to co-operate with the lion within the latter's stomach.

The United States did not think much of this suggestion and Great Britain echoed its remarks. The Soviet Union pressed the point. Now it took a historical view of the problem. During the

Second World War, it asserted, the neutrality of the Turks was against Russia. A bill of particulars was presented.

The Turks allowed the German patrol boat *Seefalke* to pass through the Straits on its way to the Black Sea in the summer of 1941, and this in contravention of the international pact which forbade the passage of belligerents' warships while Turkey was neutral. Not only that, the Kremlin charged, but Italian naval units were also permitted to pass through the Straits into the Black Sea, and the Soviet note mentioned specifically the Fascists' auxiliary warship, *Tarvizio.*

Yes, the Soviets said, during the war they had protested several times to the Turks against the violations of the Montreux Agreement but to no avail. There were the cases of the warships and auxiliary boats of the *Ems* and *Kriegstransport* classes, thirteen units of varying tonnage. During the war the Russians had also warned the Turks about the Germans' intention of dispatching 140,000 tons of auxiliary warships through the Straits as merchant vessels. These Axis troops helped the belligerents one-sidedly by participating in the Germans' naval operations.

To all of this the Turks answered that if anything of this kind had happened it was without their knowledge. They were not authorized to question a country's declaration about the nature of tonnage it was sending through the Straits. Under the Montreux Convention they had no right to inspect the vessels. If the Axis powers disguised warships as merchant vessels, the deception could not be detected. In order to prevent camouflage in the future, they suggested that the Convention should be modified by conceding them the right of checking the belligerents' manifests.

America's New Role

In connection with this very old problem, a new twist arrests the observer's attention. In the past it was Great Britain that took up the cudgel against Russia's attempts to smash the bottleneck of the Straits. This had been the historic struggle which had given rise to the Eastern Question.

The role of Washington in those days was almost nil. The pacts which Washington concluded with the Ottoman Empire in the last century were routine treaties of commerce and navigation. The United States was not a signatory of any of the treaties referring to the Straits in the interwar period: the treaty of Sèvres in 1920, of Lausanne, of the Convention of Montreux of 1936, even though the signatories included the names of Bulgaria, India and Japan.

The roles were reversed after the Second World War. Now it was the United States that took the first step in beating back the Russians on the diplomatic front. Usually, Washington made a proposal and a few days later London provided the echo. It was, no doubt, not the intention of the two English-speaking countries to demonstrate their changed roles. Just because it was unintentional, this illustration of the relative importance of the two countries in the matter of the Straits was tremendously revealing. Thus the United States assumed Britain's historic role in frustrating the Russians' warm-water thirst.

A historic change had taken place in world relations, and again many of the chapters of that change were written in invisible ink. What had accounted for Britain's part in the history of the Dardanelles? Obviously, the fear that should the Russians exercise the normal right of the stronger power against the weak, they would extend their sway to the approaches of the Straits, from which their huge shadow would fall across Britain's Mediterranean imperial lifeline.

The post-Second World War controversy revealed the fact that unbeknown to the rest of the world the Mediterranean lifeline was now that of the United States, part of the global lifeline fitted into the imperial structure of the country which was to be the guardian of the *Pax Americana.*

The *Pax Britannica* now belonged to the past. Was there still a British Mediterranean imperial lifeline? As a historic memory, perhaps, and as an auxiliary line. A dramatic change, indeed.

From a long-range point of view, was there any solution for the problem of the Straits? Supposing there was to be a change of regime in Moscow, replacing the Soviets by a different rule? Since the future is often revealed by the projection of the past into the present, what is it that we can learn?

Russia, since becoming a major power, has never been content with her role in the Straits. When history's real language will be deciphered—not the one people read in the books of literal-minded "historians," who see only the words and not the substance behind them—it may be found that many of the world's troubles have been caused because of Russia's great frustration.

The other major powers solved similar problems in a different way. Let us recall how Britain acquired Suez and the United States the zone of the Panama Canal. That was because both of them operated within the framework of the *Pax Britannica*, while Russia had to operate outside of it. There has always been an England and now there is a United States, successor to Britain's imperial heritage.

The Czars wanted the Straits, could not help wanting it because of the inner dynamism of Great Powers. The Soviets at first kept aloof from the Dardanelles and went so far as to support Turkey's claims. However, they, too, were to follow the pattern once they achieved Great Power status, not only in name but in essence, after the war.

In a change of regime in Moscow the final policy would depend upon its strength. Assuming, for argument's sake, that it would fit into the pattern of *Pax Americana* and would become the satellite of the West, it still would not be able to emancipate itself from the driving force it displayed under the Czars and the Soviets. Provided it was to accumulate an autonomous force of its own in due time.

What, then, is the solution of the problem of the Straits? There was much merit in the American proposal about complete freedom of movement of Black Sea Powers. The trouble is it would not work at the very time the largest Black Sea Power would need it most. The only way it could be made to work would be if relations between Russia and Turkey were friendly, as they were between the two wars under the regime of the founder of republican Turkey, Mustafa Kemal. At the present moment all one can say is this: History alone can tell if such a *modus vivendi* between the two nations may be re-established.

CHAPTER 5

The Imperial Lifeline—Suez

Two Monuments

At Port Said, northern entrance of the Suez Canal, there is a monument to its creator, the French diplomat and engineer, Ferdinand de Lesseps, a man who combined the unusual gifts of having great dreams and great executive gifts.

At the other end of the Canal there should be another giant statue, dedicated to the "Monumental Stupidity of Great Statesmen." In particular, it should be dedicated to the immortal Lord Palmerston who, as a practical statesman, did not permit himself to be deluded into daydreams about Suez Canals.

That such a project was an absurdity was well known in his day. In scholarly language scientists explained that there was a difference of twenty-nine feet in the levels of the Red Sea and the Mediterranean which the Canal was to link. Should it be cut, the waters of one sea would be dumped into the other with unforeseeable consequences. As a result, all of Europe might be engulfed in a tidal wave.

But assuming the absurd, if such a canal were to be cut, who should do the building? The Great Power that did not do it would feel its safety imperiled and there were always Great Powers and, above all, there was always Britain.

First, permission would have to be obtained from the Ottoman Empire, the nominal ruler of the region. It was then a huge body with hardly any brains, a modern dinosaur; not amenable to sense. It may have been amenable to the lure of gold, but where was one to get such a big pile? Then, too, the site of the proposed canal was in the midst of a forbidding desert and that created a couple of difficult questions: 1) how could a canal be built with no sweet waters for the builders; and 2) where was one to find the manpower?

Besides, what was wrong with the existing route, the one around the Cape of Good Hope, down West Africa, up East Africa? A king's ransom had been invested in that route, in its harbors, coaling stations, safety of navigation. Even if the canal route would be 5,000 miles shorter between Bombay and London, and even if around the Cape the trip took several weeks more?

M. de Lesseps, however, thought that it was an important part of human progress to shorten routes and bring people closer together, facilitating travel and the movement of cargoes. By thus shortening distance, travel and transportation could be cheapened. He talked so much about this project that some people thought he was a maniac. But others thought he was a genius.

Before seeing how this strange man fared, let us cast a glance at the Suez road in the past.

"I Am a Persian"

The Middle East of the past was so much the center that it was impossible to overlook this route. There had to be a link between East and West, and in those days there was no lifeline around Africa.

There was a Suez route in distant times, but it blended sweet water with salt, not salt with salt, as at present. The sweet water was the easternmost branch of the Nile, which was diverted into the Wadi Tumilat, a tributary of the Red Sea. Filled with Nile water all year round, the wadi—dry riverbed normally—was the missing link. Eventually, the canal silted up and it was for Darius the Great, the world conqueror, to have it restored in the year 521 B.C. as attested by a monument which reads:

> *I am a Persian and with Persia's power I conquered the the world. I ordered this canal to be dug from the river called Pirava [Nile] which flows into the land of Egypt to the sea issuing out of Persia [Red Sea].*

The work of Darius was overtaken by the fate of all canals in ages of decline, and in the first century of the Christian era it was supplanted by the "River of Trajan," as the Romans called it, remaining in use until the third century. Then Rome's hands faltered and Byzantium the fabulous, eastern Rome, took over. Its rule, too, was overtaken by the destructive hand of careless use by the time the Arabs arrived, in the seventh century. World rulers, they reopened the waterway under the name of "Canal of the Prince of the Faithful," which remained in commission until the end of the eighth century.

During the remaining centuries of Arab and, later, Ottoman rule there was no canal. However, there was an important East and West trade. The refined East provided the crude West with its spices and silk, jewelry and gems. These were transported via the great transversal highways of Persia and Anatolia. Later, also, the Red Sea was used, transshipping the goods across the Sinai peninsula to the Mediterranean.

On the western end of the road it was the Venetians and Genoese who carried on this trade. Then the destructive Ottomans severed this western lifeline, so that a new route to the Orient was needed. There were now more rich people in the Occident than before and they needed the eastern treasures.

It was for Vasco da Gama, the Portuguese navigator, commissioned by King Emmanuel I, to make the revolutionary voyage. When turning the tip of Africa, he drew good hope from that important fact. Reaching Malindi on the east coast, he set his sail across the Indian Ocean and reached Calicut. This was some six years after the discovery of America.

Thus was discovered the route to India around the Cape. Some people think that it was a rediscovery. Now it was Portugal and also England that were in favorable location toward the new route. Venice and Genoa found themselves in a blind alley, a dead-end street. The Low Countries also entered the contest for the Oriental trade. Finally, it was England's merchant adventurers that won the race.

Then Came a Frenchman

France had been both an Atlantic and a Mediterranean power, but with the discovery of the route of the Cape her importance in the latter sea had declined. One of her great ports, Marseille, once a Queen of the Mediterranean, was about to become a dead city, *città morte*. France had lost the battle for India, and lost India herself. The way to improve her position was by finding a speedier route.

There were enterprising French merchants to sail down the Mediterranean to Alexandria, then cut across the Nile Delta to Cairo, crossing from there to the Gulf of Suez on the edges of the eastern desert. However, this was a complicated operation.

It was natural for Frenchmen to turn their inventive minds to the idea of a better way. One of them advised the great Cardinal Richelieu that the Kingdom of France could regain her supremacy in the East by cutting a canal from Cairo to Suez, "such as had been effected under the ancient Egyptian Kings, and, perhaps, under King Solomon."

The restless brain of General Bonaparte also entertained this thought and he wrote to his acolyte and Judas, Talleyrand:

"The time is not far distant when we shall feel that in order to destroy England we must possess Egypt."

An Empire Dies

The Ottoman Empire was falling apart and first to go were her peripheries. In the first part of the last century the real ruler of Egypt was the viceroy, Mehemet Ali Pasha, an Albanian by birth, adventurous, ruthless, bold. Under his progeny the Ottoman Empire, nominal suzerain, retained tenuous threads on the land of the Nile. It was then that de Lesseps appeared on the scene.

Vicomte Ferdinand Marie de Lesseps was a member of a family of diplomats. His father Matthieu had been French consul general in Egypt. Ferdinand also entered the consular service and was assigned to a post in Cairo. It was in 1832 that he first thought of constructing a canal across Suez.

Because of an epidemic at the time of his arrival in Egypt, he was forced to spend several days in a quarantined ship outside Alexandria harbor. To while away the hours he read copiously, and came across a memorandum about a project of an isthmian canal across Suez. This plan set his fancy on fire, as he foresaw that its realization would help France, Egypt, and mankind in general.

A good many years passed before the first serious steps could be taken to implement the plan. The time was now the early fifties and the occupant of the French throne was Emperor Napoleon III, whose help was needed if de Lesseps wanted to do something about the canal. Several steps had to be taken previously, however.

De Lesseps found that there was, after all, no difference in the level of the two seas, so that there was no need for locks. He also found the solution of some of the thorniest problems, such as providing the working crews with water. The longer he immersed himself in the study of this question the more clearly he saw that the Suez Canal was feasible, and also that it would pay.

The first of the permissions he needed was that of Egypt. Should he be able to obtain it he would need an authorization from the nominal ruler, the Sublime Porte, in Constantinople. Since it was then under the thumb of Britain, he would have to work via London. In this diplomatic wire-pulling he needed the backing of his country's ruler. Then he would need funds, but . . . first things first.

Luckily for de Lesseps the viceregal throne of Egypt fell to that son of Mehemet Ali, Said Pasha, who was his personal friend. The new viceroy saw great benefits for himself and Egypt from the execution of the project of the canal. It would bring in additional trade and that meant revenue, and the chance to fill up the treasury coffers. More important still, the canal between himself and his Turkish masters would introduce a new strategic line of defense. In the year of 1854 he gave de Lesseps his consent to build the canal.

Next the Frenchman had to approach the Sublime Porte, but he knew that the real decision was in the hands of Lord Palmerston, who became Britain's Prime Minister the year after the viceroy's consent had been obtained. It was said of Palmerston that he held office with more general acceptance than any minister since Chatham.

Speaking on the subject of the canal in the House of Commons, Palmerston declared, "It is an undertaking which I believe as regards its commercial character, may be deemed to rank among the many bubble schemes that from time to time have been palmed off on gullible capitalists."

In the interview the Prime Minister had with de Lesseps he told him frankly that he was opposed to the canal scheme for yet another reason. Its building would promote the interests of France and therefore would be detrimental to Britain. But, he added with an air of assurance, the Suez Canal was not feasible from the technical point of view.

"Maniac" and "genius" that he was, de Lesseps surveyed the field with penetrating eyes. He had gone to Palmerston in order to get the Sultan's consent. The Prime Minister refused him pointblank and so he was going to Britain's capitalists. He sought to convince the merchants and shipowners of London that the building of the canal would be of greatest benefit to them, masters of the seven seas. The City of London remained unimpressed. Too much money had been invested in the route around the Cape. Also it considered the canal no more than a French cabal, an attempt to regain lost power and prestige.

To Napoleon III de Lesseps now appealed. The Emperor of the French was not the hated man in Britain his uncle had been. In order to lend this step more weight, de Lesseps also approached the "ruler of the rulers," the people; especially the people who could increase their weight by means of gold. He founded the Suez Canal Company, *Compagnie Universelle du Canal Maritime de Suez,* and offered its shares to the public.

The mythical "average" Frenchman is known throughout the world as a thrifty individual. However, he likes to have his fling when an exotic enterprise catches his fancy. In the days of de Lesseps and thereafter, the French *rentier* was known for his disposition to take chances overseas. The Suez Canal definitely caught the average Frenchman's fancy, and the offering of the shares was a notable success.

When a Frenchman invests his money in such an enterprise it is as good as giving his vote of confidence. Then he expects his government to back him up, if such a backing is needed.

Napoleon III was not the man to overlook a chance to increase his popularity and here was a clear mandate from the people, weighted with gold, to promote the interests of the canal company. What devious steps he took we do not know for sure. Probably he, too, operated through London. The fact is that in the year of 1859 the Sublime Porte granted de Lesseps and the Suez Canal Company the permission to build the canal.

While de Lesseps was right that no locks were needed in building the waterway across the desert, he ran into formidable difficulties because of the forbidding terrain, the insupportable heat of the summer days, the sudden drops of temperature at night, the force of desert wind and the shortage of potable water. One of the major operations was the building of a subsidiary canal to provide sweet water for the construction workers.

Only a man who was both a "maniac" and a "genius" could overcome the difficulties which man and nature placed in his way. There were tense moments when it seemed as if all the work were to go to waste. But the indomitable Frenchman saw to it that the obstacles were overcome.

Finally, in the summer of 1869, the waters of the Mediterranean and of the Red Sea mingled. It was a gala affair of worldwide significance. Where there had been only sand before there was now water, shortening the distance between East and West by thousands of miles. Heading the procession of distinguished craft was the imperial yacht *Aigle,* with the beautiful Empress of the French on board.

"Thus are realized the great hopes," the French official journal exulted, "which were entertained of this mighty undertaking, the joining of the two seas."

Failure in Success

The Canal was built; but was the great Palmerston to be right, after all, that this was not a viable financial venture but a superbubble scheme? The British did their best to make the Prime Minister's prophecy a reality, and their might was great. The Cape of Good Hope line was Britain's imperial lifeline, and Suez appeared to London to be no more than another French bid to beat a successful rival. In the midcentury world, British shipping was the most important and it could wreck the Canal by keeping aloof. Indeed, not more than five hundred ships used the Suez route in the first year of its existence and its revenue barely reached five million francs.

Then, in 1875, the dramatic event occurred that has been immortalized in many forms. The ruler of Egypt was now Ismail Pasha, who had the title of Khedive, and he was a spendthrift, in debt above his head. He had mortgaged nearly everything he had and was soon to mortgage his country as well. Before doing so, he still had his bloc of Suez Canal shares, a large part of which he had received in return for the concession. This was the largest bloc in the hands of one man, 176,602 shares, a 44 per cent interest in the company.

The Khedive's agents were in contact with a French syndicate in regard to the sale of this stock. At that point Lord Stanton, the British consul general in Cairo, got wind of these parleys and promptly sent a dispatch to the Foreign Office in London. He was able to notify Lord Derby, the Foreign Secretary, shortly thereafter that the khedivial shares could be obtained by Great Britain for a hundred million francs. There was the danger that the French syndicate was going to buy the shares and therefore the British government's answer was needed within twenty-four hours.

The Prime Minister of Great Britain was then Benjamin Disraeli, a man of vast imagination. He knew, of course, that in the past his country had been committed to the success of the route around the Cape, but he also knew that unless diplomacy were flexible it did not deserve its name. Disraeli certainly was flexible. Whether the City of London liked it or not, the Suez Canal was one of the world's most valuable waterways, shortening the way to India by thousands of miles and Britain was the world's greatest maritime power. It would be absurd to let the Canal definitely glide into other hands.

At that particular time, however, Parliament was not in session and money could not be had without legislative action. Disraeli could not be bothered with such small delays when confronted with a great emergency. He promptly turned to the greatest international financiers, the House of Rothschild, headed by such men as himself, who were not lacking in the power of imagination. Before the expiration of the twenty-four hour period, the money was advanced and the deal consummated. Britain now had the largest single bloc of shares in the Canal company. It turned out to be one of the best investments of the financial world. The mighty Palmerston, the man with the infallible intuition, had been completely wrong. The following year after the shares were bought, Disraeli went to the House of Lords with the title of the Earl of Beaconsfield.

Egypt Needs Protection

Ismail Pasha fell into the clutches of loan sharks and nowhere are they as inexorable as in the Middle East. The Khedive was unable to tell the difference between the public treasury and his own pocket, so that Egypt's finances became a madman's nightmare. Both Britain and France were now interested in Egypt. They acted in unison and deposed the Khedive. By what right, since nominally Egypt still belonged to the Sublime Porte? By the right that the Sublime Porte, in turn, belonged to Britain, and France was London's acolyte.

To be certain that nobody should think they meant to help Egypt, they replaced Ismail by Tewfik Pasha, his most ineffective son. Also, they introduced the system known in history as the Dual Control over Egypt's finances. That control was exercised jointly by Britain and France.

The control of the pursestring meant the control of the government and that was so also in Egypt. The next step would be the loss of independence and in that case Egypt would have no armed forces of her own. These were the considerations disturbing the thoughts of a group of Egyptian army officers headed by Ahmad 'Arabi Pasha, a cashiered colonel who sought to redeem himself by espousing a popular national cause. This was in the year 1882, a fateful date in the history of the Middle East.

'Arabi led the revolt against the European rule in Egypt. Fighting broke out in Alexandria and elsewhere; many lives were lost. It was 'Arabi's alleged plan to destroy the Canal. In order to forestall their action, the British landed troops. In distant Constantinople the shadow-Sultan stormed and fumed, impotent to act. France was embroiled in domestic brawls and was either too slow or did not want to take a hand. It was Britain alone that crushed the revolt, occupied Egypt and thus the Dual Control ended. England was now directly in the Middle East, not just pulling the wires of the Sublime Porte, which was sublime no longer.

The legal fiction of Ottoman overlordship in Egypt ended on the eve of the First World War, when Great Britain officially assumed protectorate over the land of the Nile.

The Canal is Free But . . .

A great international waterway should belong to all countries and not the one in whose territory it is situated . . . especially if that nation is weak, as Egypt was. The international treaty of 1888, known as the Constantinople Convention, provided:

> The Suez Maritime Canal shall always be free and open, in time of war as in time of peace, to every vessel of commerce or of war, without distinction of flag. Consequently, the High Contracting Parties agree not in any way to interfere with the free use of the Canal, in time of war as in peace. The Canal never shall be subjected to the exercise of the right of blockade.

Freedom of navigation was thus writ large over the gates of Suez. That meant freedom of navigation for the strongest maritime power—Great Britain. In agreement with the international covenant she kept the Canal open, closing it, however, when she deemed her interests to be imperiled.

Three years before the outbreak of the First World War, a German military expert, Paul Rohrbach, wrote:

> England can be attacked and mortally wounded only in one place and that is Egypt. The loss of that country means not only the end of her dominion over the Suez Canal and of her communications with India and the Far East, but would probably entail the loss of her holdings in Central and East Africa.

When the First World War broke out, Britain observed the letter of the Constantinople Convention, in that she did not order enemy ships to clear out of the waterway. It was Egypt, "protected" by Britain, which gave such an order. London was careful not to break the pact.

Several enemy ships, caught in mid-passage, sought the sanctuary of the Canal ports in reliance upon the Convention. However, the Alexandria Prize Court decided that the Convention was not applicable to ships using Port Said "not for passage through the Suez Canal or as one of the ports of its access, but as a neutral port in which to seclude themselves."

Because of this decision of the Prize Court, manned by the British, Britain's ships escorted enemy vessels that were trying to hide in the Canal, outside the three mile territorial limit, to the open sea, where they were free to escape. However, the escort vessels were always faster than the quarry, so that the latter's freedom did not last long. Yet the letter of international law had been observed.

During the First World War the Ottoman Empire attempted to establish itself along the Canal but was chased off. Throughout that war the waterway played an important role in the Allies' schemes.

In the hectic interbellum years the Canal was kept open even when Italy used it for her invasion of Ethiopia. Britain did not like this Fascist adventure which upset the African balance. Yet the British did not close the Canal to Italian ships carrying arms and men. In those days London thought that the Fascist dictators could be appeased.

During the Second World War the western gate of the Suez Canal was slammed in the Allies' face. The Mediterranean became a closed sea, *mare nostrum,* of the Axis powers. Axis dominance severed the trans-Mediterranean British lifeline, and the Allied world had to revert to the alternate route around the Cape. Their vessels had to carry their heavy loads down the coast of Africa, then up again along the eastern coast, into the Red Sea and Egyptian Allied Middle East command supply centers. Or they had to tote the goods into the Persian Gulf, and from there via trans-Iranian railway to the Caspian, there to link up with the Soviet transportation system.

The Suez Canal Today

The Suez Canal of today is somewhat "bigger and better" than was Lesseps' ditch. It has now a depth of thirty-four feet and is to be deepened two feet more in order to make it available for the world's largest ships. Its width on the surface is about four hundred feet, and half of that at the bottom. Two-way operations are to be facilitated by means of a bypass of seven miles. The Canal is a little over a hundred miles long.

The Canal company turned out to be a gold mine which has paid for the construction, administration and maintenance many times over. In one fairly typical year, for instance, after the Second World War, the company paid $32 in dividends on $50 nominal share value. In 1948 some 55 million gross tons passed through the canal, compared with Panama's 29 million. Two years later traffic through Suez rose to 82 million tons. Of these, 64 per cent was due to Persian Gulf oil tankers and little Kuwait alone provided nearly 10 million tons of the total haul. Many people were wondering what would happen to canal traffic with the opening of the great transdesert pipeline. The partial answer was given in 1951, when the canal tonnage declined to 76 million tons. This was still a highly impressive figure.

Egypt has received disappointingly little of the Canal bonanza. Under the original concession she was to receive 15 per cent of net profits, but she ceded that right for a small loan many years ago. Even now she has only an inconsequential stake in the company's financial success, being entitled to the pittance of 300,000 Egyptian pounds a year and 10 per cent tax on the dividends. However, Egypt's products are exempted from Canal tolls, and small boats up to three hundred tons may use the waterway gratis. Naturally, most of these are of Egyptian registry. This does not mean much, though, since Egyptian tonnage was only 0.3% of the total in 1950. The employees of the company, most of whom were foreigners in the better-paid positions, are to be replaced by Egyptians. The number of the Egyptians on the board of directors was to be increased.

The Aqaba Canal

The Suez Canal concession expires on November 17, 1968, after which the sole right to operate the waterway will revert to Egypt. The concession may be renewed, of course, but unless conditions change radically before then this is not likely to happen. The nationalist tidal wave that has struck the Middle East militates against the renewal of such arrangements. If the concession is not renewed, what happens to this lifeline of the western world? Also, will Egypt be able to operate the Canal?

It was doubts about the future that brought to the fore discussions about a parallel "ditch." It has been proposed to link the Mediterranean with the Red Sea via the Gulf of Aqaba, forming the eastern boundary of the Sinai Peninsula, of which Suez is the western boundary. The Aqaba Gulf bites deeply into the desert and offers the possibility of a parallel canal.

At the head of the Gulf stands the Jordan village of Aqaba, at the junction of four frontiers: Jordan, Egypt, Israel and Saudi Arabia. Very close to this village, which consists of about a hundred mud huts, is Israel's frontier settlement of Elath. It is that country's toehold on the Red Sea.

That Aqaba happens to be within the Hashimite Kingdom of the Jordan is due to a historic incident which casts light on the possible role of that sun-scorched village in the midst of a forbidden stone wilderness.

Aqaba's strategic importance is not new. In the Old Testament it was mentioned as the desert station which Moses passed with his people in their wanderings to the Land of Moab, from whence he was to set his eyes on the Promised Land. Aqaba was the port from which King Solomon was believed to have launched his many ships on an expedition to Ophir, where he was to extract the building material for his temple. After countless generations the crusaders built a castle there, the remnants of which are visible even today. This was at one time an assembly point for Mecca-bound pilgrims.

World history and this mean mud village renewed their kinship early this century when the nominal sovereign of most of the Middle East, the Ottoman Empire, claimed Aqaba, while Britain laid down the law that it belonged to Egypt, which was then British-protected.

During World War I the Turks did take the village for a time, ready to repulse their then British foe from the side of the sea. The attack came, instead, from the side of the land, under the leadership of Lawrence of Arabia. The land was then attached to Hejaz, under the rule of Sherif Husayn, nominal leader of the Arabs' desert revolt.

The tiny village thus became a pawn in a Big Power chess-board game. Egypt's relations with Britain cooled and the possibility of an alternative canal was canvassed. Coming from the desert, Ibn Saud contested Husayn's right to Hejaz and, at one point of the campaign, besieged him at Aqaba. Had he stormed into that village, he would have acquired a key position. But the British stopped him several miles away, in spite of the fact that they were on good terms with him. They were on better terms, evidently, with Abdullah, Husayn's second son. The frontier was drawn in such a way as to leave Aqaba within the newly constituted country of Transjordan.

The technical difficulties of cutting a canal from Aqaba to the Mediterranean are said not to be insurmountable. While the terrain is more difficult than the isthmus of Suez, it is not more rugged than the Panama zone. However, the Gulf approach to the proposed canal would present some problems. The entrance would have to be cleared of coral reefs, so that shipping could be protected from sudden squalls sweeping down from the bare boulders on both sides. Yet, the Gulf has a sheltered port near the rocky islet of Gezireh Fir'um.

The difficulties of building an alternative route today are greater because of politics. The shortest route belongs to Israel. There is no reason, of course, why that enterprising young country should not welcome a new canal entirely on its territory, having its Gulf of Aqaba entrance at Elath. Not much has been heard about this plan in recent times, indicating that it may have been dropped. However, it is an alluring plan, on which work may be resumed.

Funny Man Goha

In 1936, Britain released Egypt from her protection and in that year the two countries concluded the Anglo-Egyptian Treaty of Alliance, to run for a score of years. The British were authorized to keep a watchful eye over the security of Suez by stationing 10,000 troops and 400 airmen with the necessary staffs in the vicinity of the Canal. Naturally, no Egyptian troops were to "protect" any part of Great Britain so that the pact was not bilateral. "Absolute certainty that the Suez Canal will remain open in peace as well as war for the passage of British ships," said a prime minister of the United Kingdom between the two wars, "is the foundation on which the entire defensive strategy of the British empire rests."

Britain's way of putting off the final day of evacuation by pacts running for twenty years, reminded the Egyptians of a story. It is about the funny man Goha.

This funny character was in urgent need of cash and so he appealed to the Grand Vizier (Premier) with a most original idea. He proposed to teach that mighty person's mule to speak in ten years. In return for this remarkable feat he asked for a considerable amount of gold.

Intrigued by the offer, the Grand Vizier accepted it. However, he would not part with his gold without being sure that he was going to receive value for it and so he attached a string. He gave the gold to Goha, but if he failed to fulfil his part of the bargain and teach the Grand Vizier's mule how to speak, the string was to be used to hitch the funny man to the gallows.

Goha told Fatima, his favorite wife, about his luck. "Oh, you fool," she remonstrated, speaking up boldly, "you know very well nobody can teach a mule to talk."

"Who should know that better than I do, oh, you ass of a woman," the funny man replied. "But remember this: lots of things can happen in the ten years to me, the mule and, I most fervently hope, to the Grand Vizier."

Cairo did not want to wait for the expiration of the term, and in 1947 brought the case into the United Nations, maintaining that the validity of the 1936 treaty was superseded by the formation of the United Nations. That body was now available to safeguard the Suez Canal. Also, Egypt held, the maintenance of armed forces on the territory of a member nation was in violation of the spirit of the Charter.

The Security Council, however, did not agree with this argument. An international treaty, it said, was in force until its expiration date, and therefore the United Nations was not authorized to dissolve it.

Then, in the autumn of 1951, the Egyptian government startled the world with a solemn declaration that the treaty under which the British were maintaining their armed forces in Egypt was null and void. Also the Egyptian parliament declared the condominium status of the Anglo-Saxon Sudan at an end and proclaimed the reigning ruler, Farouk I, King of Egypt and the Sudan.

The British refused to recognize the validity of the unilateral denunciation of treaties. Serious riots broke out in the Suez Canal area and in Cairo, where frenzied patriotism made an alliance with the equally frenzied desire for loot. Famished farm workers who never received anything but kicks from their country died with the hallowed name of Egypt on their lips. The insensate intensity of these flash riots was appalling. The British rushed naval and air units into the Suez Canal zone. The government in Cairo took fright, clamped martial law on the country, resigned, and then was followed by a succession of cabinets. In the autumn of 1952 a military government took over, headed by Major General Mohammed Naguib, Commander in Chief of the Egyptian armed forces.

Not all of Egypt wanted the British out of the Canal zone. It seemed that an important sector of Egypt's ruling circles felt more confident when British forces were stationed close to the capital. The point had been reached when anything could happen in the land of the Nile.

What was the solution of the problem of the Suez Canal? The leading western powers announced that its security was of prime concern to the world. Recognizing the fact that the Suez Canal was a highly important international waterway, the guard on it should consist of several nations primarily interested in its safety: Egypt, Great Britain, the United States, France and Turkey, to begin with. Eventually other Middle Eastern countries would join in the defensive setup.

Great Britain subsequently presented another tentative idea to the effect that she was ready to evacuate the Canal Zone . . . but her experts in civilian status were to keep the waterway prepared for immediate action by the Allies in case of trouble.

This was reported by a major Alexandria newspaper under the heading: GENERALS IN MUFTI.

Then the still, small voice of Scandinavia was heard. Since the Suez Canal was such an important waterway, it said, and since the world now had the United Nations, serious consideration should be given to the United Nations. However, serious consideration was not given to the idea, perhaps because it was sensible.

Sudan Means Black

Suez and Sudan have been bracketed together in recent times. When the Egyptian government abrogated the Anglo-Egyptian pact about Suez, it did likewise with the 1899 treaty under which the Sudan had been given a joint rule, or condominium. In this case that meant that while Egypt helped to govern the region in name, real power was wielded by Britain. The system worked this way:

Great Britain recommended and the King of Egypt "appointed" the Governor General of the Sudan. Throughout the more than half a century of "joint rule" the Governor General has never been an Egyptian, always a Britisher. As a salve for wounded Egyptian national feelings, the green banner of Egypt, with the white crescent and the three stars, was waving next to the Union Jack over the Governor General's residence at Khartoum.

Sudan is one of the larger countries of the world with a territory close to a million square miles. Its estimated population is about eight million. Her annual revenues amount to less than sixty million dollars, and her expenditures even less. The Sudan is a poor country, so Britain's interest cannot be accounted for by this African country's wealth. The only major export item which her chamber of commerce—if she had one—could advertise would be gum arabic, a small item in total world trade. Nor does Britain make a profit by trading with the Sudan—the amounts are too trifling. The condominium is not profitable enough to create a strong vested interest among colonial administrators.

The Sudan is a hard country, with endless wastes of tropical deserts and mosquito-infested swamps in the region of the Nile. Most of her inhabitants are low-level subsistence farmers, primitive cultivators, semi-nomads, tribesmen, mere food gatherers and huntsmen. In the western wastes of Kordofan the local population still lives on an incredibly low level. Some of them may but recently have been weaned from cannibalism. The native king (*ret*) embodies the ancestors' spirits in the more backward regions. It is not because of their physical valor that these kinglets are feared but because of the occult powers attributed to them and which they are believed to have inherited from their ancestors. Should the kinglet fail to deliver the badly needed rain for the wilting crops, the incensed subjects feel free to cut him down. The god that has failed is a god no more.

Slave trading was lively in some of the backward regions, beyond the reach of central authority. Both the prospective slaves and the slave traders inhabited the same country, the slaves living in the south and the traders in the north. British authority has exterminated this nefarious occupation.

The north of the Sudan is an extension of the vast Arabic world, where the leading language is Arabic and the majority of the people worship Allah. The southerners, on the other hand, are mainly negroid or Negroes, speak native tongues unrelated to Arabic and worship the forces of nature. This region cuts right across the heart of Africa and straddles the great divide between black and white. Just because it is a black and white country, there is danger that it might fall into the hands of the one or the other, with highly unfavorable consequences for some of the people. That is one of the reasons the British believe they are performing a mission there as umpires and not as one of the contestants.

Two Sides to the Same Story

The greatest natural wealth of the Sudan is the Nile. "The land of the Nile is one valley," said an Egyptian premier in 1952. "What Allah has united let no man tear asunder." Allah has given the world the miracle of the Nile, the Egyptians say, but man can undo His handiwork and turn the world's richest land, the Delta, into a howling wilderness. Like a wild animal in the bush, the desert is crouching to reclaim its realm from the water.

The Egyptians say that the power holding the Sudan can force them on their knees in at least two important ways. First, it can impound the water for its own use, employing that most essential of all resources with no regard to the vital needs of Egypt. Also, a power occupying the Sudan can divert the water of the river. This the British have already done below Khartoum the Egyptians claim, where the waters of the Blue and White Niles meet.

Secondly, Egypt would be completely at the mercy of the unfriendly masters of the Sudan in a time of war. The threat that the waters of the Nile will be diverted would be sufficient to compel Cairo to do Khartoum's bidding.

Furthermore, the Egyptians say that they need the Sudan on which to settle their surplus population. Egypt is overpopulated, whereas the Sudan is underpopulated, they continue. Within fifty years the population of Egypt has increased from two to twenty million and if it keeps growing at this rate, millions are bound to die.

The Egyptians also say that the British are using the Sudan as a raw-material-producing country, that they have done little to educate the native population and to train a native-born higher officialdom.

The British point of view is, of course, diametrically opposed to that of the Egyptians. The Sudanese people live far better than the Egyptians, and this in spite of the fact that the former occupy a more backward part of the world, the English administrators say. It is also intimated that the extremes of wealth and poverty prevailing in Egypt do not exist in the Sudan. This latter country is not the land of disease and poverty.

The British further state that they must ask the Sudanese what they want; they cannot dispose of their fate. They also point to the fact that British blood was shed in order to free the Sudan from tyranny in the latter part of the last century. It was mostly the British, under the martyred "Gordon Pasha" (a reincarnation of "Chinese Gordon" of Taiping revolutionary fame) who fought the berserk Fuzzy-Wuzzies of the fantastic

Messenger of Allah, the Mahdi, who had proclaimed himself the Messiah. Eventually, Britain delivered the Sudan from these fantastic hordes.

There are certain arguments which Britain cannot advance. The Sudan is a keystone of the imperial edifice extending from one end of Africa to the other. If it were to be removed, the entire structure might topple into dust. Nor can the British come out openly with another problem. Once they leave the Sudan, the Egyptian office-seekers would move in and that would be the locust plague. What would happen to the Sudanese who have loyally co-operated with Britain? They would be penalized under the new regime for their faithful service to Great Britain.

What About the Natives?

It is hard to speak about articulate public opinion in the Sudan, where no more than 12,000 people are newspaper readers. One must bear this fact in mind when appraising the importance of the country's political parties.

The picturesque name of one of these groups was *Ashiqqa,* Blood Brothers, also known as the "National Front." This group favored an autonomous Sudan under the Egyptian crown. Its head was Sayyid Sir Ali el Mirghani, a strong personality who was also a religious leader. The followers of this group were drawn mostly from the north, where the influence of the Egyptian Arab was strong. This was probably the larger of the two main groups. Generally, it was supported by the merchants and the townsmen.

The other group was known as the Nation, *Umma,* and also as "The Independence Front." It sought independence, but, realizing that the Sudanese lacked as yet nation-building qualities, was ready to work with the British. The followers of this group wanted no Egyptian King even as the head of an autonomous Sudan. Their leader was Sayyid Sir Abrdur-Rahman el Mahdi, posthumous son of the late "Messiah" (Mahdi), and he too was a religious leader. His followers originated mostly in the South, and they were more typically African than Arab. Pivots of this group were the influential cattle and camel men. Their opponents called them British puppets.

The Sudanese legislative assembly was largely under the influence of this British-sponsored party. After Egypt's unilateral action, the assembly passed a self-government law providing for an elected bicameral legislature and a responsible all-Sudanese government. However . . . and there is nearly always a "however" in connection with such plans, the law also provided for certain "safeguards" in the form of powers reserved to the Governor General. The Sudanese keystone was not to be knocked out of the British imperial structure after all. *Self-determination of the Sudan by the end of 1953* was the motto of the dominant group in the legislative assembly.

After the ousting of King Farouk, the problem of the Sudan continued to bedevil Anglo-Egyptian relations. Finally, the British had the *Umma* party draw up a Constitution which they approved. Elections were to be held in the Sudan out of which was to come an all-Sudanese government which was autonomous in domestic affairs, subject to certain veto powers in the Governor General's hands. In foreign affairs, the British government maintained that the Anglo-Egyptian condominium continued, and, in the words of the London Foreign Office, "responsibility for the external affairs of the Sudan belongs as before" to Egypt and Britain. General Naguib, in turn, reached an agreement with the Sudanese liberation parties under which neutral commissions were to be formed to supervise elections. Then, a period of three years of self-government in the Sudan was to be followed by self-determination on the issues of complete Sudanese independence or some link with Egypt.

The differences between the British and Egyptian versions of the solution of the problem of the Sudan were to be ironed out.

What was the solution of the problem of the Sudan? There appeared to be no warrant for the belief that the Sudanese could govern themselves effectively or that Egyptian administrators would have been superior to the British ones. Yet the fact could not be denied that Sudan's master could easily become Egypt's master as well. One solution would have been the formation of the supranational Nile River authority comprising the regions that depended upon that miraculous stream.

The first step in that direction may have been taken when the British and Egyptians agreed on creating a vast irrigation project to harness the silty waters of the Nile. Under this plan a new irrigation dam was to be built in the Sudan and an existing one was to be raised, both for irrigation and flood control. Egypt was allotted more Nile water for irrigation so that her arable land could be increased to ten million acres within twenty-five years. Another plan called for the building of a hundred-mile drainage canal in southern Sudan's Sudd swamps. Meanwhile, the British had been building large water power dams at Owen Falls and Lake Albert, in their Uganda colony. With the completion of all these projects, which might take a quarter of a century, almost the whole of the Nile would be harnessed.

CHAPTER 6

People From Afar

A Synthetic People

"The Arabs are a manufactured people," said T. E. Lawrence, leader of the First World War desert revolt.

All people are, of course, manufactured, but the Arabs, perhaps, a little more than the others.

Three great groups inhabit the Middle East: Semites, Iranians and Turanians. The largest is the group of the Semites, most of whom are Arabs. They are Arabs not for ethnic reasons, since they belong to many "racial" groups: Dinaric, Alpine, Mediterranean, Nordic. They are Arabs because they speak Arabic, a Semitic language. There is another, smaller group of Semites in this region, the Israeli, who have revived and modernized their ancient Semitic language, Hebrew. But first, let us turn to the manufactured people.

The original Arabs were the people of the Great Quadrangle, a desert folk who erupted into the sown area of the Middle East in the seventh century and imposed their tongue and many of their ways upon most of the Mediterranean world. We have seen them sweeping across the top of Africa, crossing the Straits of Gibraltar into Spain, vaulting the Pyrenees in an apparently irrepressible urge of world conquest. We recall that Professor Toynbee speculated on what would have happened to our western world if Charles Martel had succumbed at Tours and Poitiers. In that case, would this book have been written in Arabic?

Upon the conglomerates of ethnic groups left in the wake of the suppressed western cultures Arabic was superimposed. Today's Egyptian is an Arab because he speaks Arabic and because of his Arab ways of life. He may be called "derivative Arab" to distinguish him from the "original Arab," coming from the original homeland of the Arab world, the Arab peninsula.

His ancestors may have been the pyramid builders, who were not Semitic but Hamitic; or soldiers in the armies of Alexander the Great, who were not Semitic either but were "Aryan" Macedonians; or soldiers of one of the armies of Persia—Iranians and considered among the original Aryans.

The Lebanese is Arab, too, for the same reasons. Yet, his eyes may be as blue as those of the Scandinavians and his ancestors may have come from Europe's north. The bones of those ancestors may be moldering within the confines of Acre's crusading fort. For all we know, there may be more Greek and Roman blood in Lebanon than Arab, or for that matter, Jewish blood; but most of today's Lebanese consider themselves Arabs. They and the others—Syrians, Jordanians, Iraqi, Saudi Arabians, Yemenites—regard themselves as Arabs belonging to countries with their own symbols of unity, national aspirations and common goals. The Saudi Arabians and the Yemenites only occupy sites of the "original" Arabs and yet their blood is mixed, too, with those of the people from Africa and the penetration of the influence of the Sown.

If it is the language that makes the Arab, do they all have a universal language? It would be too much to expect of a cultural group spread over many millions of miles, separated by some of the world's most forbidding deserts, living occasionally in such isolation as to defy comparison anywhere in the world. There is the Muslim's Sacred Writ, the Koran, which might serve as the language base. However, there are many non-Muslims among the Arabs. Also, the relation of the Koran to the spoken tongues is similar to that of Latin to the "vulgar" languages of Italians, Iberians and the French.

Moreover, in the Arab world there is not only a horizontal difference among the dialects, depending upon the territory, but a vertical one linked with the social classes. It makes a world of difference if one learned Arabic in one of the modern schools of Lebanon or in a one-class village school or no school at all. People on different educational and financial level just do not speak the same language, even though they are next-door neighbors. One cannot really speak of a common heritage of language throughout the Arab world. However, one can speak of related heritage and, perhaps, common cultural aspirations. When the "Voice of America" speaks to the Arab world, it employs "literate" Arabic, a compromise between the classical and colloquial —which it hopes many people will understand.

Language is the dividing line we draw among the Middle Eastern people. Related to Arabic is Hebrew, which modern Israel has revived. It had to be streamlined, of course, to be able to express such modern concepts as jet planes and atomic bombs. Today it is the living language of hundreds of thousands and the only tongue which many members of the younger generation speak. This revival of an ancient tongue is a unique accomplishment in the contemporary world. The Irish have tried it, too, but one cannot say that Gaelic has become the majority's living language.

Biblical Hebrew was related to Phoenician, Aramaic, and Assyro-Babylonian. Jesus and his contemporaries spoke Aramaic but read the Bible in old Hebrew. Hebrew is also a Semitic language and it is derived from *'Ibhri*, people from across the river, while the name of Jew was derived from *Yehudi,* he who belonged to Judah after the Babylonian exile.

There is boast in the name of the Turk, which means "power" and, strangely, also "maturity." We can see him flexing his muscles so as to frighten the weak into submission. The Turkish tongue was born in the heart of Central Asia, in the vast land we today call Sinkiang, Soviet Kirghizia or, perhaps, Kazakhstan. Unlike the Arabs, who came from the southeast, the Turks came from the northeast, in relation to the present site of their republic. In the spread of Turkic tongues we may detect the historic march of that martial race, all the way from the Balkans to distant Siberia, spanning the enormous distance of 140 degrees.

The language the Turks speak is not Semitic but Ural-Altayan, which once was called Turanian. In the Turkish tongues a comprehensive scheme of vowel attractions governs the euphonic interest, so that they are melodious. Oddly, this sweet-sounding tongue seems to have never created great poetry of internationally recognized merit. The Turks were a warrior folk and were not dedicated to a delicate way of life. Neither were the Arabs, and their language sounds much harsher; yet they have produced poets of great merit.

The hallmark of the Turks has never been cultural creativity. They never had an alphabet of their own but adopted the Arabs' script probably at the time they embraced Islam. It is also typical of the Turks that they were able to cast off this script at the stroke of a pen after the First World War. Then they adopted the Latin alphabet, a practical and withal symbolic move, to express a complete about-face from East to West. No Arab reformer would have dared to take a similar step, or if he had dared to do so, his success would have been doubtful. The reputedly most revolutionary regime of the twentieth century, the Soviets, made no attempt to tamper with their cumbersome Cyrillic script.

The Iranians are the only major people in the Middle East speaking a language like our own English. It is called "Farsi," from which the word "Persian." It is an Indo-European or Aryan tongue. The latter word means "noble," "aristocratic," and it may have been in that sense that demented racial "experts" were trying to employ a linguistic term for ethnic use. There is a controversy as to where Persian originated. Some say it came from the Caucasus range, between the Caspian and the Black Sea, spreading to East and West, encompassing also India and Iran. Others maintain that the home of prehistoric Aryan must have been Central Asia, moving from there into Europe, Iran and India.

In exceptionally rugged countries, and Iran is one of them, linguistic differentiation is bound to be great. The cultural elite in Iran speaks a literary Persian which is linked to the southern type of Middle Persian. On the peripheries of the land a variety of languages are spoken. Toward the East, the people speak an Iranian variant, *Pushtu,* which is also the dominant tongue of adjacent Afghanistan. The supremely individualistic Kurds in the western mountains, spilling over into Iraq and Turkey, speak another Persian dialect. In the northwestern corner of the country the dominant language is neither Iranian nor Arabic, but *Azerbaijani,* which is a Turkic tongue.

Since the Iranians occupy one of the Old World's most important crossroads, they had to be hospitable to other languages. Many American and British soldiers working on the Trans-Iranian Railway returned home with the mistaken notion that Iran's language is Arabic. That was the language they heard in the port cities, and in much of the oil country of the Zagros range. Iranian, too, employs the Arabs' script and, naturally, absorbed many Arab words.

We have seen that there are many Arab countries in the Middle East, with a total population estimated at some forty million. We have also noticed that the dependent Arab world extends far west in Africa, much farther west than the longitude of Paris.

Why are there so many Arabias and not just one? The late T.E. Lawrence of Arabia wrote:

> Some of us judged that there was latent power enough to spare in the Arabic peoples (the greatest component of the old Turkish empire), a prolific Semitic agglomeration,

> great in religious thought, reasonably industrious, mercantile, politic, yet solvent rather than dominant in character. They had served five hundred years under the Turkish harrow, and had begun to dream of liberty; so that when at last England fell out of Turkey and war was let loose in the East and West at once, we who believed we held an indication of the future set out to bend England's efforts toward fostering the new Arabic world in Hither Asia.

The Middle East was in parturition then, and might it not have been possible to weld all the Arab regions formerly under Ottoman rule into one country? The trend of the times favored greater integration. This was the age of large units—mammoth corporations, large nations, everything big. Many of the articulate Arabs favored a pan-Arab Commonwealth. The British might have found one satellite easier to handle than half a dozen. Yet, a pan-Arabia did not come into life.

A United Arabia needed an Arab George Washington, a Simon Bolivar, a Great Unifier, to serve as an organizer and as a symbol.The Sherif of Mecca, the nominal leader of the Arab desert fight, was not a born leader of men. Other countries beside Britain claimed a voice in the determination of the fate of Hither Asia, and France was aggressive. The process of disintegration began right there. The Arab leaders were not very sure what they wanted, either. As soon as vested interests were created in the formation of several countries, the best chance for union was lost.

Unity in the Middle East is also disturbed by the presence of numerous nationalities. In certain enclaves these "minorities" form majorities. As is to be expected, most of them occupy difficult mountain terrain, nature-made sanctuaries of dissidence. There these splinter groups have perpetuated themselves in the face of great pressure and also of frenzied religious intolerance. Where the conforming trend of the creed failed to achieve its aim of unification, it seems as if the nations of today were going to be more successful. The modern nation is the great unifier, the enemy of nonconformism.

Before looking at the majority groups of the Middle East, let us cast a glance at the minorities. At the intersection of Turkey,

Iran and Iraq we encounter the Balkans of the region. Where the shape of the mountains becomes less intractable we come across the "Macedonia of the Balkans," where cultural disaffections are fermenting.

The Balkans of the Middle East

Largest of the minorities are the Kurds, occupying the border regions of Turkey, Iraq and Iran. Modern regions have no place for minorities and so the Turks call their Kurds the Mountain Turks, while in Iraq there is a tendency to call them Mountain Iraqi. Yet they speak neither Turkish nor Arabic, but a variety of Persian mixed with words they have picked up in their unfriendly setting, together with execrable manners.

The Kurds have memories of independence in the mistiest of dim pasts when anarchy ruled the mountains and a pair of ruthless hands meant might and fief. In the fog of contradictions the origin of this ancient race is lost.

There are perhaps four million of them, a number to justify the existence of a country of their own. Jordan and Lebanon have smaller populations. There was an attempt to create a Kurdish nation when the "self-determination of nations" was a rallying call after the First World War and when nationalism ran wild. Since then there have been only traces of nationalist self-assertion among the Kurds. It is believed this was in response to the Kremlin's call. The Kurds are ready-made "subversive elements."

Kurdish manners are bad. The manners of people constantly kicked around and treated like dogs must degenerate. The Kurds' villages are often built into crags and from afar they look like nests of prehistoric monsters. They look down upon some of the world's most ancient trade routes, which have served as constant temptations for mountaineers. Living on poor land, they wanted to improve their fare by pouncing upon the caravans. They became not the Robber Barons but the Robbing Beggars of the East.

This kind of life helped them to develop a fierce spirit of independence. They were preying not only on the caravans but also upon the weaker groups in their midst. This prevented the crystallization of a spirit of unity upon which a governing class could impose itself, bringing about collective action.

They were roughly handled by the Ottoman Empire under the heels of which they lived for many centuries. As the Empire's hands began to falter, the Kurds caught a glimpse of a better day. While unable, because of their disunity, to start kicking the Sultan, they did create a problem for the not-so-Sublime Porte.

The Sultans thereupon resorted to a well-known device: that of turning the footpads into gendarmes. Constantinople appointed the lawless Kurds the guardians of mountain law and order. They were free to prey upon their industrious Christian neighbors, the Armenians. The Kurds are Muslims and it was represented to them that by slaughtering the Christians they were collecting merits for their entry into the blissful Seventh Heaven. Besides, they had a good opportunity to collect a lot of loot.

A large number of the Kurds graze their herds on the summer grass of the high mountains, driving them into the valleys with the arrival of the autumn rains. We have encountered this vertical nomadism under the name of transhumance. In the hill country they are on their native land, but in the valley they are on the sufferance of settlers from whom they either buy or extort the right of pasturage. During the annual migration the caravans march under the supervision of sheykhs, supported by savage-looking strong-arm men who see to it that the despoilers are not despoiled.

Christians are Fair Game

Unlike the Turks, the Armenians are a very old people in the Middle East. Their original habitat was probably to the south of the Caucasus range.

"And Noah was five hundred years old: and Noah begat Shem, Ham and Japheth." Because a grandson of Japheth was named Haikh, the Armenians call their country Haiasdan. The dynasty of "Haikh" was said to have ruled over it until Alexander the Great came along. "The Armenians are perhaps the oldest established civilized race in Western Asia," Professor Toynbee wrote

in a book about the Armenian massacres. The Armenian Kingdom is said to have been the first organized community in the world to embrace Christianity. Their chief habitat was the jagged mountain region in eastern Turkey over which Mount Ararat soars. It is the country of the district of Lake Van, the largest in Turkey. Armenian land sprawls across the Soviet boundary, midway between the Black and Caspian seas, south of the Caucasus range.

They lived in peace in their mountain country, they say, long before man began to record his history. Their hills looked down upon the valleys which were the natural highways between Europe and Asia, and so they were brought into close proximity with trade. Also, they became a highly mixed people. They speak an "Aryan" language; but many noses in the hills are hooked, which ignorance mistakes for a sign of "Semitic" origin. These noses are Oriental because the Armenians are an Oriental people. In the mountains the peasants are usually tall and handsome while in the valleys they tend to be short and thick-necked. Most of them are swarthy-skinned and straight black hair prevails.

The Armenian minority formed a Christian island in the Muslim world. All around them mankind embraced Islam, but the Armenians' loyalty to their church remained unshaken. They are not Roman Catholics, nor are they Orthodox, nor have they ever been in communion with Russia's official church. They are Gregorian Catholics.

The "Rome" of the Armenian Gregorian Church is the town of Ejmiadzin, and there is the seat of the Supreme Pontiff, Catholicos. He touches the candidates for the bishop's office with the holy hand of Saint Gregory, one of the most sacred relics of early Christian times. With his own hands he prepares the holy oil employed in the Armenian church service. Three times the baptized are plunged in the font to commemorate Christ's three days of entombment. During the Mass the priests' acolytes rattle a cross with jangling rings—once called Queen Cleopatra's war trumpet because she is said to have used it in a decisive battle. This strange instrument looks like an Egyptian sistrum and may have been a device originally used to exorcise evil spirits. The Armenian clergy may marry, but the monks are celibate. The priesthood stands in much higher esteem than the Russian clergy did in czarist times.

The language of the Armenians sets them apart, too. It has no kinship with Turkish but is Indo-European. In the Ottoman Empire they and the Greeks, as well as the Jews, were traders. To stoop to trade, finances or arts and crafts was degrading to the Turks. Islamic fatalism further accentuated the difference. Heavenly rewards must be earned on earth, the gentle Armenian believed.

"The Armenian Nation"

The Armenian question was unknown in Turkey until the later nineteenth century. For hundreds of years the Turks made no attempt to suppress the Armenians, allowing them to form an *Ermeni Milleti,* Armenian nation, as they allowed other Christian groups to do likewise, so as not to have to besmirch their hands by having to deal with the infidel dogs. The Armenians had their own constitution in those days and their own national assembly. The two and a half million Armenians were at the crest of their good fortune when disaster overtook them.

As the Ottoman Empire was falling apart, Sultan Abdul-Hamid II, who ascended its throne in 1876, needed a scapegoat. The Armenians were Christians and many of them were prosperous. Obviously, they were the cause of the downfall of imperial Turkey. "The way to get rid of the Armenian question is to get rid of the Armenians," said Abdul-Hamid. It was in the Russo-Turkish War of 1878 that the Armenian Question first became an international issue. The Russians occupied a part of Armenia, along with other Turkish territory. In the Treaty of San Stefano they forced the Ottoman Empire to guarantee the security of the Armenians against the Kurds. This made the Turks extremely suspicious. They would have called the Armenians "Fifth Columnists" if the term had been familiar to them. But they were familiar with its meaning.

The Great Powers interfered at this point. This was one of the exit gates by which the Russians wanted to get closer to the south, while the English were obsessed with Russia. St.

Petersburg thought it was a good idea to have a Christian minority in Turkey serve its aims. The Armenians were not schooled in the duplicities of the Foreign Offices. They thought they would get Great Power help if they organized themselves for self-defense. It would be better for them to have an organization in case the Ottoman Empire fell apart. They formed a revolutionary organization, *Hunchak,* in Turkish Armenia. The Czarist government thought this was a very good idea and so it helped the formation of the Armenian *Dashnak* society in Russia, teaching refugees how to carry arms. The Ottoman Empire decided to teach the Armenians their place and the Kurds received word that loot and heaven, too, would be theirs if they sanctified themselves with Armenian blood.

The Armenian Massacres

The great Armenian massacres were the result. They occurred in the early years of the First World War. This is how the Armenians' own report explained the causes of the tragedy:

> The Ottoman Empire needed money for the prosecution of the war. She was the Ally of Germany, but the Reich itself was short of funds. The Armenians themselves were reputed to be the bankers of the Ottoman Empire. Many of them were rich, and the Germans were convinced that their wealth would tide the Turks over the first two years of the war.
>
> The Germans wanted the Turks to win the war with them, but not for themselves. They regarded the Turks as a decadent race which would always make a mess. After victory, they wanted to take their country over. The Berlin-Baghdad Railway was merely the entering wedge. They believed that the Sultan's country could be made to yield huge dividends, and they wanted those dividends for themselves. By exterminating the Armenians they helped to stamp out prospective rivals in banking, industry and trade. The Armenian massacres were part of the preparation of the right of way for the Berlin-Baghdad line.

The great Armenian massacres took place during the First World War, when about half a million of these unfortunate people were slaughtered. Many saved their lives by sneaking across the frontiers, mostly into Russia. The final destination of most of the Armenians was the murderous deserts near Deir ez Zor in eastern Syria, their place of deportation. Many of them died on the road, and others after arriving there.

"On the road I found four little children," a missionary wrote. "Their mother sat on the ground, her back against the wall. The hollow-eyed children ran up to me, stretching out their hands, crying: 'Bread, bread.' When I came closer to the mother I saw she was dying."

"In one village," wrote a New York Armenian newspaper in the autumn of 1915, "a thousand Armenians were crowded into a wooden house, which was set on fire."

"Forty Days of Musa Dagh"

On the mountaintop of Musa Dagh, in the district of Antioch, within sight of the Mediterranean, a visiting American-Armenian, trapped in his native country by the outbreak of the war, organized the Armenians of the neighborhood in self-defense. The choice was either surrender, or deportation, which could mean death along the way. They decided to fight, and for almost six weeks they held out. Epidemics and starvation decimated their ranks, Turkish cannon and internal discord ravaged them. In the long history of man's struggle against overwhelming odds their heroism is almost without parallel, immortalized in Franz Werfel's *The Forty Days of Musa Dagh.*

Many Turks tried to save their neighbors, but few succeeded. The persecution was organized, the defense was sporadic. The Turks were indoctrinated to look upon their Armenian neighbors as their enemies' allies, saboteurs of the most pernicious type. Several Turkish officers refused to carry out orders, but they were replaced. Whenever the Turks quailed at so much butchery, Armenian papers aboard reported, the German soldiers had no scruples.

There are Armenian minorities scattered all over the Middle Eastern countries, in Syria, in Egypt and in a few cities of Turkey. Most of them however live in the Soviet Union and particularly in one of its component republics, the Armenian Soviet Socialist Republic.

After the Second World War that republic issued a call to the

Armenians abroad to return to their new homeland. More than anywhere else, the call was heeded in the Middle East. What was the reason for this call? The Kremlin may have wanted to produce a more densely populated Soviet Armenia in order to bolster its claim against Turkey for the return of the latter's northeastern districts, Kars and Ardahan. These belonged to the Russians between the Balkan war of the 'seventies and the end of the First World War. A large number of the population of the districts consisted then of Armenians. After that war the Soviets returned this region to the Turks in a gesture of good will toward a country which they considered their only friend. The friendship over, the Kremlin wanted to have its toys back.

Meanwhile, the Armenians continue to be the footballs of world politics.

He Who Gets Slapped

The number of Christians in the Middle East is estimated at three millions. One of the most harassed of these groups, although small in numbers, is the one calling itself Assyrian. Yet, it seems to have no links with that ancient race that practiced one of the most hideous of human crimes, race extermination, or genocide.

The modern Assyrians are also known as Nestorians, after the patriarch of Constantinople, Nestorius, whom the fifth century council of Ephesus condemned as a heretic for having taught his followers that the divine and human features of Jesus were joined in perfect harmony of action but not in the unity of a single individual.

The followers of Nestorius became one of the splinter creeds that tried to lose themselves in the Middle East mountains. They are still in the rugged hill country, their rudely built churches dimly lit, bare of images save the Cross, which they worship with the most devout veneration. A group of these mountain Christians, called the Chaldeans, entered into communion with the Holy See in Rome some centuries ago. As the language of their liturgy, both of these sects use Aramaic, the language Jesus spoke.

These non-Muslims, too, like many others, had their own

religious-political organization, the *millet* system, under the Ottoman regime, governing themselves within the limits set by the capricious Sublime Porte, but largely at their own discretion. Like most of the other non-Muslims, these Assyrians were not familiar with the modern concept of nation. They did not consider themselves nationals of the empire, but a "separate nation." As such they tried to make common cause with the enemies of their host country, and joined hands with Russians and the British. The Turks, however, did make a distinction, and when they caught Assyrians they slashed their throats, the punishment for traitors. Those, too, who were not working for the foe were captured and massacred, and at the sight of the mass massacre the civilized world recoiled with horror—but did little else.

The golden age was hailed among the Assyrians when the Ottoman realm collapsed. The Christian nations were triumphant and Christ was now the King of the Middle Eastern world. The Ottomans had invested the Assyrians with autonomy, and the Christians would surely give them their independence. Then the time would come for them to settle accounts with their Muslim neighbors.

Instead of that, Islamic countries were established, under Christian tutelage. Most of the Assyrians were assigned to the Kingdom of Iraq, which was a Muslim country. The British needed reliable native forces to keep the unruly Iraqi under control and the Assyrians filled the bill. The mandatory authorities assembled the Assyrian Levies against the rebellious Iraqi and they saved the British army from utter disaster, in the words of a British high official.

However, the time came for the Iraqi to gain their freedom and this happened in 1932. Freedom was hailed as a wonderful thing all over the country and people celebrated by massacring Assyrians. "I saw and heard many terrible things in a war," noted an English military observer, "but what I saw in Simel [scene of a massacre] was beyond human imagination."

About ten thousand Assyrians fled into adjacent Syria and there they had to battle harsh nature and even harsher neighbors. Some twenty-five thousand of them, however, remained in Iraq and there, again, tragedy struck during the Second World War.

Even after Iraq had gained her independence the British had the right to retain their armed forces in that country. At the height of Axis victory an ambitious Iraqi politician, Rashid Ali, launched a revolution against the British and their influence in the government. Again London called the Assyrian Levies into service and the rebel leader was crushed. "Few communities have shown more courage than the Assyrians," an English historian wrote, ". . . and their gallantry was duly rewarded by a long alternation of massacres and migration."

What is the solution for the Assyrian problems? They are suspect in the Middle East because of their association with the Christian powers. Also, the Assyrians are far from peaceful little lambs; they have been toughened and made ruthless by the many slaps they have received. Their number is too small to form a nation and their ranks are not serried.

The Mountain of Churches

Farther down the coast, Christianity came into the world groping for its light. What was the nature of Christ? This was the question which shook the Christian world from one end to the other end. The Son of God was consubstantial with the Father, of the same substance, the Nicene creed held. The other view held that the Son was essentially like the Father but was not identical in essence with him. The former view was that of the homoousian and the latter was homoiousian. In semantics the one letter "i" made all the difference, and what a difference it made!

There were other disagreements too, again mostly about the nature of Christ. A certain measure of uniformity was established elsewhere but not in the heart of the Middle East, so close to the scene of the great religious controversies, so close to the birthplace of the creed.

Nature provided the dissidents with a sanctuary in the form of the mountains of what is today the small republic of Lebanon, the highest in the region. The Lebanon Mountains are the mountains of churches and of countless creeds. Not far from these church-covered peaks the Apostle Paul was initiated into Christianity, at Damascus. At Antakiya, the former Antioch, St. Peter is said to have founded the first Bishopric.

This region became officially Christian early in the fourth century, when the Roman Empire embraced that creed. When the conquering Arabs subdued the Levant in the seventh century they encountered a predominantly Christian population. Many of them joined the victorious creed of Islam, but some of them remained steadfast to their fathers' faith. They sought refuge in the mountains and found a sanctuary there.

When the Crusaders had to yield to the dominant forces of the Middle East, many of the survivors must have found the mountains nature-made temples for their faiths.

One would have to go very far to find so many religious faiths as in the Lebanon. A considerable number of these are not practiced outside of this region. Some seventeen religions have been identified in this area, not including the Protestant ones, which are summarized under the heading of "miscellaneous."

One of the larger groups is that of those who call themselves right thinking, orthodox, and whom the world knows popularly as the Greek Orthodox. They belong to the Holy Orthodox Catholic Apostolic Eastern Church, which is the church of most of Russia and of the Balkans. This religion originated in Constantinople, after the split-up of the Roman empire. It differs from the Roman Catholic Church in some basic questions, such as the nature of deity and liturgy.

Another important Christian sect of this region is that of the Copts, who form a very important minority in Egypt. It is said that the name means "Egyptian" in a mixture of Arabic and Greek. The Copts maintain that they are the purest representatives of the ancient Egyptians. Their language is derived from late Egyptian mixed with many Greek words.

The Coptic peasants speak Arabic, but the liturgy employed in their churches is ancient Coptic. The nature of Jesus plays an important part in their creed. *I believe that this is the life-giving flesh which thine only Son took from the Holy Mary,* the Coptic credo says. *He united it with His divinity without mingling, confusion and alteration. . . . I believe that His Divinity was not separated from His Manhood for one moment of the twinkling of an eye.*

The Coptic creed originated in the early church of Alexandria. In the history of that much-persecuted church the desert monasteries played an important part. For that reason none but a monk of one of the desert monasteries can qualify today as the head of the church, invested with the title: "The most Holy Pope and Patriarch of the great City of Alexandria and of all the Land of Egypt, of Jerusalem the Holy City, of Nubia, Abyssinia and Pentapolis, and all the preaching of Saint Mark."

In spite of this magnificent title, the jurisdiction of the Coptic Pope is limited to Ethiopia and Egypt.

The Syrian Orthodox community is one of the dissident churches. It gained its name from the sixth century Bishop of Odessa, Jacob Baratai. Members of the church are also known as Jacobites and, like the Copts, they are "monophysite," maintaining that there was but a single nature in Christ, the divine and human constituting one composite nature.

To make the complication even more complex, some of the Middle East Christian churches split off their parent bodies in the past and entered into communion with Rome. Thus, some of these churches have their doubles in the form of Uniates, subscribing to the articles of creed and dogmas of the Roman church but retaining certain features of the old liturgies and the occasional use of a language other than Latin.

The Maronites form one of these Uniate Churches, the most numerous in the Lebanon; their native language is Arabic and their liturgy old Syriac. They also have retained the married clergy.

A few years ago members of separate "nations" within the Ottoman Empire under their own ecclesiastical authorities, these Christians of the Middle East today render their allegiance to their Arabic countries. The day of the church as the source of authority in the Levant is largely gone, and the day of the nation has arrived.

Islam Means Submission

Most of the people of the Middle East are Muslims, followers of Islam. It is the religion of the majority in all Arabic countries except Lebanon, where the Christian Arabs have a small edge. Today nearly all the Turks are Muslims, and the majority of the Iranians hold the same creed. Even in Israel there is an Islamic minority.

The veritable heartland of Islam is in the Middle East, whence it had its global march. Today it is a world religion, whose followers are estimated at more than three hundred million people.

Islam is dominant across the tremendous waistline of the Old World, from the Atlantic Ocean in the west, across steppe, desert and jungle, covering most of the lower part of Asia, including the countless islands of the South China Sea archipelago and the Republic of Indonesia, deep into the Pacific, tapering off into the Philippines. Islam's offshoots penetrate far into Soviet Central Asia, into the bulk of western China on the one side, and the Balkans on the other. If we include Bahai as an offshoot of Islam, as it, indeed, was originally, then Islam is a global creed. It was only recently that the foundation stone of a magnificent Bahai temple was laid on the outskirts of Chicago. The city of Washington will soon see one of the handsomest mosques to be seen in the Western world.

A brief survey of the Islamic world discloses the following facts. The Muslim creed is supreme in its birthplace, Saudi Arabia, in Yemen, the Persian Gulf protectorates of Oman, Trucial Oman, Qatar and the Bahrein islands, where fully 99 per cent of the inhabitants are the Prophet's followers.

Turkey is also all Islamic, but for 2 per cent, while Syria is four-fifths Muslim. Because of the mountains, Lebanon is more Christian than Islamic.

Across the Persian Gulf, Iran is almost all Islamic, and only one per cent of the people of Afghanistan are followers of other creeds. Pakistan, which came into existence two years after the Second World War as an officially Islamic nation, claims 86 per cent for that creed.

Many, many thousands of miles from Mecca, the birthplace

of the religion, in Soviet Central Asia, some of the Soviet component republics are nearly 100 per cent Islamic. There are about twenty-five million Muslims under the Kremlin's sway.

Adjoining that region, in the distant land of Chinese Sinkiang, about three-quarters of the natives are Islamic. At the other end of the world, in Indonesia, some 90 per cent of the inhabitants pray to Allah. There the largest political unit is the "Muslim party."

The entire northern littoral of Africa is Islamic, beginning with Egypt, where they form 92 per cent of the population, while the rest are mostly Copts. All the way to the Spanish Sahara on the Atlantic Ocean the Muslim religion holds sway.

The Nile belongs to the Prophet's followers, and those of the Sudanese natives that are not nature-worshipers are Muslims. The influence of the creed penetrates deep into torrid Somaliland on the east coast of Africa, on the Equator, where almost 100 per cent of the inhabitants subscribe to Islam. France's Madagascar "down under" and England's Tanganyika have sizable Muslim populations, and so have isolated island clusters all over the Indian Ocean.

The jump from there to the heart of Europe is enormous. There are a million Muslims in Yugoslavia, just a few hundred miles from Vienna the sophisticated and ultracosmopolitan.

It is amazing how this religion has spread and is still spreading, in the face of the well-organized missionary activities of the Christian churches. What is the explanation? But first let us see what is this conquering faith and who was its founder.

His Name was Mohammed

His name was Mohammed ibn 'Abdullah ibn 'abd ul-Muttalib, but history knows him as Mohammed the Prophet, and Mohammed means the Praised One. He was in his early sixties when he died in 632 A.D. He may have lived part of his life with the ill repute of an eccentric or a self-styled seer, but he died as one of the great teachers.

In his native town of Mecca he observed a crude and cruel life. The people worshiped the obvious phenomena of nature, including a black stone. It may have descended from heaven in another age and what was more natural than that people should worship it? They worshiped the things they feared, and they sacrificed their children to these evil powers. Soon the country around him might be depopulated and the town of his birth would be no more.

Mohammed was a posthumous child and his mother, too, found an early death. Was it unnatural that a parentless child should be seeking a greater father, to invoke his help? With the mysteries of heaven he was in constant communion as a shepherd boy—with the life-giving sky, out of which came the winter rains and the summer sunshine.

On his travels with an uncle, the boy saw great cities inhabited by Christians and, perhaps, also Jews. They lived in houses which amazed Mohammed. The inhabitants of those towns and houses practiced no infanticide. It was the western world which irradiated the desert, and not the Iran of Zoroaster, nor the India of the Hindus. Looking toward the West, his eyes fell upon a much higher level of life. Perhaps he thought it was even better, since his imagination must have been strong.

He withdrew occasionally into a cave near his native Mecca, and he saw visions, when the spirit was upon him. He was subject to epileptic fits. The East treated such people either with reverence or scorn. The radiant countenance of Archangel Gabriel was upon Mohammed, and the angel was the herald of Allah, the desert-born creator of the world. Allah was not merely one of the many, but the Only One.

Then Mohammed went among his people and proclaimed: "Allah Akbar" (Allah is Mighty), and he continued to preach: "There is no god but God," and man must submit to him, Islam, and do His bidding. Men are equal, Mohammed said, and those who have bread must give to those who have not.

He had a contagious belief in his strength and therefore he was scorned and all but stoned. He had to flee his native town and he found a sanctuary in Yathrib, higher up the coast, where there were monotheists, Jews. So he honored the place of his sanctuary by calling it the City, Medina, the name under which it is known to this very day. His flight from Mecca to Medina in the year 622 of the Christian era was the beginning of the Muslim calendar, and history knows that flight as Al-Hijra.

Then Mohammed forced the towns and the desert to listen to him, and there was drought on the land, and people were inclined to listen to anybody, even to a Prophet, even to a person who sought to speak the truth. And so Mohammed forced his own contemporaries to honor him as a Prophet in his own country. It was he whom Thomas Carlyle selected as the prototype of the Hero as the Prophet. "To the Arab nation," he wrote, "the appearance of the Prophet was as a birth from darkness into light; Arabia first became alive by means of it. A poor shepherd people, roaming unnoticed in its deserts since the creation of the world: a hero-prophet was sent down to them with a word they could believe. . . ."

The Prophet performed no miracles and claimed no divine descent. Edward Gibbon praised him highly as one who lived the life he preached. Nothing but water and dates were his nourishment, Gibbon wrote. For weeks there was no fire on his hearth. No royal pomp for him even when he could afford it.

This Prophet of the desert did not deny that many Prophets preceded him. The frequency of such names as Suleiman (Solomon) and Musa (Moses) betokens the respect in which Old Testament figures are held in the Muslim world. The greatest Prophet before him was Jesus, but Islam's founder proclaimed that he himself was the fulfillment. The Koran is crammed with references that the Jews had adulterated the Bible and suppressed the glad tidings of the Prophet's coming.

"A Bona Fide" Book

Koran means "recital," reading matter. It is even more to the Islamic world than the Old Testament is to the religious Jew. The Testament is the Sacred Writ but the Koran is also codified law, and there are countries where even today it is the civil and criminal code. In other Muslim countries it lays down the rules for judges in many walks of life. In parts of Islam the only classification among men is according to their knowledge of the law, and great veneration is the share of the most learned doctors.

The number of commentaries on the Koran is endless, and a

ninth century commentator was the author of some thirty volumes of exegesis. The comments of some of the others were even more numerous. On every occasion the Koran may be cited, recited in the great crises of life, sometimes in one single sitting. Every word of it is admired as the acme of wisdom. But for a few interpolations of the Prophet's own words, it is represented as the very words of Allah.

As to the non-Muslim, it is hard not to agree with Carlyle's appraisal: "We, too, can read the Koran; one translation of it, by Sale, is known to be a very fair one. I must say it is as toilsome reading as I ever undertook. A wearisome confused jumble, crude, incondite; endless iterations, long-windedness, entanglement; most crude—insupportable stupidity, in short!"

Real Carlylean language, refreshing in an age which finds virtue in hiding its thoughts. Yet, Carlyle found the Koran stamped with the hallmark of greatness in spite of all its imperfections, a "bona fide book," genuine, sincere, dictated by a man who was struggling heroically to express himself. And that man got across the substance of his message.

Mohammed seems to have been an illiterate, with no first-hand knowledge of the Bible, about which he knew of only by hearsay. He liked the beautiful Biblical stories, which became maimed and stunted in his version, sometimes grotesque, lacking in the necessary build-up and the magnificent simplicity of great writing. Also, numerous errors slipped into his narrative. The Koran describes that evil person, Haman, who was chief minister of the Persian King and who hated Esther, as a pharaoh's steward in Egypt. It identifies Mary, the mother of Jesus, with Miriam, the sister of Moses.

You Can Prove Everything from the Book

Since the Koran is the source of all authority, it must cover all situations. This was proved a generation and half ago by a famous doctor of Koranic law, Sheykh Mohammed Abduh, as told by Bayard Dodge, former President of the American University of Beirut.

The learned man was asked one day about the Koran's stand on Darwin's theory. Although the sheykh was a doctor of the traditional law, he was also a modern man. With no hesitation he opened the writ at the right place: "Behold, your lord said to the angels: I am going to place a successor (Khalifah) on earth." This has been interpreted to mean that the Prophet should have a successor on earth, but the sheykh pointed out that the successor of the animal was the man. Darwin's point was proved.

On another occasion the learned man was asked to express his opinion on Pasteur's theory. Again he turned to a famous Koranic passage which told about the invasion of Mecca by the Ethiopians in the Prophet's day. In connection with it, the Koran described a strange calamity which befell the invading hosts. "Did he not turn their strategy to naught," the Koran asked, "and turned against them swarms of flying things?" The sheykh's decision on the Pasteur theory was based upon this passage.

"The flying things were bacteria, and it was an epidemic. The Pasteur theory is proved."

In the Prophet's days there were no American soft drinks being marketed by large corporations. One of these wanted to do business in a country where the Koran was the law, and the learned men were in a great quandary. Finally one of them, who was more learned than the others, found the solution. There was a passage in the Koran referring to water in the camel's hump and obviously this could also be applied to soft drinks.

The name of the Koranic law is *sharia* (highway), which means the highway of justice. There are different highways in different parts of the Muslim world because of its size. However, they all agree on certain rules of life.

The Pillars of Islam

There are five main pillars of Islam. The first is bearing witness that there is but one god: the profession of faith. Another one is prayer five times a day. There are two other liturgical obligations. One of these is the fasting, during the month of Ramadan, from dawn to dusk and the other is the pilgrimage to Mecca, if feasible, at least once in a lifetime. The fifth one is giving the appointed and legal alms, *zakat*.

Before Islam the Arab world was probably not so conscious

of poverty and misery. The extremes must have been great, and the word must have been that not only the poor but also the rich must have always been with us. The *zakat* is a regular tax, described in detail and measured according to the almsgiver's ability to pay. Upon the possession of five camels, for instance, it is one goat or sheep. The Prophet commanded the Muslim society to take care of its poor, and that in itself was an important step. He also created the concept of the consecrated community in which everybody bore the responsibility for the others' welfare. Thus the rich were made to purge themselves of the sin of covetousness, and the desert was to be purged of chronic famine. Indeed, the very word *zakat* means purification, as well as charity.

There were other duties too which Islam was to observe, and they are of interest because they serve to show that the Prophet's social conscience was very highly developed. The believers were enjoined from eating the meat of the pork and drinking wine. There have been explanations for the prohibition of pork, such as the danger of trichinosis in a hot climate. It is believed today that this was not the real reason. There were many other similar dangers, all of which could not be considered. The desert country of Mohammed's environment lacked the surplus food on which pigs feed, and they would have had to subsist on the necessities of the poverty-stricken people, thus widening the gap between rich and poor. Wine was not forbidden because of its intoxicating effect, but because it was a luxury which the Prophet's sense of justice could not bear.

Where the entire community is dedicated, submitting to the will of God, there is no need for special consecration and thus there is no regular clergy, hierarchy, in Islam. The only difference between believers is their knowledge of the Book. Also what wisdom they have derived from it. A person in an orthodox Islamic country may become a judge (*qadi*) with no special training. If one is conversant with the Koran and possesses wisdom (*hikma*), one can become a judge. The teachers and interpreters of the law (*'ulama*) also reach their position because of their erudition and wisdom.

The Islamic world is so large, dispersed over such a vast area, that divergences from the norm are to be expected. Conditions were somewhat different in the Ottoman Empire until the end of the First World War.

The Ottomans had gained their position in the world because of their military spirit and they were converts to Islam, which was not originally their creed. A measure of regimentation was their way of life. It was not for them to adhere fully to the desert Arabs' spirit of freedom. Therefore they brought into being some kind of a hierarchy, headed by the Sheykh-ül-Islam, Head of Islam, who was not only a religious but also a secular dignitary, Chief Justice. There and elsewhere in the Islamic world there was no real distinction between "church" and state, the religious and the secular, since the entire community was consecrated and no distinction could be made between its various aspects. There is no head of Islam today in Republican Turkey but, strangely, there is one in the Soviet Union, which has a vast Muslim population.

It was also the Ottoman Turks who grafted such offices as the *mufti* and grand *mufti* on the main trunk of Islam. The mufti was an officer charged with the duty of collecting common-law precedents upon which to base future judgments, and the grand mufti was the chief officer of the region. The British took over this custom after the First World War and appointed their worst enemy, Hajj Amin al Hussaini, Grand Mufti of Jerusalem—an appeasement that failed.

Iran was also a convert to Islam and did not perhaps for that reason comprehend its democratic spirit. In that country there is a clergy playing a highly important role. For generations it was an impediment to progress. After the Second World War it was a *mulla* (clergyman scholar), Sayyid Abol Qasim Kashani, who played an important role, mostly through terrorism, in forcing the nationalization of British oil.

The Hold of Islam

Islam swept the world with incredible speed and is still gaining converts. What is the explanation of its present success, in Africa, for instance, where the former nature worshipers are more likely to follow the Muslim creed than Christianity?

For one thing the Prophet's creed seems to appeal to oppressed people since it imposes no clerical rule on them, no priestcraft or superior creatures claiming divine guidance. Islam is democratic.

Also it draws no color line. The Christian creeds in many parts of Africa are associated with the white man and his oppressive tactics. The missionaries are sometimes suspected as the agents of "imperialism." There can be no such charge leveled against Islam, partly because it has no missionaries and partly also because the Muslim countries live mostly in a colonial status. The Koran speaks emphatically for the poor as well as the slave. While slavery still exists in the Arab world, it is more a form of paternalism than submission to the will of an earthly master.

Islam speaks the language simple people understand. It was composed by an illiterate and it seems to appeal to illiterates. Its desert setting is that of a large part of mankind which finds little in common with the Christian and Jewish Testaments. Furthermore, since Islam has no official clergy, it is flexible and tolerates many of the practices that have grown up in the bush.

The Muslim creed speaks to the poorhouse of the world, where people are thirsty and hungry, people of the desert but also of the savannah and the jungle. The Prophet himself grew up in a flaming valley where water was scarce.

In the poorhouse of the world life is sad but there is a beautiful and gay world, after death. The Koran itself says little about its joys, which are intimated rather than described. However, there are traditions and they emphasize the future world.

In the Muslim belief there are seven heavens, each of them in the realm of a precious treasure, under the guardianship of a great figure of the Testaments.

The first heaven is of pure silver and there the stars are hung out like lamps on golden chains, and in that heaven Adam and Eve dwell. The second heaven is of pure gold, the land of Jesus and John the Baptist. The third heaven is of white pearls, under the eyes of Joseph. The fourth heaven is of white gold, according to one version, or ruby, according to the other and it is the heaven of Enoch. The fifth heaven is the realm of red gold and therein dwells Aaron, the man of peace. The sixth heaven is that of garnet, and it is Moses' abode. The Seventh Heaven is the highest, the land of the Shining Light that no tongue can describe, the domain of Abraham. There the blessed lounge in green satin garments, their easy chairs resting on multicolored carpets, drinking the waters of crystal-clear springs. The trees around them provide the blessed with cooling shade and the sweetest of grapes please their tastes. Keeping company with them are the gazelle-eyed *hur,* described by the Koran as "damsels with retiring glances whom nor man nor *djinn* hath touched before them." The distance between each heavenly region is five hundred years' journey, Mohammed said.

Not only physical but also spiritual joys are the dwellers' share in the highest heavens. "Ye shall sit on seats, facing one another: all grudges shall be removed from your hearts."

For people coming from life where feuds were endless and many of whom must have lost their lives in wars, there could be no greater bliss than peace. "Your salutation shall be peace [*salam*]," the great blessing.

Naturally, women were to occupy an inferior place even in heaven. They were admonished to purge themselves of hate and envy, finding solace in pious talk.

The lot of the sinful is the fiery pit of the *jahannam* (hell), corresponding to the Hebrew gehenna (Ge-Hinnom, Valley of Hinnom, where sacrifices to Baal and Moloch were offered). Hell also has seven sections. Those of evil heart are tantalized by the monstrous *zaqqum* tree, bearing a fruit that looks like Satan's head. A body of infernal guards operates the chains and neck irons. The pains of the body are further intensified by torments of the spirit, maledictions, self-accusations and belated pleas for redemption.

Islam Also Means Dissension

Within Islam there are various sects, of which the most important is the *sunna* (custom, divine law). It encompasses by far the largest part of the Muslim world. The followers of sunna are the Sunnites and they supplement the Koran with the traditions (*hadith*) handed down by the Prophet through his companions and their followers. The Sunnites recognize all the successors of the Prophet.

The next most important sect is that of the *shi'ah* (partisan), whose followers are the Shi'ites. They do not accept the sunna traditions, reject the first three caliphs, and are followers of the fourth of them, Ali.

A typical hadith was quoted by T. P. Hughes in his *Dictionary of Islam:* [1]

> Abu Kurain said that Ibrahim ibn Yusuf ibn Abi Ishaq said to us from his father from Abu Ishaq from Tulata ibn Musarif, that he said, I have heard from 'Abd ur-Rahmen ibn Ausaja, that he said, I have heard from Bara ibn 'Azib that he said, I have heard that the Prophet said: Whoever shall give in charity a milk-cow or a leather bottle of water, it shall be equal to the freeing of a slave.

The great dividing line between these branches of Islam is the question of the successor to the Prophet, called the Caliph.

All in all, the Prophet had ten wives but left behind no son. He had an adopted son 'Ali, who was also his nephew and the husband of Fatima, Mohammed's eldest daughter.

When the Prophet died, he was succeeded as Caliph by Abu Bakr, father of Mohammed's favorite wife, 'A'isha. Abu Bakr was an old man when he took office, and he was followed by two successors before 'Ali could fill the place.

After 'Ali's death, one of his sons, Hasan, followed him as Caliph, but he abdicated, retired to Medina and was assassinated there in a harem intrigue. He was followed by his brother Husayn, who, in turn, was slain in his feud with a caliph. This occurred on the tenth day of the Muslim month of Muharram (October 10, 680) which is the great Shi'ite holiday.

The "partisans" think not only that 'Ali was the first of the Prophet's genuine successors, but also that his followers (*imams*) were invested with esoteric knowledge, were infallible in the interpretation of the law, were sinless, became supreme vehicles of divine inspiration, and temporal rulers by divine right. The

[1] Quoted in *The Caravan,* by Carleton S. Coon, p. 99.

Caliphs, they held, were not by human appointment as the Sunnites claimed.

The partisans further believe that the twelfth imam, who disappeared in 874, is still alive, will reveal himself as the Messiah on the Day of Days and will gather all humanity into the fold of Shi'ah.

There are other differences, too, between the Sunnites and Shi'ites. The former abhor carved images and any representation of man. The partisans, on the other hand, worship saints, particularly the tombs of their great heroes: 'Ali, "The vice-regent of God"; Husayn; and the "unstained" Fatima. Also important is the fact that they consider the other Muslims unbelievers.

Shi'ah is the official religion of Iran in the form called *Ithna-'Ashariyya* which recognizes twelve imams as the Successors of the Prophet. This creed is also important in Iraq, and it has followers elsewhere, especially in Yemen, which follows a special brand of Shi'ism. Religious differences complicate the life of the republic of Lebanon. There the Premier is always a Sunni Muslim, the President of the republic a Maronite, the Foreign Minister a Greek Catholic, the Speaker of the House a Shi'ite, the Vice-President of Parliament a Greek Orthodox, and so on and so forth.

Nationalism in Religion

Iran was won over to Islam in the seventh century. Before that her creed was a bastard form of ancient *Zoroastrianism.* That creed recognized two Divinities—the God of Light, Ahuramazda, and the God of Darkness, Ahriman—and it was the duty of the faithful to help the former to triumph.

This ancient creed of Persia also believed in the return of the divine person, Messiah. Before Islam came into the country, the Iranians combined their Zoroastrianism with the worship of the King, a main support of the God of Light.

It is easy from this to see why the Iranians embraced the schismatic form of Islam and not the traditional one. This was the expression of their revolt against the creed which had been forced on them. Persia's Shi'ah is Islam, but it is shot through with old Persian religious practices and cults. 'Ali and his sons are reincarnations of the Zoroastrian God of Light, while his Caliph predecessors are the embodiments of the God of Darkness.

Furthermore, the seed of 'Ali became Iranians themselves. His son Husayn is said to have married the daughter of Yazdegerd, the last of their dynasty, Sassanians, before the Arab conquest and the adoption of Islam.

The cult of 'Ali and his sons is the center of the most spectacular part of Iran's Islam. Their New Year, *Nawruz,* is a great holiday because on that day Mohammed had conferred the Caliphate on 'Ali. Foreigners who have ever visited a Shi'ite country, especially Iran, remember most vividly the weird passion plays performed in the first ten days of Muharram, the first month of the year.

These plays culminate in the religious procession in which long lines of participants of all ages form. They carry chains and steel with which they lash their bodies, as they move out of dark alleys garbed in black in sign of their deep sorrow. In a shrieking tone they chant the names of 'Ali's two sons, whom they consider martyrs. It sounds like *Shahsy-Wahsy* but the words are: Shah Husayn wah Hassan. (King Husayn and Hasan, too.)

The climax is reached on the tenth day of Muharram, traditional anniversary of the assassination of Husayn at Karbala. This time the zealots are carrying swords, with which they slash away at their skulls until the path of their march is marked by blood, and all the while the hideous wail of chant goes on endlessly: *Shahsy-Wahsy.*

On such occasions foreigners do best to watch the procession from vantage points where they cannot be observed. The frenzied mob occasionally turns against outsiders, who are not engrossed in the grief for the loss of the partisan heroes. In the middle thirties Iran's reform Shah, Reza Khan, forbade the bloody processions of Muharram, but how could he prevent the performance of these eerie passion plays in Iran's forty thousand villages?

From the veneration of 'Ali as the Prophet's authentic successor there was only one step to consider him God. There are, indeed, some Ali-worshipers in Iran known as *'Ali Ilahis.*

The greatest dissension among the Islamic dissenters has been about the number of imams, rulers and interpreters of the law. Iran holds to the number twelve, while others believe in seven, which is considered a magic number. These seveners are, in turn, split into several groups, among which the religious affinity is small and sometimes it is difficult to realize that they all are Islamic offshoots.

Best known among the seveners are the Ismaili, so called because of Ismail, son of the sixth imam, disinherited on account of unworthy conduct.

Unworthy or not, he attracted attention and soon a group was on hand to proclaim him the worthiest of the worthy, whose inspiration was divine.

The western world became acquainted with this sect in crusading times. The Ismailis were then under the command of the Sheykh el Jebel, Chief of the Mountains, known to the West as the Old Man of the Mountains, a reputed descendant of the Prophet. His strongholds were in north Iran's Elburz mountains and in the Syrian hills. From there he dispatched his retainers to amass glory for their stay in the Seventh Heaven by assassinating the infidel Christian intruders.

Iran is an important opium-producing country and must have been one then, too. In order to stimulate the religious ardor of the warriors, the Old Man of the Mountains seems to have drugged them with opium (hashish). These dreaded foes became known to the Crusaders as "*hashishin,*" which they distorted on their western lips to sound like *assassin,* and that became a household word in the languages of England and France.

In the twentieth century the reputed descendant of the Old Man of the Mountains, the fabulously rich Agha Khan, attracted much attention with his wealth and good luck around Deauville's racing stables. It is claimed for him that he is the forty-ninth direct descendant of Mohammed. Today some of the "assassins" live in northwest Syria, in Iran and in India. They are known for their probity as hard-working peasants, scraping enough out of the soil to make a living and to contribute large amounts to their supermillionaire religious head on his birthdays.

'Ali was God, holds another group of the partisans, known as the *Alawi*, in northwest Syria and the Turkish borderland. They have also adopted some Christian practices at the crossroads of the great religions, such as the celebration of Christmas. Vestigial remains of paganism in the form of fertility ceremonies are a part of their creed. They too live in the mountains, where dissidence from established ways may be maintained.

A strange offshoot of the Islamic partisans are the *Druzes.* There lived a mad caliph in Cairo at the turn of the tenth century, by the name of Al-Hakim. One of his least attractive customs was to have young girls of the city attend an orgy at the end of which he had them immured and left to starve while he gloated on their agonized shrieks. Another of his mad ideas was to force the citizens to work by night and rest by day. He made the Jews drag large replicas of the golden calf, and forced the Christians to carry heavy wooden crosses. It is believed that his persecution of the Christians led them to ask the West for help, which eventually resulted in the crusades. One day the royal madman was murdered or, according to another version, he mounted a white ass and lost himself in the desert.

Around this royal insanity a man of Persian blood, ad-Durazi (hence the name of Druze), built a religion. The madman is to re-appear one day as the Herald, Messiah. The Druze people live in the dark hills of the Jebel Druze in southern Syria, in Lebanon and Israel's Galilee. Sometimes they live together with Christians and Muslims, and yet their lifelong neighbors know nothing about their rites. They are secretive to the limit, meeting for worship in undistinguished houses protected by guards from curious eyes. In Arabic they are called *Bani Ma'ruf,* children of good deeds, and are known for their hospitality. They help the weak, protect those in quest of asylum and aid those striving for independence. However, some of them at least went berserk during the last century, killing Christians, and causing an international incident. During the war of Israel, the Druzes in the Galilee made common cause with the Jews, against the Arabs.

The Druzes practice concealment (*taquiya*), which goes so far as to deny their creed among foes. Some say they worship the golden calf, while others say that they heap execration on it in their secret rites. It is also said that the faithful belong to several groups, among which is that of the initiates, who know the major secrets of the creed, while a larger number know only some of the mysteries. The majority of the followers are commanded to ask no questions and to obey.

In this Middle Eastern "kitchen of religions" the Devil Worshipers deserve a passing notice. They are called the *Yezidis* and they seem to show how hard old ways die in the tradition-bound Middle East. They may be descendants of the die-hard supporters of Zoroastrianism, with one basic distinction. Their ancestors must have reached the decision that since the God of Light was good by nature there was little sense in kowtowing to him. There appeared to be far more sense in paying homage to the sinister God of Darkness, and, indeed, the Yezidis are said to worship the devil. Also they salute the sun at dawn and hold the belief that one day Christ will return. Though they pay no attention to God, they practice filial piety, neighborly love and provide the poor with alms. They believe in the immortality of the soul and perform expiatory rites at the graves. They eat no pork, but otherwise limit their relations with the Muslims. Some of these Yezidis are Kurds, living in northeastern Syria, while the communities of others are in the hill country of Iraq and even in Soviet Armenia. All in all, this is a synthesis of many ancient creeds, including also atavistic strains of shamanism.

The Gate and Reform

Out of the Middle Eastern incubator of many creeds recently issued a religious philosophy which seems to be the offspring of previous faiths with a dash of modern spiritualism and humanism. Originally it was an Islamic sect, but it has developed into a religion with universal scope. It is *Bahaism*.

Its founder was Sayyid Muhammed 'Ali, born in Iran's Shiraz early last century, another reputed descendant of the Prophet. He was a devout Muslim of the shi'ah sect and his followers called him the Bab (Gate) because through him they would be able to communicate with the long awaited Messiah, the Hidden Imam, also known as the Mahdi. The Consecrated Messenger was thought to be able to confer favors on his followers even before his earthly return.

The inevitable development occurred and he who had been thought to be the Gate now claimed to be the fulfillment, the Messiah. At the hand of fanatical foes, who thought his claim sacrilegious, he died a martyr's death.

His followers dispersed and a group of them found sanctuary on the coast of Palestine, in Acre and Haifa, in the latter city of which they had their most beautiful shrine until the American Middle West wrested its laurels. From the Holy Land the creed spread to other parts of the world.

"Splendor of God" (*Baha-Ullah*) was the name of a successor of the Bab and the present name of the sect is derived from him. In spite of its Islamic origin this creed has no links with the Prophet or Hidden Imam. It is a philosophy of the mind and action holding fast to the belief that universal brotherhood is the supreme end of all true religions. Bahai's main aim is peace among man. It is tolerant of other religions pursuing similar paths, and has neither set ritual nor formal prayer.

Islam has never passed through an age of basic change, such as Christianity witnessed during the age of the Reformation. However, it has several reform movements of limited scope of religious content or geographic location. Best known to the world is the Wahhabi movement, because it prevails in Saudi Arabia, famed for Mecca, its oil and its King. The name is derived from a late eighteenth century religious reformer, Ibn Abdul Wahhab. This is known as a puritanic sect, since its followers frown upon many luxuries, such as silk and flamboyant mosques. However, the Wahhabi King, Ibn Saud, had probably the world's most gorgeous fleet of custom-made American cars. Obviously, the Koran had not forbidden luxury in motorcars. A deeply religious man, he performed all the rituals in the Holy Script. At the same time, he charged a hundred dollars for each pilgrim who wanted to visit Mecca, a religious obligation. That meant that pious people had to scrounge and save before they could amass an amount which represents a vast fortune in the Islamic world.

Another puritanic sect, the Sanussi, burst into being in the deserts of Cyrenaica, to the west of Egypt. The sect was so named after the early nineteenth century religious reformer, Sheykh as-Sanussi. Members were placed under obligation to interpret the provisions of the sacred law literally. Their return to the religious practices of early Islam was facilitated by self-induced ecstasies.

These sects in the poorest parts of the desert obviously "rationalized" their puritanism. Since they had so little, they might as well turn their poverty into an obligation and a virtue.

In Exaltation There Is Solace

Revivalist meetings are well known to the Muslim world. The whirling dervishes are still inducing trance through rhythmic motions. The hypnotic power of the group, an expectant audience and the intoxication of physical exhaustion enhance the effect.

There are more exalted types of religious intoxication, too, including the creed of the mystic Sufi, mentioned already in Omar Khayyam. *Sufi* means wool because of the shirts the zealots wear. Since it is a form of mysticism, its essence is hard to put into words. It has been described as the "search for God as a disembodied spirit," but that applies also to other creeds. The Sufi followers try to realize "existence in abstract and spiritual essence," whatever that means. In Sufism "world and soul are transformed into and absorbed by Deity, serving as its mirror and reflecting divine beauty, wisdom and love." A teacher of Sufism came to grips with its substance in these words: "What thou hast in thy head in the form of ambition, resign; what thou barest in thy hand, throw away; and whatsoever cometh upon thee turn not back."

If this sounds like an occult form of neo-Platonism, let the reader be content with that description. If, on the other hand, it sounds more like the pantheistic philosophy of Spinoza, that "God-intoxicated man," then the writer of these lines will agree.

Sufism has its greatest hold on Iran, the land so close to India, land of mysticism. It had its start in Persia's northern mountain regions and her jungle country. Perhaps it was distilled into its present form out of the faiths of many deities, sublimated into mystic thoughts, re-creating the projections of man's primordial hopes and fears.

The Never-ending Sayyids

In the Islamic world one constantly encounters the *sayyid,* a descendant of the Prophet through his daughter Fatimah, by 'Ali. This was bound to happen in a region where Mohammed continues to be an ever-present reality. Particularly numerous are the Prophet's reputed descendants in certain parts of Iran. Man's eternal desire for distinction may be the explanation, since it is unlikely that the Prophet's seed should have been spread so far.

Anomalous situations are created by the vaunted offsprings' claims to high esteem and their frequently low standards of virtue. A foreign contractor building a road across the country's northern range some years ago was forced to draw upon the man power of a village whose inhabitants claimed Mohammed as their forebear. They were ready enough to accept the wages but were loath to work. In similar cases a solution was offered by the bastinado, but what to do with the exalted men?

At last, the contractor's shrewd local minions found the solution. Politely they requested the sayyids whose mortal frames were to be chastised to remove their green turbans denoting their august descent. Reverently these were placed upon immaculately white sheets. Then the punishment was administered.

After the descendant of the Prophet had been helped back again to his feet, the contractor's henchman picked up his turban, kissed it with the utmost reverence, and replaced it on the sayyid's head.

The high esteem shown the headgear removed the sting from the punishment, even though the sluggish body had been treated harshly. Thus stimulated to greater zeal, the sayyids resumed their work to the general satisfaction, for a time.

CHAPTER 7

The Dead Man Lives

The Amazing Turk

He saw visions, as Mohammed had done, but he belonged to the twentieth century and so his visions were different.

His name was Mustafa Kemal, his countrymen gave him the names of "Ghazi" (Victorious) and "Ataturk" (Father of the Turks). He did not create modern Turkey—no individual person could do that—but he began to harness her dormant potentialities, without which he could have accomplished nothing. It was Turkey that created him and he re-created Turkey.

He was a blend of the divine and diabolic, a man without fear, with an abundance of hypnotic power, a very unusual man and a very great man. It is still a question whether his own countrymen understood him fully.

When he came there was a dynasty, the Ottomans, and he needed a nation, Turkey. He looked at the East and did not like what he saw: countries mired in the past, dreaming about it, always dreaming, a lazy world and a sick world, full of diseases of the body and the mind.

He looked at the West and did not like it too much either. But it was better, because people had medicine and schools and more food, so they did not die so quickly, and they became strong. Mustafa Kemal knew what few of his eastern contemporaries knew, that you cannot have a strong nation composed of weak individuals, and that a country cannot be strong if it is ridden with disease, ignorance and poverty.

There was one thing, particularly, he did not like about the western nations. And yet that was the substance of the West: the spirit of extreme competition among the nations, scoring points at the neighbor's cost, driving to the very limit of possibilities—and no balance, no balance whatever. He wanted his nation to be the creator and not the destroyer. The great nations of the West he wanted to copy were destroyers, always for good causes, because they were better than the other countries, always much better.

He did not want Turkey to be better, just good, within her own sphere and not beyond it. No Manifest Destiny for him. The Ottoman Empire had pursued that chimera, pushing always onward, hitching its security to the most recently acquired post and then driving onward to secure security. He saw what had happened to that empire, and so he wanted to have nothing more than a Turkey, inhabited by the Turks.

Mustafa Kemal had a cold and cruel vision, outside of conventions. The piling-up of consecrated absurdities did not create a consecrated cause. He dared to turn his country upside down, inside out, to shape it into a new mold. He was a George Bernard Shaw among the nation builders, a man who dared to assert the opposite of what people had been repeating for ages and which for that very reason had become the norm. And, behold, he was right. Goethe would have been delighted to see him and perhaps would have told of him: *Voilà un homme.*

Others tried to follow in his footsteps, but they were bunglers because the spark was absent . . . in them, or perhaps in their nations. Mustafa Kemal's country also lost the spark, but about that later.

Overlooking the Aegean

It is fascinating to study the antecedents of greatness; drunkards, syphilitics, in so many cases. But what do we know about the ancestors of great people in the Muslim world, where so many people claim descent from the Prophet? No such claims were made by Mustafa's ancestors and that may have been the reason he wanted to become a Prophet by his own right. His father appears to have been a minor clerk in the Salonika offices of the Ottoman Debt Administration, an Albanian. The Turks liked to place aliens in such unpopular posts. Sometimes the government ran out of funds and then the father, Ali Riza, had to do without any salary. Finally, he vacated the bureaucrat's chair and went into the lumber business.

Mustafa's mother was not Turkish either. Zubeida was a Macedonian, tall, blue-eyed, flaxen-haired. A Slav, maybe, or an offspring of the Vikings, or of an English sailor. People from all over the world visited Salonika, the leading Aegean port. She wore a veil, like other Muslim women, and was confined to the house. But she had a will of her own, and occasionally she left her husband's house. Mustafa's temperament was hers, not only the color of his hair and eyes.

Salonika had a very large Jewish population in those days, at one time the majority of the people. These were descendants of Spanish Jews. Years later, when Mustafa Kemal had become immortal, the Jews of Salonika said there could not be the least doubt about the fact that his family had been a member of a pseudo-Jewish sect, well known in town. But then, it is an occupational hazard of famous people to be claimed by everybody, once they are famous.

"The Father of the Turks" was not the son of the Turks and that was not unusual either. The offspring of an Albanian and Macedonian, he had to be the man to lead the revolt against Turkey's extinction. As a child he may have been teased because of his origin and so he had to develop a countervailing sense of being a Turk.

Also, he lived on the very edge of the huge Ottoman Empire. A sense of nationalism on the frontier can occasionally become a very aggressive sense of patriotism. On the frontier, people are on guard; and this was particularly so in Salonika, surrounded by alien and hostile Balkanites. If you were a Turk, especially a frustrated Turk, then you could easily become an aggressive Turk. Mustafa Kemal shared this quality with many nationalist leaders. Think of Napoleon the Corsican frontiersman; of Hitler the Austrian; or of the leaders of French nationalists, from Alsace-Lorraine.

Mustafa was magnificent at his studies. At the Cadet School in Salonika his mathematics teacher, a Captain Mustafa, gave him a name to distinguish him from other Mustafas and from himself—he called him Kemal ("Perfection"). "A brilliant but difficult youth with whom it is impossible to be intimate," was his headmaster's description of him at the Senior Military School of Monastir. Perfection Mustafa was in his studies but not in his relations with people. He became the father of a neighbor's daughter when he was fourteen. His reserves of energy were too great to be drained, no matter how dissolute in love affairs. That he remained, incidentally, up to the very end of his life.

He was twenty at the turn of the century, a member of the secret society, "Vatan" (Fatherland)—a wild-eyed youth talking endlessly in the Café Gogno of Salonika about the coming revolution. In his daydreams whom did he try to imitate? Nobody, presumably, and again he copied nobody when the time came to give body to daydreams. Great creators are originals and not copyists.

Money was, of course, a sordid thing in the radical youth's eyes, but he felt better when he had it and evidently he ceased to be impecunious when his widowed mother married a well-to-do man. Mustafa Kemal's newly acquired affluence helped to keep afloat a revolutionary plot. He swore in new members as a leader of the youthful conspirators, and kept up their morale with a flood of patriotic oratory. In his leisure time he kept on drinking and knew no limit in love affairs, composed vitriolic poems, cursed and shouted, spent his nights in dens, with his vitality unexhausted.

The attention of the authorities was, of course, attracted to him. A member of his secret society was an agent of the secret police, and so one day Captain Mustafa Kemal, the young prodigy, was escorted into the redoubtable Red Prison of Constantinople. It was also known as the death house. One day he was called for, and this time he was escorted into the office of a high official who drawled: "His Majesty has deigned to extend clemency to you. . . . Your fate will be determined by your conduct. . . . A second chance you will not have."

So he was put on a sailing boat and soon he found himself in Damascus. There he set up a branch of the "Vatan" and kept on organizing, talking, ranting. But Damascus was far out of the way of events rushing toward a climax, and so Kemal decided to return to Europe without the approval of the higher authorities. If this was desertion let them make the most of it. In the Balkan region of the Ottoman Empire the revolutionary *élan* was rising.

In Salonika, Mustafa was easily recognized. He got away for the moment, but a warrant was issued for his arrest. The police commissioner's aide was a fellow plotter and he helped him to get out of the country, to Greece, Palestine, then back to Damascus where he informed his superior officer, also a plotter, about the Balkan events. For this he was transferred to a higher position in Salonika.

This was 1908, and the Committee of Union and Progress acted. Kemal plunged into the work of the creation of a new Turkey, not dynastic but nationalistic. Enver Pasha, unscrupulous, picturesque, frenzied, appealed more to the popular fancy than the morose Kemal, who was pushed out of the way.

The Ottoman Empire was falling apart, one wall of the edifice collapsing here and another one there. Italian troops landed in Libya in 1911, to claim that nominally Turkish territory for Rome. On the battlefield Kemal was to show his mettle. But the Italian navy commanded the sea, and the British the land approaches to the attacked region. London wanted to detach Rome from the bearlike embrace of Berlin and so she closed the route to Turkish troops.

Kemal disguised himself as a desert Arab, crossed Syria and Palestine, arrived at the Egyptian frontier. He made his way into the war zone, where he was to show the world who Kemal was, the new Turkey, bold and adventurous.

The first object he noticed was a resplendent desert tent to the occupant of which the tribesmen bowed. It belonged to Enver. Kemal's career in Africa was short-lived, since Enver would rather see Libya lost to Italy than have anybody else save it for Turkey. Kemal was back again in Constantinople; then went to the Balkans, when war broke out there. But Enver continued to be Turkey's great man, the idol of the people, full of grandiose ideas of uniting many millions of Muslims under a puppet Caliph-Sultan. These were mad ideas but fascinating, because they turned hopelessness into exaggerated hope.

Kemal the Watchdog

There was this advantage to being under a half-crazed man like Enver: tomorrow he was sure to do the opposite of what he was doing today. So Kemal found himself at an important command in the early days of the First World War. He was at Rodosto, on the Sea of Marmora. It was a good place for an ambitious Turkish officer early in 1915, or a very bad place, depending upon his luck. For Mustafa Kemal it turned out to be a very good place indeed.

The western Allies had decided to break the blockade of the Straits which was maintained by the Central European powers. It was important that they should do so, because if they managed to get past the Bosphorus into the Black Sea they could supply Russia with arms via the short way and that might make a great difference to the outcome of the war. If the czarist forces could pin down many German divisions, the appalling deadlock in the West might be broken.

So they tried to smash their way across the Dardanelles. Rodosto was not far from the scene of action and Kemal was ordered to the Straits. The Allied forces—Australians, New Zealanders, English and French colonials—were trying to bypass the joint Turkish-German sea defenses by an invasion of the Gallipoli Peninsula.

In the tangled hills of the peninsula Kemal's troops held a night maneuver during the early hours of April 25, 1915, and were surprised to see a body of Turkish soldiers climbing the hills in great haste. From them Kemal learned that the enemy Allied forces had landed at the neck of the Gallipoli Peninsula some fifteen miles from its tip, entertaining the plan of cutting off the Turks operating in that neighborhood and seizing the crest of the hills overlooking the Dardanelles. From there they were to drive straight into the capital and uncork the bottle for the Russians.

Indeed, the Turks were taken by surprise, having had no hint that the Allies were to land there. As a matter of fact, the Allies had meant to land elsewhere, and had disembarked there by mistake. Since the Turks were unprepared at that spot, this might have been a lucky error for the invaders. But there was Kemal, a favorite of the gods, unwittingly catapulted into the crucial battle.

He knew that his forces were weak and he had no way of sizing up the Allied strength. Prudence counseled him to keep the bulk of his troops in reserve, should the main enemy force land elsewhere. If, however, this was the bulk of the forces of the foe, it was best for him to throw all his reserves into the fray. He had to heed his intuition, which told him that this was the main thrust of the enemy—and he was right. The Allied strategy of surprise was completely wasted. Also the wild terrain helped his soldiers, who climbed like goats.

The Allies were forced to evacuate the Dardanelles, and this incident, of which Kemal was the hero, had a part in it. Turkey was saved for the moment and czarist Russia was doomed. Mustafa Kemal was recognized as the savior of the capital of the Ottoman Empire.

He had the "lucky hand," of that there could be no doubt. So he was sent on different missions, glamorous but useless. The end of the war found him commander of the Seventh Army Corps, operating in the south. The British were now in full march across Palestine, supported by the revolting Arabs of the desert. Turkish deserters overran the countryside, lines were breaking everywhere, onward the British-led troops swept, a human avalanche.

Kemal saw that this was the end of the old Ottoman Empire, but he hoped that this was the beginning of new Turkey. He should have hitched his wagon to the British star, and he was ready to do so, but the march of events was inexorable. That was the first time he adumbrated his future policy. He saw no reason at all in fighting for the Arab lands, which had belonged to the empire. Turkey was the country of the Turks and not a global caravanserai. He relinquished ground to the advancing enemy, because it was Arab ground, and because he could not have saved it anyway. The step he took turned out to be not only good diplomacy but also good strategy. He took his stand along the mountain ramparts, on the border between the land of the Turks and the Arab land. The future prophet of Turkish nationalism had made the great decision: Turkey was to be Turkish or she was lost.

The Agony of the Sick Man

This was the moment the world had feared, the agony of the "sick man" of Europe. The final blow was delivered on the Greek island of Lemnos in the Aegean. There, in the town of Moudros, an armistice was signed on a late autumn day of 1918. Turkey was stripped of everything worth having. Every major Ally and some of the minor ones were authorized to tear out a quivering limb of the dying empire. Not only the British and French were to have their chunks but also the Italians and, later, the Greeks, who were to receive Smyrna, the Queen of the Aegean, and a considerable part of its hinterland. The Straits were opened to all warships and placed under an international commission. A vague shadow of a country up on the high plateau of Anatolia was to be the remnant of Turkey. These gory remains were now at the mercy of any or all countries ready to deliver the fatal blow. In the east of what had not long before been the Ottoman Empire the Armenians and even the Kurds were to have their way.

This armistice was shortly thereafter followed by the Allied occupation of Constantinople, and key points of the country. This is what the Turks say about the condition of their country at that time:

> The Turkish army was demobilized and all its equipment was seized. The country was exhausted and impoverished. The Turkish people who had been fighting almost continually in various wars since 1910 had suffered heavy casualties. There was no foreign power to whom they could turn for assistance. The minorities in Turkey were plotting and causing serious trouble in many parts of the country.
>
> The Sultan and his cabinet in Constantinople, shorn of all prestige, were ready to agree to any terms dictated to them in order to ensure their own safety. There was no doubt that the terms of the final peace treaty would be extremely severe and would be tantamount to the extinction of Turkey as an independent State.

This is, indeed, what happened in the Treaty of Sèvres. The Turkish source continues:

> The world was sure that the sick man of Europe was dead, and that the only thing which remained to be done was to bury him and share his possessions.

Without waiting for the appearance of a national leader, the Turkish record states, various national resistance movements had sprung up in many parts of the country in opposition to the victors and the central government. But to render this opposition more effective it was essential that these various national resistance movements should be co-ordinated under a unified command.

The Sultan, Mohammed VI, was a puppet and apparently he wanted to remain one, rather than an ex-sultan. He and his court camarilla were suspicious of the dour Mustafa Kemal Pasha. A man with his piercing eyes was capable of doing anything, even starting a war of independence. And the Sultan was tired, the courtiers were also tired, and the nation had too many wars. It was better to have a tiny country up in the highlands than no country at all and that was to be Turkey's fate if dour persons like this General Mustafa Kemal had their way.

So they kicked Kemal upstairs with the magnificent title of Inspector General of the Northern Area and Governor General of the Eastern Counties. There he was, an Inspector General and Governor General with nothing to inspect and nothing to govern.

On a tramp steamer Kemal Pasha sailed eastward along the Black Sea shore, but the haste and secrecy of his trip aroused suspicion. The British stationed in Constantinople were particularly distrustful, and they dispatched a warship to track him down.

Kemal reached the seaport of Samsun a few hours before his pursuers and promptly moved inland to the picturesque town of Amasya on the Yeshil Irmak river, where he found refuge in the old rock castle of the town. This is the site of a historic miracle, when the Mongol horde of Timur was defied there for months.

In that town was born Kemal the Prophet, performer of one of the greatest deeds of the East. Thenceforth his life was the history of Turkey.

The national revolution began when the Greeks occupied Smyrna on May 15, 1919. To the Turk this was the abomination of abominations. He knew the Greeks as the infidels over whom he had ruled for centuries and with whom he did not want to dirty his hands. For that reason the Greeks in the Ottoman Empire were allowed to have their own autonomy (millet). There were plenty of Greeks in and around Smyrna, in one of those nationality enclaves which had survived the great Turkish flood that had engulfed Constantinople almost five centuries before.

And now this "scum of the earth," these Greeks, came over from their gutters to lay their hands on Turks—the people who once had the mightiest of empires, the greatest Islamic country in the world.

This feeling of outrage provided Kemal with the powerhouse which he set into motion. He himself was an unbeliever in Allah and he had never thought too highly of the Ottoman Empire, but there was an eternal and immortal Turkey which no force on earth had the right to extinguish.

This is how it all began, at the Congress of Erzurum in July, and at the Congress of Sivas in September, 1919, where the delegates of the eastern provinces at first, and of all the country later, swore that the motherland was an indivisible whole within its national frontiers, and that no foreign mandate or protectorate was accepted. Now Mustafa Kemal became an international figure, the head of a Representative Council, which was to become the nucleus of a later government.

Then in April of next year there was the opening of a new parliament in Ankara under the name of the Turkish Grand National Assembly. Mustafa Kemal was elected its President, and that meant he was the Head of the State. All legislative and executive powers were vested in the Assembly. It held its meetings in a classroom of the fusty agricultural school. Kemal was the schoolmaster and the deputies were the pupils. They were unruly, thinking, perhaps, that he was the old-type careerist, a man of strong words and weak actions. He had to teach them that he was different, a new type of Turk, a nationalist in the western sense of the word. He had to teach them that he had hypnotic power and that he was going to change the universe they knew.

The Knife Cuts Into Butter

The people in Turkey were tired and while the delegates to the Congresses were loud-mouthed, they would have stopped short of action. Turkey had been at war for fully ten years, and food was short, hope was short; life was short too, and people wanted to live it out to its natural end. No more wars.

The Greeks played into Kemal's hand and provided him with the national energy he needed. Turkey was dead, obviously, and the Greeks would have been fools not to open the dead man's chests of drawers to look for heirlooms. In the summer of 1920 the Greeks set out for Smyrna, marching north and east. There was nothing in front of them except Turkey and all the world knew that the long agony was over: Turkey was dead.

It was almost five hundred years before that the Turks had cleared out the Greeks, liquidating the last remnants of the Eastern Roman Empire. And now the very descendants of those Greeks were on the march, seeing themselves in the role of the heroes of classical Greece and of the crusaders. "Onward Christian soldiers!"

And they were urged onward by the British Foreign Office, which had switched over to the Greeks in response to a series of complicated challenges.

The Turks were no more, but there was the place of Turkey, a gaping hole and it had to be filled out. To the south of the Taurus, in the belt of the desert and the Fertile Crescent, involved diplomacy was filling out the vacuum: mandates, native rulers, checks and balances, and above all, divide and rule.

But something had to be done also about the Anatolian plateau, that huge chunk of land facing the Black Sea, the Straits. Beyond the sea was the sullen Soviet land, convulsed with the agonies of parturition, preliminary, possibly, to an abortion; but it was Britain's basic policy to keep the Russian bottled up and that policy had to be long-range. Perhaps Russia needed no Middle Eastern containment, but Britain would not have become a World Power if she had not been able to look into the seeds of time.

Other reasons, too, propelled the Greeks on their march. Word reached Downing Street that the Quai d'Orsay, France's Foreign Office, was lending a helping hand to the nationalistic forces gathering in Anatolia. In diplomacy it is an axiom that next to the official enemy one should most distrust the friend. Britain and France were waging their cold war on a global pattern. France, bewildered by the unexpected victory—helped to her feet by Britain—was ready now to see Britain fall.

Finally, there was Italy, salvaged by the Allies for the great victory celebration, victim of the delusion that she was really a victor and ready to gather the conqueror's loot. During the war when Britain was holding up the Allied edifice with a mighty effort she sought to prevent a cosmic collapse by promising everything to everybody. Italy had been promised a share of the Turkish booty, but now Great Britain did not want it to fall into her hand. Italy was firmly entrenching herself in the strategically located Dodecanese Islands where the Aegean meets the Mediterranean.

And so the Greeks cut into Anatolia, the pathetic remnant of the Ottoman Empire, as a knife cuts into butter. Their strategy being to move from natural defense to natural defense, they advanced to Bursa the ancient, dear to the Osmanli Turks, because there were buried Osman and Orkhan, their first sultans. And then they advanced to Afyonkarahisar, where they dug themselves in.

The nationalist army was collecting slowly. There was a shortage of arms. The French were helpful to the Turk. So were the Italians, who did not like the Greeks, and so were the Soviets, who did not like anybody.

The Greek High Command had better supplies for its army, but it was not too efficient. The commander in chief, a political appointee, disliked the winter campaign in the cold interior, preferring the warmer climate of Smyrna and, above all, the sunshine of the sidewalk cafés. He suffered from the strange delusion that his legs were made of glass and one day, it is recorded, he refused to get out of bed for fear they might break.

The war was dragging on. The Greeks had expected no resistance, but there were now soldiers in front of them, tattered beyond belief and poorly armed, it is true, but soldiers just the same. By night the Greeks could hear the weird music of creaking wheel disks on ancient carts provisioning the Turkish forces. To the Greeks this constant creaking was gruesome, but to the Turks it was celestial music. This was their country, after all, and this was the sound which they had heard all their lives. How beautiful could be the music of the creaking, unlubricated wheels. The Turkish soldiers fell into an ecstasy.

Time was of the essence because every week meant converts to Kemal's cause: young officers who saw their salvation in the continued existence of a country which would have an army; simple peasants who were open to the argument that this was their country which they had to defend. In the distance there was Smyrna the Glorious, in the sunshine of the sea, and it was full of Greeks who were traitors, and those traitors had houses which were well stocked with food and many other things. The martial instinct of the Turks was alive again.

There were cruel battles in the winter, and the Turkish highlands have their own Siberia and Alaska. Still, the Greeks advanced when spring came and by the summer they moved ahead in the valley of the Sakarya River, leading straight to the heart of the country.

A Monkey Bites a King

In the autumn of 1920 a monkey bit a king and history was written. The monkey's name is unknown, the ruler was Alexander, King of the Hellenes, son of King Constantine, whom the Allies had forced off his throne during the Greek War because he was pro-German. A year after his son's death, this King was back again in Athens, while the pro-Allied government of Eleutherios Venizelos was out.

This cooled the ardor of the British for the Greek cause considerably. King Constantine was not their friend. There was also dissension in the Greek armed forces. Kemal's army was waxing while that of the Greeks was waning. The element of surprise was lost and the enormity of the attempt to snuff out Turkey completely now began to dawn on the people. Many of the Turks may not have been conscious nationalists, but they knew that the Greeks wanted to rob them of their homes; and besides, the Greeks were infidels.

This was no longer a hit-and-run war but a campaign which threatened to imitate the World War in being a succession of wars of attrition. Mustafa Kemal was now Commander in Chief, in addition to being Head of the Government. He had many of his troops concentrated at Eskishehir, an important railway junction, and let the enemy guess that great events were impending there. In the company of several of his generals he attended a football match on August 26, 1922, and for that night he issued an invitation to a gala ball at headquarters. The enemy spies were also to know about the ball. Obviously, the armed forces could relax for the moment.

He let no enemy spies know, however, that during the night he let his headquarters move closer to the front. The Eskishehir concentration was a well-manufactured feint, and the real build-up was about a hundred miles farther down the line, at the Afyon front.

Now Kemal issued his famous Order of the Day: "Soldiers! The Mediterranean is your goal."

At four o'clock the sun rose behind the rounded top of Sultan Dagh and during that day it was to observe a historic sight. Machine guns spat angrily into the devil's own orchestration of the war. But the machine was largely forgotten when the bayonet went to work, and in that the Turks were good.

In twelve hours the historic battle was decided. The Greek army was cut in half, in Athens the King of the Hellenes recalled the general with the legs of glass, but the Turks were too fast and the commander was captured.

Few of Kemal's soldiers had shoes to last for more than a score of miles and the sea was two hundred and fifty miles away. On the Greek side entire regiments surrendered without a show of battle, their morale gone; others fled into the hills, while along the line of retreat the countryside rose spontaneously, and the guerrillas had a rich harvest, including the shoes of dead Greeks.

Up hill, down hill, the pursuers followed their quarry. When Turkish boots were worn thin, legs were swathed in rags. Then the army marched in bare feet and it marched to victory.

The topography of the country helped the Turks. The mountains, descending into foothills, straightened out into the fruit-bearing hinterland of Smyrna. The pursuers' bare feet carried them onward through a land in flames until they reached the coastal towns—above all, Smyrna.

An acquaintance of the author, Anthony J. Klados, a Greek resident of Smyrna at the time, gave the following account of the capture of the city.

> Smyrna was in flames, the scene of robbing, looting and wholesale slaughter. The survivors sought to save their lives by rushing to the jetty, in order to get into a boat and escape. As the flames spread on the waterfront, more and more people came, pushing others into the sea.
>
> Those who could swim, shouted for rescue, while making for the foreign ships in the harbor, mostly Italian and French. But the crew, evidently, had orders to have no hand in rescue operations because in many instances the ropes which were grasped by the unfortunate victims were cut.

Then came other ships, mostly British men-of-war, and loaded their human cargo on deck and departed. More than three-fifths of the city was destroyed, including all the banks, business houses and consulates in the European quarter on the quay. The Greeks say that half a million people perished there but the extent of the real damage in human life is impossible to ascertain.

Turkey had had a large Greek population, very Greek and very Greek Orthodox. Many of them had taken arms against Turkey, and many others gave expression of their joy over Greek victories. Under the Ottoman Empire they had formed an enclave, little Greece within Big Turkey, and the Ottomans cared little how the infidels acted or what they felt. The Greeks of Turkey did not realize that the new Turkey had an entirely different attitude toward minorities and the national soil.

For the surviving Greeks it was impossible to remain in Turkey, and so an exchange program was drawn up. The Refugee Settlement Commission of the League of Nations lent the two countries a helping hand. The Near East Relief helped to feed and shelter the exchanged population. Some 1,200,000 Greeks were repatriated to Greece and some 400,000 Turks were sent to Turkey. The city of Salonika, where Kemal was born, lost its entire Turkish population. Never before has history seen an organized exchange of population on so vast a scale, and never before has so colossal a task of this nature been accomplished with so little friction. The problem was less grave for Turkey, which disgorged more people than she received. Her large open spaces were crying out for settlement. But Greece was an overcrowded little country, and local tension developed occasionally between "old" and "new."

The Empire is Dead, Long Live the Republic

The Ottoman Empire was dead, but its successor, Turkey, was very much alive. The Treaty of Sèvres which had all but wiped Turkey off the map was replaced by the treaty of Lausanne, which was negotiated in midsummer, 1923. The following incident will illustrate the difference in the attitudes of the conferees at the beginning and the end of the parley.

Turkey was represented by Ismet Pasha, who was to be the country's second president, as Ismet Inönü. Just before the conference at Lausanne started, Ismet noticed that easy chairs had been provided for the other delegates but only backless ones for the Turks. He asked the cause, and the embarrassed reply was that no more easy chairs were to be found. "Very well then," he said affably, "we'll be back when you have found them." (P. S. He got the easy chairs.)

The Turks hailed the Lausanne conference as a "great diplomatic victory" which acknowledged Turkish freedom and independence. The "spheres of influence" were forgotten and the region inhabited by Turks was restored to them. There was some argument about the Mosul region, which is today part of northern Iraq, and about Alexandretta in northern Syria. Constantinople and its environment remained with Turkey, but the

Straits were demilitarized. The badge of dishonor, the system of capitulations under which aliens were tried by their own native courts in Turkey, was removed.

Then events followed one another in quick succession. Vanguard of the new Turkish national idea was the Republican People's Party, founded in the summer of 1923. The Allied forces were withdrawn from Constantinople in the autumn. A fortnight later Ankara superseded the former city as the capital of the country, and in a few more days the Turkish Republic was proclaimed, with Mustafa Kemal as its president.

The removal of the capital from the metropolis on the Straits to the Asian town in the highlands had both practical and emblematic significance. Constantinople had been, during the Ottoman Empire, a cosmopolitan city. One of Kemal's greatest strokes of genius was, in an English commentator's words, to call the Turkish people to turn, both in spirit and by the actual transfer of the centers of administration, from the debilitating coastal plains with their heritage of Byzantine corruption and imperial decadence, and to withdraw to the forefathers' harsh uplands.

A large part of Turkey is that tough Asiatic plateau of rigorous climate and infertile soil, where the struggle to exist breeds the toughest peasant stock—an excellent illustration of Professor Toynbee's theory of challenge and response.

A paradoxical move this was, from West to East, as part of the process of westernization. It was a contradiction only in a geographical sense but not in a higher sense of symbolic substance. Turkey signalized the change from the a-national dynastic State of the East to the national, western country by moving from the international city into the national interior.

Revolution from Above

The foreign policy of the Ottoman Empire was clean-cut during the period of its early dynamism. Then, it was adopted by the leading Great Powers, first Britain and then the Reich. What was that foreign policy?

The answer pointed to Russia, the "global" country, covering the top part of most of Eurasia. When Turkey was still virile it spread into the county north of the Black Sea. Then Russia acquired a measure of dynamism, whereas the Ottoman Empire lost it. It was then Russia's turn to push the Ottomans out of the land of the steppes and to take the offensive. Should that country breach the dikes of containment, might it not overwhelm all the world? Then it was that Britain assumed command, while Turkey occupied an advance post. A strange company indeed it was, no longer linked with religious or ideological factors. Christian Britain fighting Christian Russia by means of the Islamic Turk. The Ottoman Empire had many major wars with the Russian empire, an average of one every twenty-five years.

The secular feud left its mark on the Turk. The peasant in that country has a strange way to denote the enemy. He calls him "Muscovite," whether Italian, Greek, British or Russian. In my visits to Turkey, older peasants frequently confided to me: "We have fought the Muscovites."

They fought them in 1911 and 1922, too. Told that in those wars the enemies were Italian and Greek, they remonstrated: "The enemy was the Muscovite!"

The Ottoman Empire had been forced to waste its substance because of that scrapping and that was the plight Kemal found. Turkey was to remain the Great Powers' victim as long as this situation continued. He concluded a friendship pact with the Kremlin, thus reversing the Turks' traditional policy. This friendship was sealed in a tangible way. The Russians had returned to Turkey the two provinces of Kars and Ardahan which they had annexed a generation before. The Soviets helped out Turkey's five-year plan with an eight million dollar loan. The two countries were to be friends, not enemies as in the past. Being friends they would prosper, helping each other. Thus the most troublesome problem of the past—the Eastern Question—was to be answered. The sultans and the czars must have been rubbing their ghostly eyes in their various sections of the Great Beyond.

Revolution on All Fronts

Had anything been overlooked in the Turkey of Kemal? Was there any other country in the world that shook itself so completely loose from the hold of the past? What was past was wrong because it was the past. The foe was dependence on kismet, fate. The name of the enemy was the minaret and the mosque, the place of worship and its slender tower. It was the muezzin's nasal wail calling the faithful to the twilight service. The vicious foe was the turban and the fez, the woman's veil and the peasant's ignorance, the illiteracy of the shepherd and the people's indifference. He was the vermin and the Arabic script, high mortality rate and the village madman. He was tradition and slothfulness and stupidity. The foe must be smitten and whoever resisted was the foe.

In Turkey the battle of the hats was on. The turban and the fez were not merely headgears, functional articles of clothing, but they were also the ritual, religion, Allah, the true faith. Anybody who dared to touch them was accursed and to the *jahannam* he was to be consigned. A few people went to their death because they refused to exchange the cap for the fez. Most of the people accepted the change, because the Turk was brought up as a military man and he was used to accepting orders, and Kemal Pasha was a general, he had authority. Also, because experience showed that Allah did not smite dead those who took off the fez but the State was ready to smite those who failed to wear the cap. The nation was mightier than Allah, all the world could see. It was the new God. And was not that, after all, the spirit of the West?

Mustafa Kemal had his pictures taken in a dress suit. They were displayed everywhere in Turkey and were printed on the stamps, as they continue to be printed to this very day. The good Turk wore European dress and the fez belonged to a dead era.

They erected monuments to him and he could not have enough of these. Not merely because he was vain but also because this was part of his nation's education. These monuments were graven images expressly forbidden in the Koran and yet Allah's lightning did not topple them from their pedestals. The Script was the Republican Constitution and it did not forbid the erection of monuments.

Turkish music in the past had grown out of religious recitation, blended into it, as it issued out of the nostalgia of nomadic strains. To western ears their undertone was monotonous, sad or savage. That was the spirit of the East: extremes of sadness and of joy, the atmosphere of the hungry steppe and of the campfire, with men leaping around the flames. The new Turkey was to be different. The West was symphony and it was jazz. So Kemal gave orders that the republic was to listen to Tin Pan Alley syncopations and Wagner dirges.

The Army of Light

The year 1928 of the Christian era was the Year One of the Cultural Era of Republican Turkey. Blackboards were set up in the bazaars and the marketplace, where fiery-eyed youngsters awed graybeards with the esoteric secrets of the Latin script. Blackboards were set up in the government offices and Excellencies became pupils. Blackboards were set up in the Grand National Assembly, where the people's teachers went to school. The Latin script must be learned, the government told public officials, or out you go! The Latin scrip must be learned, the government told jailbirds, or out you do not go! At first the newspapers were printed in both Arabic and Latin, and then only in Latin script.

The Army of Light was organized and off it marched into battle against the hosts of darkness. "Offensive on all fronts!" was the insistent command. Members of the Teachers' Congress of Ankara took the pledge: "We will teach every Turk to read and write." Two million Turks learned the Latin alphabet in a few years, and those who refused to learn were castigated. The new script was a link with the West.

The Turanian renaissance was to be heralded by the schools. Education was made compulsory, a lofty ambition still very far from fulfillment. A decade later "Village Institutes" were established—something new under the Middle Eastern sun. In tens of thousands of villages teachers were badly needed and there was no time for long training programs. People in this region are flexible, learn very quickly. So, children just out of the elementary schools were to become teachers, if they were smart. They were—and still are—transformed from children into teachers in a five-year training program, half study, half practical work. From the most traditional, and most useless, type of education, Turkey turned immediately to the innovations of John Dewey. The schools were also to teach plumbing, farming and, in the coastal villages, fishing. The young teachers not only teach the three R's but also show the way to village improvement.

The Turk was to learn the trades his fathers despised. Junior high schools were opened to encourage the liberal arts and humanities, the broader human view. The University of Istanbul was raised to western levels. When the German Nazis decided that they preferred darkness to light and ejected the torchbearers, the Turks employed many of them promptly. Another university was opened in Ankara. Adult education was to be fostered in the People's Houses (*halkevis*), where older Turkey was to learn about itself and the outside world.

And so the reforms were launched on all fronts. Old Turkey was debilitated with all the plagues of the Orient, full of running sores and early death. New Turkey was to train physicians and was to open war on the deadly epidemics which sloth tolerated.

Polygamy was now outlawed—there had been very little of it anyway. If a man was rich enough to want several wives, let him get them in the ways of the enlightened West. However, only one of them was to be the legal wife.

"The progress of the nation is measured by the status of its women" and "a country in which women are excluded from political life is a half-paralyzed body." New Turkey announced: "Men and women must help one another and tread the paths of life together."

Women acquired similar rights to men, to hold property, hold office, to be designated legal guardians to minors. Divorce, extremely easy for the male under the law of the Koran, was now made more difficult for him.

In the ten years up to 1935, Turkey was turned upside down and inside out. What had been, was no more. The past was adjudged guilty. New law codes were adopted, based upon the most advanced codes of the West. The State was secularized and Turkey was no longer wedded to Islam. The Gregorian calendar was adopted to replace the Muslim year and Friday as the weekly day of rest had to yield to Sunday. Everybody had to adopt a distinctive name. That is how Mustafa Kemal became Ataturk and his successor in the presidential chair, Ismet, became Inönü.

The Kemalist Revolution having done away with the system of capitulations, under which foreigners were not subject to Turkish courts, ceased to be a colonial area. The foreign investors were no more. Neither were there many minorities left.

The Revolution had found acceptance not only because Kemal knew how to give orders and his nation knew how to obey them. He was the founder and the molder of the republic, its first president, the head of its only party, the Republican People's Party. Kemal pulled his people out of the slough of despond, and showed them the new way. It led to a Promised Land which was not that of Islam but of Turkey. It was the home of the Turk. In that land there were not too many rich effendis. In that land the young people were not outcasts, as they had been in the Ottoman Empire. The women, more than one half of the population, now had a vested interest in the republic. They were treated now as human beings.

On November 10, 1938, Ataturk died, having worked, drunk and loved himself to death.

The following day the Grand National Assembly elected Ismet Inönü President of the Republic.

Turkey on the Edge of the War

At the Casablanca Conference in January 1943, President Roosevelt and Prime Minister Winston Churchill agreed that the latter should "play the cards" in Turkey for both. Britain, after all, was an old hand at that game. The Turkish republic was an ally of both England and France.

Shortly after Casablanca, Churchill met President Inönü at Adana, in southern Turkey, and there assured him that pressure to enter the war would not be brought to bear on him at that time. Just the same, both the United States and Britain would supply Turkey with arms and ammunition. Turkish resistance was deemed very important, however, in case of an Axis attack or a German demand for passage through the country. Eventually lend-lease aid was extended to Turkey.

Was Turkey helping the Allies more by staying out of the war or was she to fight the Axis? There seemed to be one view that regarded the Turkish republic more valuable as a powerful roadblock in the way of the Axis "lifeline" toward victory, the deathline of the anti-Axis world. This view held that the most useful function Ankara could perform was to stand guard on that highway. Should it go to war against the Germans . . . anything could happen. Nazi might seemed to be overwhelming in those days. What could a country like Turkey do against it? By waging war on the Third Reich, Turkey was inviting disaster for herself as well as for the Allies. A short cut to the oil wells of the Middle East would be opened to the Axis in that case. From the East the Japanese steam-roller would be set into motion and the tongues of the global pincer would meet somewhere near the Persian Gulf.

The opposite view became more vocal when the German juggernaut had been forced into reverse at Stalingrad. Declaring war on the Axis would force the Third Reich to thin its lines in the Soviet Union. Behind the German lines near the Straits disaffected Balkanites might rise in revolt. In Yugoslavia there was already an Underground Second Front of liberty-loving people. The end of the war could be hastened by inducing Turkey to fight the Reich.

This was the attitude of the British government and Churchill became its advocate. His plan was to open a mighty second front in the east of Europe. Turkey was to occupy the center of the front, flanked by Russia on the right and Britain on the left.

The Soviet Union supported the British plan, and with some reluctance the United States consented. The Big Three finally agreed to request Turkey to enter the war, and early 1944 was to be the date of her entry.

Turkey said, "yes . . . but. . . ." She needed arms, supplies, transports. Meanwhile the Ankara government kept on sending some of the most vital war material to Germany: copper, iron, steel and, above all, chrome ore. Were these to come back into Turkey fashioned into bombs, killing the purveyors?

It did not look as if the Turks meant their promise to go to war against the common foe and Mr. Churchill suggested energetic action. Just because Turkey claimed to be Britain's ally was no reason to afford her immunity from penalties for helping the Axis. The route of Turkey's ore shipments should be bombed.

Ankara promised to mend her way . . . 50 per cent. It was ready to cut Reich-bound chrome ore shipments by half. Negotiations about joining the fighting Allies continued. It was the impression of London that Ankara was "stalling," asking for more arms and still more arms until the war was over.

This, indeed, was the case. When the Axis was so weak it could take no revenge, Turkey severed diplomatic relations with the Reich. Finally, on February 23, 1945, the Grand National Assembly at Ankara declared war on Germany and Japan. The war in Europe was now in the stage where there could be no doubt about the imminent collapse of Adolf Hitler's "Thousand Years Reich."

An Object Lesson in Diplomacy

Thus Turkey managed to go through the Second World War as the friend of Germany and the ally of Great Britain. There may have been weighty reasons why the Turks wanted to sit out that war. Across the river Maritsa there was their neighbor, Bulgaria, under Germany's heel. Those were the years when German might drove panicky fear into the strongest nation's heart. From the West came a twentieth century Genghis Khan, as ruthless a murderer as man had ever seen, a Genghis Khan provided with the most effective slaughtering methods of modern civilization.

Then, too, Turkey had seen more wars in the past than any of the other countries. Her First World War began two years before its official beginning and ended four years after its termination elsewhere. It lasted for a full decade. The nation may have lacked the strength to resume the fight.

Also, Turkey had the good luck of being peripheral both to the Axis and the Allies, the Germans being next door neighbors on one side and the Allies on the other. If the Reich were beaten, all would be well, and the pall of doomsday would be lifted; if they were victorious, it would be suicide for the Turks to oppose them. The Soviets were the only permanent neighbors. Should they be victorious, their stock would rise and they would demand a hand in the control of the Middle East. Turkish postwar aims may have been best served by a stalemate.

Britain wanted Turkey to enter the war not merely to help in the war but also in the ensuing peace. Turkey in the Balkans might have turned out to be a balancing element against the Russians. With the wisdom gained by hindsight, this seems to have been a good policy indeed. The Turks would have strengthened Britain's hand, might have weakened the Soviets. Mr. Churchill, the most experienced of the wartime western diplomats, clearly foresaw that the era of good feeling between East and West was not to endure for long.

The policy of the United States was—as we have seen—to let the British play the Middle Eastern cards. Washington was asked for help to give the Axis the final push in the Balkans. Its answer was that all its resources were engaged on the other fronts. This refusal forced southeastern Europe upon the Soviets' tender mercies. Had the United States found it possible to participate in the final Balkan push, the Soviet power in the region would have been weakened.

Bending to the Wind

One of those beloved phrases that come rolling off statesmen's lips with the ease of falling objects is the "sovereign equality of all nations." As so many other things that are taken for granted, there is no sovereign equality of countries. The prevailing relation among them is sovereign inequality, and Turkey's recent history is a case in point.

No country could be prouder of her record than Turkey. Undaunted and unafraid, she stood up to the Russian bully. In reality, she was able to do so because she was backed to the hilt by the United States. The Turks sized up America as being stronger than the Soviets.

It fell now to the United States to contain Russia, a role previously performed by Great Britain. On March 12, 1947, President Truman addressed Congress on this subject, and what he said was history. He told a joint session of the legislature that it was the duty of the United States to provide military and economic aid for nations striving to maintain their freedom and independence. The survival of Greece and Turkey was essential to prevent the spread of confusion throughout the Middle East. "The seeds of totalitarianism are nurtured by misery and want. They spread and grow in the evil soil of poverty and strife. They reach their full growth when the hope of a people for a better life is dead. We must keep that hope alive. The free peoples of the world look to us for support in maintaining their freedoms. If we falter in our leadership, we may endanger the peace of the world—and we shall surely endanger the welfare of the nation."

The President of the United States asked for $400,000,000 in aid for Greece and Turkey, of which three-fourths was to be granted to Greece as military and economic assistance, while the rest was to be given to Turkey as military aid. The Truman Doctrine was born.

The "sovereign equality" of Turkey among the nations of the globe was now assured. Her territory became an advance base of United States defense, under Russia's very nose. Through the operation of the silent comptometer, the money Congress appropriated for Turkey's military needs was multiplied sometimes by as much as ten. Military matériel was placed on the books as American army "surplus," at one-tenth of its real value.

In the leading hotels of Ankara, East and West did meet. Never before had the relations between the two countries been as close as now. Forgotten were the nightmares of the Armenian massacres, the days of the "unspeakable Turk." The Turks appeared in the shining armor of Christian soldiers marching into war against the anti-Christ. When the Korean War broke out, the Turks wasted no time waiting for an adequate supply of arms to reach them. Promptly they moved into battle against the common foe and the enthusiasm of the West for the gallant Turks knew no bounds.

The flexibility of Turkish policy in the light of changing events was revealed anew. While German armor was smashing ahead during the Second World War, the Turkish republic was inspired to copy Nazi ways. The country still had the remnants of Armenians, a number of Jews and other nationalities. These minorities were to pay an enormous special war tax, *varlik vergesi*. The victims sometimes had the money, but more often did not. In the latter case they were dressed in the convict's stripes and sent into the mountains to build roads. The Nazis' racial policy was reproduced in the dour highlands of Anatolia.

With the victory of the West, the attitude of Turkey toward Jews and Armenians was changed. The Jews in particular seemed to be singled out to be the regime's pets. Turkey was the first Middle Eastern country to enter into normal relations with the newly constituted State of Israel.

This friendliness toward the Jews was interpreted by some observers as an extreme case of . . . anti-Semitism. During the war the Nazis kept dinning into the Turks' ears that America was *verjudet*, in Jewish hands. This lesson the Turks took to heart and wanted to show America what great friends of the Jews they were.

Etatism Meets Its Peer

Under Mustafa Kemal the Turks tried to mate a blend of collectivism with private enterprise. They wanted to modernize their country, introduce some industries. They did not want foreign capital, with which they had had very bad experience in the past. Foreign political influence usually followed foreign capital. They lacked a sufficient quantity of native funds. The best method seemed to be, therefore, to pool the resources of the entire nation and combine that with whatever private enterprise they could dig up. This was the well-known system of *étatism*. Certain industries, such as paper and metallurgy, were fully in the hands of the State, while others, such as the shoe industry, were 90 per cent State-owned. The share of the State in the mining of chrome was 80 per cent. On the other hand, most of the cotton and copper plants remained in private hands.

The Truman Doctrine changed the official Turkish attitude considerably. The world came to know the United States not only as the great land of private enterprise, but as a crusader for *laissez faire*. Freedom of enterprise was equated with democracy. (Not much was said about tariffs and agricultural policy.) The Turks liked what they saw. Then they looked toward the north, into the land of collectivism, and they did not like what they saw.

Look at the United States, the Turkish high officials said, and see for yourself the advantages of their system. Let there be far more private industry in our land. . . . This was to be the Turkish New Deal.

The Republican People's Party of the late Mustafa Kemal Ataturk had been the champion of the supremacy of the State in economic matters. It had to yield the field to a new political party, that of the Democrats.

Up to 1945, Turkey had a one-party system. The Republicans had practically no opposition. Thenceforth, however, the opposition came into being. The greater the influence of America, the stronger was the push of the Democrats, champions of free enterprise and *laissez faire*. In May 1950, new national elections were held. They ended with a landslide victory of the Democrats, while the former ruling party slid into obscurity.

Again: *Plus Ça Change . . .*

Under the previous regime, Kemal was not only the Prophet but also the National Divinity, whose words and even intentions became living monuments in the Turkish Pantheon.

Under the new regime the lip service to the national hero continued, while his basic policies were reversed.

Ataturk had altered the course of Turkey's foreign policy by terminating the traditional attitude of enmity toward the Russians. Under his policy Turkey was no longer to man the Western Powers' eastern ramparts, to be treated as expendable.

Under the new regime, again, Turkey assumed her previous role as bulwark for the West. Under the Ottoman Empire, while it was associated with attempts to contain Russia, there was also an attempt not to identify it with only one major power. Thus, for instance, a British mission was training the Ottoman navy and, at the same time, a German mission was training the army. Now, however, after the Second World War there was no balancing of foreign influence. Ours is the age not only of total war but also of total peace, in the form of preparing for future wars. The United States assumed full responsibility for training Turkey's army, navy and air force.

"Operation Bootstrap" of the Kemalist regime was also reversed. No longer was the country to pull itself out of the economic mire by means of its own resources. The new Turkish regime enacted a "Law for the Promotion of Foreign Capital Investments," to induce foreign capital to move into the country. Obviously, it was to be American capital, the only one of its kind in the world these days. The newly established Turkish Industrial Development Bank was to combine domestic and foreign private capital with government funds. However, neither large-scale, nor even small-scale, influx of foreign capital materialized. Foreign funds were wary because Turkey looked too much like a military staging area, an advance post of defense. American capital was able to find far more profitable employment at home.

The new regime went further than inviting foreign capital. It announced its policy of denationalizing some of the national industries. Here again it ran into difficulties, since native "venture capital" was neither sufficiently venturesome nor adequate, and foreign "risk capital" was apprehensive of too many risks.

American aid to Turkey was helpful, but mostly in the field of agriculture. Because of that aid the acreage under cultivation increased rapidly by some 20 per cent, enabling Turkey to export to Europe large quantities of grain. The United States provided many thousands of tractors, among other things. The Marshall Aid program to Turkey enabled her to increase coal production by one-third and chrome production by 40 per cent. Were the Turks to be content with being hewers of wood and drawers of water? Or were they to build up their industries?

A Retrospect

A generation after the establishment of the Turkish republic the time was ripe for stock-taking. Turkey had witnessed the most remarkable transformation of the Middle East: a backward Oriental country was to become a progressive Occidental nation. Her example fired the imagination of the entire region.

Country after country sought to copy the Kemalist methods. Even today whenever a new man arises in this area the world asks hopefully: Is he a new Kemal?

A person who last saw Anatolia thirty years ago would not believe his eyes, were he to revisit the government quarters of Ankara. Such a person would have every reason to marvel at so many other phases of transformation. Women occupying important positions, being members of parliament, practicing the professions. He would be pleased with the new role of youth, at the strides progressive education has made, the popularity of sports.

The visitor would notice the absence of a large and super-rich effendi class, the curse of Iran and the Arab countries. He would notice a somewhat higher standard of living for the people, as well as an enhanced measure of political awareness, greater interest in international affairs. He would also notice the more obvious changes about the people's dress and the difference in the status of Islam. He would observe that Turkey today is almost entirely Turkish, with the barest seeds of the minorities. The nationalities no longer occupy the important positions that were theirs in the past.

However, if it were possible for the visitor to see these changes as a current, he would notice that the pace slackened after the death of Ataturk. That great man took his people to the high mountains and let them catch a glimpse of the Holy Land. It is still no more than a glimpse.

The pilot projects are there and the bold blueprints are also on hand. The new quarters of Ankara are supermodern. In the factory sections of such cities as Adana and Malatya an American boom-town atmosphere prevails. That is what visitors from abroad see, mostly. They do not see how the majority of the people live in their dismal hovels. They do not see the tens of thousands of Anatolian villages looking the same as they looked in Kemal's days, looking the same as they must have appeared in the days of the Ottoman conquest five centuries ago. The thousands of American tractors are there, but otherwise farming in Turkey is still as primitive as it must have been in the crusaders' times.

Islam is no longer the State religion, but in Anatolia's thousands of villages the leader of prayers still exercises strong authority over his flock. Most of the people still lack the drive and daring which Kemal envisaged as the main ingredients of the character of the new Turk. And a dervish order is back again, called the *Tijanis,* waging a campaign against Ataturkism in a small but symptomatic way.

In other words, the great Turkish Revolution bogged down with Kemal's death. His successor Ismet Inönü, the presumed executor of his will, never had even a particle of Ataturk's frenzied drive. Ismet Pasha's successor in the presidential chair, Celal Bayar, leader of the Democratic Party, never even wanted to have such a drive.

It is not hard to find the reason for Turkey's present plight. It takes generations—not mere years—to alter a nation's basic traits. Turkey has had only one generation at her disposal to bring about the change. But to plan and to begin was in itself a historic deed.

CHAPTER 8

The Curse of Too Much History

Iran First and All the Time

Shortly after the midcentury mark, Iranians were asked how they expected to operate the immensely complex Anglo-Iranian Oil Company which they had just expropriated, since they lacked the technical knowledge. In words of flaming indignation they answered that the people who gave the world some of its greatest poets, an Omar Khayyam, a Firdusi, surely would know how to run a mere oil well. They did not. Iranians have shown themselves to be afflicted with too much history.

They have, indeed, a very long history in the forefront of the world stage. Also, they have an epochal continuity of history, such as not even the Arabs can offer. In the face of the tidal waves of conquests by Arabs, Mongols and Turks, in the face of constant danger of being engulfed by the Russians and the British, they have saved their Indo-European tongue and native ways.

For a very long time their language was the tongue of much of the Middle East and of India. It was not a very long time ago that British diplomats at their Indian posts felt compelled to study Persian in order to be able to converse with members of the better classes. Persia's language was at one time the *lingua franca* of those classes all the way from the Danube to the Ganges.

Empires overran the Middle East, established themselves, then receded. New conquerors came and the map of the region underwent constant changes. In the midst of this maelstrom, Persia remained a remarkable phenomenon of withdrawal and return. What were the main reasons for this seeming miracle?

Persia, which today calls herself Iran, occupies a transition zone and was therefore not sucked into the East or West, but was able to maintain herself outside of the Roman and Byzantine empires. She was also able to stand outside the Ottoman Empire and the realm of the Grand Moghuls.

Topography helped, too, the rugged country, with its savage mountains, the Elburz and Zagros; its savage deserts, Dasht-i-Kavir and Dasht-i-Lut; its places in the moon between desert and peaks; the cosmic upheavals of nature's forces.

More important, the pride of the Iranian ruling classes has sustained their country. They are strong people because they are proud people and the steel of their pride conquers enemies better equipped with arms. A nation feeling that superior cannot be subdued.

And now a paradoxical cause of this strength. Partly at least Iran's strength may be due to the fact that she is and has long been weak. Iran's location on the peripheries of Great Powers may have been her salvation. If she had been strong she might have presented a danger to these nations, but it was not deemed necessary to bother about her.

The Long Night of Despotism

One of the greatest occupational hazards in Iran for centuries was to have been born a monarch's brother. One of the first steps a Shah, the newly enthroned ruler, did was to remove his next of kin, whose only possible defense was to be the first with the flashing dagger.

For many centuries Iran was a despotism, the nature of which is indicated by the ruler's title: "Son of a Shah, King of Kings, Great Chief, Refuge of the World, Shadow of God, May Allah Exalt His Sultanate." Let us glance at the Shah as he exercised his power until well into the nineteenth century. There was a revival of royal despotism which was ended only during the Second World War. Although it was extinguished, it continued in another form: the tremendous power of the leading families.

In the past it was from the Shah alone that even the most exalted governors of the realm derived their authority, which was lost as soon as the royal countenance was shrouded in the dreaded cloud of displeasure. The Sultan's Shadow was the name of the prince who was allowed to live out his allotted span of time.

This system exterminated the aristocracy of the country. The absence of aristocracy helped despotism stay at the helm. Strange as it may sound, the grandees would have mitigated the extremes of tryanny. However, it seems to be contrary to human nature to have no restraints put upon even the most autocratic of authorities. In the course of time such a restraint was built up in Iran within the circle of the religious teachers, (*mulla*), and even more of the *mujtahid*, "one who strives," the scholarly clergyman. As the hand of the despot began to falter, that of the clergy was strengthened. It followed the royal pattern in imposing a reign of terror upon the little people, claiming sanctification for evil deeds.

Bad Old Times

The memory of these bad old times is not washed out as yet. There are people who remember the reign of Shah Nasr ed-Din, whose life closed at the end of the last century. He was the last of the old-fashioned tyrants, but only to his people, not in foreign relations. His country had become the political football of Britain and Russia by that time.

This Shah followed the hallowed custom of living on the fat of the land of his people, moving from place to place with his imperial retinue. After the passing of the court, the countryside looked as if it had been devoured by the locust plague. One region of the country, however, appeared to be prosperous in the midst of desolation, and the secret of its success was found to be this:

The people of the region had dispatched a deputation to the Shah, who had just ascended the throne, to express to him their abiding loyalty. It also carried a gift of great value which it was ready to lay at His Majesty's feet under one condition. That condition was that the August Personage give his gracious pledge on the Koran never to set His blessed foot on the soil of their land. The monarch accepted the gift, made the pledge on the Writ, kept it and, as a result, the region was prosperous.

Since the Shahs were living on the fat of the land, they could indulge in great luxuries and one of these was to have many wives. Shah Fath Ali, a contemporary of Napoleon, was said to have emulated Solomon in having a thousand wives, which was far more than the Koran counseled. However, he complied with the Law by taking most of them as his concubines. At the time of his death his offspring was reported to have numbered many hundreds.

There were thousands of Imperial Highnesses in Iran when the observant German diplomat, Friedrich Rosen, was posted there toward the end of the last century. Many of these exalted personages filled extremely modest stations in life. When the Ambassador stopped over at Kermanshah on his way from Baghdad to Tehran, he found that many of the petty officials in that town were Iranian Imperial Princes.

In Baghdad he engaged a cook who was most anxious to return to Kermanshah, where he had left his Princess wife. The royal lady was so grateful to Ambassador Rosen for having brought back her spouse that she spontaneously volunteered to wash not only his linen but also his retinue's, which was large. For this she took no money and the Ambassador sent her some sugar loaves. So delighted was she with this that the husband cook called again on the Ambassador to tell him that because of his generous gift his wife, Her Imperial Highness, was graciously pleased to grant her benefactor the unusual permission to inquire about her august health.

Nasr ed-Din was more modest than his predecessor and according to Rosen he had only two to three hundred wives. Sometimes the diplomat caught a glimpse of these unfortunate creatures when they were driven past him, and they lifted their veils furtively. Many of them appear to have been tall Circassians of extraordinary beauty, with fair complexions and dark eyes, their eyebrows artifically connected over the bridge of the nose. Trespassers on the harem intimacy were reported to have met speedy and cruel death. The Shah, who was inordinately fond of hunting, took with him on his expeditions several "sections" of his beautiful wives.

This last of the absolute rulers of nineteenth century Iran was no longer absolute in his relations with the major powers. Since they knew how impotent he was in the international field, they treated him accordingly. When one of the foreign spokesmen handed him a note he considered insulting, he responded with the sickly smile of a laughing hyena in the foreigner's presence. No sooner was that man out of sight, however, than the Shah let himself go, exploding in a stream of vulgar expressions, including his choice phrase: "I defile his father's grave."

"The King and They"

Under such rulers it was an art for the subjects to remain alive. How was one to escape being despoiled by the imperial gangsters? To save one's head and fortune the subject had to practice deception and that, too, became an art and science. Successful dissimulation may have meant all the difference between life and death. It is in this light that one can understand a prominent Iranian's answer to the question of what was his country's main contribution to the contemporary world: "If it were not for Iran, the world would be at a loss for liars."

However, the Shahs were bound to lose importance as the major powers began to trespass on their country's independence. After the First World War there was another attempt to reform Iran, followed by an attempt to bring back the days of yore when despotism was in flower.

Power Corrupts

Throughout the years Lord Acton's words resound: "Power corrupts, absolute power corrupts absolutely."

This must have been the cause of the downfall of Shah Reza Khan Pahlavi.

Iran's throne during the First World War was occupied by the do-nothing Shah, Sultan Ahmed, a member of the Qajar dynasty, who felt far more at home in Nice than in Tehran.

The Shah liked the arrangement under which Britain and Russia ruled in his place, while he spent his country's money in France. After the First World War the Soviets had to abandon Iran temporarily, leaving the field open to the British. Since the Shah was busy playing the roulette, and the country had no strong aristocracy to have its say, there was nobody in the country to interpose a veto, except the people and they did not count. Iran was on the point of falling to Britain when Reza Khan, Commander in Chief (*Sardareh Sepah*) of the Persian Cossack Brigade, stepped in. That Brigade had been set up by the Russians before the war, but now it was not under Soviet influence.

Reza, unlike the ruling dynasty, was of Persian origin. He entered the service of the Brigade at the turn of the century, and sheer ability enabled him to rise in the ranks. He had no important family links. It is said that he was illiterate and learned to write his name much later.

At the time the British appeared to be ready to take over Iran, he received a call from influential members of the clergy, representing the only strong public opinion in the country, to act. This was in 1921. With the four thousand troops at his disposal, he marched on Tehran. The British would have been ready to take over the country, but they could not afford to fight for it. In Tehran, Reza made himself Commander in Chief of all Iranian forces and Minister of War. He saw to it that the country was not to become a British protectorate.

Meanwhile the Soviets were playing high-level politics by relinquishing the special rights the Russian imperial government had acquired in Iran. Then, after they had gained Tehran's good will, they induced it to sign a pact as a counterweight to the British. Its most significant article contained the following provision:

> Both of the High Contracting Parties are agreed that in case there should be attempts on the part of third countries to realize a rapacious policy on the territory of Persia [Iran] through armed intervention or to turn her territory into a base for military action against the Russian Soviet Federated Socialist Republics . . . the government of the latter shall have the right to send its troops into Persian territory in order to take necessary military measures in the interest of self-defense. . . .

Shah Sultan Ahmed was deposed by the *majlis*, National Assembly in October 1925, and thenceforth he did not need to worry about interrupting his pleasurable stays in Europe.

A few weeks later, the legislature elected Reza Khan hereditary ruler under the name of Reza Khan Pahlavi, Shahanshah, King of Kings. A few more days and the Royal Prince, Shahpur Mohammed Reza, was proclaimed *valiahd*, Heir Presumptive to the throne. Thus the crown of Darius the Great was made hereditary in the family of the former Cossack officer.

Iran had descended to the nadir of life and became the doormat of the world. *Ex Occidente Lux* was then the dazzling motto: "Out of the West Comes Light." Cast off your tattered garments, the East heard, and adopt the ways of the West, the ways of the victorious new day. Improve your roads, build factories, start irrigation projects, free yourself from foreign countries, stand on your own feet. The Mustafa Kemal regime was showing the East just then how to do it, and progressive people throughout the region fell under his spell. Reza Shah was set to become the Kemal Pasha of Iran.

He appeared to have the making of the New Man of the East; not the endlessly philosophizing type that can solve all problems in endless discussions but cannot drive in a nail. He was a man of action who had fought his way to the top, with nobody to help him. He knew how to command and he had bold concepts.

However, in Iran he faced odds greater than those which Kemal had encountered in Turkey. The Iranians lacked the deference to authority which characterized the Turks. Also, the Iranians were less flexible, perhaps because they were more indigenous to the soil and did not have to adjust themselves to a new environment. The Turks had had to adjust themselves to their setting, to which they had come from afar.

Iran, furthermore, was more a conglomerate of peoples and ways of life, and not as homogeneous as Turkey had become. In Iran headstrong tribal leaders proliferated, Kings within the Kingdom. The title of the Shah was descriptive: King of Kings.

Reza could not disestablish Islam and thereby place his country on an entirely new foundation, that of a secular nation. In Iran the Shi'ah sect was always considered a national institution and to tamper with it was tantamount to tampering with the nation.

The Shah did attack the antiquated bases of the old, sometimes with great courage. He changed the law system from the Koranic Shari'a to a secular code along French lines. He took pains to improve education and invited European experts to the Tehran University. He introduced reforms to improve health and sanitation. He ordered women to discard their veils.

The Shah knew well that westernization meant industrialization. He was well aware of the fact that Iran was bound to be dependent on foreign countries if she was to be dependent upon their imports. His country had little more than handicrafts and it was not easy to start from scratch. The limitations imposed upon him were serious. The country lacked important industrial raw materials. Where was it to get the technical knowledge, managerial and business ability?

He did undertake the task of industrialization. During his regime some 150 industrial and mining enterprises were built. Iran, too, was deficient in capital that the rich men wanted to risk. They could get far more money by lending it to the peasants at usurious rates. In Iran, too, the government had to go into business. It operated about one half of the new plants, but that was the more important half.

Proudest achievement of the Reza regime was the Trans-Iranian railway, to span the country from the Persian Gulf to the Caspian Sea. How badly it was needed we may judge from the fact that when it got launched, all of Iran had just a little over 200 miles of railways, and this for a country of 628,000 square miles. Tehran's own "railway station" served a line only five miles long, to suburban Shah Abdul Azim.

The Trans-Iranian is 910 miles in length, built under the supervision of an international syndicate which included Americans, Germans, then Swedes and Danes, who were considered neutral in this region. Much of the labor force was recruited in Italy.

The importance of foreign policy even in railroad building was well exemplified by the trials and tribulations of the Trans-Iranian. When a railway is built, especially if the country is poor, it usually seeks out the densest human settlements. In the case of this line that could not be done because then the Trans-Iranian would have run toward the Soviet frontier, against which the British protested, and toward the British-controlled Indian boundary, which appeared highly objectionable to the Kremlin. This is the reason why the Trans-Iranian passes through empty country, terminating in a land of nowhere on the Caspian Sea, definitely away from the Soviets.

As finally drawn, the line turned out to be a highly difficult engineering feat with more than two hundred tunnels, from sea level to an altitude of ten thousand feet. Within the radius of less than a thousand feet the line traverses six bridges and four tunnels in one stretch, and in another, sixty miles out of ninety consist of tunnels.

The capital, Tehran, was to be a monument to the greatness of the Shah. The city was modernized. There was the Avenue

ShahReza which Second World War Americans dubbed Tehran's Park Avenue. However, from the magnificence of that street one stepped back a thousand years in a matter of minutes.

In front of the magnificent new buildings the western visitor is still shocked by Tehran's amazing multipurpose water and sewer system, in which people wash their filthy garments, into which they urinate and from which they drink. No wonder that the death rate is still appallingly high. Some Iranians who can bear no criticism of even the worst features of their country point out that this multipurpose system is really democratic, since it makes water available to the poorest.

The Age of Decay

Some observers spoke about Reza's split personality, which followed the Zoroastrian pattern; Reza the Good, Ahuramazda; and Reza the Evil, Ahriman. That split personality appears to have been not so much of the man himself as of his position. When he reached the pinnacle he suffered a dizzy spell. Naïvely, he expected gratitude from those he had favored. He received a shock, resulting in frenzied wrath, by the ingratitude of the chief court favorite, Abol Hossein Khan Teymourtashe, Minister of the Court. The monarch had trusted this man of reputed sterling character until the day he found out the truth.

Shah Reza was modern not only in what he was trying to do for his country but also because he wanted to make a pot of gold on industrial enterprises. In the spirit of the modern times he had bought shares in leading enterprises, and much to his dismay he found that invariably they failed. Investigation disclosed that failure was due to the actions of the trusted Minister who exacted an unreasonable amount of protection money from the plants. One inquiry led to another and then the truth began to dawn. The miscreant parading as the faithful steward had been gathering the wires of the government in his greedy hands. The Shah now suspected him of having his eyes on the throne.

Full of bitterness, the Shah had the erstwhile favorite flung into jail, from which only his mortal remains were removed. This may have been the Great Divide in the monarch's life.

Thereafter he became the proverbial Oriental despot, the hermit of the peacock throne.

The rest of Reza's rule took place behind a steel curtain. There was an impenetrable censorship. No longer was there any law in the land. Whatever struck the King's fancy he took from his subjects, and his secret police terrorized the land. Those who incurred his displeasure were reputed to have been killed in a ghastly way. Air bubbles were introduced in the victim's veins and he died a thousand deaths of untold agony.

The reform movement now yielded to misgovernment. The bank note circulation increased fivefold within half a dozen years, and the land's gold supply was ebbing away. The more vicious the rule the louder were the sycophants' paeans, fearful for their sinecures and lives. To the masses of the people, however, the royal reign of terror conveyed little meaning. With the profound wisdom of the eternally downtrodden they knew that no matter who skinned the poor, he skinned them alive. Some of these common people may have derived pleasure from the knowledge that the horrors of the torture chamber were now visited upon the mighties of the realm.

Traveling Salesmen and Statesmen

During the "Age of Hitler" the Nazis told the Iranians that they were people of superior blood, authentic Aryans, and that pleased them greatly. They also told them that the large Iranian province of Kerman really meant German, and that, too, pleased the people. If a nation's blood was good, everything was good, and if the Iranians were Germans, it was so much the better. That seemed to take care of everything and one did not need to worry about the famine in the province of Kerman, about epidemics in another region, the collapse of morale and national bankruptcy.

The authentic Aryans were admired by the leading Nazis, including the Minister of Propaganda, Herr Josef Goebbels, who told the Iranians how wonderful they were and that the rest of the world should draw inspiration from them. He picked up dysentery in drinking-water but it was not a disease that affected anybody's blood. General von Blomberg also paid a courtesy call, but it seems reasonably certain that in spite of the Iranians' dazzling blood he found little in their military system which the Germans could copy. The ubiquitous Dr. Hjalmar Horace Greeley Schacht, financial wizard and destroyer of Germany, also came to admire, but he left the country disappointed. Faultless money management, it seems, was not a function of superior blood.

Nazi propaganda films were in great vogue in Tehran, Shiraz and other places because they showed what could happen to people with inferior blood, such as the French, and even to people who rated a passing mark, the Dutch. It was all highly instructive, showing that it was profitable to do business with Hitler.

The British Embassy in Tehran insisted that the German traveling salesmen were not of the genuine variety, and for once the Soviet representative agreed with his British colleague. Thereupon the British and Soviet embassies undertook a joint *démarche* at court requesting the Shah to expel the Nazi spies parading as businessmen. As usual, the Shah was cross, and he replied that he had no objection against expelling all foreigners. Thereupon the British and the Soviet agreed that if anybody was to be expelled it should be His Majesty. Their troops began to move upon the capital from north and south. Reza Khan was placed on a plane headed for South Africa, after he had been asked to sign a patent of abdication. His twenty-two-year-old son, Mohammed Reza Pahlavi, was proclaimed *Shahanshah*. The young man had a Swiss education, appeared to be western-minded and seemed to favor democracy. The Anglo-Soviet-Iranian agreement was signed on January 29, 1942, setting up the British and Soviet spheres in the country, providing that the "guests" were to respect the territorial integrity, sovereignty and political independence of their host and that they were to withdraw their troops from Iran not later than six months after the end of the hostilities.

The Iranians disliked the British, feared the Soviets, were resentful against both because of their occupation of Iran. They looked to the United States for aid—everybody else did—and America made Iran eligible for lend-lease, sending her also all kinds of advisers, including economic and military experts.

President Roosevelt became interested in Iran and sent one of his emissaries, Patrick J. Hurley, on a special mission to Tehran. He received a report from him early in 1944 which he summarized in a memorandum to Secretary of State Cordell Hull (reproduced in the latter's *Memoirs*), where he said:

"Iran is definitely a very, very backward nation. It contains really a series of tribes, and 99 per cent of the population is, in effect, in bondage to the other 1 per cent. The 99 per cent do not own their land . . ."

Stirrings in Azerbaijan

There were several versions as to what happened in Iran under the regime of the British and the Soviets. Dr. Goebbels, who was an interested party, reported the following in his Diary on May 14, 1942: "Most appalling conditions are reported from Iran under the Bolshevik-English rule. A terrible famine is said to have started there. Englishmen do not know how to organize a country. At best they know only how to exploit it in the most vigorous manner for their war effort."

Less prejudiced observers, on the other hand, reported that both the British and the Soviet had introduced long overdue reforms. The Soviets in the north launched a vigorous campaign against malaria, and they joined the British in fighting the terrible locust plague. As to the Soviets, it seemed that they would like to continue their program of reform even after the expiration of their lease. In other words, they lingered on and seemed to settle down in Iran's northwestern region, known as Azerbaijan, one of the most fruitful territories, densely populated by people speaking a Turki language and related to the Soviets' own Azerbaijani across the boundary. The capital of the Iranian province had a railway link with Russia but not with the capital of Iran.

Under Reza Shah, Azerbaijan was treated not so much as a province as an occupied territory, and at one time that mighty potentate prohibited the use of Turki. He also employed harsh methods in despoiling it of its food supply.

During the Reza regime there was an underground Socialist

organization in Azerbaijan which the authorities ferreted out and broke up in the middle thirties. At about the same time there appeared at one of the Azerbaijani frontier posts a nondescript group of people asking for admission on the ground that as Iranians they had been evicted by the Soviets. After some bargaining the group was admitted into Iran. One of their members was a man called Jafar Pishevari, who was to play a role in Iran's post-Second World War history.

All of a sudden this Pishevari appeared, before the end of 1945, as the President of the Azerbaijan Autonomous Republic. Previous to that there had appeared a party with the name of Tudeh, meaning "masses," with a program calling for most of the reforms the region needed, such as, for instance, land reform, a democratic constitution, and social security. Now the Tudeh changed its name to Democratic Party, disarmed the local organs of law and elements of the Iranian army.

Shortly thereafter a Kurdish Peoples' Republic was established in the nearby mountains. Iran was powerless to act against this sudden onslaught of republicitis but this was also the business of Britain and the United States. Should the Soviets take over Iran in the Middle East, the balance of power would be upset. From that vantage position the Kremlin could foment disaffection in the Arabic countries and there would be another rich harvest of ripe fruit.

The West took the case of the Azerbaijan Autonomous Republic and the continued stay of the Soviet forces in Iran to the United Nations. Public opinion in the West was alerted. Finally, about two months after the original deadline, the Soviet troops moved out of Iran. But the autonomous republic of Azerbaijan remained. Then, one day, the Iranian army began to march into Azerbaijan, found that the Soviets troops were gone and that the autonomous government was gone, too.

The iron curtain of Iran was rung down then and the world learned little about what was going on there. Some years later Supreme Court Justice William O. Douglas visited the region and reported that the land reform and social security system set up by the former autonomous government had been scrapped. The revolutionary regime had set up schools, clinics, hospitals, liberalized tenant-landlord relations. There was no trace of these reforms either by the time the Justice called. The return of the loyal troops signalized the beginning of wholesale slaughter and a denunciation was sufficient to establish guilt. The landlords were back again, acting very patriotic when laying heavy hands on the people. Any hint at the need of overdue reforms was a confession of guilt of Communist sympathies.

In the rest of Iran the Tudeh party was allowed to carry on for some time, under the shadow of suspicion that it was crypto-Communist. Then it was forbidden, and it submerged into the underground, to emerge intermittently as the inefficiency of the organs of law and the provocation of frenzied patriotic bodies allowed it to function.

Subsequently, it was reported to be operating under several names, the best known of which was: Association to Combat Imperialism. It took a strong stand in favor of Iran's nationalization of oil and just as strong a stand against Britain and America. Thus it was operating on a common front with the superpatriotic bodies which combated it and which it fought, in return.

The Camel Jumps the Ditch

"It is easier to make a camel jump a ditch than to make a fool listen to reason," a Middle Eastern proverb says. In midsummer 1952, the camel appeared to be ready to jump the proverbial ditch.

A series of portentous events were taking place in the boiling cauldron that was Tehran. Riots flared up in the streets and people were killed. Iran's Premier, Dr. Mohammed Mossadeq, received dictatorial powers to deal with the crisis. A strange man he was, engaging in tricks that did not betoken strength. For days he did not dare to budge from the parliament building for fear of his foes. Perennially sick, he transacted state business in his bed. He cried at the least provocation when the audience was large enough. What was his strength in the face of many weaknesses openly flaunted?

He was not the spokesman of the common man but protected their interest when this served his purpose; whenever he needed numbers to buttress his policy, in other words. A rich man himself, he was the friend of the rich. He was shrewd and utterly unscrupulous: a man who could see simple, significant relationships and act decisively when action was needed. He told Iran that she was poor because she had been robbed by the British oil company. That was a good point to arouse the people and to divert their attention from those whom an eminent American in another age called the "malefactors of great wealth." However, conditions in Iran grew worse, not better, and something else had to be pulled out of the hat.

Dr. Mossadeq was supported by the octagenarian speaker of parliament, Ayatollah Kashani, the little ancient with the blue eyes that were always inflamed. One of the political clergy in whom Iranian history abounds, this man of religion operated a gang of cutthroats to terrorize the land. A strange sight, indeed, it was to see this team of oldsters manipulating the wires in one of the world's oldest countries.

The foreign press reported the details of the land reform previously described but did not seem to be concerned about where the money was to come from. Certainly it would not come from the coffers of the State, which were all but empty, so that government officials could not be paid. Luckily for Dr. Mossadeq and Ayatollah Kashani, the Soviet Union is contiguous with Iran and they knew only too well that this fact was worth much money. The United States had already started pouring funds into Iran in the form of Point Four programs: natural resources, industries, communications, transportation, housing, labor, education, farm and health projects. Indeed, Iran was the first country in the world with which the United States signed a Point Four agreement. In mid-1952 more than forty million dollars of that aid was reported available for Iran and more was to come.

These funds may finance the officially announced reforms. Experience, however, has taught the student of Iranian life that announcements are not synonymous with reforms, and that between the word and deed many a slip may occur. If the reforms were really carried out, the democratic world would have cause to rejoice. A tragedy in Iran would have widespread repercussions on the rest of the world as well.

Meanwhile . . . there was the Soviet Union whose frontiers ran parallel with those of Iran for a thousand miles. And also meanwhile . . . American officers were trying to train an Iranian army and in Iran there was no army to train. But there were people in uniform of the Nazi type flaunting the swastika of "racial purity." Their number was small to be sure, but several of them were parading in front of the Soviet delegation. Then there were the Pan-Iranians who wanted a Greater Iran, including also Soviet territory. What kept the Kremlin from simply walking into the Land of Darius and turning it into a satrapy? The apprehension, no doubt, that by doing so it might unleash a major war. And so the world was looking at Iran with deep concern.

CHAPTER 9

The West in the East

Israel Builds a House

It is a dot on the map, the tiny State of Israel, a small island in the midst of the Arab world. But its contrast with the surrounding pattern of life is significant. Great inequalities characterize the social structure of the Arab world, while Israel strives to make the Prophets' admonition for social justice take shape.

Who should know more than the Jew what it means to be the underdog; he, the most cruelly persecuted of all minorities.

It is only on the map that Israel is in the Middle East. Culturally, she is in the very heart of the West. This presents a problem and an opportunity. A problem because a small slice of the West in the East is an anomaly, an alien body, to be cast out by its environment, lacking the stimulation of well-matched rivalry, in danger of being sucked into the gaping hole of D.I.P.

This is also an opportunity for a country to serve as a bridge between East and West. From this focus the constructive features of the Occident may be transferred to the Orient. Our civilization can offer much to the East in the form of higher living standards, better health, organization, security. Nor is that all. There is close connection between material and cultural values. How can one speak about the higher values of life where every third child dies before reaching its first birthday? How can one speak of civilization, when he is bound to perish before he is afforded a chance to show his value?

In return, the East can offer us indestructible values, of which our ancestors were recipients in the past, and which seem to be lost in the fog of the great contemporary obscurity. It was the mission of the Middle East to fill the empty vessel with spiritual content. Even today it can show us how to look at ourselves within the framework of eternity. It can teach us not to drive the pursuit of material interests to the very limit, the point of no return, and beyond that, to the point of self-destruction, the point of race suicide. The Israeli think that they can help to bring about the happy blend—the West in the East, synthesizing the values of both.

Few countries have been written about as much as Israel, young nation of an old people. There is no point in repeating what has been said so often and sometimes very well. This chapter confines itself mainly to Israel's current problems.

In the Beginning . . .

It began with a treason trial and the time was the end of the nineteenth century. The accused was a certain Captain Alfred Dreyfus of the French General Staff, a patriotic Frenchman, and an officer of impeccable record. At that time two Frances were fighting for their futures. The one was republican and liberal and the other one was monarchist and reactionary. It was this second France which wanted to come to grips with the French republic. Captain Dreyfus was a Jew, in the army of the French republic. He was accused of having sold military secrets to the German Reich.

He was found guilty of treason and imprisoned on Devil's Island, off the tropical South American coast, truly the devil's own land. At first the outside world knew nothing about the case, but the French army knew and gradually others, too, began to learn about it. It became a *cause célèbre,* which started a "cold civil war" in France. The case dragged on and on. In the end the convicted man was vindicated and received the decoration of the Legion of Honor, while his detractors, perjurors, were unmasked as the enemies of the republic.

The Dreyfus case stirred up, among many others, the Paris correspondent of Vienna's leading newspaper, *Neue Freie Presse.* Dr. Theodor Herzl was a native of Budapest, long-time resident of the Habsburg capital on the Danube, a highly respected citizen of Austria. Although born a Jew, he was not really aware of it. But the Dreyfus case jolted him out of his cosmopolitan attitude. If this could happen in France, what could happen elsewhere? Under the impact of the case he revised his attitude toward the Jews and wrote one of those books that make history. The title of the book was *Judenstaat* (*Jewish State*) and in it he wrote: "Our national character is too historically famous and in spite of every degradation, too fine to make its annihilation desirable."

That is how modern political Zionism began, Jewish nationalism, the return to the Holy Land of those who want to go there, the persecuted Jews. Then came the massacre of the Jews in the Russian empire, an empire in agony, needing scapegoats, and they were very conveniently on hand. They slaughtered Jews in Kishenev, in Gomel, insulted them in many other places. And this was at the beginning of the twentieth century.

This jolted many members of the Jewish community out of their complacency. Zionism was in the air. Young Jewish people from eastern Europe started going to Palestine, to live and work there. Not just to die there, as some of the oldsters wanted. These young people were rejected in their birthplace, in the Jewish Pale of Russia, treated as intruders, at best to be tolerated, but not for long.

Palestine, the country of their dreams, turned out to be a nightmare, ridden with malaria, poverty—miserable hovels on heaps of stones in the midst of pestilential swamps. It had spots of beauty, too, but they were few and far between. Once it had been Canaan and now the young people wanted to re-create that land. To make the desert bloom like a rose. Then came the First World War and the Balfour Declaration: His Majesty's government viewed with favor the establishment in Palestine of a national home for the Jewish people. . . .

The war was over and Britain assumed the mandate over Palestine. Then the trouble began. Jews kept on going into the little land, mostly young people and mostly from eastern Europe, where the new Polish nationalism barely tolerated them. There were only 55,000 Jews in Palestine at the time of the First World War armistice. Two decades later there were some 600,000 of them.

The majority of Palestine people were poverty-stricken Arabs. The effendi landowners sold much of their land to the Jewish National Fund at high prices and then started stirring up the fellaheen, by telling them that the Jews were robbing the people of their land.

The notorious Grand Mufti fomented a series of uprisings, the most violent of which was the Arab Rebellion, beginning in 1937 and lasting until the outbreak of World War II. Jewish settlers had already organized their resistance forces which took the form of *Haganah,* a paramilitary body.

We have seen that it was Britain's policy to fill out the Middle East vacuum with Arabs, and therefore she adhered to a pro-Arab policy in Palestine. As the international horizon was getting darker in the face of the threat of aggressive Fascist powers, the situation in Palestine was also becoming tenser. The danger threatened that the Arabs would make common cause with the Axis. It was in an attempt to keep the Arabs in line that His Majesty's government published the White Paper of 1939, which the Jews considered a betrayal of the Balfour pledge. Under the White Paper, Jewish immigration into Palestine and the transfer of land from Arabs to Jews were to be severely restricted. And this at a time when Europe's Jews were facing extinction at Nazi hands.

During and After World War II

The Jews felt they had been double-crossed. Yet, when World War II broke out the Palestinian Jews had no doubt as to where their interests and sympathies lay. They entertained no thought of impeding the British war effort; on the contrary, they were more than eager to join the British forces fighting the Axis in the North African desert. Jewish units fought creditably in those campaigns and also in the invasion of Italy.

The Zionists, meanwhile, were preparing the stage for the postwar period. The American Zionist Organization, meeting in a conference under the chairmanship of the veteran leader, David Ben-Gurion, convened in New York in 1942, and formulated the so-called Biltmore Program, named after the hotel where the conference was held. This served as the Declaration of Independence of Palestine Jewry. The Program called for the earliest establishment of a Jewish Commonwealth in Palestine, the creation of a Jewish army and the repudiation of the White Paper. Meanwhile the gates of Palestine were to be kept open for immigration under the control of the Jewish Agency, which was the highest executive organ of the Zionists and other friends of Zion. The Agency was also to undertake the development of the barren land in the Holy Land.

During the war most of the European Jews were exterminated by the German Nazis and their satellites. When it was over there was a tremendous pressure on the part of the survivors to reach the Holy Land, so as to forget the horror they witnessed and get away from the scenes of the slaughter of their kin.

There was no eagerness, however, on the part of the British government to meet this demand. The helm in London was now in the hands of the British Labour Party, strongly pro-Zionist while in opposition, but anti-Zionist now, in power.

The United States also entered the conflict, the two great political parties and the Presidential candidates calling for the admission of larger numbers of Jews into Palestine and the softening of the British attitude.

Since the inception of the mandate there had been about twenty important commissions to inquire into the Palestine problem. Now the British called upon the United States to help solve it. An Anglo-American Commission was appointed to find a solution, but its recommendation was not accepted. Then the British government decided to submit the issue to the United Nations, which in turn produced a program envisaging the partition of Palestine into an Arab and a Jewish region. The city of Jerusalem and the surrounding area, altogether 289 square miles, were to be placed under a special international regime. The Assembly of the United Nations approved the plan in spite of the Arabs' violent opposition. The Jews of Palestine accepted the general idea of the partition, while objecting to some of the details of the territorial division.

Months of uncertainty followed, marked by vacillation in the policies of the western powers and strife between Jews and Arabs. At one time the United States government favored partition and then changed its mind and advocated a United Nations regime in the Holy Land. Politics and diplomacy were at grips in this case, the White House representing the first and the State Department the second. Our foreign policy followed that of the British in this respect, but there were very few Arab voters in key states of the Union. The American Secretary of Defense, James V. Forrestal, was to write in his diary on October 21, 1948, that actually our Palestine policy had been made for "squalid political purposes." He hoped that some day he would make his position on this issue clear.

In the spring of 1948 the British decided to wash their hands of the whole mess and announced that they were pulling out of Palestine. This withdrawal began officially on May 12th. Two days later the General Council of Palestine Jewry met in the all-Jewish city of Tel Aviv and proclaimed the establishment of *Medinat Israel*—the State of Israel.

This was the signal for all the neighbors of the new State to take the large-scale hostile action they had threatened. The United States government promptly recognized the State of Israel, and the announcement came from the White House. The United Nations was debating the issue. Meanwhile the armed forces of Egypt, Jordan, and Iraq began moving into Palestine, where there was also a local Arab force in operation.

Later these were reinforced by contingents from Syria, Lebanon, and a token force from Saudi Arabia. The Arab countries allied against Israel had a total estimated population of some 35 million, while the defenders represented a nation of some 600,000 people. The Israel army numbered about 75,000 members at its peak, and it was supported by women's auxiliary services.

The Arab countries were well supplied with arms, while the Israelis were not. Jordan's Arab Legion, equipped and officered by the British, was considered an exceptionally formidable unit. If ever there was a hopeless military situation, Israel seemed to be facing it.

David and Goliath

Near the spot where the Biblical combat of David and Goliath had taken place, the ill-matched armies met. Miraculously, history repeated itself. In this case, however, David would not have won if Goliath had not helped by knocking himself out. The armed forces of that proud nation, Egypt, presented a disgraceful spectacle. The Arab Legion of Jordan was effective, but it did not help the Egyptians. The Syrian army was not too bad, either, but it did not want to support Jordan. This was the principal trouble, backbiting and jealousy. There was no unified command, of course. The morale of most of the Arab units was bad. The common soldiers were ignorant and uninformed, and they must have been asking themselves what they were fighting for. Would a victory benefit them or their pashas? The physical condition of most of the Arab soldiers was poor. Weakened by disease and poor diet, they lacked the physical stamina to fight.

The Israeli on the other hand knew very well what they were fighting for. For them it was a simple matter of survival. If they were defeated and pushed out of this little land, where could they turn? The plans and dreams of generations of Zionists would be ground into the dust.

The United Nations ordered a truce, then appointed a mediator in the person of Count Folke Bernadotte of Sweden, President of the International Red Cross. He prepared a plan for the restoration of peace in Palestine but was assassinated while passing through the Jewish quarter of Jerusalem in September

1948. His place was taken by an American, Dr. Ralph Bunche. In January 1949, he was able to arrange a truce between Egypt and Israel, and the other Arab States soon took similar action. The United Nations then continued to wrestle with the task of working out a genuine peace acceptable to both sides. The armistice frontiers of Israel enclosed an area of 8,100 square miles, the size of New Jersey, and its rapidly growing population totaled about a million and a half four years after the end of the war.

Problems Without End

The government was barely established when a host of urgent questions arose, and foremost among these was the problem of immigration. The conventional solution would have been to allow the country to recover from the war before turning to this question. The Israel-Arab war had rendered the position of hundreds of thousands of the Jews in the Middle East untenable, and quick action appeared to be the only way to head off the gathering disaster.

A large number of Jews were languishing in Europe's DP camps, their morale visibly sinking. An answer was demanded also to the problem of Jews in the satellite countries. Rumania had the largest number of Jews, next to the Soviet Union. The Peoples' Democracies were prejudiced against the middlemen, and the Jews were the traditional tradesmen of the region. A large number of them were professionals, the type of people wanting to ask questions that are not to be asked in authoritarian countries. All this added up to anti-Judaism, even if not to anti-Semitism.

The backward Middle East was to provide many of the immigrants, and how were they to blend with advanced Europeans? Democracy meant little in regions from which many of the settlers were to come, and how were they to be fitted into a system which Israel hoped was to become a model of democracy? Government meant oppression in the lands from whence many of the newcomers were to come. Would they carry over their natural aversion to despotic government to Israel's democratic state?

Then, too, land was scarce in Israel, but it would have faced a problem even if good soil had been abundant because conventional farming cannot support a large population. A rapid and large increase of people calls for a higher degree of industrialization. Small European countries with extremely limited resources have been able to create high living standards by turning to industry. Again a host of difficulties arose. Industries may grow in war when a country is already highly industrialized, but it is hard to get them started when there is no peace. It is still harder to get them launched when neither primary raw materials nor markets are close at hand.

"Kibbutz Galuyoth"

Israel's picturesque language calls it the *kibbutz galuyoth*, ingathering of the exiles.

When the new State was born, it already had a large population on hand. The resources of the little country were scant, while the ravages of the war were great. A large influx of immigrants with no knowledge of the special conditions of their new homes forced people to live on aid from abroad, supplementing the meager resources of the land.

"We love immigration but only few among us love immigrants," Prime Minister David Ben-Gurion twitted his countrymen.

As a matter of fact, the ingathering of the exiles was accepted by all parties. The Prime Minister called it the "greatest event in Jewish history." Under his leadership Israel's government threw the country's gates open to all comers with no delay. The majority of the people was ready to eat less and live in smaller quarters: immigration was not to cease.

This reaction was the result of several causes. When the older settlers looked over the applicants for admission, they could not help exclaiming: "There, but for the grace of God, go I." Surrounded by their own kin in the sanctuary of the Holy Land, the older settlers recognized the tragic plight of the newcomers, often the sole survivors of a family.

Then too the people of Israel tried to peer into the future. They were still surrounded by a hostile world, a small island in the ocean vastness. In case of a second run of war they would need more hands holding more rifles and the larger the number of people the greater the country's security.

More immigrants meant more consumers, to be sure, but in time they also meant more producers. America's incredible growth impressed them as partly the result of its past liberal immigration policy. More people possessing a large variety of aptitudes were needed if Israel was to become the "West of the East," a workshop at the crossroads of the world.

By admitting all prospective immigrants, Israel was acting as the instrument of Jews all over the world. Thus acting for them, the country could expect the others to help carry a portion of the burden.

In about two and a half years after the proclamation of the State, the population doubled. Immigration into the United States at its peak never represented more than an annual 2 per cent increase in the country's total population. Four years after independence the country's population was about 1,600,000, but thereafter the increase was less rapid because of the economic conditions.

"Operation Ali Baba"

In the previous period nearly all immigrants to Palestine came from Europe and only 9 per cent from the Middle East and North Africa. In the period of 1948-51, about one half of the immigrants came from Africa and Asia.

The extremes of cultural differences among the arrivals in Israel could not be much greater. The two poles of one great tragedy were represented by the well-groomed German physician and the Yemenite mendicant. Nazism set in motion a Palestine immigration the backbone of which was formed by highly educated people. The newest wave, however, brought the Jews of North Africa and the Levant to Israel. In less than two years "Operation Magic Carpet" evacuated over 45,000 Jews from their ancestral homes in Yemen, while the more recent "Operation Ali Baba" has transported 122,000 Jews from Iraq to the new State.

The difference between the two types of immigrants was illustrated by the following stories.

A constant murmur a visitor to Israel some time ago heard attracted his attention. The visitor stepped closer, and found the sound came from a chain of workers handing bricks to one another at a new building. As the laborers passed the bricks they said: *'Bitte, Herr Doktor," "Danke, Herr Doktor."*

As to the Yemenites, they had never seen silverware and when they first caught a glimpse of it in operation, it is said that many of them thought that forks and knives pushed into the mouth were instruments of torture to punish delinquent servants.

Friction was inevitable in the "Israelization" of all human elements. While the older settlers of Jewish Palestine had raised standards of living, health and education far above the general level of the Middle East, the physical standards of the Yemenites and some North Africans were depressingly low. Some Israeli Occidentals looked down at them as people from the other side of the moon.

Some of the older inhabitants assumed a superior "master race" mentality. They tried to engage the "blacks" at lower wages and to treat them as second-class citizens. However, the government and national labor federation took special measures to protect these newcomers.

The Yemenites turned out to be highly adaptable, hard workers who entered into the spirit of the West with greater ease than might have been expected. Also they showed themselves to be People of the Book. Nothing captivated Israel's heart so much as tiny Yemenite children reading the Bible fluently, two of them facing it upside down and the other two in reverse, a habit forced upon them in their former home by the chronic shortage of the Holy Script.

Perhaps a greater problem arose from the influx of the immigrants from North Africa and Iraq. The inhabitants of the appalling Moroccan and Algerian ghettos were exposed to the contradictory influences of East and West, depriving them of a ready social balance. Many of the Iraqi Jews, too, found it hard to adjust themselves to the highly advanced State of Israel. Longer than history remembers, their ancestors had lived in the Land of the Two Rivers and become adjusted to its ways.

The Israel "Pressure Cooker"

Is it possible to integrate such vastly varied cultural strains into the community life of a new state? The realization of a common fate is the most vital integrating factor. People do not uproot themselves, especially if their roots are in the tradition-bound East. The Yemenite Jews, for instance, had never seen a motorcar, heard a radio or known anything about twentieth century inventions. For countless generations they belonged to the Yemenite soil. The challenge must have been great when people with such deep roots decided to move.

The government of Israel was alive to the difficulties of blending so many ingredients into one common way of life. Whenever possible, living quarters in settlements, old and new, were so arranged as to merge the different strains. The school was the main instrument of integration, as it has been in the United States. Its effectiveness was impaired by the fact that the Israel education system itself is not unified. One of the country's great educational agencies and a highly effective tool of the blending process was the army.

It was inevitable that there should be attempts among the earlier arrivals to dig themselves in. Seeking to gain status on the basis of one's date of arrival in a new country is as old as human nature. The Mayflower mentality is no more absent from the Middle East than it is from the Middle West. The earlier pioneers among the Palestine Jews came from the empire of the czars: Russia and Russian Poland. Thus, the Israel equivalents of the Mayflower descendants are the Polish and Russian Jews.

Surveying the saga of Palestine immigrants, Israel was reminded that Israel Zangwill, the novelist, had coined the imperishable term of "melting pot." The Israeli hold that under the prevailing conditions the melting pot can no longer serve them efficiently enough and what they now need is a "pressure cooker."

Building a New House

The economic problems the young country faced were towering, because it is small and poor in natural resources. It lacks the great industrial raw material twins, iron and coal. Its water-power resources are small, capable of only limited expansion.

The greatest known natural wealth of Israel at present is in the Dead Sea and in the country's coastal farming region. The Dead Sea contains huge amounts of chlorides, particularly magnesium (estimated at 22 billion metric tons) and sodium (about 11 billion). Also it has potassium and calcium chlorides. However, only one-fourth of the sea lies within Israel's present boundaries.

The area of another body of water, Lake Hulah, is said to contain some 20 million tons of peat. The Negev has some manganese, copper and mica; recent mining operations have brought to light phosphate rock and glass sand. Elsewhere in the country, local requirements of gypsum and fireclay have been met.

Most of Israel's famous citrus groves and vineyards are concentrated on the coastal plains and the Vale of Jezreel (Emek). The latter is largely under mixed farming, as are the hills of Galilee, raising grains and fruit. The Negev—covering more than half of Israel's area—is largely arid, with an increasing number of settlements which grow crops with irrigation and water storage.

The water potentialities of Israel are dramatically revealed by the fact that the Jordan drops nine hundred feet within nine miles between Lake Hulah and the Sea of Galilee. Within a hundred miles the river spans the climatic zones of an entire continent. However, much of that region now belongs to the Hashimite Kingdom of the Jordan.

"Is There no Balm in Gilead?"

The land of Palestine is consecrated with ages of history, compounded of memories of heroic struggles, of exile, and man's eternal desire to have a place he can call his own. The goal of Zionism has been the return to Zion and within that aim has been imbedded the craving to till the consecrated soil. Throughout the ages the Jew was made to feel that he had no home. Thus he came to create the ideal of Zion, his own dwelling place.

In the seemingly never-ending dispersion the Jew was torn from the soil, imprisoned within ghetto walls, forced to turn to the urban occupations of finance and trade. Zionism, on the other hand, revived the hope of a formerly peasant people of being remarried to the soil.

Some of them reached Zion and saw their dreams doomed. The land had been eroded by mismanagement and abuse, the soil was barren, its polished stone unreceptive to seed. Many of the pioneers persisted and eventually the boulders began to loosen up, the barriers placed by human indifference and nature's hostility were overcome.

Other impediments were to be vaulted. Winter rains carried the eroded soil down the hills, depositing it in the estuaries of streams. Palestine's prevailing wind crosses the seas from the west and it piled the sand high on the shores, choking off narrow river mouths. A chain of coastal marshes was created in which the malaria-bearing mosquito made its home. The pioneers set about draining the marshes, tying down the sand with eucalyptus trees. They created Palestine's citrus industry on the coast.

When Israel became a state in 1948, a new impetus was given to farming there. Within four years about 320 agricultural settlements were begun, while during the previous seventy years only 270 such colonies had been launched.

During the first three years of Israel's life, farm production increased some 80 per cent. During the farm-year 1949-50, the country's cultivated area grew to 600,000 acres, an increase of 50 per cent. The largest increase among all crops was that of vegetables—82 per cent during one year.

The field crops were favored in the past since they required less capital and specialized knowledge, and they filled stomachs more quickly. However, Israel's constricted area proved to be inadequate for modern methods of grain growing. The country's plans therefore called for a larger proportion of industrial and citrus crops, more profitable and easier to export. The farmers had 500 tractors at the time of Israel's declaration of independence, while three years later they had 2,200.

The importance Israel attaches to farming was revealed by the place assigned to it in the three-year development program the government outlined in the autumn of 1950. The program was to be financed by $1.5 billion, of which Israel undertook to provide the equivalent of $500 million, with aid from foreign countries other than the United States, while the rest of the sum was to come from America in the form of a $500 million bond issue, private investments, gift funds, grants-in-aid.

The amount earmarked for agriculture was $320 million, expected to double the national income derived from farming and increase the farm population to 20 per cent of the total.

Two years after this announcement word came from Tel Aviv about a master development program over a ten-year period. The largest investments were to go into irrigation, building, electricity, railway and road transport. The bulk of the amount to finance the master development project was to come out of the reparations funds to be paid by West Germany.

Mayim, Mayim!

Water plays a highly important part in Jewish sacred literature and folklore. One of the first words the visitor to Israel learns is Hebrew for water—*mayim*. The range of rainfall is very wide for so small a country—from 36 inches in Safad, on top of a Galilee hill, to 9 inches in Beersheba, in the northern Negev, declining further as one proceeds south. Northern Israel has more water than land, while southern Israel has more land than water. The great problem is how to effect the flow of the excess into the deficiency area.

The most ambitious proposed solution of this problem was named after Walter Clay Lowdermilk, former assistant chief of the United States Soil Conservation Service and author of the Jordan Valley Authority (JVA) plan, under which an irrigation canal is to link the north and south. This in turn is to be combined with the Mediterranean-Dead Sea Hydroelectric Power project, which would take into account the most dramatic feature of the region, that the Dead Sea lies nearly 1,300 feet below the level of the Mediterranean and that channeling Mediterranean waters into the lower Dead Sea could generate a great amount of water-power.

In the dramatic story of irrigation in Israel the Negev is cast for a special role. It is the great inverted triangle with its apex at Elath on the Gulf of Aqaba. There are already some collective farms on the northern margins of the Negev. One of them had a reservoir to catch water, while another one was experimenting with afforestation. Some of the small settlements installed water pipelines of limited dimensions. Other plans called for the replacement of these pipes by larger ones, all the way up to 24 inches. Some of the resources of the Yarkon river—moving out to sea farther north—were utilized, but much more could be salvaged.

There is some water in the more northerly parts of the Negev, particularly where the Hebron range serves as a cloud precipitant. But there as well as elsewhere the rain races down the denuded slopes into the wadis and into the sea, there to be lost to irrigation. Ambitious plans have been drawn up to connect the Negev triangle with a waterpipe gridiron extending from the Hulah Lake to the Yarkon river on the outskirts of Tel Aviv and so on farther south.

Another important problem of the country is this: too many people live in town and not enough on land. After the wave of the "Lovers of Zion" in the eighties came those to whom Palestine was not always the first choice. Some of them just wanted to make a living and to do that on the land was extremely hard for people unused to that type of work. Only about 17 per cent of the people live at present on the land, including the villages, and the rest of the population lives in urban centers. One-fifth of the total resides in the united cities of Jaffa-Tel Aviv. Only about 18 per cent of those gainfully employed live by farming and fishing. Agriculture's part in the national income during 1949-50 was only 9 per cent of the total. From another angle, the primary production of farming and fishing represented 13 per cent of the total net value of the production of services and goods.

A Great Experiment

World-wide interest attaches to the Palestine collective settlements, "*kibbutzim*" (sing. *kibbutz*), which literally means gathering. In these settlements property and earnings are owned collectively and work is organized on a communal basis. These are the only idealistic contemporary organizations of this type.

In Israel membership in the collective is voluntary, while in Russia it is compulsory. The Israel collectives do not run on money economy, while those of the Soviet Union do. Those entering an Israeli settlement of this type join a community in which the motto is: One for all and all for one. They get what they need, but they receive no pay.

These farm settlements maintain communal institutions such as central dining rooms and kitchens, children's quarters, central stores, social and cultural centers. The number of members ranges from 60 to 1,700, and the settlement is governed by the general assembly of all members. While they are mainly agricultural, more and more of them have been turning to industrial sidelines. The oldest of them, Degania, was founded in 1909.

Out of Israel's total rural population of 161,000, only about 63,000 were kibbutz members, while the others were either independent farmers or belonged to different types of co-operative (as distinguished from collective) settlements. Only about 5 per cent of the newcomers had gone into the collective settlements from the foundation of the State, and this is even lower than the proportion of the collective members in the national total.

Why Enter the Collective?

People became members of the communal settlements because they wanted to dedicate themselves to the cultivation of Zion's soil without wishing to turn their ardor into cash. Also the country was mostly desert and the individual alone could not change it into citrus groves. Even less promising was the attempt of the individual to turn Judaea's hard stone into fruit trees.

Return to the Holy Land meant for many of the pioneers an attempt to turn away from the money economy of the ghetto, its stores and countinghouses. The collective seemed to offer the advantage of sparing its members the hazards of business cycles. The member knows no prosperity, to be sure, but neither does he know the horrors of depressions. If he and his dependents are incapacitated by accident, sickness or age, the collective looks after them.

There are weighty reasons why Israel's collectives are losing ground. While the actual difference is vast, the communal life looks reminiscent of the labor camps which many of them had just escaped. The collectives are in the open country, and many immigrants crave the comforting presence of the town. An Arab village may be near the kibbutz, and the survivor of Bergen-Belsen horrors cannot bear the thought of potential enmity so near. Many of the immigrants are so exhausted from the type of life they had led for many years that they lack the strength to go into pioneer labor on rugged land. It is easier for them to return to the urban work of their own past.

Yet, the new State needs the work of the communal settlers for the type of farm work which cannot be made profitable for the individual. Also the country needs the type of people the collective farms have produced—people who know that their own salvation is linked to community welfare. Various attempts have been made to induce newcomers to settle on such farms, but their success has been indifferent.

Is there a solution to the collectives' problem? Many members admit that the new settlers' reluctance to enter communal life without preparation is understandable. Let them overcome their fear, get settled and see the collectives in their proper perspective, then the newcomers may realize that these settlements represent an Israeli dream—mutual help in a setting that saves people's energies by not forcing them into the turbulent stream of overcompetitive life.

Ardent supporters of the collective ideal point to the many flourishing settlements with their happy, well-fed children, the adults' public-centered lives and superior social institutions. The past speaks to them with an eloquent tongue, and they hold fast to the belief that the kibbutzim speak the language of the future.

Industries to the Fore

The Middle East is nonindustrial. Only Egypt and Turkey show signs of incipient industrialization, while elsewhere the bazaar and handicraft industries abound.

It was the soil that demanded immediate attention in Palestine under the British mandate and little attempt was made to create larger industries. However, industry began to grow as new Jewish skills were accumulated. The Nazi regime sent a wave of German immigrants who had been trained by a dynamic industrial life.

World War II stimulated industrialization in Palestine. The Middle East Command in Cairo sent out an emergency call for locally produced industrial goods, and the Jewish community in Palestine responded to the call.

The industrial centers that have come into being in the course of years are pivoted mostly on the coastal plains, around population centers, along travel arteries and close to the ports. The largest of them centers around Tel Aviv and is sometimes described as the Petah-Tikva-Rishon-le-Zion region, containing about 67 per cent of Israel's industrial plants. These factories produce mostly processed foods, beverages, pharmaceuticals, chemical materials, leather goods and plastics.

While the Haifa region, centering around Israel's all-weather port, contains no more than 15 per cent of the plants, these represent about 40 per cent of Israel's industrial investment. This area produces electricity, cement, machinery, chemicals, sanitary equipment, ceramics, glass and tools. It is also the location of the country's large oil refinery, which has been partly paralyzed by the Arab neighbors' hostile attitude.

Jerusalem has only 8 per cent of the country's industries, mostly handicrafts and printing, but its economic importance is on the increase. The remainder of the industries is dispersed, some of them in farm collective settlements. The diamond cutting and polishing industry (said to be largest in the world after Antwerp) is in Nathanya's business center, on the coast. Gross investment in Israel industry was the equivalent of $32 million in 1949 and $53 million (at 1949 prices) in 1950. The State's new Investment Center assisted in the establishment of 980 new enterprises in four years.

These are small figures, of course, both absolutely and relatively, but this is the Middle East and not the area of Pittsburgh. Ambitious plans for industrial expansion were announced by the government. They included an assembly plant for heavy farm machinery, a machine-tool production plant, a tool and die factory, a plan for the processing of Dead Sea chemicals, modern lime kilns and plants for plywood production.

Heavy industry planned to have another center on the shores of Haifa Bay, near the city of Acre. The plans embraced steel pipe shops, a rolling mill and a steel foundry with electric furnaces. Expansion of electric power was essential for increased industrial and farm production.

Plans and Frustrations

Middle Eastern and not Middle Western standards have to be applied to these projects. Nothing would be more beguiling for the Israeli than to devise plans as if Haifa were a Mid-East Pittsburgh, but the new State's realism rejects such assumption. Israel wants a well-balanced industrial-agricultural economy, such as that of France, fitted to its location and taking available resources into account.

It takes time, however, before new settlers are integrated into the country's productive life. There is a huge gap between imports and exports resulting in chronic dollar shortage, and too much dependence upon the United States.

Israel can neither get goods from her neighbors nor sell to them. Some of those neighbors have farm surpluses, and yet the new State has to haul high-priced food from distant points. Israel's own natural market would be the adjacent area. Arab boycott retards the country's ambitious plans of industrialization.

Still another problem is that of capital for new investments. The exiles' ingathering saddled the country with a huge financial load. Most of the newcomers came with little more than what they could carry on their backs. Israel's legislature, the Knesset, passed a law in the spring of 1950 under which foreign investments were encouraged. Foreign investors were allowed to withdraw specified proportions of their capital and their profits in the currency of their original investments. Israel shares the unenviable lot of most of the world's other countries in that the Israel pound is not convertible into such "hard" currencies as the dollar. The country passed through a period of inflation resulting in a greatly reduced real value of the Israeli pound.

One of the reasons why large-scale foreign capital appeared

to shun pioneering in Israel was the belief that the country was Socialist. That was true to the extent that some of its important parties were labor. On the other hand, four years after the declaration of independence some 80 per cent of the country's industry was owned by private individuals and corporations; the rest was owned by the companies of workers, while the government itself owned only the usual public utilities.

Industrialization for a country like Israel may mean the difference between success and failure. Experience shows that high living standards cannot be realized on agriculture alone. The tremendous productivity of the machine multiplies the work of man many times and enables him to raise the tone of his life. The surrounding Middle East has shown what happens to a region which tries to live almost exclusively on farming: poverty and the effendi rule. Also, Israel needs industries in order to maintain herself in the midst of a hostile world. Industries also mean arms and ammunition.

Geographically Israel is situated in Asia, but by choice she is a western country. Yet, the region to which she belongs is part of the huge colonial area extending all the way to Japan in the east and the Union of South Africa in the south.

Besides, making the country less dependent upon imports would also increase its weight among the nations. Industrial countries play a more important role in foreign affairs than farming regions.

Israel must also consider another aspect of the problem. Normally, industries tend to cluster in large metropolitan regions. The new nation cannot afford to become an overgrown Tel Aviv, extending virtually from one end of the small country to the other.

With these factors in view a system of "industrial zones" was receiving serious attention in the government. The plan called for de-urbanization and scattering of new industries all over the land in a highly original way.

These industrial zones were compounds of factory buildings or prefabricated factory sites. They were to be provided with power and water, road and possibly rail transportation, on land which was less costly than the metropolitan areas. These zones were to be set up in the foothills of Judaea, in the Negev, other rural areas and also in the suburbs of less industrialized towns. Jerusalem was to be one of them, and in one of its outlying western sections some hundred acres were set aside for this purpose.

This plan still awaits realization. Industrial zones might help to siphon off some of the excess metropolitan population, creating a better balance between town and country. Less turbulent times, however, must wait upon the realization of these zones.

Remarkable parallels in the situation of Israel and Switzerland invite attention. Basic industrial raw materials are deficient in both countries. The Swiss do have a little iron ore and manganese, which may also be present in Israel's Negev. After all, near its frontier settlement of Elath is believed to be the site of "King Solomon's mines." Curiously, the most important mineral product of both countries is salt. Yet Switzerland has shown the world that it is possible for a country so short of resources to become highly industrialized and even rich.

Both of these countries have the most precious of all "raw materials"—intelligent, hard-working, determined people. Also the Swiss have known how to turn their barren country to best advantage in the tourist world. Natural beauty is an asset which Israel also has. Some of her scenic attractions can be appreciated only now that roads have been built into two Galilees. From a tourist point of view the new State has also the advantage of being built on some of the holiest sites of Christianity and Judaism, for that reason, too, the future of her tourist industry should be bright.

Israeli therefore see the country of their future as an eastern Switzerland. That, incidentally, was the part which the nation's first president, the scientist-statesman Dr. Chaim Weizmann, envisaged for his country.

The realization of this aim may, of course, run into snags. Switzerland is surrounded by countries producing many of the raw materials she needs, while Israel is not. But the new State has a seacoast, and maritime transportation is less costly. A more serious handicap is that while Israel has many brilliant scientists, she is short of craftsmen, technicians, or just plain handymen.

That deficiency will be met in time, as the new challenge elicits the suitable response in the Israeli's confident view.

A Unique Labor Union

Nowhere else in the world is there such a labor union as Israel's *Histadrut,* General Federation of Jewish Workers in the Land of Israel. It covers most of the workers of the country in all fields, and all the labor unions, of which it is the most important, and which embrace some 90 per cent of the workers, including farm labor. The unique feature of the Histadrut is that it is the country's largest employer as well, besides being in charge of important social services.

This situation came about under the British mandate in response to an inescapable need. Britain was ready to provide the social services an enlightened colonial administration was expected to grant to a backward region in Asia. These services were superior to those the Arabs were getting under their own governments in the adjacent countries. However, Palestine's Jewish people were not Middle Eastern "natives," and Britain was not prepared to provide them with the government services the English were receiving at home.

Thus the Histadrut became a jack-of-all-trades, and that is the factor that might develop into a problem. The Jews of Palestine under the British mandate needed the government services a highly advanced community expected to receive from its own country and which it failed to obtain because of the British attitude. The Jewish labor federation was thus forced to become a government substitute.

In addition to the usual functions of a trade union Histadrut took over the most important social services, such as the sickness and unemployment funds, old age insurance, invalids' homes and vocational training courses. It runs one of the country's most important dailies, *Davar,* as well as weeklies, trade papers, libraries, a publishing house and sports associations. It organizes concerts, exhibitions and runs one of the nation's best theaters, *Ohel.*

Israel's labor federation owns one of the largest contracting organizations of the country and, perhaps, of the Middle East—

Solel Boneh. This, in turn, operates a wide variety of industrial establishments, including lime and stone production, battery works, rubber plants, general building materials and many others. Histadrut owns a bank, insurance and shipping companies, wholesale purchasing and agricultural marketing co-operatives. Affiliated with it are the major transport co-operatives and most of the farm collectives. Only a few of Histadrut's varied activities can be mentioned here.

The problem is this. Now that there is a forward-looking Jewish State, should it not look after social security and related questions? Then, too, Histadrut in business may turn out to be a deterrent to private investment and especially foreign capital. The conclusion may be reached that the labor federation maintains a tight monopoly.

How will Israel's labor federation be adjusted to the new conditions? The temptation in similar cases is always strong to carry on as heretofore. The labor federation has created the usual vested interests and the equally inevitable tendency for "empire building."

The pressure will continue strong to maintain many of the federation's activities as an employer, but the counterpressure may also pick up strength, especially in the United States. Luckily for the country, the Israeli show signs of developing the art of not creating "problems" where time might be expected to provide the solution. It is possible, in the long run, that the ancillary functions of Histadrut not directly relating to the protection of the workers' interests will be absorbed by the government. There is also another solution: the transference of those functions to autonomous government agencies.

Whatever the ultimate fate of the labor union, Palestine history is bound to reserve one of its important chapters for the work of the Histadrut. Many Israeli feel that it was largely through its instrumentality that their society has been saved from falling into the Middle Eastern pattern of enormous extremes between the "have nots" and the "haves."

"The Portable Fatherland"

What is the new nation's binding force, since the people of Israel have sprung from some three score of nations? Some of them look as Oriental as the High Yemen Arabs, while many of them are as Nordic as Minnesota Swedes.

There was one binding force for Jews throughout the endless epoch of dispersion, and that was what the great German poet, Heinrich Heine, called the "portable fatherland" of the Jew, the Bible. Wherever there was a Bible, the Jew felt at home. That is why the religious bloc of Israel lays special stress on the cementing force of the Jews' ancient creed. It was conflict between this bloc and Prime Minister Ben-Gurion's Socialist Mapai supporters which precipitated Israel's first coalition cabinet crisis early in 1951. When the July elections in that year failed to give Mapai a clear majority, the government was reconstituted on the same basis as before—a coalition of Ben-Gurion's party and the religious bloc.

The bloc consisted of several branches, two of which were middle-class parties while their two affiliates were labor groups. One of these branches was the "*Mizrachi,*" a name which is abbreviated from "*Merkaz Ruhani*"—Spiritual Center—and which literally also means "Easterners," since Palestine is in the East with regard to Europe. The party's motto is, "The Land of Israel for the people of Israel on the basis of its Holy Law."

Israel was intended to be not merely the Jewish people's dwelling place, but also the Jewish spirit's abode. It was the ancient creed that lent the Jews the strength to survive endless waves of persecution, steeled their arms against the Arabs and enabled them to perform the miracle of the creation of the State. In their new homes it is their religion which will hold together the disparate elements, and without it they could not continue to develop.

This party has a labor wing, *Hapoel Hamizrachi,* the motto of which is "Law, Torah and Labor." It went to the polls in the 1951 summer elections and won more votes than the mother party.

The more extreme orthodox are represented in the *Agudath*

Israel, "Association of Israel." It opposed Zionism originally as a rank heresy because of its view that the return to Zion could be brought about only by the Messiah and not through secular political parties. The Second World War, however, impelled this group to turn to Zionism, and it accepted the Jewish State with the intent of making the Holy Law the law of the land.

Far more has been heard in the outside world about the small superorthodox group in Jerusalem, calling itself *Neturei Karta,* "Guardians of the City." During Israel's war with the Arabs, members of this group attempted to prevent food trucks from reaching Israeli soldiers on the Sabbath, since under their interpretation of the Holy Law no work whatever was to be performed on that day. The importance of this fanatic group of a few hundred people is small, but their publicity has been great.

The entire religious bloc advocates an enforced Sabbath observance, religious law courts, all food sold to conform to dietary laws, the granting of power to religious authorities over religious schools, inheritance, marriage and divorce. The religious bloc does not include the "Guardians."

Pure Sabbath observance means, among other things, no public vehicles moving on the Sabbath and other holidays. The religious bloc demands strict observance of dietary laws in the entire land. At present, they are observed in government institutions, including hospitals. Also, at present, jurisdiction in matters of personal status, religious foundations and endowments is exercised by the rabbinical courts for Jews, and by their own religious courts for Christians and Muslims, this system having been inherited from British mandatory days and, before that, from the Ottoman Empire. The religious groups claim the right of completely free selection of schools not only by established residents but also by immigrants in work camps.

The opposition to the bloc maintains, on the other hand, that religion is a matter of inner feelings and not of public compulsion. The ultimate goal is the western idea of separation of church and state. Israel has not only Jews but also Muslims and Christians, and it should not become a theocratic state.

The Struggle of Ideologies

The Israeli come from the most advanced democracies and the most backward autocracies. The earlier settlers came from Czarist Russia with her strongly anti-Semitic views. Many of these settlers were attracted to opposition groups, particularly socialism. Some of the best work of these was done on collective farms. Their way of salvation seemed to lie in common action, keeping their standards above the distressingly low levels of the Middle East. It was natural that the labor parties scored highest after independence was declared.

Israel has a multiparty system, more like that of France than Britain. However, the main ideological conflict is between labor and antilabor groups. Two important labor parties have made their mark, one left of center and the other one left. The first one is the Labor Party, *Mapai,* while the other one is the United Workers' Party, *Mapam.*

The Mapai defined itself as a Zionist Socialist Party aiming at the ingathering of the exiles, the building of the State of Israel and a Socialist regime founded on spiritual and cultural freedom. Its domestic policy called for democracy and State-planned economy based on the development of constructive private enterprise.

Its foreign policy tended to be increasingly amicable to the West. Also, it wanted to strengthen the authority of the United Nations.

It was Mapai that gave the country its first prime minister, David Ben-Gurion. He headed a coalition cabinet, which also included the religious groups and the spokesmen of two smaller parties. In the midsummer 1951 elections it obtained 45 out of a total of 120 seats.

The other labor party, Mapam, stood for a classless, socialist society and supported a firm bond between the "workers of the world" and the Soviet Union. However, the party has always been strongly Zionist (to the Communists, a nationalist aberration), believing that political leadership in the new State should belong to the farm collectives and not to the industrial proletariat. It accepted no "party line" from the Kremlin. Within Mapam there were several well-defined ideologies, so that it was not at all monolithic. However, the more left-wing *Hashomer Hatzair* seems to have gained the upper hand. The small Communist party of Israel is not much less critical of this party than of other labor groups. While Mapam is not the Tito brand of communism, it shows some resemblance to it.

What is the explanation of the Soviet-friendship of the Mapam? It may be a carry-over from Czarist times when the present leaders were young people fighting an anti-Semitic regime. Also, many members of the party, no doubt, see the Soviet Union more as an incarnation of theory than as a reality, appearing different in the fata morgana of time and space. The party had 15 seats in the second Knesset.

The General Zionists defined themselves as a liberal party in favor of private enterprise and a unitary national educational system independent of party politics. They stressed the economic advantages of laissez faire and were strongly opposed to many activities of the Histadrut. They picked up great strength in the first three years of the existence of the country, having had only 7 seats in the first parliament and 20 seats in the second. Israel's first President, Dr. Chaim Weizmann, did not belong to any political party but was ideologically close to the Progressives. Late in 1952 they joined the cabinet.

The Communist Party of Palestine, *Makai,* was "weak numerically and in terms of power," to quote a United States Congress publication on the strategy and tactics of world communism. It had 4 seats in the first parliament and 5 seats in the second.

Leading Political Personalities

The Constituent Assembly, known as the First Knesset, passed its first law in February 1949, laying the permanent foundations of the permanent organs of the State. The President of the Republic was elected by the unicameral assembly, his term of office to run for the duration of the Knesset and thereafter until three months after the convening of the new legislature.

The position of President was described as being like that of the King of England, a national symbol shorn of power. Israel's political system was closely patterned on the British parliamentary regime, except that she had proportional representation instead of single member constituencies. As in Britain, the dominant personality was the Prime Minister, the chief executive and also the leader of the majority party in parliament, thus linking in his person both the administrative and the legislative functions of the government.

The country's first Prime Minister, David Ben-Gurion, is considered its ablest statesman. He started his Palestinian career as a farm hand in 1906 at the age of twenty. Then he became a watchman. The Turks expelled him from Palestine because he failed to support their effort during the First World War. He came to the United States and helped recruit pioneer workers for Palestine. He joined the Jewish legion, which lent a hand in ousting the Turks from the Holy Land. During the mandatory regime he played a leading role in the creation of the Histadrut and the Mapai. In Israel a web of legend has been woven around him, a "providential statesman." The historic decisions leading to the dramatic establishment of the new State are mostly credited to him. A man of action and a scholar at the same time, he not only produced ideas but also superintended their execution.

Israel is too young a country to have a large number of prominent statesmen. Among those who made an impression in the country's early life is Moshe Sharett, Minister of Foreign Affairs. He was twelve when his parents took him to Palestine, and he shared the pioneers' hard life in those early years. Under the British mandate he filled important posts as a leader of Mapai and head of the political department of the Jewish Agency for Palestine. There are probably few foreign ministers with his aptitude for languages, nine of which he speaks well.

One of the picturesque political leaders of the country is Mrs. Golda Meyerson, who speaks English with a Middle Western accent. Before she began her Palestinian career of raising chickens, she had been a teacher in Milwaukee, Chicago and New York. She has filled several important government positions, including Israel's first ambassadorship to the Soviets and cabinet posts

Americans became familiar with the person and work of Abba Eban, Israel's permanent representative to the United Nations and its ambassador to the United States. Among the seven languages he speaks fluently are Arabic and Persian, besides the more conventional tongues. The late Professor Harold J. Laski used to say that Eban's English was as sonorous as Churchill's.

The Problem of the Schools

Core of the struggle between the religious groups and the other parties is the school system. It had its roots in the mandatory regime when the British provided so little education that the Jews had to take matters into their own hands. Today there are four main trends of elementary schools in the land of Israel.

In 1952 the most important of them were the labor schools, which aimed to provide the student with a Socialist orientation and the elements of manual training, in addition to general education. The Jews received no technical training in many countries and they need a large number of skilled craftsmen. These schools enrolled about 37.3 per cent of the students.

Then there were the nonideological, general schools teaching about 32.7 per cent of the student body. They provided education without any special religious or political bias.

The school of the Mizrachi had about 18.5 per cent of the students, and they provided education with a pronounced religious trend. They accepted all those who wished to register, while the Agudath schools accepted only those children whose parents were strictly religious.

Many Israeli believe that this is a grave problem and that the State should run all the schools or at least that the children of the newcomers should attend State schools. They see great dangers in creating separate educational compartments.

The new State is also trying to improve and extend education for the Arabs. After nearly thirty years of British rule, not more than about one-third of the Palestinian Arab children of the proper age attended schools, and of these only 18 per cent were registered in government institutions, while the rest attended private Christian and Muslim ones. When Israel took over the country, nearly all the Arab women were illiterate. Even today it is far from easy to get Muslim girls out of their traditional seclusion and turn them into teachers. However, a beginning has been made.

It is highly significant of the "Israel dream" that among the modern Jewish buildings of the Holy City none is more prominent than the Hebrew University of Jerusalem and the adjoining Hadassah Hospital occupying the heights of Mount Scopus. The university looks back upon a quarter of a century of existence, helped into life by an American, the late Judah L. Magnes, its first chancellor and president.

Mount Scopus, although under Israel control, is behind the boundary line of the Hashimite Kingdom of the Jordan. The university had the alternative of either suspending work or trying to find new quarters in the already overcrowded New City of Jerusalem. The decision was made to continue the work. The university is not only in operation but is expanding greatly. A new faculty of medicine and a department of education have been developed. The university's scientific research program and especially its agricultural research have become the most important in the Middle East, matched only by the work of the Weizmann Institute of Science in Israel's city of Rehovoth. Some of the latter's work is noteworthy in the Middle East, as, for instance, experiments to transform electrical and chemical energy into mechanical energy without any intermediary machine.

The handicaps under which the university has been laboring may be easily grasped. Its unique collection of Orientalia, for one, is immobilized on Mount Scopus, and the school must manage on highly inadequate library facilities. So widespread are its functions that it had to be accommodated in more than a score of buildings. The trials and triumphs of this school indicate the importance Israel's people attach to higher education.

A Minority Becomes a Majority

For the first time in two millennia the Jews became a majority in their own country, with a minority in their midst. That is the Arab minority, estimated at some 170,000 persons, of whom 69 per cent are Muslims, 25 per cent are Christians and the rest are Druze. This Arab community has been growing through very slow re-immigration and infiltration.

The Israel Arabs, as their kinsmen elsewhere, are ethnically mixed. They, too, are called Arabs and consider themselves as such because they speak Arabic. Pure-blooded Arabs of the desert type are hard to find in Israel except among the Bedouins of the Negev.

A visit to an Arab village in Israel ought to be an anthropologist's delight. The diverse strains one finds there are obviously the heritage of hosts that passed through these global crossroads in the course of centuries.

The bulk of the Israel Arabs is concentrated in the hills of Galilee; at the foot of the hills of Samaria and Judaea, known as the Little Triangle; and in the Negev wilderness. There are also sizable Arab enclaves in such urban centers as Haifa and Acre.

The Palestine Arabs under the British were considered better off than their kinsmen in their own countries and under their own administrations. Even though in attenuated form, the social pattern of the Middle East applied to them. Most of them were fellahin with a few effendis in their midst. The majority of the former were living close to the margin, afflicted with many plagues of the Levant.

When the war broke out between the Arabs and the Israeli, nearly all the effendis and most of the fellahin left. The Arabs say they had been terrorized by the Jews. On the other hand, the Jews say they had been warned by the Arab countries to quit their homes temporarily, so as to leave the field clear for the invading armies' operations. They were to return home again in the wake of the expected Arab victories. These victories never materialized. Meanwhile many Arab villages in Palestine were wiped out.

How many Arabs were left stranded? The figures range from 600,000 quoted by Israeli, to more than a million, the Arabs' estimate. The United Nations' guess is between the two. These pitiful people became the football in a gruesome game. Israel did not want many more Arabs. The Arab countries did not want them either, with the exception of Jordan. The Arab governments wanted to keep them in their tragic condition, to use them in their policy against Israel. King Abdullah of Jordan accepted them, since he needed a larger population to increase the importance of his country. This was one way to fight his fellow Arab monarchs. In Jordan the refugees received citizenship rights. An attempt was made to integrate them into the economic life of the country, especially on new irrigation projects.

Most tragic was the refugees' plight in the coastal Gaza strip occupied by Egypt, and the suspicion was voiced that they were being kept in that condition on Cairo's order to use them for diplomatic moves. Obviously, ex-King Farouk and the pasha group could have done far better to relieve the refugees' misery. The relief officials of the United Nations and Christian groups received little co-operation from the Arab countries, with the notable exception of Jordan. Israel was criticized on the refugee issue, but she pleaded that the Arab countries made effective aid to the homeless people impossible by not concluding peace.

The Sons of Ishmael in Israel

Among the Arabs of Israel about two-thirds were laborers. Some of the deserted effendi land was distributed among them but not according to a definite plan. Reliability from the Israeli point of view seems to have been an important yardstick.

The condition of the small farmers among the Israel Arabs seems to have improved. Since the State is in great need of farm products, prices are high and most of the Arabs are farmers. The Arabs pay next to nothing in taxes, spend little, buy gold on the black market and hoard it in the bank—the only type they know, an earthenware jug.

The rest of Israel's Arabs are ex-landowners, merchants and ex-government officials. They are not easily absorbable and are extremely unhappy in Israel.

The government of Israel views the Arab problem with concern. Arabs form about 10 per cent of Israel's population—a sizable proportion. The authorities realize that prosperity, especially in a small country, is indivisible. If there is a large slum region among the Arabs of Israel, the economic standards of the entire country are bound to suffer.

The problem is vividly illustrated by walking from a Jewish settlement to a nearby Arab village in, let us say, the Little Triangle. In a matter of minutes one drops back hundreds, if not thousands, of years. The Jewish village, on the other hand, has a rich cultural life, also electricity and the most modern machinery.

Another problem is linked with this. Many of the Arabs were bent on destroying the Jews under the British mandate. Are these residents of Israel the same people who were engaged in those wild anti-Jewish attacks? Would they become a dangerous Fifth Column if there were a "second round"?

Whatever the answer to these questions, the government is bent on modernizing Israel's Arab life. Some of the villages now have electricity. Some have tobacco nurseries where rows of beds are covered with scrub to protect the seedlings. These and other cash crops occupy less space than grains, and the fields thus vacated are occupied by the Jewish National Fund for settlement in strategic locations—just in case. This is what the Arabs call the "Jewish National Fund Line."

The government is also sending farm machinery into the Arab regions. There is not enough of it as yet, but its quantity is growing and the fellahin are not averse to adopting improved methods.

The plague of the Levant is the middleman, whom the government would like to eliminate from the Arab regions of Israel. The fellah sometimes gets no more than about one-third of the market price for his produce. Co-operative marketing seems to be the solution, and that is what the government seeks to promote. Arab laborers are encouraged to join the various Histadrut groups, and in many other ways, too, every effort is made to protect their interests. Wages for the Arabs of Israel are much higher now in purchasing power than they were under the mandate and still are in Arab countries.

Rights and Restrictions

It is said that in the all-Arab city of Nazareth there are more portraits of Theodor Herzl, founder of Zionism, than in any Jewish city of its size. On Israel's mid-May Independence Day some of the Arab villages are more demonstrative of their joy at "liberation" than their Jewish neighbors. No important cases of sabotage against the State are known, and except for cases of illegal entry, the Arab criminal record is surprisingly good.

The Arabs have the right to use their own language in the legislature and government offices. Jewish officials dealing with them are expected to be fluent in Arabic. Freedom of movement of residents in military areas, however, is restricted. This applies to Jews as well as Arabs, but very few Jews live in these regions. In the Galilee and the Negev regions they are allowed to travel without government permit only in the district where they live, while in the Little Triangle they need an authorization to leave their town, and that is granted only for good cause—or a good story.

What is Israel's long-range policy toward her own Arabs? The government has announced that it will try to get them out of the fatal D.I.P. stage of the Middle East and will expect most of them to respond to these efforts. The "cake of custom" is particularly hard in that part of the world, and it may not be easy to accomplish this aim. People are too deeply rooted in the Oriental "*malesh*" (what does it matter?) tradition and may not be able to follow progressive leadership. In that case, Israel's authorities say, their unassimilable Arabs should be given a chance to settle in the Arab countries where they would feel more at home. That solution—if it is a solution—will have to wait upon the return of peaceful times.

Facing the Arab World

Israel feels herself part of the West but her government would also like her to be a loyal member of the Middle Eastern comity of nations, seeking to raise the standards of the region in co-operation with her neighbors.

The Arab countries have so far refused to recognize Israel

not only *de jure* but also *de facto*, so that the country's boundaries are mere armistice lines. The relations between Israel and the Arab countries can be characterized as "bad neighbor policy."

There have been some shadings in the relations between Israel and the Arab neighbors. Occasional outbursts of temper apart, they were best with the Hashimite Kingdom of the Jordan. The late King Abdullah appeared to be ready to come to terms with Israel. The new State's northern neighbor on the Levant coast, the small republic of Lebanon, is captive of the Arab League and would, no doubt, be happier to entertain normal relations with Israel.

A curious paradox faces us when we come to consider the special problems between Israel and the Arab countries. There are no such problems between her and the governments most violently opposed to a settlement. The only country which has a number of problems to settle with Israel is precisely the Jordan Kingdom whose late king was ready to come to terms.

Israel bars Jordan's way to the most valuable outlet of the Mediterranean, and she also bars the road to Bethlehem. On the other hand, the Hashimite Kingdom bars Israel's shortest way between Tel Aviv and Jerusalem by holding the small Latrun salient. Jordan has the Jewish Quarter in the Old City of Jerusalem with its Wailing Wall and holds the road to Mount Scopus.

Generally, the Arab countries object to Israel on the ground that the creation of the new State was contrary to the wishes of the majority of Palestine's inhabitants and that its existence is illegal. The Arabs claim that Israel's ingathering of the exiles is accumulating further explosive material by piling up a surplus population which is bound to exert pressure on the neighbors, thereby leading to "imperialism," because the Jews will need more space.

In response to Israel's claim that she is ready to help build up a better balanced economic system in the Middle East, the Arabs contend that this would be a colonial regime under which they were to provide raw materials and buy the new State's finished products.

On the other hand, the Israeli say that there are more deep-seated reasons for the Arab countries' violent antagonism. They assert that the Arab leaders fear that the new State will start social fermentation among the fellahin, creating a desire for social services and higher standards. If Israel showed that a high standard was possible for the masses the game of the effendis would be lost.

If I Forget Thee, oh Jerusalem . . .

The largest number of the monotheistic creeds' sacred shrines are in Palestine. Most of the Christian shrines are in the walled-in Old City and so is the Wailing Wall, venerated by Jews, and the Mosque of Omar, sacred to Islam—all in Jordan's hands. Israel's share of Jerusalem, the New City, has only the Church of Dormition and the Coenaculum. The other Christian Holy Places in Israel are mostly in Nazareth.

The fate of the Holy Places has aroused world-wide attention. The United Nations proposed several projects, of which the latest was the internationalization of the Jerusalem region. It was, however, rejected by both Israel and Jordan, whereupon the United Nations decided to "study" the problem further.

As usual, the study is expected to produce no new results, especially since neither country will now allow any part of its territory to be internationalized. The most they are prepared to accept is a United Nations supervision of the proper maintenance of the Holy Places.

On the Israel side, not only the major shrines but also the minor ones are prominently marked as being under special government protection. Jordan has a custodian of the Holy Places with the rank of a cabinet member, and ample care of the shrines is likely to continue. Throughout the times, Palestinians have learned to respect religious sites which they feel in honor bound to serve as trustees. Islam reveres the great Old and New Testament figures as its own prophets. In the past it was the feuding Christian sects and not the Muslim authorities under the Ottoman Empire that caused the gravest man-made damage to the shrines.

In the Midst of the Cold War

Israel is bound to play a more important role in world affairs than is normal for so small a country because of her location in the heart of the Middle East, her articulate population and dynamic leadership.

We have seen that the special problem of this territory is that it represents a power vacuum, even though the countries of the Middle East are nominally independent and under the effective domestic jurisdictions of their own governments. Against Great Powers they would be unable to hold their own. The Arab States were not able to stand up even against Israel, an infant among the nations. Because of the fatal effendi-fellahin relationship the Soviet Union may have an edge on the other powers by claiming leadership for the oppressed. It could rightly assert that the Arab ruling classes in most of these countries understand only the language of force.

Israel has to tread her wary way in this cockpit of the world, so close to great treasures. Most of the country's people feel that they are linked to the West. They have set up a democratic government and want to keep it democratic. It is not a "fair-weather" democracy, and is not easily swayed by the whims of the passing moments. In a crisis not precipitated by the West they know on which side to take their place.

The United States falls in a special category as far as the Israeli are concerned. They are thankful to America for her prompt recognition of their country, without which their problem would have been much greater. Without American financial aid the work of reconstruction and development would have been unmanageable. America's first ambassador to the new State, James G. McDonald, prominent educator and public servant, was Israel's outspoken friend.

Great Britain left many bitter memories in Israeli hearts. Yet, the times have changed and countries must pursue a realistic policy. Today the relations between the two countries are cordial.

Originally, Israel's foreign policy was described as "nonidentification," a term coined by the country's director general of the

Foreign Office, Dr. Walter Eytan, to express Israel's freedom of judgment and action and her rejection of permanent political allegiance to any other country.

Eventually Israel spoke of an "independent" foreign policy, described by the same spokesman as "having ideas and ideals of its own which it is prepared to advocate on its merits and defend against criticism, from whatever quarter it may come." Later, she moved further toward the west.

Facing the Future

The "Old New Land" of Herzl, founder of Zionism, is still a very young old country, still in transition and face to face with many perils. There is some danger that bureaucracy might become too powerful, and there is also danger of too much political favoritism and, in general, too much politics. It is inevitable, perhaps, especially where an administration has to be improvised on such short notice, that not always the ablest but the more aggressive should forge to the front.

There is danger of setting up a too one-sided urban civilization, and this in spite of the fact that rural development was given top priority. The economic problems, especially that of inflation, are immense. There is peril in depending too much upon outside help, particularly upon aid from the United States.

The Arab neighbors keep on threatening a "second round" of warfare. This danger, probably, is not as great as it seems, because of the Tripartite Pledge by the United States, Great Britain and France: "The Three Governments, should they find any of these States [Arab countries and Israel] preparing to violate the frontiers or the armistice line, would, consistent with their obligations as members of the United Nations, immediately take action both in and outside the United Nations to prevent such a violation."

Israel deserves credit for remarkable achievements during a short time in a region where progress is halting. This was the view of the United Nations Survey Mission for the Middle East, which summarized its findings:

"A cool examination of the relevant figures is apt to provoke wonderment at the magnitude of the task Israel's government has set itself. But there are forces which cannot be measured in figures, and these forces sometimes decide issues in apparent defiance of reason. Israel has accomplished astonishing things already."

Mr. Ben-Gurion expressed the sentiments of his people: "All down the years, from Joshua, son of Nun, to the Battles of the Defense Army of Israel, we have been the few withstanding the many. . . . This small but wonderful people, with its ethical and intellectual qualities, is not one iota inferior to the greatest among the nations."

When the Israeli look at the difficulties of the future, they are disposed to say: "He who does not believe in miracles is not a realist."

CHAPTER 10

Cherchez l'Huile

Philanthropy Plus Fifty Per Cent

It was a professor laden with wisdom who admonished his eager students always to document their statements with appropriate footnotes. He advised them further that in case not even the most copious footnotes could unlock history's jealously guarded secrets they should draw wisdom from the most profound of all maxims of history: *Cherchez la femme.*

Modern youth needs no such advice, knowing that a matter seemingly as unimportant as the twist of Cleopatra's nose might have altered the course of history. The wise professor of today would have to modify the old adage to read: *Cherchez le pétrole.*

There is much oil in the Middle East. This is truly an amazing story, this discovery of oil in the barren wastes. But a few years ago they seemed to contain nothing but stone and sand. Today we know that the region's vast underground caverns are filled with treasure which would eclipse the treasure troves of the Arabian Nights. The region has been found to contain more than half of the known oil reserves of the world, the rest of the world including such rich wells as those of the Americas, the Soviets and the Far East. As an authoritative publication puts it:

> The significant fact is that the Middle East is a veritable "power house" of oil where wells often produce at an almost miraculous rate as compared with most of those in other areas. Oil is there in such quantities as possibly to be a determining factor in the shape of things to come.[1]

It was in the frontier days of oil exploration in this region that an American expert was impelled to exclaim, "There is oil here for hundreds of Rockefellers." Today he would probably amend his statistics to read: "There is oil here for thousands of Rockefellers."

This has an important bearing on international relations. The Middle East oil regions are in close proximity to the Soviet Union, which is watching the scene with gnashing teeth. All the oil in the region belongs to the westerners, none to the Russians, and this in spite of the fact that the petroleum area is at their threshold.

This oil is also important because it supplies the largest part of Europe's needs. The United States also will need greatly increased oil supplies.

On the history of the Middle East, too, this tremendous bonanza is bound to exert its effect. The poorest of the poor regions suddenly obtained a windfall in the form of one of the world's greatest concentrations of natural wealth. Hundreds of millions of dollars go each year into Middle East pockets. The great question is: Whose pockets? How will this shower of gold affect the future of this poverty-stricken region?

It was the empire builder, Cecil Rhodes, who once startled

[1] *Middle East Oil in United States Foreign Policy,* by Halford L. Hoskins, Public Affairs Bulletin No. 89. The Library of Congress Legislative Reference Service.

the world with the statement that the empire's basis was "philanthropy plus fifty per cent." The percentage applies also to Middle East oil. What will be the share of philanthropy?

Five Cents for a Square Mile of Gushers

As far back as the days of Herodotus, oil seepages were known in Iran and Mesopotamia in the area of the Persian Gulf. In the former country's Zagros Mountain region the eerie flames of oil leaks must have filled the natives with fear. Asphalt from the petroleum seepage to the south of Hit on the Euphrates was employed in the masonry of buildings in ancient Ur. A native oil industry in Iran's Kasr-i-Shirin is reported to have been in operation for centuries. The petroleum of shallow pits was garnered, subjected to primitive refining and sold to caravanserais along the routes.

The biggest business of the Middle East got its start with what might be described as the bargain of the century. The hero of this life-size tale was an Englishman with a Midas touch, William Knox D'Arcy. In the Mount Morgan district of Australian Queensland he touched rock which, lo and behold, turned out to be gold. Encouraged by this phenomenal success, he had his eyes open for similar coups. He had a businessman's vision in foreseeing that the exotic horseless carriage might one day become a serviceable means of transportation. Spurred by this belief he told his amanuenses to be on the lookout for petroleum.

The next gold nugget was found lying on the terrace of the Café de la Paix of Paris. At just the right moment there happened to be a person on the terrace of that famous caravanserai of France whom history remembers as "a certain M. Kitabishi." This gentleman of uncertain background was looking for a soft touch and found one . . . himself. He had obtained from the Iranian government the promise of a concession covering the exclusive right to look for and produce oil on half a million square miles of that country. This was some time before and M. Kitabishi was sorry about the whole business. Iran's credit rating was very low and what was he to do with oil, even if it were found? M. Kitabishi must have been one of those people who thought that the horseless carriage was a passing fad. So, he was ready to sell his concession for $20,000. Mr. D'Arcy's agent said that it was an awful lot of money for so little, but he had a couple of good stiff drinks and then pretended he was acting under their influence when he displayed interest in Iranian oil. The deal was consummated in 1901 and it was then that the history of Middle East oil began.

History's Seesaws

The first exploratory drills failed and it looked as if D'Arcy had made the worse part of the bargain. Years passed in inconclusive search until one day oil was struck in Iran's forbidding Zagros Mountain region, in the very shadow of a fifteen-thousand-foot peak, Serdeh Kuh, in a place called the Temple of Solomon, Masjid-i-Sulaiman.

Now that oil was found, capital was needed, and so the original entrepreneur canvassed the market. He found the Burmah Oil Company enterprising enough to take a risk. Thus came into being the pioneering oil company of the Persian Gulf region, Anglo-Persian, which later changed its name to Anglo-Iranian. A chronicler of these events recorded: "It would surprise many people to know how very nearly there was no Anglo-Persian Oil Company at all." [2]

In London there was then a gentleman whom his subordinates called the "oil maniac," First Sea Lord Fisher, who was transforming units of the British fleet from coal to oil burners. There was also another oil maniac, the First Lord of the Admiralty, whose name was Winston Churchill. Largely at the prompting of these men the British government acquired an interest in the Iranian oil company which eventually waxed to 56 per cent. This was on the eve of the First World War.

Early this century a fantastic Armenian, about whom more will be said later, Calouste Sarkis Gulbenkian, made a comprehensive report on the oil possibilities of another part of the Persian Gulf region, Mesopotamia, which belonged to the Ottoman Empire. Sultan Abdul-Hamid was so impressed by this

[2] E. De Golyer, leading oil geologist, at a conference on the Problems of the Middle East held at the School of Education, New York University, June 5-6, 1947.

report that he had immense tracts of land in Mesopotamia transferred from State possession into his own private domain.

The British took a deep interest in this tract of land and so did the Germans. These latter were working on the plans for the highly important Berlin-Baghdad Railway, and in the course of their work they ran into a veritable "lake of petroleum." This delighted them greatly. A tug of war ensued between the British and the Germans, with the Sultan serving as an umpire. Then came the Young Turk Revolution, which appeared to favor the British. The Sultan was kicked out and Mr. Gulbenkian helped into life the Turkish Petroleum Company, in which German, British, Turkish interests and he himself were the shareholders.

Then came the Great War which the Germans lost. The Ottoman Empire was no more, and Mesopotamia was no more. Instead of that there was the Kingdom of Iraq, sitting over the oil wells, and the real masters were the British.

It is an old, old adage that to the victor belong the spoils and this was particularly true after a war in which the victors proclaimed that they had done the fighting for high ideals and wanted to make no money on it. The French in the past had nothing to do with Middle East oil, but now they were in the region as mandatory powers in the neighbor Levant States. So the French demanded that the Germans' one-fourth share of the Turkish Petroleum Company should be turned over to them.

The San Remo Cocktail Party

The British frowned upon this idea but the French were insistent. If England's oil companies wanted to get their petroleum on the market, they had to have pipelines to the Mediterranean coast and those had to traverse French mandates, Syria and Lebanon. This is where the French had the British by the throat.

A conference was called in San Remo and there, in the spring of 1920, the oil peace between the Allies was signed. France was to receive the Germans' pre-war 25 per cent share. The Turkish Petroleum Company was renamed Iraq Petroleum Company. Peacemaker in this oil war was Mr. Gulbenkian, who received 5 per cent of the shares of the company. Later he acquired the reputation of being one of the richest men in the world. His collection of paintings which both Britain and the United States had a chance to see certainly supported the belief that he was fabulously rich.

It was before San Remo that the War of Independence of American Oil against British Oil began. Because of the favorite beverage of high-level diplomatic gatherings, the historic event deserves to be immortalized as the San Remo Cocktail Party. Its results, however, were long delayed.

Oil executives are famous for having the most highly sensitive noses. As soon as it became clear that the Middle East was rich in oil, American petroleum interests began to display a lively interest in it. The opening gun was fired when they asked the British to admit American oil-exploring parties in Iraq. The British said no, and now that San Remo sealed the friendship with the French, the latter also said no. The excuse was that they were mandatories in this region and had to protect the interests of the natives. At about the same time the caustic and witty late Count Carlo Sforza of Italy made the remark: "Mandates . . . are bashful formulae to render more decent our colonial greed."

The British launched a counteroffensive, charging that American oil interests were engaged in Middle East politics and had encouraged the Turkish republic to lay claim to the oil-rich Mosul district in northern Iraq, under British mandate. They also charged, according to George E. Kirk (*A Short History of the Middle East*) that while the United States was clamoring for the Open Door, she had "conspicuously failed to grant it to other nations in the Philippines and other parts of their economic empire."

One of the largest American oil companies appealed to the Department of State for redress and was told that it was ready to protect the interests of the entire industry, not one of its members. Thereupon the leading members of the industry appealed to the government.

Shortly after the First World War there was a case of national jitters about a forthcoming oil shortage in the United States. Said the Director of the United States Geological Survey in January 1920: "The position of the United States in regard to oil can best be characterized as precarious." A few months later he said: "Americans will have to depend on foreign sources or use less oil." A voice from the same office: "Within five years—perhaps three years only—our domestic production will begin to fall off with increasing rapidity, due to the exhaustion of our reserves." He foresaw the need of importing large quantities of oil and, perhaps, using shale. In reality, American oil extraction has increased tremendously and, of course, consumption, too.

The United States Senate indulged in angry outbursts in the spring of 1920, discussing the "near stranglehold the British government had upon the undeveloped oil areas of the world." Congress accentuated its strong views by passing the Mineral Leasing Act under which the Washington authorities were authorized to reject applications for leases of public lands to citizens of foreign countries which denied like privileges to Americans.

"Open the Door to American Oil" was the call of Washington diplomacy. Finally, after many years of wrangling on the highest level, American oil won in 1928. The American Near East Development Company was admitted into the I.P.C. (Iraq Petroleum Company). It consisted of Standard Oil Co. (New Jersey), Socony-Vacuum Corp. and the Gulf Oil Corp. (in 1934). Later Gulf sold its share, leaving the two previous-named companies in control of the American holdings. Twenty-three and a half per cent each was the share of the Anglo-Iranian, Royal Dutch-Shell, Near East Development Co. and the Compagnie Française des Pétroles. The remaining 5 per cent belonged, of course, to the Old Billionaire of the Mountains, Mr. Gulbenkian. This was the modest way American oil entered the Middle East field. Since then it has assumed leadership.

The Persian Gulf Oil Rush

The outside world took little interest in such a remote subject as the Middle East oil. However, oil companies did. Rising out of the steaming waters of the Persian Gulf there is a group of islands called Bahrein (Two Seas) which suddenly turned out to be rich in oil. After a brief tussle between British and American oil interests, the petroleum of the islands enriched the

American pool. It must be said that in the ensuing years American oil was more enterprising and readier to take risks than its British counterpart. Also it reaped greater benefits.

Eventually, world attention was attracted not to Bahrein but to one of the least-inviting coasts of the world, the shores of the Arabian mainland some twenty-five miles from the islands.

How American oil companies obtained this concession has now become a veritable lore. One of the most popular versions was the following:

Oil was found underneath the flaming plains of the Saudi Arabian Kingdom. There was a headlong rush of the leading companies of the world to obtain the concession. Among the powers represented were not only Britain and America, but also Germany and Japan. It so happened, according to the story, that the highest bids were made by Berlin and Tokyo, and the lowest from the United States.

"Get out the oil," good King Ibn Saud told the Americans and then in a stage aside:

"These Yankees are only after oil and not my country."

Then there is another popular story, which has received wide currency. An American philanthropist was prospecting for water to quench the thirst of native tots. He was apprised by the King's emissaries that their exalted master would like to talk oil with Americans. He put them in touch with the right persons.

Still another version of this Arabian tale tells of an official of the Bahrein Oil Company gazing wistfully from his island toward the distant line of haze indicating the shore. If there was oil on Bahrein why should there be no oil on the mainland? He engaged in some drilling which indicated an oil structure, to be known as the Dammam Dome.

Drilling was begun in 1934, but at first the results were discouraging. However, on October 16, 1938, oil was discovered in commercial quantities in the Dammam field. There then ensued a rush by various parties, particularly representatives of the Axis nations (Germany, Italy and Japan) to obtain concession in Saudi Arabia. The Iraq Petroleum Company was also on the scene, but the California Arabian Standard Oil Company was the successful bidder. The total concession area held for the exclusive use of the company was about 440,000 square miles, equal to about one-sixth of the area of the United States.[3]

A million miles from nowhere, with no transportation facilities, no population centers from which to draw the labor force, no nearby markets, it required imagination to see the possibilities of the Hasa coast of Saudi Arabia as a great oil center. Eventually the Standard Oil Company of California, associated with the Texas Company, formed the Arabian American Oil Company, which was to achieve fame and success under the well-known name of "Aramco." The deed was sealed with the payment of 30,000 gold sovereigns into Ibn Saud's royal palm. Later the original operators were joined by other American oil companies.

Gadgets and Gold Planes

Many hundreds of millions of dollars were to descend from heaven in years to come, representing royalty payments. The "descent from heaven" is not a figure of speech. Desert Arabia is very slow in most things but its alacrity when expecting gold has no match. Therefore planes carrying gold have become regular features of the Middle Eastern sky. The desert loves the dollar which it knows to be a good currency but, after all, it is only printed paper. There is nothing like pieces of gold sovereigns.

If prosperity requires a large measure of business acumen, what is holding Arabia back from forging to the front? Does any other part of the globe possess as much business sense, refined to the nth degree? Consider the case of these gold sovereigns themselves. The story is told by Aramco officials with relish.

The sovereigns in question have a nominal value of $12.84 a piece, and the most common ones among them bear the likenesses of Queen Victoria and King Edward VII. Oil officials noticed a bizarre thing in connection with these gold pieces. The Queen's sovereigns sold at a discount in the bazaars. The American observers assumed that this was because of the lower rank of a queen than a king, being a mere female. However, they found out eventually that women are inferior in the desert but

[3] The International Petroleum Cartel, U. S. Government Printing Office.

gold is gold whether bearing the features of man or woman. What was wrong with the Victoria sovereigns was not the sex of the ruler. Victoria's reign preceded that of Edward VII, therefore the gold pieces have been longer in use and more of the gold particles had been rubbed off. That accounted for the discount. Do not desert Arabs qualify as brilliant businessmen?

What other changes have been effected by the gold shower? The most spectacular ones concern the direct recipients of oil royalty, primarily King Ibn Saud. Trade in the leading jewelry stores of New York's Fifth Avenue must have increased tremendously as a result of the royal bonanza. It has also changed life in the heart of the desert, which had never seen the like of what oil royalties can do.

Take, for instance, the case of the royal palace in Riyadh, capital of Saudi Arabia. It is a hell hole of creation, right in the heart of the dusty desert. If you do not like the heat you should not have been born an Arab.

But that miraculous land of America, which knows how to turn the saddest desert sand into the richest mine of wealth, has also known how to turn the earthly inferno into an anticipation of the Seventh Heaven with its crystal-pure air. In other words, it has become possible to air-condition royal suites. This is precisely what American engineers have done in the royal capital. It looked very good to King Ibn Saud, whose chambers were now filled with the entrancing scent of mountain air.

Reflecting on what wonderful things can be accomplished with the miracles of modern technique, he stepped onto the terrace of the royal mansion one day, ready to enjoy the magnificence of the star-lit heaven. Then he found to his great dismay that the terrace was not air-conditioned.

"You have forgotten to air-condition the terrace, my terrace," he told the American engineers.

They informed him that air-conditioning was meant only for indoors. However, the King cut them short.

"You Americans can do everything."

Such innocent faith in the national genius could not be disappointed. The engineers set out to air-condition the desert. This they did by building a large plastic bubble over the royal terrace, and then installing a jumbo air-conditioning duct that discharged cool air. Now the stalwart King could do his star-gazing in air-cooled serenity and his faith that no sorcerer of the Arabian Nights could hold a candle to an American engineer was confirmed.

The Lamps of Aramco

At first the Middle East received very little out of its oil wealth, instead of the huge royalties and taxes it had every right to expect. The oil royalty holders in Venezuela, for instance, received 86 cents per barrel (one metric ton is about 7½ bbls. of Middle East crude petroleum), as compared with 13 to 33 cents in Persian Gulf ports in 1948. The Iranian government received only 16 cents on the net profit dollars of the Anglo-Iranian Oil Company. "All is well in love and warfare," commented an Iranian wit; "also in oil royalty accounting."

Even before the Anglo-Iranian issue had exploded, Aramco had raised Ibn Saud's share to 50 per cent of the net operating revenue. Until 1950, the Kingdom of Iraq received 22 cents per barrel from the I.P.C. Then the government's share was raised to 33 cents, doubled to 66 cents in the following year, and further increased in 1952 to 50 per cent of the company's profits from its operations. Fifty-fifty became the rule in the Middle East oil world.

Compared with the lamps of the oil companies, even the fabulous lamp of Aladdin paled into insignificance. After all, what did that famous son of Mustafa the tailor get out of his lamp? Merely untold wealth for himself, a palace and the Sultan's daughter. And if we know royal ladies well enough, the chances are she was a shrew. Compared with that, the list of benefits the Middle East has been receiving in the form of oil royalties sounds almost like the fantastic wealth resulting from radio prize contests.

In all seriousness, some of the sheykhs of the Arabian peninsula must be rubbing their eyes at what is happening to them. There is, for instance, the Sheykhdom of Kuwait which is little more than six thousand square miles of desert, a sparsely settled British protectorate. Its nominal ruler, Sheykh Abdullah al Salim al Sabah, used to have a civil list so slender that it reminded one of the salary check of an American college professor. However, he could live on that in the desert.

The latest information we have about him is that he has received no less than $140,000,000 oil royalties in one single year. With that he can not only increase Fifth Avenue's jewelry trade but also bring in water for his subjects. It is rather unfortunate that the possibilities of his small protectorate are closely confined by nature. "Allah gives nuts to those who have no teeth."

Or there is the case of the Sheykhdom of Qatar, an even smaller Arabian protectorate so far removed from the world that the last estimate of its population was taken during the First World War: some 25,000 persons. The Sheykh of Qatar, Ali Bin Abdullah Bin Qasim Al Thani, receives up to $14,000,000 a year on the basis of the present annual oil output of two million tons. He never had it so good.

It is estimated that annual oil revenue in the Middle East, royalty payments, wages, current expenditures of oil companies, will soon amount to half a billion dollars. That is a tremendous amount for the poorhouse of the world, likely to bring about some changes. Are these bound to be revolutionary or evolutionary?

The Common Man Done in Oil

When Aramco went into the desert it was ready to pay its labor more than the going wages, which it found distressingly low. It wanted to have a full day's pay for a full day's work in a climate which is particularly trying. The officials found that the going wages amounted to seven cents a day and they were supposed to pay no more for fear of wrecking the local labor market.

Today the wages are higher, what with a little high-level diplomacy on the part of the company and with inflation. It is an unusual sight indeed to see a large corporation trying to increase the pay of its workers.

Most of these employees are unskilled, not so much because they could not be trained to perform more highly qualified work but because the companies are reluctant to make themselves expendable. Should there be an adequate staff of highly screened and qualified native workers, the governments might conceive the idea that there was no sense in splitting profits with the foreigners. However, a new agreement with Iraq provides for the training of native employees both in the oil fields and at British universities.

The foreign oil companies, especially the Americans, have done much to improve the working conditions of labor in their plants. Indeed, they have launched a full-fledged New Deal regime of which the much-maligned Washington teams could be proud.

The number of oil company employees is somewhere around a hundred thousand, and is increasing rapidly. The companies have established schools for them, their children and, in some cases, anybody else who cares to come. Besides the usual subjects taught in Arabic, oral and written English are also on the curriculum.

Social services of a considerable scope have been set up. These include health services in hospitals and clinics, of a nature to which people in the area are not used, and on a truly impressive scale.

The benefit of oil royalties is also beginning to seep down to the level of the people, but it is only the beginning and the "seepage" is limited. It is the benevolent dictatorship of the type of Saudi Arabia's that appears to be in a better position to do more for the people than the so-called democracies of the region. Several improvements were projected for the Saudi Kingdom, mainly out of oil royalties. Most important of this is the railway, between the oil center of Dammam and the capital Riyadh, by way of the oasis of Al-Kharj, which has already been opened. The next major project seems to be the reconstruction of the Pilgrims' Railway, from Damascus to Medina, which Lawrence of Arabia's men had wrecked.

Several new paved roads are expected to be built, one linking the holy cities of Mecca and Medina. These highways may be of special benefit to the royal court, owner of a famous fleet of supermodern motorcars.

Irrigation, of course, is the great issue of desert Arabia. At several strategic points centrifugal pumps have already been installed to increase the water supply. One of these is at the edge of a large limestone pit at Al-Kharj, where a new farm development covers 3,000 acres.

Many of the improvements are more closely connected with oil production, although benefiting the region as a whole. A large pier was completed at Jidda, Saudi Arabia's Red Sea port. Entirely new harbors were built in the oil region, Dammam and Ras Tanura, the latter of which is the terminal of a great pipeline and an oil refinery site. An air service has been established linking the Red Sea with the Persian Gulf. Telephone and radio communications are being installed and improved. It is contemplated that a quarter of a billion dollars will be set aside for the further development of water supplies, electrification, hospitals and schools. Saudi Arabia's minister of health has become an important purchaser of American medical equipment.

Off the coast of Saudi Arabia, on Bahrein Island, the oil company has been sponsoring farm development. It has drilled Artesian wells, launched a project of water conservation, imported selected seeds and distributed them among the local people. A seawater distillation plant capable of providing a million gallons of fresh water a day was built in Britain for the Sheykhdom of Kuwait.

We should not underestimate the importance of the effect of the American way of life on the Middle Eastern way. The American, and also the British, oil towns seek to reproduce home life with all its luxuries, and sometimes even more. American Middle East oil towns look like improved replicas of Texas. In that setting a washing machine and the innumerable kitchen utensils of well-equipped American homes are miracles.

Some of the American employees have exhibited a missionary zeal in converting the younger generation of the oil-producing Arab countries to the cult of sports, particularly baseball. American soft drinks are naturals for this part of the world which is hot as blazes and cannot indulge in alcoholic "long ones," largely because of their cost and Islamic prohibition. These soft drink companies are also acquainting the leading Middle East countries with the American way of advertising. Occasionally there are strange by-products of these esoteric publicity campaigns. An Egyptian daily, for instance, having been overlooked in the allotment of the advertising budget of an American soft drink company, launched a campaign against it with the charge that pork fat is used in the manufacture of the drink. And as all the world knows, any part of the pig is taboo in the Muslim world.

What is the effect of this incredible wealth upon the poverty-stricken Middle East? It is too early to make a forecast, since this development is quite new. People do not respond so quickly to changes, especially not in this area which is used to slow motion. Most of the people are not directly affected by the oil bonanza.

Yet, it is a source of constant surprise to see with what speed news travels where there are no newspapers. People hear about life in the new oil towns, and they see that such things are possible. The great oil companies, which may be counted among conservative organizations, are exerting a revolutionary influence. The fraction of the population affected by the "oil rush"—productive of incomparably greater wealth than the gold rush of past times—may become the "critical mass" which will cause the chain reaction, to employ the term used in the language of the atom bomb. Middle East oil is lubricating the revolutionary changes in the region.

The Story of the Pipeline

It is not enough to have oil; it must also be transported to its markets. From the head of the Persian Gulf, where so much oil is concentrated, oil had to be taken in tankers to the Mediterranean. That meant seven thousand miles, coming and going, to the closest Levant port. That was costly and there were also Suez Canal toll charges, amounting sometimes to as much as $40,000 on a single shipment.

The Iraq Petroleum Company was the first with a pipeline, from its base at Kirkuk. In the desert it bifurcated, one branch ending in the Lebanese port of Tripoli and the other one in the Palestine city of Haifa. The latter branch was closed down by the Arabs during the troubles with Israel. This pipeline was only

12 inches, later paralleled by 16-inch lines. Anglo-Iranian constructed several pipelines. The flow of Iraq oil was later trebled by laying a 30 inch pipeline from Kirkuk to Banias on the Lebanon coast.

Then came the "Tapline," one of the world's major pipelines in operation, 30-31 inches wide, linking the Saudi Arabian wells with the Lebanese coastal town of Sidon.

The building of this line was another Arabian desert epic. Tapline had to cross some of the world's hottest and unfriendliest wastes. The temperature along the line of construction sometimes rose to 130 degrees in the shade, but where was that shade? A careless worker touching the sun-scorched metal lost his hand. Humidity in the desert is so low that crew members had to drink as much as two gallons of water a day, but the desert had no water. Therefore wells had to be drilled and they did bring in water. Over part of the route, fiery winds buffeted the desert and overcame the crews with avalanches of fire. Finally the line was completed. Today it is flanked by settlements attracted to it by the new water holes.

How Much Oil Underneath the Sand?

It is difficult to forecast the future production capacity of petroleum regions. One can speak more confidently about past achievements. The Middle East is so important to the petroleum industry not merely because it straddles the richest pool but also because its wells are incomparably more productive than those of any other part of the world. For one thing, that reduces costs greatly. The average daily production of a well in the Middle East of 1949 was 3,700 barrels, against 11 barrels in the United States. The figure for Venezuela was 201 barrels a day. As the experts put it, Middle Eastern oil is drawn from richly flowing wells, while those of the other regions must be artificially lifted.

Correspondingly, the cost of production of crude petroleum must be much lower in the Middle East than elsewhere. That is, of course, a closely guarded trade secret. However, some information about it did leak out in a Congressional committee hearing investigating the national defense program. It disclosed that about the time the Second World War was over, the cost of production of a barrel of crude oil in Bahrein was 25 cents, in Saudi Arabia 41 cents, compared with the cost of production of a barrel of oil in Venezuela three years later—$1.54. The oil companies charged $2.22 in the Persian Gulf, which, naturally, did not include transportation charges. This was the same as United States Gulf Coast price, in a high production cost area. Eventually, the companies reduced their price to $1.75 at the Persian Gulf. Adding 66 cents per barrel in transportation cost, this made the price $2.41 at Sidon, on the Mediterranean. Much of that oil was sold to the Government of the United States. The Justice Department in Washington instituted proceedings to recover $50,000,000 from four Middle East oil companies for alleged overcharges.

The Federal Trade Commission published a report in the middle of 1952 about the world petroleum supply and demand. Based upon figures that were some two years old, it revealed a graphic picture about the increasing importance of Middle East oil for the United States. It showed the Middle East producing 2,250,000 barrels a day, of which it consumed only one-tenth. On the other hand, the United States consumed more than it produced: 7,350,000 barrels a day, against 6,700,000 barrels of daily production.

Oil production figures in the Middle East are dated just as soon as they are uttered. Here is just one set of figures on the oil production in the Sheykhdom of Kuwait. It started at the end of the Second World War and was 16 million barrels in 1947. Three years later it was 125 million barrels and one year later, in 1951, it shot up to 204 million barrels, increasing further to about 280 million barrels in 1952. This was the largest increase in the Persian Gulf area and was partly due to the fact that the Anglo-Iranian Oil Company was nationalized by Iran in 1951. At the rate the remaining oil companies were operating there was to be no loss to the western world because of the loss of the Iranian fields.

Oil for the Lamps of America

Attention was called to the distressing fact in recent times that the United States constitutes no exemption to the laws of nature and that its natural resources are also subject to exhaustion. This applies to oil as well, although the early fears of an imminent drying-up of the wells have not materialized.

In a pinch, America can draw upon a variety of reserves. The continental ledge of the sea may be richer than it is assumed to be.

If worse comes to worst, oil may be squeezed out of oil shales and even out of bituminous coal. Also, this country has considerable amounts of natural gas. It is believed that these potential oil reserves could cover America's needs at the present rate of consumption for over a thousand years.

However, it has not been shown conclusively, in the language of the Legislative Reference study of oil, that the quality of the products and the cost of large quantity production in terms of steel, labor, investment, are such as to relieve the demand for crude petroleum:

"It may be, as a representative of the Oil and Gas Division of the Department of the Interior has said, that 'ultimately, synthetics can and will supply the bulk of our liquid fuels from resources that are found abundantly within our borders, but in view of the present situation, ultimately may be too late.'"

In midcentury the Middle East fields covered the bulk of the requirements of Europe—about three-quarters of it, and a large portion of that was for the common defense. France alone was using some thirteen million tons of oil, and similar requirements were increasing along the line. If mankind was destined to destroy itself, it was floating into destruction on the tidal wave of oil.

An International Cartel and a Cold War

The Federal Trade Commission report [4] said five American and two foreign oil companies have been operating as a cartel to control world prices and production. The concerns named were the Standard Oil Company (New Jersey), Standard Oil of California; Socony-Vacuum, Gulf, Texas Company, Anglo-Ira-

[4] *International Petroleum Cartel.* Staff Report to the Federal Trade Commission. Submitted to the Subcommittee on Monopoly of the Select Committee on Small Business. United States Senate. Washington: Government Printing Office, 1952.

nian, and Royal Dutch-Shell. These companies were said to control 55 per cent of the production, 65 per cent of the reserves, 57 per cent of the refining capacity and 66 per cent of the private tankers of the world, excluding the Soviet Union and its satellites.

This shows American and British oil interests dominating the field. But at first there was a "cold war" between the Allies: the United States and Great Britain. And it still continues in a strange form, in spite of the "cartel."

The most exciting battles of this war have taken place in the sound-proof rooms of hush-hush board of director meetings, staffs of grand strategy. The sounds of battle occasionally penetrated into the outside world, as in the *Memoirs* of Cordell Hull, for many years America's Secretary of State.

We recall that the British were holding onto the Middle East petroleum fields, keeping out Americans, and that it was the continued effort of the State Department in Washington that enabled United States producers to participate in the Iraq Petroleum Company. This was the triumph of the Open Door policy.

Then came the American big battalions: in Saudi Arabia, on Bahrein Island. During the Second World War the British saw their chance to recoup some of their losses. Saudi Arabia was in a bad fix because of the suspension of large-scale oil operations. Britain was in the habit of assuring the loyalty of Arab kings by placing them on the payroll. This time too Britain proposed to help out Ibn Saud with a considerable amount. However, now there was not only England but also the United States.

Mr. Hull suggested: "If Saudi Arabia is permitted to lean too heavily upon the British, there is always the danger that the British will request a quid pro quo in oil . . ." [5] So, Mr. Hull suggested that the American government share the subsidy on an over-all basis. Not only that, but the government in Washington contemplated buying up the Saudi Arabian oil wells. That, in turn, was not palatable to the American oil companies even though the government appeared to be fighting their battle.

By that time the British oil companies were on the defensive

[5] *The Memoirs of Cordell Hull,* Vol. II, p. 1515.

and so it was in their interest to call a halt to the cold war. The year was 1944, and the war was drawing to its end. This was the era of good feeling, when the fellow-Allies were angels and only the Axis nations were the blackest of devils. Still, one could not know about the Soviets. They revealed tremendous strength. Would they use it in realizing their old ambition, getting down to the Persian Gulf? Next door to them were the largest oil pools of the world. It would be safer for the western Allies to get together on the question of oil. And so they did, by negotiating an "oil peace treaty" in Washington and London.

The resources, observed the Secretary of State, which were held to a substantial extent by American and British interests could not be adequately developed unless the two governments reached an agreement providing for close co-operation. Other governments were eventually bidden to join. The agreement sought to promote friendly co-existence among the Great Powers of oil in the fields of production as well as distribution. Among other things it provided that adequate petroleum supplies should be made available to the nationals of all peaceable countries at fair prices; that there should be equal opportunity to acquire rights of exploration and development in areas not already under concession; that there should be respect for all valid concession contracts; that oil resources should be developed in such a way as to encourage the sound economic advancement of countries in which the deposits lay.

This was the language of diplomacy. Translated into everyday language, it said: Don't loot the natural resources of the host countries! Don't cut the other fellow's throat!

The Foreign Offices of the two countries approved the documents, which were duly signed and sealed. Then came an exciting interval about which we know nothing. It must have been one of those intramural battles in the padded rooms of the Board of Directors. What we do know is negative. The Senate of the United States decided to ignore the document—the silent treatment. Evidently some influential people thought that the pact was an attempt on the part of the weaker British to restrain the Americans' aggressive hands.

This was not the end of the story. The following year another attempt was made to pass the pact in an even more diluted form. "The signatory governments agree," a revealing declaratory passage of the proposed pact said, "that the international petroleum trade in all its aspects should be conducted in an orderly manner on a world-wide basis."

This was again diplomatic double talk. Translated into ordinary language, this was a warning: Gentlemen will please check their daggers at the door.

The pact was signed in due form, and it also was allowed to expire in a Senate pigeonhole. British fears were realized. American oil marched triumphantly into the Middle East.

In March 1951 the Iranian parliament nationalized the Anglo-Iranian Oil Company. The world is familiar only with surface events. The ruling class of Iran seems to have reached the end of its road and so it needed the usual scapegoat. This is probably part of the story. While the controversy was raging certain hints were made in even the most representative section of the British press indicating that petroleum competitors may have had a hand in the game. But this is again something which is locked in the most secretive of all secret archives, the strongrooms of the oil companies.

The fact is that by 1952 American oil dominated the Middle Eastern scene. The British, who, at first, monopolized the field, had only 14 per cent of the total output. America's foreign oil investment, mostly Middle East and South America, now amounted to 3½ billion dollars in 1950, a large increase since the end of the Second World War.

Then came the charge of the international cartel. It is not in contradiction with the facts of the "cold war" among the American and British producers.

"If you can't lick 'em, join 'em"—and that is what the companies did after the Second World War. The combatants decided to get together under various systems of joint ownerships and exchanges of stocks. Out of this has grown one of the most baffling corporate complexes of modern times. The report describes it as follows:

> Jersey Standard, Socony, Royal Dutch Shell and Anglo-Iranian are linked through their joint holdings in Iraq Petro-

leum Company and its nest of subsidiaries: Gulf and Anglo-Iranian jointly own Kuwait Oil; Standard of California and Texas have many joint relations through the California-Texas complex and are tied to Jersey Standard and Socony through Aramco and Trans-Arabian. . . .

And so on and so forth.

The story of Middle East oil promised to be a gusher. In the autumn of 1952 a leading American oil distributor visited Iran, looked over the Anglo-Iranian plants, the wells, talked with the Prime Minister and other leading personalities. The sensational portion of the Iranian press spoke about impending events of great significance, but, then, it is not addicted to understatements.

A few weeks later Iran broke diplomatic relations with Great Britain. Why Iran should be so angry with the country which it despoiled would have been a mystery only in a more sensible age. Certainly, Iran would have dared to do nothing of this kind when she stood in awe of the formidable power of Britain. This time she did not stand in awe, either because the British empire no longer inspired it, or else because she felt to be protected. The world was wondering—by whom?

CHAPTER 11

Great Powers in the Middle East

A Highway and a Vacuum

In the heart of the Middle East where the road debouches from the hills of Samaria to the Plains of Israel the small village of Megiddo stands today. So great was the military significance of that point that the Biblical Apocalypse names it as the site of the last great battle among the nations before Judgment Day—Armageddon.

"There is probably no older road in the world than that which can still be used by caravans from the Euphrates to the Nile, through Damascus, Galilee, Esdraelon, the Maritime Plain, and Gaza," wrote George Adam Smith in his classic book, *The Historical Geography of the Holy Land.*

On this lifeline of the Middle East Thothmes, Ramses, Sennacherib, Cambyses, Alexander, Pompey, Saladin, Napoleon, Allenby and Montgomery have led their armies.

Those war leaders who took roots in this region expanded their realms, while those that failed were quickly swept away. Alexander moved into this region in 332 B.C., and his name is commemorated in Alexandria, Alexandretta, many legends and folklores. When he secured the pivotal point of the Middle East, the world belonged to him—the world worth having.

Julius Caesar made his bid for world dominion in the name of the "city," Rome, which was to be pivoted on Egypt. That the seat of the Roman realm should be transferred to Alexandria was the serious thought of Mark Antony. No less a person than Napoleon passed this information on to us. The choice fell on Constantinople, another world anchorage in the Middle East. This Second Rome survived the first well nigh a thousand years.

Next, it was the Arabs' turn and they are still there, heartland of a vaster Muslim world. The Crusaders came and they failed, their rule remembered only in magnificent ruins. After them the Tartars. . . . Their realm was vaster than anything the world had seen or was to see. They were not able to establish themselves in the Middle East and their world empire was to crumble.

The Ottoman Turks came and they stayed, finding a vacuum caused by waves of devastation, which they filled. At first their hold was strong because they represented the powerful and ruthless men of modern times. But then they lost their self-confidence and began to weaken. Then the Eastern Question emerged. Who was now to fill out the vacuum?

A Meteor on the Middle Eastern Sky

Elemental forces in the shape of man were always attracted to the Middle East. We have heard Napoleon say that Britain's might could be shaken only in Egypt. His attempt to conquer the Middle East was based upon a deep knowledge of global strategy. In the shadow of the Pyramids he was to lay low England's might, and not across the Channel. With the global pivot in his hands he was to be the master.

On Saint Helena he told a little-known incident of his experience in Egypt. It was the story of how he was to become a Muslim and thus gain the adherence of the Islamic world.

During his campaign in Egypt he called upon Islam's famous school of higher learning, Al-Azhar, and met its venerable sheykhs. The learned Sheykh Cherhaoui was deeply impressed by this famous representative of the *Franji,* to whom he made a strange proposition:

"You and your valorous army should become Muslims. In that case a hundred thousand of our men will flock to your flag. You will train them, and establish a great Arab nation. After that it will be up to you to subdue the East."

"I objected," Napoleon recorded, "the necessity of circumcision and the prohibition of wine. The French soldier could not live without his drink."

The sheykh admitted that these objections deserved to be seriously considered. A few weeks later he offered a solution. Circumcision, he said, was important but not one of the main commands of the law. However, he admonished Napoleon, he had to warn him that the uncircumcised could not enter Paradise.

Entering Paradise did not seem to worry Napoleon and so there remained only the problem of wine. That required an even longer meditation but the solution was eventually forthcoming. If that evil beverage was so essential to the *Franji,* well and good, but . . . in that case they must be prepared to increase the amount of their contributions to charity.

There the matter rested, perhaps because Napoleon was forced to face thornier problems. He had to evacuate Egypt and abandon the idea of destroying Britain's might at the foot of the Pyramids.

He did not give up the thought altogether. He tried again, at the other extreme of the Middle East. The next attempt was made in Persia.

The conqueror's restless mind conceived the idea of employing the overland route in his attempt to subdue England in India. To that effect he was to march across Russia, debouching in Persia. The Shah of those days—the one with the thousand wives —was in favor of the idea. He had trouble with the Russians but lacked time to beat them, presumably because of his domestic preoccupation. Napoleon appeared to be the right person to help him in his quandary. The French Emperor promised to send him military instructors. Thereupon the Shah wrote to him:

Every word in your noble lines is like a drop of amber on camphor or like the perfumed curls on the rosy cheeks of the beloved with a bosom of lilies.

This style of writing employed by the Shah is understandable in view of his main interest in life.

However, the French military instructors did not arrive. Instead of them, it was the Russians who appeared, carving another chunk of Persia for themselves.

Then Came the British

Late in the nineteenth century it was the British who established themselves in the Middle East. They appeared to be on the pinnacle of their power, and their ability to weather future storms depended on their control of the Middle Eastern core. Also they controlled the Ottoman Empire "as the noose supports the hanged man." It was a basic British policy, Foreign Secretary Lord Lansdowne announced in 1903, that his country would regard the "establishment of a naval base or a fortified port on the Persian Gulf by any other power as a very grave menace." Previously, Disraeli and Lord Salisbury had staked out the entire Ottoman empire as Britain's defense position against Russia.

It was inevitable that in his mad quest for world rule Hitler should send his forces into this region to challenge Britain's might. When his Afrikakorps suffered its disastrous defeat in the desert warfare of 1942-43, the Third Reich entered upon the decline that was to end in utter ruin two years later.

When head of the North Atlantic Treaty Organization, General Eisenhower declared, "As far as sheer value of territory is concerned, there is no more strategically important area in the world than the stretch that begins at the Persian Gulf and swings westward."

Speaking to Congress on May 24, 1951, President Truman said about the Middle East: "No part of the world is more directly exposed to Soviet pressure. The Kremlin has lost no opportunity to stir these troubled waters, as the postwar record amply demonstrates. Civil war in Greece; pressure for Turkish concessions on the Dardanelles, sponsorship of the rebellious Tudeh party in Iran; furthering of factional strife in the Arab States and Israel —all reflect a concerted design for the extension of Soviet domination for this vital area."

The Middle East is a highway at the crossroads of the world, but it is also something else—a negative quality with strong positive potentialities. It is still largely a power vacuum at present, filled by nations that lack the strength to defend themselves against major powers. Highway and power vacuum form a dangerous combination and the Middle East, indeed, is a *terre fatale*. Let us cast a glance at the major powers having special interests in the region today.

Great Britain's Pax

Great Britain has been involved in the Middle East longer than the other Great Powers. Historians usually mention only those facts which were written with visible ink in the annals.

First there was the Turkey Company of England in the sixteenth century, an age which saw the mushrooming of the great trading companies of merchant adventurers. Then it combined with the Venice Company and the two of them now became the Levant Company which Queen Elizabeth chartered. This was confirmed by James I and Charles II and, supplemented by usage, it formed the basis of British consular jurisdiction in the East. The Levant Company was so strongly linked with the government that it paid the expenses of the ambassadors sent into the region by the government. It did not go out of business until 1825.

Then Britain moved more boldly into the Middle East when she occupied Egypt in 1882 and proclaimed her protectorate over it with the outbreak of the First World War. The visibly written chapters of history make much of the fact that the United Kingdom became a dominant factor in this area only during and after the First World War. During that war by organizing Arab resistance and after the war by being the mandatory power in Palestine, Jordan and Iraq, as well as by pulling the wires in the background of Syria.

The fact of the matter is that when these things happened England had been in the Middle East for centuries. However, that part of the record was written in the invisible ink reserved for the most important phases of history. The reader interested in that period of British events should look for them in books under either of two headings: "The Ottoman Empire" or "The Eastern Question." The most important part of Turkish history for several generations was English history. It was Britain in the background, and not the Ottoman Empire in the foreground, which maintained the watch in the Middle East so that outsiders might not trespass. Especially, it was Britain which contained Russia, so as to keep her from reaching her warm-water goal.

This role of Britain was inevitable in view of the part she played in history. She operated the system of balance of power: no nation was to disturb the status quo through the acquisition of an excess of power. Britain had to play an important role in the Middle East, because of the juxtaposition of patent weakness on the part of the Ottoman Empire and presumed strength on the part of monumentally massive Russia.

In normal times Britain appeared to be no more than one of the major powers, on a footing of equality with the other Great Powers. All of them were supposed to operate within their own spheres, sanctioned by custom and pacts. These Great Powers often had satellites of their own, over which they exerted a gravitational pull.

Britain's special role was revealed only in times of crisis, when one or more of the Great Powers sought to overstep the bounds of their own spheres, trying to establish a dominant position.

This was particularly the case in the presence of a power vacuum. The next-door neighbor of the Ottoman Empire, for instance, was Russia, which wanted to fill out that void, thereby upsetting the existing balance. It was bad enough that the empire of the czars had become so bloated with land loot. Had she also obtained favorable positions in relation to sea routes she might have become unmanageable. For a long time Britain's feud with Russia was the most important event of history.

Before that came to pass, however, Britain's eyes were fixed on France. That country revealed a dynamism that threatened to engulf Europe. It was therefore in the interest of Britain to create counterweights to France, the system of divide and rule. Only when that system failed and France actually set out to become the dominant power in Europe did Britain take to war.

The last time France made such an attempt was during the meteoric rise of Napoleon. It was no coincidence that alone among the other Great Powers, Britain was always part of the coalitions which were to bring about the French Emperor's fall.

After this was brought about, France was fitted into the British system of satellites. It took several generations before the French kingdom, empire and later the republic found their proper place in this scheme of things. Many French statesmen were notoriously blind to the appropriate position of their country. Every time France forgot about her role, Britain reminded her of the facts of life. Gradually, the French republic occupied the position assigned to her by London. When that happened, France was no longer deemed a potential competitor and Britain assigned her parts of colonial realms which she did not want herself. In many of these cases the French republic served as *locum tenens* for the British Empire. This was particularly the case in Africa. Early this century England gave the highest recognition due to a satellite by assigning to her the most vital part of Africa, in Morocco at the strategic point where the Atlantic Ocean and the Mediterranean meet. Britain had to be convinced that France was too weak to upset the world balance before London approved this arrangement.

The real position of Britain was thence not only one of the Great Powers but of an umpire and a policeman. She was really a World Power, the first among nominal equals. The system which she operated was productive of the *Pax Britannica.*

There were certain factors which conspired to assign this role to Britain. First of these was her island location. Situated on small islands within sight of the huge Eurasian continent, Britain was a fragile structure indeed. However, this very fragility was a challenge to which she gave the proper response. Because of her physical weakness she had to develop a countervailing strength. In order not to be dominated she had to dominate the threatening continent. This she could do by taking advantage of the mutual jealousies of the great continental nations, promoting the interests of the weak, breaking the arrogance of the strong. She was helped in this respect by the Continental Powers themselves, which responded to this treatment, constantly weakening themselves by trying to weaken their neighbors.

Rome had shown Britain how to turn weakness into strength. The "city" organized its world empire by building roads and giving law to its world. England had this advantage over Rome, that nature had given her countless roads, all of them radiating from the British island's heartland and linking her with all parts of the world. It cost Rome much money and labor to build those indestructible roads, but it cost little to Britain to use nature's own sea routes. She had to see to it, however, that her navy was stronger than that of the other nations. To be on the safe side, Britain established the rule that her navy must be at least as strong as the navies of the next two most important maritime powers. When the German empire sought to ignore this rule, the First World War became inevitable.

Britain also had another qualification to become the World Power. In the course of centuries her capital, London, became the financial center of the world and her currency, the pound, acquired the sterling qualities which made it the standard of all other currencies. He who pays the piper calls the tune and Britain was able to pay several pipers at the same time.

Between the two World Wars of this century Britain still appeared to be the World Power. In reality she was that no more, partly because she was no longer the mistress of the seas and also because London was no longer the financial center of the world. America was now the strongest power, but she believed that she could withdraw into an isolation from which only the evil-minded could flush her out. That was, of course, the great mistake for which mankind had to pay with the Second World War.

Meanwhile, Britain tried to fill out the Middle East vacuum. We were told by Lawrence that the Arab nations were to be the cement. London may not have noticed that they lacked the strength and ability to perform that role. Only the Arab states' war with Israel revealed the intrinsic weakness of the Arab countries. Britain, too, was reminded that a nation could not be stronger than the sum of the strength of her citizens.

The evil genius of Hitler detected the flaw in the world's organization—Britain was too weak to be the World Power. He proclaimed the supremacy of the German, the racial crown of creation. The most dynamic country was to rule Europe and he wanted no more.

However, Britain knew that he who ruled Europe was sure to rule the world. This was not a question of conscious policy, but a historic necessity. Again Great Britain headed the coalition that was to see the fall of the madman's Third Reich.

This was the end of Britain's role as the World Power. Yes, she won the war but was bound to lose the peace. She could hope for no more than to be a respected elder statesman to the next World Power. Nations do not like to reveal their weakness and yet Britain had to do that in the year of 1947. It was in that year that she abdicated her throne, which she offered to the United States. In that year London told Washington that she was no longer able to watch the ramparts in the Balkans against the Soviet pressure. This was the time when London told Washington that America would have to assume the burden of halting the Communists in Greece. Such seemingly unimportant matters reveal the greatest secrets of history. Then President Truman uttered the historic words which came to be known as the Truman Doctrine. "The King is dead, long live the King!" Great Britain ceased to be the World Power, the Pax Britannica was gone. It was now for the United States to resume the work of Britain—the day of the Pax Americana has dawned.

The United States Faces the Fertile Crescent

The political record of the United States was almost a blank until quite recently and it is revealing to compare it with the closely written pages of American history in the Middle East today.

The few events to be recorded were negative or abortive. There was the case of the Barbary Pirates ("pyrates," in the spelling of Thomas Jefferson) at the beginning of the last century. A part of the region still paid tribute to the Ottoman sultan. Morocco had a government of her own, or it would be more correct to call it an anarchy of her own. At any rate, the United States was able to buy immunity from Moroccan piratical raids for $10,000, a bargain even for those days.

But there were the "pyrates" of Algeria, Tunisia and Tripoli. They had been kept in check by the British navy; but when the American colonies revolted, the protecting navy vanished from the seas. London looked with glee at the activities off the Barbary Coast.

It was in October 1800 that the Dey (viceroy) of Algeria forced the S.S. *George Washington* to haul down her flag and hoist the banner of Algeria. Then the Dey instructed Commodore William Bainbridge to sail to Constantinople bearing presents to the sultan. When the Commodore remonstrated, the Dey replied: "You pay me tribute, by which you become my slaves. I have, therefore, the right to order you as I might think proper."

This was the first contact of the young republic with the Ottoman sultan and the Middle East.

Half a century passed before history records another contact between the United States and the Ottoman Empire. That was the "Koszta Affair."

Márton Koszta was a Hungarian who seems to have fought in his country's war of independence of 1848 against the Habsburgs. Then he came to the United States. A businessman, he went to Smyrna, Turkey, before he became an American citizen.

He got into trouble there, probably because he was bragging. How else could the Austro-Hungarian authorities have known who he was? At any rate there was an Austrian war vessel in Smyrna harbor then, which kidnaped him and it was understood that he was to be taken to the Austrian port of Triest, charged with high treason.

At the same time there was an American sloop-of-war in Smyrna harbor, Captain Nathan Duncan Ingraham commanding. Captain Ingraham learned about the kidnaping and he sent an ultimatum to the Austrian ship to release Koszta. The Austrian captain answered that Koszta himself did not claim that he was an American citizen. Captain Ingraham had the muzzles of his cannons bared and repeated the ultimatum. Koszta was returned to the American sloop.

America's first active act in the Middle East was hailed by none other than Karl Marx, writing in the Aug. 12, 1853, issue of *The New York Tribune:*

"Americans have abstracted another Hungarian from the claws of the Austrian eagle. It is cheering to see the American intervention in Europe beginning just with the Eastern Question."

During those years the United States signed a commercial treaty and established diplomatic relations with the Sublime Porte, obtaining privileges as favorable as those enjoyed by the most favored European nations, including capitulatory rights, under which American nationals had the advantage of low customs duties and special treatment in law cases.

Another half a century passed before we hear again of the United States in the Middle East, and again in a comparatively unimportant incident. In 1908 Washington backed a group of American businessmen in planning a railway line in what is southeastern Turkey and northern Iraq today. Not only that, the group was also to acquire the privilege of exploiting the right-of-way for twenty-five miles on both sides of the line. (P.S. It would have been the great northern Iraq oil pool.) This was known as the Chester Concession. However, the group of backers withdrew and the plan fell to the ground.

America's concern with this region was almost purely missionary and cultural until recent times. The first American missionaries arrived in the region around 1820, and fourteen years later they set up an Arabic press in Lebanon. In 1886 the American Protestant College was opened in Beirut, later to become the American University of Beirut. Americans established the equally famous Robert College and American Women's College in Constantinople, the American University in Cairo, and numerous secondary schools.

Archeological exploration by Americans also acquired significance in this region. Beginning with 1838, the noted Biblical scholar and explorer, Edward Robinson, initiated an important program of historical explorations, aided by Eli Smith, ardent missionary and distinguished Arabic scholar. Their success encouraged other Americans to study the Levant.

Until recently, American trading interests in the region were scant, and it was only between the two World Wars that the United States began to realize the region's potentialities in connection with the discovery of oil. The United States also took a deep interest in the implementation of the Balfour Declaration and the establishment of Israel.

During the Second World War the United States air forces established a string of bases to link Africa with the Far East, and the hub of the system was the Middle East. America also had a hand in the operation of the Middle East Supply Center and of the Trans-Iranian Railroad, to help embattled Russia receive the wherewithals of her resistance.

Shortly after the war the United States assumed leadership to present the case of the West in connection with the problem of the Straits. Also, America took the initiative in pressing for the evacuation of Soviet troops from Iran. The United States moved to defend Greece and Turkey, and she dispatched military experts to Iran.

Naturally, the United States was the source of the funds reaching the Middle East in various forms, for the implementation of the Truman Doctrine, Marshall Plan aid for Turkey, Export-Import Bank loans, World Bank disbursements, grants to the United Nations Relief and Works Agency for Palestine

Refugees in the Near East, disbursements under the Mutual Security Act, under the expanded technical assistance program of the United Nations and under the Point Four Program.

The United States now had diplomatic and consular representatives in parts of the Middle East which had never seen them before. The representatives of various government organizations were to be found in all parts of the region, engaged in all kinds of work. American representatives were found in the most off-the-beaten-track places, in the Persian Gulf protectorates, in the High Yemen. When a large number of Mecca-bound pilgrims remained stranded in Lebanon, it was the United States air forces that undertook their free transportation to the airport near the holy city.

NATO's Southeast Command was situated at Izmir (formerly Smyrna) on Turkey's lovely Aegean coast.

The United States was active in organizing the defense of the Middle East, which obviously was still a power vacuum. However, because of fear of "imperialism," lack of co-operation among the Middle East countries, and the state of war prevailing between Israel and the Arab lands, the effective organization of defense ran into a snag.

Motherly Russia

In the political testament of Peter the Great, the authenticity of which is challenged, that remarkable man is said to have admonished his people to "get as near Constantinople and India as possible." Russians should, therefore, "excite continuous wars, not only in Turkey but also in Persia."

However, there is nothing spurious about the authenticity of the resolutions of the Sixth Comintern (Communist International) meeting in 1928, which outlined the methods of communism to destroy capitalism and annex the Middle East to the Soviet World. It was part of this plan to effect temporary co-operation with the spokesmen of nationalist movements.

> The United States reminded the Soviet Union [1] that on Nov. 25, 1940, a proposal of U.S.S.R. People's Commissar for Foreign Affairs Molotov to German Ambassador Schulenberg to reach an agreement with Nazi Germany on

> the limitation of spheres of influence between the Axis powers and the U.S.S.R. provided among other things, that the U.S.S.R. be enabled to establish "a base for land and naval forces" within range of the Turkish Straits and that "the area south of Batum and of Baku in the general direction of the Persian Gulf is recognized as the center of the aspirations of the Soviet Union."

The official line may not have changed much since that Comintern meeting. The Voice of the Kremlin keeps on telling the people of the region that their principal foes are the "imperialists." This, of course, does not displease the ruling clique of the Middle East countries. The Soviet Union has also been trying to operate through the national minorities but has met with scant success.

It is safe to assume that Communist pressure in the Middle East is strongest through the party. Let us therefore look at it.

Communists of the Middle East

It is not easy to speak about Communists in the Middle East because, with one exception, the party is suppressed everywhere. Before its suppression, however, the portraits of Stalin were seen on many walls and he was known even to unlettered people as *Abu Shanab,* Father of the Moustaches. He is still known under that name.

The view seems to have gained ground, particularly in the United States, that communism is repugnant to Islam. After all, the Kremlin is atheist and the Islamic countries are religion-centered. This may be true in some cases, but not true in others. On the contrary, one of the Communist talking points in the Middle East is their contention that Mohammed and Marx were ideological twins, since both of them wanted social justice, a better life for the common man. To show the alleged similarity, excerpts of the Koran and of the Communist Manifesto are juxtaposed.

Whatever opposition there may be to communism is mostly not on that score. It is on the ground that communism is international, not indigenous—part of the current xenophobia.

[1] U.S. Note, Dec. 19, 1951.

Who are the Communists in this region? The answer to that question is not easy and one is dependent on more or less intelligent guesses. In Alexandria it was found that some 50 per cent of them were students, 10 per cent were professionals, and 40 per cent were factory workers. Naturally Alexandria has sizable industries, while most other Middle East cities lack them. In Iran, too, the Communists are reputed to maintain a stronghold in industry; and Abadan, containing the world's largest petroleum refinery, is said to be a Communist town.

Among the factory workers there are Communists, no doubt. A larger percentage of them appear to be intellectuals, "bookish men," not necessarily the evil-plotting type but people who find no other solution, only the great housecleaning. It is mostly this bookish type that gets caught in police dragnets.

What do Communist activities consist of? Based upon his reading of a representative portion of the Arabic press, Moshe Perlmann sought to answer this question at the 1950 Harvard University conference: "The Great Powers and the Near East."

It seems from the press that the Middle East Communists discuss publications, reproduce leaflets and pamphlets on matters of public interest and seek to distribute them in factories, streets and schools. In Egypt they have their own lingo. Thus a "specialist" is a party member, a "patient" is a worker, the "hospital Kasr-al-Ayni" means the party's Cairo branch, and a "microbe" is a policeman. The Communists also appear in the wake of riots periodically convulsing the region.

How large were these Communist parties? In 1947 the Communists claimed a party membership of twenty-four thousand in the entire Middle East, while the non-Communist estimate was about half of that figure. Turkey, Saudi Arabia and Yemen were said to have no Communists.

In Iraq, where at one time there was much ado about the Communists, they may have had no more than two hundred members and most of these belonged to the national minorities. In Egypt their number was said to have been some five hundred. The only sizable parties were in Lebanon, Syria and Palestine, and they were the objects of a study of the Committee on Foreign Affairs in the Congress of the United States.

The largest number of Communists was found in the smallest country, Lebanon, with an estimated party membership of fifteen thousand. This little country is far more exposed to outside influences than any other Arab land because of its port, Beirut, and because of its function as a transshipment area. Also, it has a considerable number of intellectuals.

Curiously, the appeal of the Communists appears to have been strong to the very religious-minded Armenians and to members of the Eastern Orthodox Church. The Armenians remember that Russia offered them sanctuary at the time of the greatest persecution and it seems that to many members of the Eastern Orthodox Church Russia is "holy" whether she is Czarist or Communist. There is more to this, however, than appears on the surface. Many Christians needed a protest organization, and this was the only one available. The other groups were no more than Tweedledee and Tweedledum. The Soviets also appealed to the restless Kurdish tribes in Iran and Iraq.

Some Muslims also joined the Communists and the first to do so was the typesetters' union, consisting of people of more than average articulateness. Furthermore, the Lebanon Communist Party had an effective ruler in the person of Mustafa el-Aris, best known of the party leaders in the entire region. He was launched in life the hard way as a printer's devil at the age of twelve, earning more slaps than bread. At twenty-three he was an avowed Communist, and a very effective one, too. He became acquainted with the French jails, where he had the leisure to perfect himself in Marxist theory. When the French left, he was simply transferred to a Lebanese prison where he continued his studies with signal success. While the Communist Party is outlawed in Lebanon it is said still to control the strong Union of Land and Transport Communications and other labor groups.

Another colorful Communist is the former leader of the Syrian group, Khalid Bakdash, an intellectual because he graduated from a secondary school. A member of a Muslim Kurdish family, he was familiar with the life of a minority. He became editor of the Communist daily, *People's Voice*, and he fought Syria's Vichy government in the early days of the Second World War. For this he was jailed. When the Free French came in they freed him as a hero of the resistance, then imprisoned him as a Communist.

In the Middle East, communism and nationalism move hand in hand. Khalid Bakdash revealed a strong nationalistic vein, combating "western imperialism," opposition to Zionism and to the establishment of the State of Israel.

Soviet Policy in Palestine

The devious policy of the Soviets in Palestine has attracted much attention. Russian communism has been traditionally opposed to Zionism for more than one reason. First, it saw in it a disturbing form of "nationalistic atavism." The trend was toward internationalism, the Communists said, and that trend should not be disturbed by creating another country.

The Jews among the Communists had an additional reason for fighting the Zionists. Back in Russia, under the Czars, they were engaged in a feud with another left-wing group, the so-called Bundists, who were both Socialists and Zionists. The enmity to the Bund was thus transferred to the idea of Zion.

The Communist Jews of Russia could not help seeing midway between the two World Wars that anti-Semitism was rampant in various parts of the world. The persecuted Jews had to go somewhere and it was then that the bright idea occurred to the Kremlin that the Soviet Union was just the right place for the oppressed of all countries. It was thereupon decided to create a new Promised Land for the Jews. The place selected was in the taiga of Far Eastern Siberia, in the great bend of the Amur river in a territory called Biro Bidjan. Perhaps, the Soviet leaders were hoping that some of the funds collected for Palestine would be diverted to Siberia. Needless to say, the undertaking was a failure.

Then came the great Palestine controversy. This would have been just the right time for the Kremlin to turn its anti-Zionism into political cash, come out against Palestine as the Jewish State, and thus gain the gratitude of the Arab world. Very much to the surprise of everybody, the Kremlin reversed its attitude, expressed its approval of the idea of partition, which the Jews favored and the Arabs rejected, and then was among the first to recognize the State of Israel.

What was the explanation of this change of front? Possibly the Kremlin thought that what the British did not like must be good for the Soviets—or that Israel would be less hostile than the Arabs—or that the creation of Israel would introduce a disturbing element into the Middle East—or that the Soviets could more easily obtain custody over Greek Orthodox property in the Israeli Holy Land than in an Arab country. The Communist line seems to have changed again. In the "treason trial" of former Communists in Czechoslovakia at the end of 1952 a strongly anti-Israeli and even anti-Semitic line was revealed. Devious, indeed, are the ways of Kremlin policy. Perhaps the Soviets wanted to make up with the Arabs.

As to the Communist party in Israel, we may accept the word of the United States Congressional Committee investigating this problem in the Middle East. It found that communism "presents no serious danger of immediate control" in the entire region, including Israel but with the possible exception of Iran. There the Tudeh party kept on operating in broad daylight, even though officially suppressed. On its banner was written the motto: IRAN FOR THE IRANIANS. That meant that Americans and British should keep out.

Watchman, What of the Night?

"American democracy is ill fitted to conduct foreign policy," wrote Count Alexis de Tocqueville. "Fortunately, it has none."

Now, however, Washington must have a foreign policy or there will be no United States and, perhaps, no world, either. What kind of a policy should it be?

When Lord Milner was appointed undersecretary for finance in Egypt as a young man to serve under Lord Cromer, Britain's renowned proconsul in Egypt, he was shocked to find himself in a web of international intrigues. He took his troubled thoughts to Lord Cromer with the remark that something should surely be done to put an end to the seemingly limitless diplomatic cabal. Cromer listened to the young man with the wisdom born of experience but could offer him no solace.

"You must remember," he said finally, "that one of the fundamental axioms of foreign policy is that every nation hates every other nation."

"But if we can get them to understand one another better," queried the inexperienced young man, "may we not in time get rid of much of this hatred?"

"I am afraid, my dear Milner," countered Cromer with resignation, "that the better they understand one another, the more they will hate one another." [2]

The United States, as the new World Power, or candidate for the post, enters a field about which Immanuel Kant wrote: "It is the desire of every State or of its ruler to arrive at a condition of perpetual peace by conquering the whole world, if that were possible."

Adam Smith, whose acuity of observation has never been doubted, observed: "No nation ever voluntarily gave up the dominion of any province, how troublesome soever it might be to govern, and how small soever the revenue which it afforded might be in proportion to the expense which it occasioned."

And another axiom to be remembered: "In great affairs there is much more in the minds of events (if such an expression may be used)" said Lord Grey of Fallodon, "than in the minds of the chief actors."

Was de Tocqueville Wrong?

The United States was highly successful in developing a productive domestic policy. Now that we have to learn to find our place in the world we must cultivate a constructive diplomacy, and the Middle East is the right spot to begin. In the first place, we must keep clear of the mistakes the British made in this region.

They made the great mistake of underwriting the existing regimes in the Middle East. The British supported the pashas, who represented "law and order."

The policy for America is not to underwrite the existing regimes which are bankrupt anyway. What is the point of iden-

[2] "The Endless Adventure," by F. S. Oliver, quoted in *Power Politics,* by Martin Wight, Royal Institute of International Affairs, p. 34.

tifying ourselves with the dead hand of the past? Let us not forget the "mind of events" about which Lord Grey spoke. Our "permanent revolution," presented in the proper form, can become a highly important export article.

It is not the type of revolution some people mean, including a member of the Supreme Court of the United States. Our country has no right to stir up revolutions. Where to begin, where to end? We cannot afford to operate as a Holy Alliance or even as a Holy Alliance in reverse.

The continuous revolution of America does not consist of thrusting arms into peoples' hands and exhorting them to rise against their rulers. It simply means that we should lend our help to give a chance to every person who deserves it. And that would facilitate the end of the pasha rule.

We are investing billions of dollars in the Middle East, in the forms we have enumerated. We can see to it that this money, which is tremendous for this region, should be used for the most productive purposes . . . and on a mass level. In other words, our money should not get stuck in pasha pockets. Of course, the Middle East is short of people who can be used for this purpose. But that is where our technical assistance program stands us in good stead. They have a shortage of technically trained people and we have an abundance of them. Some western European friends are also long on talent. In this case a Foreign Legion of Technicians and Engineers is more than justified.

There is no shortage of possible projects in the Middle East and there is an overabundance of unskilled hands. We have learned from the oil companies in the region that those hands are unskilled, mostly, because of lack of training. Once they are properly trained, they become skilled—on short notice. The stress should be on projects where labor is the main factor.

Yes, but the pashas will not let us have our way. They are afraid that we upset the prevailing system of extreme polarization. Of course, we should make every effort to convince them first that what we are trying to do helps them more than it helps us. We are trying to save their necks. They ought to know that if the Soviets move in, they will get short shrift.

Supposing they are so obdurate they will not even know what we are talking about, that they do not want to hear us. That is possible, too. In that case we have to turn to more drastic measures. In calm, measured tones we must explain to the *people* of the Middle East what we are trying to do. We have the means to do that, through the various Voices. The unrepentant pashas will not like this but that is something we can bear. Once they see we mean what we say, many of them will decide to listen.

We must do something else, too, which is not very spectacular but is highly important. There is no better indoctrination of our way of life than personal demonstration. At present there are some 30,000 foreign students in the United States. They are from all over the world. This sounds a lot, but it is too little. There should be more of them from the Middle East alone, especially in our technical schools, so that the young people of these countries should learn from us how to become gadget-minded. They need that very badly. You have to do a lot of looking in Damascus before you find a decent plumber. But you just whistle and there will be a horde of first-class lawyers on your trail. The education of the Middle East has been too one-sided and both they and we are handicapped in our plans.

Just as important as the selection of the right work projects and of exchange students is the choice of our representatives abroad. Here is an item printed in the July 29, 1952 issue of *The New York Times,* filed by Albion Ross in Tehran:

> Resentment has grown because of the numerous United States officers, officials and experts in Tehran whose mode of living is ostentatious. The average Iranian thinks that these Americans live and act like princes.
>
> There are three American clubs here that cater to these Americans who seem unable to live without entertainment and who show their "wealth" even more obviously in a few hotels and restaurants. Such foreign "institutions" are not popular in ultra-nationalist Iran.
>
> Another problem is that Iran is a Muslim land and alcohol, according to the Muslim faith, is evil and is associated with the infidel. Americans are almost never seen outside working hours without something to drink. . . .

This is not the exception. Many people in various parts of the world have been disturbed by the quality of our representatives abroad. This may seem to be a trifling point, but it is really of tremendous importance. In the western world we care little what clubs a man frequents, what beverages he drinks. We do not even notice it. But the Middle East is different. There an American is about as inconspicuous as the Empire State Building. He is not only the citizen of a country but he is a landmark, an institution. He does not know how many people are actually watching him and how the grapevine works. It works with incredible rapidity in places where few newspapers are read. The grapevine is their gossip column which everybody reads.

Many Americans live not only like pashas, but as super-pashas. They live in an enchanted circle, belonging to a world the average man cannot enter. They are dressed like royal personages, travel in fabulous cars, eat the best food and, above all, drink the best beverages, rent the best houses, boost prices. There *is* an iron curtain between them and the people. That is not America's permanent revolution.

It is not easy to associate with many people in the Middle East. Soap is a luxury and many people do not smell good. That is the point. Americans accredited to these countries must realize that upon their behavior the future of our relations with the region may depend. More than that, our future. . . . They must be more than our ambassadors. They must be our missionaries who can never be paid adequately for the work they perform. They must be the type of people who know that a lowly mission to the backwoods of Iran is a consecrated mission, even if it deals with the extermination of phylloxera. They must be dedicated persons.

Such people can save the Middle East for us . . . perhaps also they can save us. If they do not live up to their mission, anything can happen. It is in our power to funnel the potential dynamism of the region into creative work.

On the Edge of the Volcano

And what about the agenda of the great problem area of the Middle East, the Arab countries and Iran? Is there still time to take action or have the books already been closed?

These countries had reached the threshold of great decisions. Iran particularly showed ominous symptoms of a country falling apart, held together only by the cementing force of a common hatred. And it was, partly, an artificial hatred directed against an alien oil company. The observer could not help comparing the condition of Iran with that of France before the Great Revolution. There was the disintegration of authority, the frenzied mobs, the stifling atmosphere that precedes the storm. There were even the weak kings, in France as well as in Persia, guileless victims of tragedy they did not cause.

In the Arab countries there were ominous rumblings, too, the far-off sound of the volcano before the cataclysmic eruption. There were halfhearted attempts at solutions, but never a coming to grips with reality. To come to grips with it would have been to deny the very nature of the ruling regime. So there were plans and projects and schemes, tentative, only too tentative. There were hurried visits from America, and truly creative plans and more plans. And the people were losing faith because they had seen so many attractive projects. Meanwhile the cultivable land in Egypt had gone up during a half a century only one-sixth of the population increase, which was twofold. And other countries were faced with similar problems.

What did the people want? They wanted to live, of course, and not merely to vegetate, worse than animals. Bread, that's what they wanted, and occasionally a little meat. They wanted to have a piece of land, and some work paying wages on which they could live. But how were they to reach that glorious goal? That is precisely what they did not know.

They were told by their rulers, echoed by the Soviets, that all the trouble and all their misfortunes were due to the "imperialists." A convenient explanation, indeed, expressed in one word which, as everybody knows, is the best explanation, especially if you are too hungry to think, and too tired.

It did make sense to many of them. They recalled the arrogance of the colonial administrators, stalking in their bazaars in resplendent uniforms, smelling of soap, clean, oh so very clean. They recalled the Jim Crow cars into which the people of Iran were crowded during the war, on their own trains in their own railway cars. First-class cars were occupied by people who came to teach the world the benefits of democracy.

So there is a hiatus in the life of the coreland of the Middle East because the people know what they want, in a hazy way, but do not know how to get it. That is why there have been so many "revolutions" recently, or, as they are sometimes called, "bourgeois revolutions." But where are the bourgeois in the Middle East? That is just the point. It is a region without a middle class that could serve as an intermediary, balancing the extremes.

That is why all of a sudden there have emerged all these "strong men" in the Arab countries, colonels and generals. Are they tiny replicas of Napoleon? Most likely not. They seem to be stopgaps, people to prevent the falling apart of their nations. Why these generals? Because they are the only ones who are not discredited, because they can depend upon bayonets. Or can they?

In Egypt there came into power General Mohammed Naguib, and in Syria Colonel Adib Shishakli and his flamboyant Arab Liberation Party. In Lebanon too there was a strong man in the wings, General Fuad Shehab, the Commander in Chief. In Jordan it was Glubb Pasha, the king-maker, who seems to have enthroned and unthroned King Talal. In Iraq it was General Nuriddin Mahmoud, the Chief of Staff.

This is the age of the generals in the Arab Middle East. Yet it is not the terminal station, but merely a junction. Something else is bound to come, something else is coming. What is it?

In a region which has seen the world only through the creed of Islam and which gave the world Mohammed's faith, it is natural that some people should look for a solution under the protective shelter of the Prophet's ideology. So we are witnessing the emergence of Islamic movements, striving toward political goals.

The Muslim Brotherhood, *Ikhwan al-Muslimun,* is the most comprehensive of them. Some years ago it claimed three million followers in Egypt alone. Its sway extends from the Atlantic to the Indian Ocean, it is supranational. What does the Brotherhood want? This is a disturbing question because it appears to want different things at different times. At one time it wanted land reforms, a labor code, more industries, better wages. And how did it go about accomplishing these aims? By murdering prominent politicians. Also sometimes by making common cause with crypto-Communists, while at other times fighting them.

Iran created her own Islamic political movement, *Fadean-o-Islam* (those who sacrifice themselves for Islam), and what program did it advocate? Frantically it espoused the nationalization of foreign oil, and waged a campaign of extermination against those who dared to defend programs that might really have helped to save the country. Disturbing, indeed, is the thought that the combination of Islam and politics should produce assassination.

And what about the Communists in the region? "Death to the Shah," members of the crypto-Communist Tudeh party shouted on the thirty-third birthday of the monarch, in the autumn of 1952, in Tehran's Amjadieh Stadium. The Tudeh had been outlawed but what is the effect of the decree of a government which is itself the product of hatred?

Elsewhere the Communists were outlawed and presumably unable to act. But what do we know about the potentialities when the sky has collapsed and there is a gap in authority?

And so while the Middle East awaited the arrival of a Mirabeau, it might yet see the emergence of a Lenin.

Meanwhile articulate public opinion in the Arab world was rent by a deep inner uncertainty. What line to follow, with what forces to align itself? Away from the East, some of these searchers cried; away from the land of disease, ignorance and poverty which has exhausted its life forces and which exudes an odor of decomposition. Let us turn toward the West, following the example of Turkey and perhaps going even beyond that. It is the West which is the depositary of the treasures of the new age. What is the use of producing poets when we need engineers? Of what use are the beautiful words when we need harvesting machines? *Ex Occidente Lux.*

Away from the West, the other side said, the West which has afflicted us with all its diseases and has given us nothing, except insoluble problems. The West has dynamism, it is claimed, but what good is a dynamism which destroys its operator, as is happening in the Occident? The Arab world has great potentialities, upholders of this view proclaimed, but they have never been fully exploited. Return to the crystal clear water of the fathers' ways, the ability to think things through and to act with no feverish haste. Let us return to the fountainhead of the Koran, which was ahead of its time with its deeply human social philosophy.

Finally, there was the group that would like to mediate, would like to see the Middle East as a bridge between East and West, to absorb what is best in both ways, to employ the machine but not to be tyrannized by it, to infuse technique with spiritual meaning, to establish man as the measure of value.

Which one of these schools of thought would win? Again we come back to America's role as the leading power of the West: first to understand the problems of the region in the light of its own experiences, then to lend a hand to the most constructive forces, strengthening their influence wherever we can. We must offer them genuine help and not the position of a satellite. By thus helping them we are bound also to help ourselves.

Only then will the Middle East cease to be a power vacuum, inviting aggression. The Middle East is a world without end and may therefore become the site of a new beginning.

A Note On the "Great Controversy"

Is it the Middle East, the Near East, the Middle and Near East, the Middle and/or Near East, or is it the Hither East, or is it the Levant?

Until the nineteenth century no distinction was made between the various parts of the East. The western world had little to do with it.

Anything east of "western Christendom" was called the East. For some time the Far East was called the High Levant. But generally, the troubles besetting the Ottoman Empire were summarized under the heading of Eastern Question.

Then, during the last century the West became confronted not only with the Eastern Question, but also with the problem of China. The common denominator for all Asia was no longer sufficient. The terms Near East and Far East came into existence, the first to describe the Ottoman Empire which in those days embraced also much of the Balkans.

Between the First and Second World Wars of our century the British became greatly involved in the Arab countries, several of which were mandated to them. They needed a new term and Britain's highest geographic authorities coined the designation Middle East. It was to encompass the region between the Bosphorus and India. They assigned the name Near East to the Balkans.

During the Second World War the name Middle East was dramatized. It was the region where the war might be decided. There were the British Middle Eastern Armies; there were Lord Alexander and Lord Montgomery. The Middle East Supply Center also invited much attention. The Jews called this area the Middle East and the Arabs called it the Middle East—a remarkable concordance.

Today British government publications employ the term Middle East to describe the area from Malta in the West to Ethiopia in the East, including all the Arab countries and the rest of the region all the way to Pakistan, and sometimes even to the boundaries of China. The Near East of British official usage includes the Balkans and Turkey. Non-official usage prefers the designation Middle East to include also Turkey, but not the Balkans.

The United States government agencies employed the term Middle East during the Second World War. But all this changed after the war. Then, the Department of State organized six regional bureaus. One of these was the Bureau of Near Eastern, South Asian and African Affairs; it was placed under an Assistant Secretary of State.

Within this Bureau there is the Office of Greek, Turkish and Iranian Affairs; the Office of Near Eastern Affairs; apart from two more offices dealing with Africa and South Asia. The Department at one time described the Near East as encompassing the countries around the eastern end of the Mediterranean, from Turkey to Yemen.

Thus the official United States terminology knows no Middle East.

On the other hand, the Brookings Institution in Washington, which often seems to reflect State Department policies, has published a paper entitled "The Security of the Middle East."

The United Nations, in turn, favors the Middle East, but not quite consistently. It set up, for instance, an Economic Commission for the Middle East; established the United Nations Survey Mission to the Middle East, but . . . its Food and Agricultural Organization has a Near East Office in Cairo, while its World Health Organization had an office for the Eastern Mediterranean Region in Alexandria. The United Nations' International Labor Organization sought to make everybody happy by organizing a conference on the problems of the Near and Middle East.

The French often use the term Levant to describe the Mediterranean coast of Asia Minor and Syria and Lebanon. The British sometimes use the term Hither East.

Turning now to private organizations, the National Geographic Society endeavored to bring order out of the chaos by describing the Near East as all countries, including Egypt, which are south of the Soviet Union and West of Iran. It described the Middle East as including, mainly, India and Pakistan.

Two of the three major publications in America, dealing with this region, call it the Middle East. Columbia University, the Middle East Institute, Asia Institute organized conferences to deal with the problems of the "Middle East," while Harvard University called Near East conferences. The School of Education of New York University had a conference on the Middle East.

Most of the books dealing with this subject have the Middle East in their titles, and that name seems to be favored also by most lecturers and authors of newspaper and magazine articles.

The general confusion on this subject was well illustrated in *The Times Literary Supplement* (London) which recently printed a review about a book entitled *The Near East and the Great Powers,* under the caption: "Middle Eastern Problems." It appended the following remark to the review: "In passing, it may be mentioned that in the United States the term 'Middle East,' now generally used in Europe, has not yet displaced the older title which figures in the name of the book."

The writer of this book has employed the term Middle East because it is more prevalent in the world at large; its usage is spreading in the United States and, generally, it appears to be better known to the reading public, possibly because of the wartime publicity and the work of the United Nations.

Somehow, the term of the Middle seems more appropriate to the region. Finally, it seemed to the author that by following the internationally more deeply rooted usage he may make at least a small contribution toward the cause of world understanding.

Other Reading

For a detailed bibliography the reader is referred to: *A Selected and Annotated Bibliography of Books and Periodicals in Western Languages Dealing with the Near and Middle East with Special Emphasis on Medieval and Modern Times.* (Completed Summer 1951.) Edited by Richard Ettinghausen. Prepared under the Auspices of the Committee on Near Eastern Studies, American Council of Learned Societies. Published by the Middle East Institute, Washington, D. C., 1952.

The following books are mostly recent publications and a few basic volumes. Because of the large number of books dealing with Palestine and Israel only a few of the most recent ones are mentioned.

Albright, W. F., *The Archeology of Palestine.* Harmondsworth Pelican Books, 1949.

Antonius, George, *The Arab Awakening.* Philadelphia, J. B. Lippincott Co., 1939.

Ben-Horin, Eliahu, *The Middle East: Crossroads of History.* New York, W. W. Norton & Company, 1943.

Bonné, Alfred, *The Economic Development of the Middle East.* London, Kegan Paul, Trench, Trubner, 1945.

Caroe, Olaf, *Wells of Power, The Oilfields of Southwestern Asia; a Regional and Global Study.* New York, The Macmillan Co., 1951.

Coon, Carleton S., *Caravan, the Story of the Middle East.* New York, Henry Holt & Co., 1951.

Cooke, Hedley V., *Challenge and Response in the Middle East.* New York, Harper & Brothers, 1952.

Douglas, William O., *Strange Lands and Friendly People.* New York, Harper & Brothers, 1951.

Fisher, W. B., *The Middle East: a Physical, Social and Regional Geography.* New York, E. P. Dutton, 1950.

Groseclose, Elgin E., *Introduction to Iran.* N. Y., Ox. U. Press, 1948.

Haas, William S., *Iran.* New York, Columbia University Press, 1946.

Hitti, Philip K., *History of the Arabs.* The Macmillan Co., 1937.

——— *History of Syria, Including Lebanon and Palestine.* The Macmillan Co., 1951.

Hourani, Albert H., *Minorities in the Arab World.* New York, Oxford University Press, 1947.

——— *Syria and Lebanon: a Political Essay.* New York, Oxford University Press, 1946.

Hurewitz, J. C., *The Struggle for Palestine.* New York, W. W. Norton & Company, 1950.

Ireland, Philip W., *Iraq*. New York, The Macmillan Co., 1938.

Issawi, Charles, *Egypt: An Economic and Social Analysis*. New York, Oxford University Press, 1947.

Jackh, Ernest, *The Rising Crescent*. N. Y., Farrar & Rinehart, 1944.

Kirk, George E., *A Short History of the Middle East from the Rise of Islam to Modern Times*. Washington, D. C., Public Affairs Press, 1949.

Kohn, Hans, *Nationalism and Imperialism in the Hither East*. London, Routledge and Kegan Paul, 1932.

Koestler, Arthur, *Promise and Fulfilment; Palestine, 1917-49*. New York, The Macmillan Co., 1949.

Lawrence, T. E., *Seven Pillars of Wisdom*. London, Jon. Cape, 1935.

Lehrman, Hal, *Israel: The Beginning and Tomorrow*. New York, William Sloane Associates.

Lenczowski, George, *The Middle East in World Affairs*. Ithaca, Cornell University Press, 1952.

Lowdermilk, Walter Clay, *Palestine, Land of Promise*. New York, Harper & Brothers, 1944.

McDonald, James G., *My Mission to Israel*. New York, Simon and Schuster, 1951.

MacMichael, H. A. *The Anglo-Egyptian Sudan*. London, Faber & Faber, 1934.

Mikesell, R. F., and Chenery, H. B., *Arabian Oil: America's Stake in the Middle East*. Chapel Hill, Univ. of N. Carolina Press, 1949.

Millspaugh, Arthur C., *Americans in Persia*. Washington, D. C., Brookings Institution, 1946.

Philby, H. St. John B., *Arabian Days*. London, Robert Hale, 1948.

Roberts, Frank H. H., *Egypt and the Suez Canal*. Washington, D. C., Smithsonian Institution, War Background Studies, No. 11, 1943.

Royal Institute of International Affairs, *The Middle East; A Political and Economic Survey*. London, Royal Institute of International Affairs, 1950.

Schonfield, Hugh J., *The Suez Canal*. New York, Penguin, 1939.

Smith, Sir George Adam, *The Historical Geography of the Holy Land*. Published in many editions in London, New York, etc.

Speiser, E. A., *The United States and The Near East*. Cambridge, Harvard University Press, second edition, 1950.

The Security of the Middle East: A Problem Paper. Washington, D. C., The Brookings Institution, 1950.

Thornburg, Max, Spry, George and Soule, George, *Turkey: An Economic Appraisal*. New York, Twentieth Century Fund, 1949.

Warriner, Doreen, *Land and Poverty in the Middle East*. London, Royal Institute of International Affairs, 1948.

Weizmann, Chaim, *Trial and Error*. N. Y., Harper & Brothers, 1949.

Index